# THE INFLATIONARY SPIRAL

## The Experience in China, 1939–1950

# TECHNOLOGY PRESS BOOKS IN THE SOCIAL SCIENCES

# The INFLATIONARY SPIRAL

## The Experience in China, 1939–1950

CHANG KIA-NGAU
Visiting Professor of Economics
Loyola University of Los Angeles

*Published jointly by*
The Technology Press of
Massachusetts Institute of Technology
*and*
John Wiley & Sons, Inc., New York

Chapman & Hall, Limited, London

*Library of Congress Catalog Card Number: 58-6083*

*Printed in the United States of America*

# Foreword

In the spring of 1956 this book by Dr. K.-N. Chang was brought to the attention of the Center for International Studies in manuscript form. The senior staff at the Center felt that the manuscript, reflecting as it did the author's exceptionally valuable personal experience and the unique sources at his disposal as an organizer of China's modern banking system, and his long association with the economic and financial problems of China, could make a real contribution to the study of the Chinese financial administration and problem of inflation during the war and early postwar period. The work deserved, in the Center's view, to be made available to students and scholars in the field.

The Center therefore agreed to bring this book to publication through the co-operation of the Technology Press. We do not present this study as representing the views of the Center for International Studies or of the Massachusetts Institute of Technology. We do, however, believe that this volume will be of great value to all those who desire a better understanding of the economic background and recent inflationary problem in Chinese history.

MAX F. MILLIKAN
Director, Center for International Studies
Massachusetts Institute of Technology

*Cambridge, Massachusetts*
*May, 1958*

# Preface

The idea of writing this book came to me soon after my departure from China in May 1949. At that time, when nearly the entire Chinese mainland had already fallen under the rule of the Chinese Communists, the Chinese currency had completely collapsed as a result of galloping inflation, and the entire Chinese economic and political system had been laid waste. Thus the moment seemed opportune to put down my thoughts on the most important factors in the tragedy of Chinese inflation and to record its course of development for future historians; and the first draft of the manuscript saw the light of the day in Sydney, Australia, where I lived for nearly three years before I came to the United States.

However, I hesitated for some time in making the manuscript public. It was addressed to a controversial subject at a time marked by conflicting views of American policy toward Nationalist China before its fall. Moreover, the acuteness of the problems during the war and postwar years gave me doubt as to how my work would be judged by my friends who were directly involved in the administration of China's economy and who had exerted strenuous efforts in fighting for the national cause. Yet not to tell the full story would have nullified my single purpose, which was to draw a lesson from the cause and effects of China's inflation.

I was persuaded to publish this account by the fact that, since the phenomenon of runaway inflation in China was in itself evidence that serious errors of policy and management had been committed, to point them out now so that similar mistakes would not be made elsewhere, especially in the many new Asian countries, would constitute a service I should perform. I cannot emphasize too strongly that this post-mortem of the Chinese tragedy has not been undertaken in a spirit of reproach or vindication. My sole purpose is to ensure, so far as I am able, that the Chinese tragedy should at least have some beneficial effect on other nations which have been more fortunate thus far.

The book has been written to lay bare the fundamental economic conditions behind the symptoms of inflation which embattled and finally engulfed Nationalist China. Yet it will be clear to the reader that Nationalist China's economic collapse cannot be attributed to economic causes alone. My approach emphasizes the economic causes which produced inflation as they appear in retrospect. The fundamental logic of the relationship between aggregate demand and aggregate supply seems to have escaped the grasp of China's leadership, but it is not so elusive as to evade scrutiny a decade after the fact. I have sought, therefore, to trace in the first part of the book the process by which aggregate demand came to outstrip aggregate supply. Modern economic analysis directs attention to these variables, and by studying their behavior in Nationalist China we see clearly how government policy brought inevitable results which may not have been foreseen by the leadership itself.

What the Nationalist government did to tame the monster of inflation to which it had given birth also deserves attention. In retrospect the government's anti-inflationary policies look peculiarly impotent, but we should understand that the leadership functioned in the context of wartime emergency and rather unsophisticated confidence in its corrective powers. The numerous perambulations of government policy—as if it sought for an elusive panacea—are recorded here in considerable detail. All of which I describe seems to suggest that it is difficult to combat the symptoms of inflation without attacking its basic causes as outlined in Part I.

Because of the lack of publication of accurate statistics during the war and postwar years, the figures I quote and some estimates I make are based upon statistics which are accessible only to me. I have made some changes in these, using for license a knowledge of them derived from personal experience. Any corrections would be welcome.

I am indebted to many friends and institutions without whose assistance and encouragement this book could not have been published. To the Center for International Studies, Massachusetts Institute of Technology, I owe much for financial assistance and publishing facilities and for securing Dr. Douglas Paauw, Associate Professor of Economics at Lake Forest College, to edit this work. His suggestions and painstaking efforts outlining the reorganization of my original manuscript to make the work more readable cannot be valued too highly. For his patient, valued, and useful help I am most grateful.

To Dr. Yuanli Wu, Associate Professor of Marquette University, go also my sincere thanks for his comments and revision in the final text, and to Richard W. Hatch, of the Center for International Studies, for his final editing of the manuscript before publication.

I wish to record my gratitude to Mr. Glesson-White, of the University of Sydney, for his indispensable assistance in the preparation of the original manuscript and to David Wei for his work in checking the tables and statistics.

I am also greatly indebted to George Greene, Jr., who was the first person to encourage and assist me to publish the book, and to Father Charles S. Casassa, S.J., President of Loyola University of Los Angeles, for his interest in its publication.

I wish to extend my deep gratitude to a group of veteran bankers and economists who brightened our professional relationships with their friendship. They assisted me in searching for a solution to the problem of inflation when I was in the Central Bank of China, either by giving valuable advice or by taking pains to do research work. Their opinions and studies provided a most useful source of ideas and materials, which I have embodied in my book. I would like to mention Messrs. K. P. Chen, Li Ming, Tsuyee Pei, Arthur N. Young, Cyril Rogers, S. Y. Liu, P. H. Ho, Lee Kan, H. J. Shen, T. Y. Wu, S. H. Chou, S. C. Tsiang, N. T. Wang, Fisher Yu, Y. L. Wu, and C. C. Chen. I am also grateful to Dr. Lewis Maverick for his kindness in helping to read the proof.

CHANG KIA-NGAU

*Loyola University of Los Angeles*
*May, 1958*

# Contents

# Part 1

## The Historical Background

Chapter 1

# The Period up to 1939

## 1. Prewar Background

### *Predisposition toward Inflationary Finance*

China has had a long history of cycles of monetary stability, deflation, and inflation. The fall of dynasties was repeatedly preceded by long trends toward inflationary finance, culminating in the complete disruption of the currency system as a result of the unrestrained creation and circulation of new means of payment. Since paper money made its appearance in China as early as the eleventh century, providing a device by which government authorities were able to expand the supply of money with relative ease, inflation became a problem whenever gold, silver, and copper currencies were supplemented by fiat money to raise the level of expenditures undertaken by China's ruling groups.

The march toward the last inflationary crest in China began with the establishment in 1905 of the Hu-pu (Board of Revenue) Bank, which was authorized to issue bank notes. Its establishment reaffirmed the fact that the leaders of the government, whether politicians or warlords, conservative or revolutionary, seldom departed from the belief that the government could spend more than its income simply by increasing the note issue. In fact, the petition sent by the Board of Revenue to the Emperor in March 1905 suggested that the Hu-pu Bank was founded with this belief in mind:

> The Bank is the key to finance and the note issue the key to the Bank. In Western countries, notes are issued in normal time to collect and accumulate gold and silver. In times of emergency the government can obtain money from the Bank which the public will accept because of its confidence in the notes. The Bank can underwrite the issue of bonds by virtue of its reserves of gold and silver accumulated from the issue of notes.

The philosophy embodied in this statement came to have great significance throughout the Republican period, and the financial policies of successive governments showed close conformity to this line of thought in the next several decades. Moreover, in the belief that the note circulation would increase according to the number of banks of issue, note issue was not restricted to one bank. By 1907 two government banks, one commercial bank, and one provincial government bank had obtained the right to issue notes. Twenty years later, the two government banks and no less than twenty-eight commercial and eleven provincial banks were issuing notes.

Agitation for currency reform—the replacement of the confusion of coins and notes by a uniform national currency—had begun before the turn of the century, and foreign experts had been invited to make investigations of the Chinese financial system and to propose reforms; but progress was slow until the Nationalist government of 1928–1937. Even then, government reform stopped short of a final solution to the currency problem. Apart from disagreement on the currency standard and the constant internal political strife, an important reason for the failure was the government's need to create a gold reserve to enforce currency reform. The blueprints for reform proposed a foreign loan to provide China with bank reserves (metallic), but the government feared that this would lead to foreign interference in internal financial matters and restrict its freedom to draw freely upon the banks.

### *The Silver Standard: A Natural Check to Inflation*

As a result of the increased influx of silver due to the favorable balance of trade in the early periods after the opening of foreign trade in the middle of the nineteenth century, and to foreign investments in China in the later periods, silver had become the basis of the currency. Silver bullion in varying shapes and weights, silver dollars of foreign and provincial mintage, and subsidiary silver coins circulated along with copper coins. Each circulated independently of the others, and each was accepted according to its intrinsic value with no fixed ratio of exchange among them. Large transactions in local and foreign trade were made through the medium of silver bullion. The people amassed silver as wealth, banks kept their reserves in silver, and the balancing of interbank accounts was done in silver.

When bank notes were reintroduced at the end of the nineteenth century, they usually circulated only in the cities, the people in the interior persisting in using silver dollars or copper coins. Demand for redemption was great at harvest time, whenever China's balance of payments became adverse and exports of silver were needed, or when popular rumor held that particular banks issued notes in excess of their cash reserve. Some provincial banks, in the belief that the seal of the provincial government was sufficient to maintain full value, increased their issue without restriction and even attempted to compel the people to accept inconvertible notes. This resulted in depreciation of these notes and the creation of strong popular resistance to accepting them. Had it not been for the public demand for redemption in silver, the predatory attitude of government authorities toward the banks would have brought about violent inflation earlier than it finally occurred.

However, this restraint did not afford absolute protection against unregulated expansion of the note issue. Both central and provincial governments frequently made attempts to suspend the mechanism of the silver standard by ordering the banks of issue to cease redemption. For instance, in 1916 Yuan Shih-kai, President of the Republic of China, needed funds for his attempt to establish himself as Emperor. He proposed to seize the cash reserves of the two government banks, the Bank of China and the Bank of Communications. Since the cash reserves of these banks were relatively small, he instructed them to cease redemption of their notes, and the public was ordered to accept notes at par. This departure from the principles of the silver standard was frustrated by the refusal of the Shanghai Branch of the Bank of China, whose note issue was larger than that of any other bank, to comply with the government's order. For several days there was a run on this bank, but it succeeded in meeting the public demand for silver. Although the Bank of Communications and the Peking Branch of the Bank of China were forced to suspend redemption, the government failed to achieve its objective because of the limited amount of silver it could appropriate from these banks, and the public showed strong resistance to accepting irredeemable notes at par with silver coins.

The provincial governments dealt with the note issues of the provincial banks in an even more primitive manner. Whenever the banks could not redeem their notes, the provincial authorities tried to maintain the exchange value of notes by threatening dire penalties to people found buying or selling notes at a discount. In Manchuria the penalty for exchanging notes issued by the Bank of Eastern Three Provinces at less than par was death. (The official rate was $50 Manchurian notes per one silver dollar.) Nevertheless, provincial bank notes were circulated at heavy discounts, and this placed a very real limit on the extent to which these issues could be increased. In 1916 the total issue of nineteen provincial government banks reached about $200,000,000 (representing silver dollars), more than half of which was irredeemable.

### *The Banks' Self-Defense against Inflation*

Despite the courageous act of the Shanghai Branch of the Bank of China in 1916, the irredeemable note issues of the Peking Branch of the Bank of China and the Bank of Communications continued to increase as a result of government pressure upon the banks. But public confidence in paper currency was badly shaken by the Yuan Shih-kai episode, and in the period 1916–1921 Bank of China issues increased only from $46.4 million to $62.5 million, while Bank of Communications issues rose from $21.3 million to $30.1 million. After a long struggle to resist further government borrowing, the two government banks managed to withdraw all irredeemable notes from circulation by 1922, and public confidence in paper currency gradually revived. By 1927 the note issue of the Bank of China had increased to $159.0 million, and that of the Bank of Communications to $65.1 million.

On March 25, 1928, the Bank of China took a positive step to enhance the value of its currency and to check unlimited expansion of the note issue. A Supervisory Committee, comprising representatives of the Chamber of Commerce, the Bankers' Association, and the Native Bankers' Association, was established in Shanghai to ensure that the bank maintain adequate reserves behind its note issue. Every three months the Committee published a report on the bank's reserve position after it had been certified by a public accountant. This supervision was designed to assure the public that the bank of issue would not permit the government to tamper with the note reserve. The same practice was subsequently adopted by the newly founded Central Bank of China, the Bank of Communications, and private banks of issue. The public became less wary of holding bank notes, and note circulation increased rapidly in the years after 1928. Sound currency gradually drove the unsound notes of the provincial banks out of circulation except in Manchuria and Canton. In Manchuria, where large amounts of currency were required seasonally for the marketing of huge harvests of agricultural products, the soundness of the money was overlooked. In Canton large annual inflows of overseas Chinese remittances gave rise to greater demand for local currency than the sound banks could provide.

After the death of Yuan Shih-kai a succession of governments relied heavily upon inflationary financing. Since the 1916 fiasco had proved the futility of using direct intervention to obtain funds from banks, resort was made to more subtle methods, the most frequently used device being the sale of government bonds to issuing banks which could hold them as reserves to the extent of 40 per cent of total note issue. Prior to 1935 the capacity of the banks to absorb government bonds had already reached saturation point.

It can be seen that under these conditions strict adherence to the rules of the silver standard was the only check on note issue, and that, if the banks had been relieved of the responsibility of redemption in silver, an inflationary process would probably have been set in force.

### *Change from the Silver Standard to Foreign Exchange Standard*

The increasingly high price of silver, caused by the leading Western financial powers' retreat from the gold standard after 1931, and climaxed in 1934 and 1935 by the American silver purchase policy, had a serious deflationary effect on China's economy. Large amounts of silver flowed from the interior to Shanghai and other ports for export. The loss of silver reserves reduced the credit base, money became scarce, and commodity prices fell. The necessity for currency change was recognized, and in November 1935 the existing silver standard was replaced by a new foreign exchange standard worked out with the aid of foreign experts, including Sir Frederick Leith Ross from Great Britain. The new currency plan provided that:

> The bank notes issued by the Central Bank of China, the Bank of China, and the Bank of Communications should be the nation's sole legal tender, the Chinese National Currency, abbreviated CNC.
>
> The use of silver for currency purposes should be prohibited, and that the public should surrender to a Currency Reserve Board appointed by the government, or to its agent banks, all monetary silver in their possession in exchange for legal tender notes.
>
> The Central Bank of China should buy and sell without limit foreign exchange at "current rates." The first official rates should be, respectively, 1 shilling 2⅜ pence per Chinese dollar for buying sterling, 1 shilling 2⅝ pence per Chinese dollar for selling sterling, and 29½ cents and 30 cents per Chinese dollar for buying and selling U.S. dollars.

The introduction of the new currency system dispelled the anxiety of Chinese businessmen that internal price levels might fall through further increases in foreign silver prices, for they were confident that domestic prices would rise through a fall in the internal value of the Chinese dollar. It also appeared that credit conditions would ease with the adoption of a more flexible monetary standard. The public appeared to be willing to surrender its silver for paper money because the new currency system had the support of the British banks in China.

But the leading Chinese bankers in Shanghai were most apprehensive over the potential dangers of the new system. Indeed, the draftsmen of the plan had not lost sight of the danger of inflation, and had warned the government that two other measures of financial constraint should accompany the currency reform. They proposed, first, that the Central Bank of China should be reorganized as a Central Reserve Bank, with capital subscribed by the commercial banks, private citizens, and the government. In this way the Central Bank would be separated from the Ministry of Finance and raised to independent status; and the supply of money would be supervised by a committee on which responsible members of the business community would have a deciding vote. Second, the authors of the 1935 reform urged that the government rationalize its finances to make a balanced budget feasible, thus reducing the government's dependence on deficit financing through note issue. In acknowledgment of these suggestions, the government pledged that it would reorganize the Central Bank in the manner indicated, and declared that it was ready to embark on a thoroughgoing overhaul of government finances to bring the budget in balance within eighteen months. These promises did not allay the fears of the Chinese bankers, who, remembering the previous twenty years, foresaw the dangers of inflation.

Unfortunately, their fears proved to have been well grounded. The Central Bank never gained independent status, and no serious attempt was made to reorganize government finances. From the time when the new currency system came into operation in 1935 to the middle of 1937 the note issues of the four government banks increased from CNC $453 million to CNC $1,477 million. Only about half of this increase represented notes issued against silver surrendered. The details of this expansion are given in Table 1.

### *Movements in General Price Level prior to 1939*

In the century prior to 1935 three major factors influenced general price levels in China: domestic agricultural harvests, world commodity prices, and the world price of silver. Two key commodities, food and clothing, which account for the bulk of consumer expenditures in a subsistence economy, led changes in the prices of other commodities affecting the cost of living. Before 1900 food prices fluctuated violently in response to the size of the domestic crops. Since the circulation of copper coins was limited, the shortage of money at

TABLE 1. NOTE ISSUE OF FOUR GOVERNMENT BANKS[1]

| Date | Notes in Circulation, CNC |
|---|---|
| Nov. 1935 | 453,000,000 |
| Dec. 1935 | 672,983,000 |
| June 1936 | 947,971,000 |
| Dec. 1936 | 1,330,960,000 |
| June 1937 | 1,477,200,000 |

[1] Including the Farmers' Bank. Based on the statistics compiled by the currency department of the Ministry of Finance.

harvest time had a dampening effect on agricultural prices. This seasonal effect was diminished as the circulation of silver dollars spread after the turn of the century. After 1900 China began to take greater advantage of imports of foreign agricultural products whenever they became cheap relative to home-produced goods through either a fall in world prices or a rise in the price of silver. Since clothing entering the Chinese markets was almost wholly imported until the 1920's, its price, too, depended on world prices and the silver exchange rate. Consequently, foreign prices of food and clothing and the price of silver were important determinants of China's internal price levels. This brought close correspondence between internal price movements and world price trends until 1930. Discrepancies between internal and external price levels did, of course, occur; but they tended to be evened out by changes in the volume of imports. For instance, a rise in the internal price levels, an increase in the value of silver on world markets, or a decline in foreign prices stimulated an inflow of imports that exercised a deflationary influence on internal price levels, bringing them closer to prices abroad. Thus, if world prices were converted into Chinese currency at the prevailing rate of exchange, with corrections for freight and insurance charges and the generally inferior quality of Chinese commodities, differences between internal and external prices were small. The comparison in Table 2 of Chinese and American prices of cotton and wheat during 1930 shows the tendency toward parallel movements in Chinese and foreign prices.

After 1930, however, fairly big disparities appeared between price trends in China and those in Great Britain and the United States. Up to the time of the Japanese invasion in 1937 Chinese price levels passed through two distinct phases, the turning point coming with the currency reform of 1935. The wholesale price indexes for the United States, the United Kingdom, and China (Shanghai), and the

TABLE 2. CHINESE AND AMERICAN PRICES OF COTTON AND WHEAT (U.S. prices converted to Chinese currency)[1]

| | Cotton (per picul) | | Wheat (per picul) | |
|---|---|---|---|---|
| 1930 | China (Hankow) | U.S. | China (Hankow) | U.S. |
| Jan. | 51.0 | 75.4 | 6.97 | 7.73 |
| April | 50.4 | 74.0 | 7.17 | 7.98 |
| Aug. | 45.0 | 71.4 | 7.00 | 7.84 |
| Dec. | 46.7 | 65.5 | 5.94 | 6.79 |

[1] Based on data in the report of Bank of China, 1930. One picul equals 2.91 bushels.

index of the exchange rate of Chinese dollars for sterling in Table 3 illustrate the reversal in Chinese price trends in 1935, and subsequent differences in Chinese and world price movements.

TABLE 3. WHOLESALE PRICE INDEX (1935 = 100)

| | U.S.[1] | U.K.[1] | China (Shanghai)[2] | Exchange Rate Index in Sterling[3] |
|---|---|---|---|---|
| 1930 | 109 | 112 | 120 | 115 |
| 1931 | 85 | 99 | 132 | 146 |
| 1932 | 71 | 96 | 118 | 118 |
| 1933 | 74 | 96 | 108 | 118 |
| 1934 | 89 | 99 | 101 | 109 |
| 1935 | 100 | 100 | 100 | 100 |
| 1936 | 102 | 105 | 112 | 122 |
| 1937 | 108 | 122 | 124 | 122 |
| 1938 | 100 | 112 | 159 | 166 |

[1] League of Nations Monthly Bulletin of Statistics, Nov. 2, 1939.

[2] Based on index numbers of wholesale prices in Shanghai, compiled by National Tariff Commission, Ministry of Finance.

[3] Quotations of TT Rate (Telegraphic Transfer Rate) for sterling in Shanghai.

In 1931 wholesale prices in the United States and the United Kingdom fell considerably (by 12 per cent and 22 per cent, respectively) while Chinese wholesale prices rose by 10 per cent. This increase was mainly attributable to a 21 per cent depreciation in the effective Chinese exchange rate on foreign countries, resulting from a fall in the world price of silver. The world depression had not yet affected China, and the drop in silver prices more than counterbalanced the deflationary effects of China's growing foreign trade deficit. In 1932, when the United States, Britain, and a host of other countries abandoned the gold standard, world prices began to level off. As a result of the rise in world silver prices following the United States Silver Purchase Act of 1932, however, prices in China began a downward trend which lasted until the currency reform of 1935. The external value of the currency appreciated by 23 per cent in 1932, by another 8 per cent in 1934, and by 9 per cent in the first nine months of 1935. Recovery of foreign demand for China's exports was discouraged, China was flooded with cheap agricultural imports, and large quantities of silver were exported. Commodity exports slumped, and internal prices of foodstuffs and raw materials were forced down by competition from foreign goods. In the years 1933–1935 Shanghai wholesale prices declined by 24 per cent, while prices in Britain increased by 4 per cent and those in the United States by 41 per cent. The fall in Chinese commodity prices would have been even greater if the government had not levied an export tax on silver equal to the differential between its internal and its external value. This reduced the outflow of silver, the main deflationary force affecting domestic price levels.

The experience of the early 1930's demonstrated the undesirable deflationary effects of rising world silver prices on the Chinese economy; and the main object of the currency reform of 1935 was to break the link between internal price levels and silver. After November 1935, when China left the silver standard, the foreign exchange rate was fixed by the Central Bank, and it ceased to follow the world price of silver. Nevertheless, the exchange rate continued to have great influence upon internal price levels until the outbreak of the Sino-Japanese war in 1937.

The new rate of exchange decided by the government at the end of 1935 represented a 20 per cent depreciation in the external value of the currency. In relation to its former silver content, the new Chinese dollar was greatly undervalued on the world market, being no less than 40 per cent below what it would have been at the ruling London price of silver. This discrepancy had a significant psychological effect on Chinese financiers and businessmen who believed that the internal value of the currency would fall in line with its new external value. In the two years following exchange depreciation Chinese demand for securities, real estate, and other domestic forms of investments rose significantly, contributing to increased wholesale price levels. At the same time, exchange depreciation raised Chinese prices of imported goods—an effect that was strengthened by increases in wholesale prices in Britain and the United States—and provided a substantial degree of protection to local agricultural and manufacturing enterprises which had fallen into a precarious state during the earlier years of the depression. In various ways, therefore, the depreciation of the currency imparted buoyancy to industry and trade. It is more important from our point of view, however, to note that the currency reform of 1935 provided the basis for expanding the supply of money with relative ease; and, in the absence of controls, it actually generated mild inflation as early as the 1935–1937 period.

## 2. The First Period of War Inflation: 1937–1939

Wartime inflation in China falls naturally into three phases. There was a period of moderate inflation dating from the outbreak of hostilities in July 1937 and lasting until the second half of 1939. In this early stage prices in Free China rose at the average rate of 40 to 50 per cent per year. There followed a two-year period, ending in late 1941, in which the people began to lose confidence in the currency. Hoarding and speculation became widespread, and prices increased by 160 per cent each year. Inflationary trends again quickened after Pearl Harbor; and in the remaining four years of the war annual price increases in Free China averaged more than 300 per cent.

### *The Impact of the Japanese Invasion on Prices in Free China*

The origins of hyper-inflation in Free China are associated with the abnormal conditions created by the war with Japan and must be set against the background of Japanese military operations. After the fall of Peiping in July 1937 the Japanese armies overran Northern and Eastern China with extraordinary rapidity, and by the end of the year they controlled a broad sweep of China stretching from Suiyuan province in the north to Chekiang on the coast. In November 1937 the Chinese Government moved to Hankow. In a few short months the enemy had gained possession of the richest agricultural and manufacturing regions of China, and had severed Free China from the vital seaport of Shanghai.

After their early victories the Japanese adopted a dual strategy of cutting China's lines of communication with the outside world by seizing control of the coast and infiltrating the provinces on the border of Indo-China and at the same time pushing west along the

Yangtze toward Ichang and Chungking with the object of severing north-south road and rail arteries and blocking east-west river communications. After September 1937 the Japanese Second and Third Fleets attempted to blockade the entire coastline to Chinese shipping, but imported goods carried in foreign vessels were reaching China in considerable volume. In October 1938 Japan tightened her grip on the coast by seizing possession of Canton, and, a few days later, strengthened the blockade of the Yangtze by capturing Hankow. The fall of these two cities meant that the vital Hankow-Canton railway passed out of the control of Free China, and that the international trade route via Hong Kong was severed. By the close of the year the Japanese occupied a third of China—regions producing 40 per cent of China's agricultural output and containing 92 per cent of her prewar industrial capacity.

In 1939 the enemy launched a new offensive in the south aimed at disrupting China's communications with Indo-China. In November they captured Nanning in Kwangsi Province, an important center of road transshipment. Meanwhile in the central provinces the Japanese armies fanned out on either side of the Yangtze with the object of immobilizing Changsha, a focal point of rail and river transport south of the river, and Ichang on the Yangtze, the last remaining link in the water communications between Chungking and the eastern provinces. The campaign against Changsha failed; but the defense forces at Ichang were overwhelmed in June 1940.

The loss of the coastal districts exerted an immediate inflationary influence on the economy of Free China. Prices of chemicals, metals, electrical goods, and other commodities normally imported or produced in the coastal provinces, began to rise very rapidly; and they continued to lead the increase in general price levels throughout the war. The capture of Canton and Hankow in the latter half of 1938 contributed to a 72 per cent rise in import prices during this period. Each advance made by the Japanese toward sealing off Free China from communication with the outside world was matched by a rise in import prices, as shown in Table 4.

The Chungking index of import prices in December 1939, after hostilities began in Kwangsi, and Nanning had been captured, was more than double the June figure. Prices of commodities transported from other provinces were similarly affected by the disruption of communications, particularly in the second half of 1939 when the Japanese carried out their large-scale attack on Changsha. In contrast, prices of locally produced goods, mainly consisting of foodstuffs and agricultural raw materials, were some six per cent lower than prewar until

TABLE 4. INDEXES OF WHOLESALE PRICES IN FREE CHINA
(Base: Jan.–June 1937 = 100)

| | Locally Produced Goods (Chungking)[1] | Goods from Other Provinces (Chungking)[1] | Imported Goods (Chungking)[1] | All Commodities (All of Free China)[2] |
|---|---|---|---|---|
| Dec. 1937 | 93 | 125 | 147 | 109 |
| June 1938 | 95 | 195 | 227 | 127 |
| Dec. 1938 | 115 | 275 | 389 | 155 |
| June 1939 | 141 | 313 | 501 | 205 |
| Dec. 1939 | 221 | 578 | 1,054 | 306 |

[1] Taken from tables of monthly statistics compiled by the Economic Research Department of Central Bank of China (simple geometric means for 22 basic commodities). Chunking was the wartime capital.

[2] Taken from tables of monthly statistics compiled by the Directorate-General of Budgets, Accounts and Statistics (simple geometric means for 22 basic commodities).

mid-1938 as the result of an unusually abundant harvest in Szechwan province. In 1939 prices of these items began to rise in conformity with the general inflationary trend.

Thus the military operations of the Japanese created in Free China very serious shortages of manufactured goods, which in turn exerted a strong upward pressure on prices. The situation was further aggravated on the demand side by a movement of population out of the territories threatened by the enemy into the provinces of Free China. It has been estimated that fifty million refugees had migrated from the war zones into the interior by 1940, increasing the population of Free China by about 25 per cent. These figures may exaggerate the size of the movement that occurred; but the influx of refugees was certainly very large, exerting considerable pressure on supplies of food and clothing. The flight of population inland even necessitated the cultivation of new types of agricultural commodities to satisfy the preferences of newcomers from the coast.

### *The Government Deficit*

In addition to the powerful inflationary forces released in Free China by the Japanese invasion there were internal causes of inflation which we must examine.

When the Japanese attacked China, the leaders of the Nationalist government pledged that they would wage a total war against the aggressor without regard for cost or concern about the potential inflationary consequences of a full-scale campaign. They pinned their hopes for solution to the problem of war finance on the willingness of the general public to make voluntary sacrifices, and on financial and military aid from friendly nations. They called upon the people to subscribe to the National Liberty Bonds immediately after the outbreak of war and appealed to the United States, British, and Soviet governments. The first foreign response came from the Soviet Union; the United States followed. The Chinese people wholeheartedly endorsed the sentiments of the government without any conception of the burden they would have to bear in respect to rising price levels. A few economists advocated heavier taxation and controls on consumers' spending, such as those employed by the Western nations in World War I; but their ideas were dismissed by the Ministry of Finance and the business community as academic and impractical for China.

In the latter half of 1938 the government launched a program of resistance and reconstruction, which had been adopted by the Kuomintang National Congress in April. The administrative departments of the government were retained intact despite the reduced area of their operations, and the army was maintained at full strength. The government turned its attention to the problem of developing industries and communications in the interior. Industries were needed to replace those lost to the Japanese and to offset the reduction in imports; communications in the interior were badly in need of reconstruction and expansion, a particularly pressing problem. Since Free China contained only about one-tenth of the total mileage of railways in China, transport was slow and costly. As the Japanese tightened their coastal blockade it became increasingly important to develop alternative trade routes through Indo-China and Burma. Hence the government expended huge sums on the development of communications and granted an unprecedented amount of financial assistance to all forms of productive enterprise. These undertakings led to an increase in government expenditure of about 33 per cent in the period 1937–1939, a very large expansion considering that in 1939 the government's activities were confined to an area about half the size of its peacetime territories.

No real effort was made in those early years to match increased government expenditures with increased revenues. As the Japanese extended their sphere of authority into the wealthy eastern provinces, revenues of the Nationalist government declined rapidly. As a result of the loss of the main tax-paying centers of the east, revenue was

63 per cent below prewar in 1939 and the government deficit rose by more than a third in 1939, as shown in Table 5.

TABLE 5. CHINESE GOVERNMENT EXPENDITURE, REVENUE, AND DEFICIT AND THE NOTE ISSUE, 1937–1939
(CNC $ millions)[1]

| Period | Note Issue | | Expenditure | Revenue | Deficit (surplus) |
|---|---|---|---|---|---|
| 1936–37 | 1,410 | June | 1,894 | 1,972 | (78) |
| 1937–38 | 1,730 | June | 2,091 | 815 | 1,276 |
| 1938 | 2,310 | Dec. | 1,168[2] | 315[2] | 854[2] |
| 1939 | 4,290 | Dec. | 2,797 | 740 | 2,057 |

[1] Expenditure and revenue for 1936–1937 based on data in W. Y. Chang, *Money and Finance in China* [in Chinese], Formosa, 1952, pp. 140–144. The unused balance of the new consolidation loan in 1936 accounted for the small surplus. Expenditure and revenue for 1937–1939 based on the statistics compiled by the Statistical Department of the Ministry of Finance.

[2] Half year, July–December.

The government planned to tide itself over the initial stages of the war by resorting to traditional policies of selling bonds and increasing the note issue. In the longer run it hoped to receive foreign aid to bolster the economy. At the end of 1937 the government issued CNC $500 million in National Liberty Bonds, little more than $250 million of which was subscribed by the public despite a nation-wide selling campaign. Excessive issue of bonds before the war had destroyed public confidence in government securities, and the capacity of the banks to absorb bonds had already been exploited to the limit. The failure of government loans in 1938 and 1939 was almost complete. In 1938 a mere CNC $18.4 million out of $1,450 million worth of bonds offered for sale was taken up by public subscription, and the record of 1939 was no better. The Ministry of Finance was forced to abandon its original belief that bond issues would be supported by the public out of patriotic motives, and had to rely on note issue and incidental sales of foreign exchange to finance the deficit. Forty per cent of the deficit for 1937–1938 was offset by proceeds from sales of foreign exchange and bond subscriptions. Creation of new money proceeded relatively slowly in this period, therefore, rising by 23 per cent from CNC $1,410 million in June 1937 to CNC $1,730 million a year later. In 1939, however, sales of foreign exchange were restricted by the depletion of the Central Bank's reserves of foreign currencies, and bond sales were negligible. Notes in circulation increased by 148 per cent to CNC $2,560 million in the year after June 1938.

In neglecting to counter the effects of its increased spending by developing new sources of revenue the government was setting in motion powerful inflationary forces in Free China. Late in 1938 the scope of the income tax was widened to include company incomes, and an excess profits tax was imposed; but the new measures were not put into effect until the close of 1939. The yield from these taxes was low and of slight importance in the over-all picture of government finance. The government failed to neutralize the rise in consumer incomes stemming from increased government spending. It is true that at the beginning of 1939 a half-hearted effort was made to fix prices of daily necessities at fair levels, to control the distribution of these commodities to a few of the major inland cities, and to ban hoarding and speculation in essential commodities; but these measures were ineffective. It was not until 1942 that the government seriously attacked the problem of preventing the increased purchasing power in the hands of the public from being automatically translated into higher prices.

In effect, the government in the early years of the war passively accepted the loss of its revenues and allowed the inflationary consequences of the deficit to go unchecked. The government's attitude reflected, first of all, the rudimentary development of central and local government administrative organization in China at the outbreak of hostilities. New and comprehensive taxes were needed, with adequate administrative machinery. Similarly, the Nationalist government had no previous experience in the application of controls on prices and the allocation of commodities. However, although these considerations explain much, the fact remains that there was a fundamental weakness of official policy. The government neglected to review its expenditures on defense, new industrial projects, and administrative services with a view to bringing these in line with decreased revenues. Economies could have been effected by reducing the number of army units, and by training numerous small guerrilla detachments living off the countryside at little expense to the government. A smaller well-equipped fighting force could have been created to replace an army whose size militated against its efficiency. The administrative system could also have been rationalized by eliminating redundant departments and by cutting down the staff of those whose activities were curtailed by the Japanese occupation of the eastern provinces. No attempt was made to economize along such lines. The need for retrenchment of government finances became more obvious after the fall of Hankow and Canton at the end of 1938. Increases in wholesale prices in Free China, which had previously averaged 2 per cent per month, now rose to 4 per cent per month. Viewing the problem of inflation in the light of cold fact rather than of national sentiment for the first time, the general public began to express anxiety about the state of government finances.

The Chinese government failed to comprehend that the essential economic problem of the war was one of achieving maximum military effort from the limited resources at its disposal. On the basis of the monetary stability of the prewar years, Generalissimo Chiang Kai-shek was overconfident of his ability to surmount the financial obstacles of a war economy. In point of fact, the silver standard acted as a brake on the money supply during the late 1920's and early 1930's, and stability was achieved despite the disturbing influence of government financial policies. The government leaders were swayed by a strange combination of traditional Chinese beliefs and modern authoritarian ideas: "Where there is land, there is money," and "Where there is absolute power, there are goods." Since the Nationalist government ruled half of China, it must have a plentiful money supply; since the Nationalist government exercised absolute power, its legal tender must be able to command the real resources required for the conduct of war. The government also assumed at this time, with characteristic optimism, that foreign assistance would soon be forthcoming as it had been on many similar occasions in the past when China had resisted an invader. Out of this unrealistic conception of the government's capabilities emerged the marathon resistance program planned without regard to the limits imposed by the economic potential of Free China and the unhealthy state of government finances. Hence the deficit grew apace, generating the inflation that was to bring Free China near economic collapse in the later stages of the war.

### *The Expansion of Bank Credit*

Free China was singularly ill-equipped to undertake the task of financing the development of manufacturing and mining industries and the expansion of food production in the interior. Prewar Chinese banking facilities were concentrated in the eastern provincial cities, with control centralized in Shanghai. Supply of credit in the interior relied heavily on small old-fashioned native banks, which in turn depended on banking facilities in Shanghai for their financing. The inherent vulnerability of such a banking structure was immediately apparent when the Japanese encircled Shanghai and the supply of credit to the interior was cut off at the source.

The responsibility for providing credit in the interior devolved upon the Central Bank of China and branches of the other government banks. In consonance with its program of resistance and reconstruction, the government encouraged expansion of credit to private industry during 1939. The outstanding balance of industrial and commercial credit granted by the government banks rose from CNC $1,471 million in 1937 to CNC $2,578 million in 1939. The government felt that this liberal credit policy was indispensable in the circumstances of war, and the policy did indeed stimulate the growth of industrial capacity in those early years. However, it placed a heavy strain on available productive resources. Coming at a time when supplies of capital goods were severely curtailed by the encroachments of the Japanese, the credit expansion was a potent inflationary factor. Experienced industrial workers were scarce in the interior, and wages rose in the competition for skilled and semiskilled workers. Thus the means of war were bought by the establishment of industries in Free China at the cost of inflation in capital goods and labor markets.

Despite a fall in bank deposits immediately following the Japanese invasion, private loans of the government banks were adequately covered by their deposits in 1937, 1938, and 1939, as Table 6 indicates.

TABLE 6. GOVERNMENT BANK LOANS AND THE NOTE ISSUE, 1937–1939 (CNC $ millions)

| Year | Increase in Deposits[1] | Increase in Private Loans[1] | Advances to Gov't.[2] | Note Issue, Dec.[3] | Increase in Note Issue |
|---|---|---|---|---|---|
| 1937 | 2,211 | 1,471 | 597 | 1,640 | — |
| 1938 | 776 | 225 | 1,451 | 2,310 | 670 |
| 1939 | 1,658 | 882 | 2,310 | 4,290 | 1,980 |

[1] Based on the report of the Joint Board of Administration of Government Banks, 1947. Figure for private loans covers the net amount granted in the year, not including agricultural loans. Figure for 1937 is outstanding balance.

[2] Based on the Statement of Revenue compiled by the Statistical Department of the Ministry of Finance.

[3] Based on the statistics of Central Bank of China.

The ratio of private loans to total deposits stood at 66 per cent at the end of 1937, 28 per cent at the end of 1938, and 54 per cent at the end of 1939. Resort to note issue for the purposes of accommodating credit demands of producers was at this time a feature of the wartime activities of the government banks rather than of private banking.

The rise of advances to the government and the increase in the amount of credit granted to industry were dual stimuli leading to the introduction of large quantities of new money, particularly after 1939. With the temporary suspension of the Shanghai money market in August 1937 and the abnormal conditions in which it operated after that date, private demands for credit did not absorb a very high proportion of the liquid resources of the banks. Advances to the government could be financed partly from deposits. The situation changed in 1939 when the government encouraged expansion of private credit, which soon came to absorb the deposits of the government banks. Nearly the whole of advances to the government were now met by creation of new currency. The government banks were in possession of a large volume of funds other than their deposits: secret reserves of foreign exchange; funds in unrevealed suspense accounts, including sums belonging to the Exchange Stabilization Fund; and tax collections awaiting remittance to the Ministry of Finance. All these resources could have been utilized for the purposes of credit extension without increasing the amount of currency in circulation before 1939. The effect of an excess of private loans over deposits was to diminish the volume of liquid assets held by the banks and to increase the demand on the note issue as a means of financing the budget deficit. However, even the activation of the balances referred to above would have had an inflationary impact by increasing the average velocity of circulation.

## *Currency Warfare and the Foreign Exchange Rate*

In addition to assuming control of the existing financial institutions, the Japanese established a number of puppet banks issuing different kinds of notes when they invaded North China. In December 1937 a Bank of Mongolia was set up in Kalgan, followed by a Federal Reserve Bank of China to act as a Central Bank, opened in Tientsin in March 1938. Two years later a Central Reserve Bank was established in Nanking to regulate the banking affairs of the central and southern coastal provinces. The notes of the Bank of Mongolia were exchangeable with Japanese and Manchukuo currencies. One dollar of Federal Reserve Bank notes was equivalent to one Japanese yen, but was only exchangeable with yen in small amounts. Exchange for yen of sums exceeding FRB $100 were subject to the approval of the Japanese, and special permission had to be obtained from the Bank of Japan for the purchase of foreign currencies with FRB dollars. Central

Reserve Bank notes were intended to circulate at par with CNC and could not at first be used for the purchase of any other currency. In addition there were two other varieties of currency, military notes and Hua Hsing Commercial Bank notes. In 1938 and 1939 military notes were issued by the Japanese to meet their expenses in Central and South China; these were withdrawn when the new Central Reserve Bank was created. The Hua Hsing Bank was opened in Shanghai in January 1939 for the purpose of issuing a kind of note that could be bought and sold on the foreign exchange market and perform the functions of a trade dollar. The Hua Hsing dollar was intended to exchange at par with CNC and was designed as the unit of account for payment of salaries of civil servants, customs duties, and other taxes. By selling these notes the Japanese planned to accumulate CNC to purchase foreign currencies sold by the Chinese government on the Shanghai market. Excluding military notes, issues of puppet banks in China (Table 7) rose from $50 million in December 1937 to the vicinity of $550 million in the same month of 1939.

TABLE 7. NOTE ISSUES OF PUPPET BANKS, 1937–1940
(in thousands, each in its own money)[1]

| Year | Bank of Mongolia | Federal Reserve | Hua Hsing | Total |
|---|---|---|---|---|
| Dec. 1937 | 50,000 | — | — | 50,000 |
| Dec. 1938 | N.A.[2] | 161,000 | — | N.A. |
| Dec. 1939 | N.A. | 458,000 | 5,070 | N.A. |
| Dec. 1940 | 99,000 | 715,000 | 5,650 | 819,650 |

[1] Based on data compiled by the Ministry of Finance of Japan, on the subject of currency conditions in occupied areas, 1941.
[2] Not available.

Operating through their newly developed financial institutions in Occupied China, the Japanese began to wage currency warfare in Free China. They endeavored to intensify inflationary pressures by driving CNC back into the interior, and to undermine the external value of CNC by raiding the foreign exchange market in Shanghai. When the Federal Reserve Bank was created in North China early in 1938 all issues of CNC were to be withdrawn within three months, with the exception of issues of local branches of the Bank of Communications, which were to be eliminated from circulation within a year. By the beginning of 1939 CNC had been entirely removed from circulation in the northern occupied areas. The direct effect of this suppression on price levels in Free China was probably not very great.

If the whole of the stock of CNC in circulation in North China at the beginning of 1938 had been driven back into Free China, the increased volume of currency in circulation over the period of a year would have been about 10 per cent at the most. Under the stimuli of the budget deficit and credit expansion, however, the supply of money in Free China was already increasing considerably faster than this; note issue was expanded by 41 per cent in 1938 and by 86 per cent in 1939. Hence, although the gradual seepage of CNC from occupied regions must have affected internal price levels in Free China, this factor was of secondary importance when viewed against the background of other inflationary influences at work in the early years of the war. The second aspect of the currency war, its impact on the foreign exchange rate, may now be examined.

During the first six months of the war the Chinese government continued to sell unrestricted amounts of foreign exchange at fixed rates as provided in the currency reform plans of 1935. Government leaders adhered to this policy because they doubted their ability to administer exchange controls and believed that such measures would be interpreted by the foreign business communities in China as unwarranted interference in their business affairs. The government, therefore, entered into a gentlemen's agreement with the foreign banks to hold the exchange rate near the existing level and to prevent a disturbing flight of capital from China. Forward buying and selling of foreign currencies was eliminated. The financial authority believed that patriotic sentiments would restrain people from buying foreign exchange in order to transfer funds to safe depositories abroad. Until March 1938 the government policy was effective; the foreign exchange rate remained virtually unchanged (see Table 8).

In March 1938 the Japanese set up the Federal Reserve Bank and announced that within twelve months all CNC would be withdrawn from circulation in the northern areas of the occupied territories. This move threatened to deluge the Shanghai market with national currency seeking expatriation. Meanwhile the Minister of Finance discovered that there was little substance in the idea that people would abstain from buying foreign exchange; the demand for flight capital was growing daily. From August 1937 to February 1938 the government lost sterling 10 million, or nearly one-fifth of its reserve of foreign currencies. Moreover, Free China was not receiving the full benefit of sales of foreign exchange since the Japanese war around Shanghai obstructed the shipment of imported goods to Nationalist-held regions in the interior. Consequently, the government decided to restrict the amount of foreign exchange offered for sale, and after

TABLE 8. THE FOREIGN EXCHANGE RATE AND INTERNAL PRICE LEVELS, 1937–1939

| | | Foreign Exchange Rate[1] (CNC per U.S. $1) | Per cent Increase in Foreign Exchange Rate | Per cent Increase[2] in Wholesale Prices (All Free China) |
|---|---|---|---|---|
| 1937 | June | 3.41 | — | — |
| | Dec. | 3.42 | [3] | 7 |
| 1938 | June | 5.40 | 58 | 17 |
| | Dec. | 6.40 | 19 | 22 |
| 1939 | June | 7.80 | 22 | 32 |
| | Dec. | 14.48 | 85 | 49 |

[1] Based on tables of quotations of U.S. dollar compiled by the Economic Research Department of Central Bank of China.

[2] Taken from tables of monthly statistics compiled by Directorate-General of Budgets, Accounts and Statistics of the Republic of China.

[3] Negligible increase.

March 14, 1938, the Central Bank assumed control of all buying of foreign currencies. There was a prompt fall in the external value of the currency, and by the end of the year CNC had depreciated 87 per cent against the U.S. dollar.

Throughout 1938 the Japanese exploited the Shanghai market by accumulating CNC in North China and using it to buy foreign exchange to finance imports of cotton for Japanese mills in Shanghai and other essential commodities for re-export to Japan. The Nationalist government was cognizant of these tactics but felt itself compelled to support the Shanghai market, the alternative being rapid depreciation in the external value of CNC. Early in 1939, with the founding of the Hua Hsing Bank, the Japanese made a strong bid to capture the foreign exchange market in Shanghai from the Chinese government by making Hua Hsing notes the main circulating currency. Two months later, however, the Central Bank of China, together with the British banks, participated in a scheme to stabilize the external value of CNC. The Sino-British Stabilization Fund was established to operate in the exchange markets of Shanghai and Hong Kong. The demand for foreign currency was mounting rapidly at this time. Confidence in the currency was shaken by a succession of Chinese military reverses, and the Japanese were flooding the market with CNC. The Fund's resources were not designed to withstand these abnormal strains, and it was compelled to suspend operations twice in July to allow the market to settle at a new rate. Toward the end of the year the Fund was greatly assisted by windfall gains accruing from the appreciation of CNC against sterling with the outbreak of war in Western Europe, and by a flight of foreign capital from Hong Kong, Malaya, and the Dutch East Indies to Shanghai provoked by the imposition of exchange controls in those places. During 1939 wholesale prices in Free China rose by 81 per cent, those in Chungking by 64 per cent, and those in Shanghai by 158 per cent; but the external value of the national currency fell by only 47 per cent against sterling, and 56 per cent against the U.S. dollar.

Thus the long standing of CNC in the foreign exchange market and the measures for stabilization undertaken by the Chinese government in conjunction with the foreign banks frustrated the efforts of the Japanese to bring about a rapid depreciation in the external value of CNC and protected it against the competition from Hua Hsing notes. The basic strength of CNC derived from its convertibility into other currencies. The notes of the puppet banks lacked this essential attribute. They could not be converted into foreign exchange, nor were they accepted by the foreign banks in Tientsin and Shanghai. Although the exchange rate was influenced considerably by the subversive tactics of the Japanese, the government succeeded in preventing the exchange rate from rising uncontrollably from mid-1938 until the end of 1939.

### *The Inflationary Process*

Only those events affecting the general level of prices which occur independently of the inflationary process itself can be considered as causes of inflation. For example, government spending may increase merely as a result of higher costs accompanying an upward movement in prices, in which case it should not be considered as an independent variable in the inflationary process. If, however, government spending increases independently of prices as a result of an exogenous factor such as the outbreak of war, it may be properly regarded as a basic cause of inflation. In attempting to explain inflation in China, therefore, we must examine (1) the factors setting the inflationary process in motion in the early stages, (2) the additional factors aggravating inflation in the later stages and arising independently of the inflationary process, and (3) the characteristics of the process itself. In this third respect, we shall be concerned with the responsiveness of the economy to inflationary pressures.

In a majority of instances, inflation in war and postwar periods has resulted from an initial rise in government demands on the national output beyond what could be satisfied by increased production plus imports. The rise in government demand has frequently been accompanied at a later stage by increasing pressure of investment and consumer demand. The situation in China was somewhat different. By the end of 1938 the enemy had overrun regions producing some 50–55 per cent of total output, and imports to Free China were falling. This abrupt reduction in supply was a prime cause of inflation. On the demand side, there was a failure of total demand to adapt itself to the reduced volume of goods available. Compared with the prewar period, government demand taken as the real value of government spending was down by 6 per cent in the second half of 1937 and 30 per cent in 1938, although the geographical area under government control had fallen by an even greater percentage. Private investment demand, however, was probably higher than prewar in both monetary and real terms. In 1939 the monetary value of government bank credit granted to private business was 306 per cent above that of 1938, and 182 per cent higher in real terms. These changes on the demand side assume a much greater significance when they are related to the reduction in available supplies. A fall of only 30 per cent in government demand in the face of a 50 per cent drop in supply leaves much the same inflationary gap as an increase of 20 per cent in government demand with a constant supply. Thus the carry-over of a high rate of government spending into the comparatively restricted area of Free China and the huge credit expansion encouraged by the government were potent inflationary forces.

The third component of total demand—consumer demand—was of less inflationary significance. Because of the flight of refugees from the coastal provinces the population of Free China may have risen from a prewar 180 million to 230 million by the middle of 1940, locating about one-half of China's total population in Free China. At first sight this rise in the consuming population may be thought to be of more significance than the pressure of government and investment demands since these latter demands are small relative to consumer demand in underdeveloped countries. However, between 55 per cent and 60 per cent of China's prewar agricultural output was produced in the provinces of Free China, crop yields in 1938 and 1939 were good, and the inflow of population took place gradually over a three-year period. Judging by the moderate rate at which food prices rose until the second half of 1939, the movement of population was not of primary inflationary importance in the early years. Of the other two demand factors, the government deficit was the main cause of inflation in the first six months of the war, the expansion of credit becoming significant after the government adopted a very liberal credit policy in the middle of 1938.

The fall in total supply and the relative shift of productive resources to government and investment uses provided the primary basis for inflation in China. On the monetary side, the budgetary deficit and credit expansion caused large increases in the currency supply, as can be seen from Table 9. In the first year of war the

TABLE 9. INDICATORS OF CHINESE INFLATION, 1937–1939
(Base of all indexes, Jan.–June 1937 = 100)

| Period | | Gov't Deficit[1] | Note Issue[2] | Wholesale Prices (All Free China)[3] | Import Prices (Chungking)[4] | Foreign Exchange Rate: CNC–U.S. $1 (Shanghai)[5] |
|---|---|---|---|---|---|---|
| 1937 | June | 100 | 100 | 102 | 91 | 100 |
| | Dec. | 148 | 116 | 109 | 147 | 100 |
| 1938 | June | 208 | 123 | 127 | 227 | 158 |
| | Dec. | 239 | 164 | 155 | 389 | 187 |
| 1939 | June | 240 | 209 | 205 | 501 | 228 |
| | Dec. | 336 | 304 | 306 | 1,054 | 424 |

[1] The deficit of the first half-year of 1937 was based on revenue excluding the proceeds of Consolidation Bonds; the proportion of deficit between first half-year and second half-year is 5 to 7.

[2] Based on the statistics compiled by Central Bank of China.

[3] Taken from tables of monthly statistics compiled by Directorate-General of Budget, Accounts and Statistics.

[4] Taken from tables of monthly statistics compiled by the Economic Research Department of Central Bank of China.

[5] Based on tables of quotations of U.S. dollar compiled by the Economic Research Department of Central Bank of China.

note issue lagged behind the government deficit. This discrepancy is partly accounted for by relatively large sales of foreign exchange and government bonds, which offset a third of the deficit for 1937–1938, and partly by the existence of idle funds in the hands of the government banks immediately after the outbreak of war. From the second half of 1938 through 1939, however, new currency issues approximated the deficit because of the expansion of private credit. It is worth observing here that the increase of notes in circulation in Free China was greater than the rise in the note issue. The volume of currency in circulation was also swollen by funds brought into Free China by refugees from the eastern provinces, and by sums transferred by people living in North China after the suppression of CNC.

Shortages caused by the reduction of supplies and the increased demands of the government and private entrepreneurs were most serious in a specific range of capital goods and in raw materials for industrial production. It is true that foodstuffs for provisioning the army comprised the bulk of government demand, but the comparatively slow rise in food prices in 1937 and 1938 indicates that government requirements were not excessive relative to supply in this early stage. The remainder of government demand and the whole of investment demand were concentrated on capital goods, and prices of these goods rose enormously. For instance, by the end of 1938 the price index for metals and electrical goods in Chungking had increased three and a half times as much as the general wholesale price index. As illustrated by the indexes in Table 8, import prices also advanced at a faster rate than other prices.

Prices of imports reacted to changes in the rate of foreign exchange as well as to internal conditions of supply and demand. The exchange rate rose much more rapidly than internal prices in the middle of 1938 and again at the end of 1939. On both occasions (see Table 7) the Chinese government was unable to keep the exchange rate in line with internal prices as a result of Japanese currency warfare and the flight of capital from Shanghai. Except for these two periods, however, the exchange rate increased more slowly than other prices and was not a source of inflation. Thus the inflation of the early war years was manifested largely in the rise in the prices of raw materials and manufactures, with prices of agricultural commodities responding slowly to over-all inflationary trends. The loss of imports and industrial productive capacity, the government deficit, and the expansion of private credit were of prime importance in generating this effect. The gradual growth of consumer demand in the provinces near the fighting front and the two major variations in the foreign exchange rate tended to aggravate these basic causes.

### *Stabilizing Influences*

At the start of the war Free China was confronted with a formidable array of potentially inflationary conditions. Yet the increase in the general level of prices lagged far behind the deficit and the expansion of the supply of credit and currency until the closing months of 1939. Thus it was two years before the inflationary process was set in motion and all prices began to rise as fast as, or faster than, the government deficit and other initiating factors.

A number of circumstances account for the economy's relatively slow response to inflationary pressures. Perhaps most important of all, the economic base of Free China became the predominantly rural sector of the interior, where prices showed less sensitivity to inflationary stimuli than in the urban sector. The supply situation was considerably eased by the development of alternative lines of communications with the outside world after China's seaports had fallen to the enemy. Before communications with Hong Kong were severed at the end of 1938, the Chinese government began the construction of a railway with a total length of 644 miles from Hunan Province, through Kwangsi, to connect with the terminal of the Indo-China railway at Chennankwan. By dint of prodigious efforts the first section of 224 miles from Hengyang to Kweilin was built in eight months at the record speed of one kilometer per day. In 1939 the project was more than half completed and a connection was established between the Hunan-Kwangsi line and the Hankow-Canton system. Japanese penetration of Kwangsi prevented the completion of the 304-mile stretch to the Indo-China border, but the finished section greatly facilitated the movement of goods brought by road from Indo-China in addition to playing an important role in the evacuation of Hankow and Canton. The construction of the Burma Road from Kunming in Yunnan Province to Wanting on the Burma border was also a significant achievement. This road, with a distance of 600 miles traversing some of the most mountainous country in China, was built by an army of 160,000 workers in eight months, and at the end of 1938 the highway was opened to traffic. China received a revivifying flow of foreign goods by way of the Burma Road, and in the first half of 1939 import prices rose less than other prices for the first time since hostilities had begun. These counterblockade measures partly overcame the difficulties caused by the loss of sea, rail, and river communications.

However, there were more important reasons for the slow progress of inflation in China. Basically, the rate at which prices increase in a time of war inflation is determined by three factors: the extent to which the supply of consumer goods is dislocated by the conditions of war; the responsiveness of consumer incomes to rises in the cost of living and to the creation of new means of payment; and the public's propensity to consume, i.e., the proportion of total income spent for consumption. Each of these factors may be examined in turn.

The supply of consumer goods in Free China was not greatly curtailed in the first two years of war, either by the loss of the eastern provinces or by additional government and investment demands on total output. Consequently, the cost of living index rose slowly in comparison to prices of producer goods. Although the Japanese occupation had seriously interrupted supplies of manufactured consumer goods in Free China, large stocks of clothing and other consumer items had been transferred to the interior at the outbreak of war by the merchants of the coastal cities. These stocks moderated the influence of the reduction in imports on prices, an effect that was prolonged by the postponable nature of consumer demand for semi-durables. Items such as housing space became scarce in districts inundated with refugees, but this experience was by no means general. Besides, the average Chinese was content with improvised shelter, and there was no marked jump in housing costs. Foodstuffs, the most important component of consumer expenditure, were in relatively abundant supply as agricultural production increased in Free China. Output in fifteen provinces of Free China in 1938 and 1939 was 8 per cent above the average of the seven prewar years 1931–1937. The failure of the Japanese campaign against Changsha enabled Free China to continue to draw products from the fertile rice fields of Hunan. From the point of view of the progress of inflation, therefore, the move from the urban coastal section to the more rural interior was auspicious.

Turning to the additional wartime demands for consumer goods, we note that government spending and private investment activities did not involve a very great diversion of products from consumer markets or of resources from the production of agricultural commodities in Free China prior to 1940. Government expenditure was not a very large component of total market demand. According to estimates of China's national income for a number of prewar years, it appears that the total expenditures of the central government in 1936 did not exceed 5 per cent of the gross national product.* On the basis of a rough estimate, government spending had increased to 12 per cent of the gross national product of Free China by 1938 after allowance for a 50 per cent loss of productive capacity to the Japanese. In 1939 government spending fell to 9 per cent of the national product of Free China. Hence, although government demands on output in Free China were highly inflationary in the longer period, since no attempt was made to reduce the competing claims on output by private investors and consumers in the early years, the general level of prices responded slowly to the deficit because of the relatively limited scope of government activities. Moreover, much of government and all of investment spending were directed toward a specific

* Liu Ta-chung, *China's National Income, 1931–1936,* Washington, D.C., 1946.

range of capital goods. The provisioning of the Chinese armies, which were spread over a very large area of the country, did not present a major problem for the government while harvest yields were high. Where the provisioning of troops or government construction workers led to shortages of foodstuffs, they tended to be confined to particular geographical regions because of the lack of communications. For example, the government amassed a large number of workers in Yunnan to construct the Burma Road, causing a scarcity of foodstuffs in that province. But, in view of high transport costs, prices had to rise very greatly before it became profitable to transship foodstuffs to Yunnan; this prevented the spread of shortages to other provinces.

However, the supply of agricultural products could have been affected by the diversion of manpower from rural production to military and strategic occupations. Government and private investment activity in the interior implied a demand for industrial labor, which, for a number of reasons, had only a very gradual effect on the supply of farm workers. Despite the rapid wartime expansion of manufacturing and mining in Free China, the additional industrial workers required amounted to a small fraction of the total labor force. The government made provision for the evacuation of large numbers of foremen and factory workers from the industrial centers of the coast to facilitate the growth of industry in the interior. It was estimated by the Ministry of Economic Affairs that 50,000 experienced factory workers had been resettled in Free China by the end of 1940. Thus the transfer of workers from agricultural to industrial employment was not of great magnitude. Nor did the government's military recruiting campaign make serious inroads into the farm population in these early years, although recruitment in regions in the vicinity of the fighting fronts and of the war capital led to localized labor shortages. Lastly, the inflow of refugees to Free China and the high degree of concealed underemployment in agriculture softened the impact of government and industrial demands on the supply of farm labor. Again, the fact that the war effort was now focused on the rural sector, with some additions of equipment, skilled labor, and products brought from the prewar industrial sector, provided unplanned advantages.

A second major stabilizing influence on the Chinese economy was the slow adaptation of incomes of major consumer groups to rises in the cost of living and the increased supply of money. To appreciate the significance of this factor it is necessary to refer briefly to the working of the inflationary process. The initial rise in prices resulting from the additional government and investment demands of a war period frequently causes a shift in the distribution of incomes in favor of merchants, manufacturers, and owners or producers of capital goods. Other income groups—laborers and salaried workers—are not prepared to accept this loss of real income and may eventually obtain wage increases through more or less forceful bargaining methods. Consumers, the government, and industry then compete to retain their share of the product of the economy's total economic resources, and further price rises occur, a process which leads to the familiar wage-price spiral. The rise in incomes of wage and salary earners following the rise in the price level is the mechanism by which a continuous increase in prices is generated. The fuller the degree of adjustment of wages and salaries to prices, and the more frequently these adjustments are made, the faster is the rate of increase of prices emanating from an original rise in the cost of consumption goods.

As might be expected, wages in China were not adjusted to the cost of living as fully as they would have been in a more highly industrialized economy. This was not the result of a lack of bargaining power on the part of Chinese workers. The absence of the trade unions of Western societies was more than compensated for by the solidarity of the workers deriving from their social organization. The principal reason for the sluggishness of wages was a sense of patriotism that restrained the demands of workers. Their ignorance of accurate measures of cost of living increases may also have been a factor. The scanty information available suggests that wages lagged behind the cost of living in the first years of the war. But in Chungking itself, in 1938, the wages of industrial workers, both in and out of factories, moved more rapidly than the cost of living, which for a time remained quite low; but, on the whole, these wages too seem to have fallen behind by 1939. Information relating to the wages of agricultural workers in Szechwan suggests that rural wages rose faster than the cost of living in both 1938 and 1939. This condition, however, probably was not typical for Free China as a whole, since army recruitment and the use of large numbers of coolies on construction work and in human transport services encroached on farm labor supplies to a greater extent in Szechwan than in most other provinces.

While it is appropriate to regard the level of wages as the basic determinant of consumer income in a mature economy, in China other sources of income must be taken into account. Since the major part of the consuming population of China, particularly in rural-based Free China, consisted of small peasant proprietors and tenants, the prices demanded by farmers for agricultural products were the most important factors influencing consumer incomes. Because of ignorance and distance from the market, farmers did not react quickly to the high prices they found themselves paying for manufactured goods. Thus, in these early stages of the war, wages, salaries, and agricultural returns must have lagged some way behind the general level of prices. Evidence is found in the fact that food prices did not rise as fast as the cost of living, which included the increased prices of manufactured goods. It was not until peasants grasped the full import of inflationary trends and began to bargain for higher prices for their products that a true sequence of related rises in prices and incomes, corresponding to the wage-price spiral of a more highly organized industrial economy, made its appearance.

The third source of inertia was overcome only gradually by inflationary pressures. In the first eighteen months of the war the propensity to consume was curbed by an increase in the demand for money for the purpose of hoarding. In the climate of uncertainty created by the war, money became the most convenient and secure form of storing wealth, and there was a general movement on the part of the public to hold assets in liquid funds. This preference for money prevailed until the public began to view the depreciation of the currency as inevitable. Some restoring of money to circulation by informed groups in the business community took place after the sudden fall in the external value of the currency in March 1938, but the comparative stability of the foreign exchange rates during the next six months was still conducive to hoarding. However, when the fall of Hankow and Canton in October 1938, the severe reverses suffered by the Chinese armies early in 1939, and the gathering momentum of internal price rises undermined confidence in the currency, hoarding of money was abandoned in the cities in favor of hoarding goods. In the more isolated provinces hoarding of money continued somewhat longer. Among the peasantry there had always been a shortage of money income relative to needs for manufactured goods. Consequently, as prices of agricultural products rose and no more manufactured goods became available, additional funds received by the farmers tended to be hoarded for future spending. For a period at the beginning of the war, therefore, the disappearance of money into private hoards was an important factor relieving the pressure of demand for consumer goods.

It can be seen, then, that the slow generation of inflation in Free China was caused by three important lags: the lag in the cost of food and consumer goods behind general price levels; the lag in wages, salaries, and agricultural incomes behind the cost of food and consumer goods; and the lag of consumer spending behind income. All of these lags resulted in large part from the fact that China's war economy was principally based on the rural sector. The respective causes of these lags may be summed up as follows. (1) Considering Free China in isolation, the loss of production and imports occasioned by the Japanese occupation of the coast was small in relation to total output available to meet the normal pattern of consumer demand in these areas. Further, the additional government and investment demands imposed on the economy, though very great in relation to the available supply of capital goods, were small in relation to the total output of consumer goods in Free China, particularly since agricultural production expanded appreciably in the first two years of the war. Hence the supply of consumer goods was not severely disrupted, and the cost of living rose moderately. Large buffer stocks of manufactured consumer goods transferred to the interior at the outbreak of war were also important in meeting increased consumer demand. (2) Wages, salaries, and agricultural incomes were largely determined by agricultural prices which did not rise as fast as the cost of manufactured goods. (3) The government policy of maintaining the foreign exchange rate helped to preserve the public's confidence in the currency early in the war. During this period the consumers' general desire for liquidity was expressed in the hoarding of money. It should also be noted that commodity hoarding would have been difficult in the conditions of the rural economy, where centralized markets were rare.

Chapter

# 2

# War Inflation: 1940–1945

## 1. The Middle Period of War Inflation: 1940–1941

### *The Influence of Supply Factors on the Inflationary Process*

The year 1940 marked a turning point in inflation in Free China. Prices of imported goods and goods from other provinces led Chungking price levels in the early years of the war, and the comparatively slow advance of prices of consumer goods was a stabilizing influence on the economy. In 1940, however, Free China experienced a severe crop failure, and the prices of foodstuffs rose dramatically. The summer rice crop in the fifteen provinces of Free China in 1940 was 20 per cent below the previous year, although winter harvests of wheat were kept the same. Consequently, the output of agricultural foodstuffs during 1940 fell by an over-all amount of 10 per cent; and the Chungking price index for rice, the most important single item in the price structure, rose from 213 in May to 1,004 in December. The decline in food production continued through 1941, when output of agricultural commodities decreased by another 13 per cent to 9 per cent below the prewar average.

The sudden drop in agricultural output in 1940, eliminating most of the factors that had operated to restrain the rate of price rises in the first stages of the war, accelerated the process of general inflation. Farmers, who had previously suffered a loss of real income because of the lag in agricultural prices behind the general price level, began hoarding their products in anticipation of further gains in prices. Flourishing black markets in the provincial towns pushed prices of foodstuffs far beyond the "fair price" quotations of the local guilds and agents of the government. There was an upsurge in consumer spending as industrial and operational workers demanded and obtained higher wages, and as farm incomes underwent an unprecedented increase owing to the jump in food prices. With the supply of agricultural commodities declining and transport and communications severely dislocated by the Yangtze blockade, the loss of railways, and Japanese bombings, Free China for the first time began to feel the strain of supporting a consuming population much in excess of its prewar size.

The deterioration in the supply situation in 1940 was not confined to locally produced agricultural products. Japanese military operations added to the plight of Free China in 1940 and 1941, although they were not so damaging as in the first years of the war. Having severed the trade route to Indo-China at the vital interport of Nanning, Kwangsi, in November 1939, the Japanese sealed the border more effectively. They first brought pressure to bear on the French authorities to stop essential commodities being shipped north on the Indo-China-Yunnan railway, and later, in September 1940, concluded an agreement with the Vichy government enabling Japanese troops to enter Indo-China from the south. When the British authorities temporarily closed the Burma Road for three months in July 1940, Free China was virtually isolated from the outside world. Following their successful attack on Ichang in June 1940, Japanese forces attempted to consolidate their hold on Hankow and Wuchow by sending expeditions against the Chinese in Southern Honan and Northern Kwangsi. In addition they again thrust south to the strategic outpost of Changsha with the object of gaining possession of the rich rice fields of Hunan. Fortunately, these operations in Central China were indecisive.

In the middle period of the war, therefore, the Japanese emphasized their policy of containment. Shortages of imported goods in the interior grew more acute, particularly since Free China no longer had access to the considerable volume of manufactures which formerly had been drawn from stocks in Shanghai and had been smuggled as far as Ichang or had entered Free China via Indo-China. Lack of information makes it impossible to estimate accurately the loss of imports suffered in the period 1940–1941, but the volume of imports into the interior in 1941 was probably not more than a third of the volume of goods entering in 1939.

After the temporary precedence of agricultural price rises in 1940, import prices regained the lead in 1941, as Table 10 records. In 1941, also, Chungking prices of goods from other provinces climbed more steeply than locally produced commodities. Rising costs of transportation, heavy interest payments on working capital tied up in shipments which often took many weeks to arrive at their destination, and high remittance fees charged on transfers of funds all affected Chungking's prices of goods from other provinces and of imports.

TABLE 10. INDEXES OF PRICES IN FREE CHINA, 1940–1941
(Base: June 1939 = 100)

| Period | | Locally Produced Goods (Chungking)[1] | Goods from Other Provinces (Chungking)[1] | Imported Goods (Chungking)[1] | All Commodities (All Free China)[2] |
|---|---|---|---|---|---|
| 1939 | June | 100 | 100 | 100 | 100 |
| | Dec. | 157 | 184 | 210 | 149 |
| 1940 | June | 277 | 266 | 327 | 238 |
| | Dec. | 601 | 441 | 415 | 391 |
| 1941 | June | 893 | 584 | 684 | 600 |
| | Dec. | 1,303 | 1,101 | 1,520 | 1,029 |

[1] Taken from tables of monthly statistics compiled by the Economic Research Department of Central Bank of China.

[2] Taken from table of monthly statistics compiled by Directorate-General of Budgets, Accounts and Statistics.

At the end of 1940, for instance, transport, interest, and remittance charges amounted to about 70 per cent of the original cost of cotton goods received from Shanghai; and the Chungking price index for textile goods increased from 439 in June 1940 to 715 in December.

Thus in the second period of inflation, inflationary trends quickened as a result of the sharp diminution in the supply of agricultural goods and a further reduction in the volume of imported goods. Somewhat mitigating the effects of the Japanese blockade on available supplies in Free China, however, was the increase in the output of locally produced manufactures made possible by the industrial development of 1938 and 1939. The production of producer goods increased by 40 per cent in 1940 and 30 per cent in 1941, and that of consumer goods increased by 110 per cent and 32 per cent respectively for the same periods.* Nevertheless, the absolute levels of output of these commodities remained small in comparison with the total requirements of Free China, shortages were severe, and prices continued to rise.

* *China Handbook 1937–1947* (New York, Macmillan, 1947).

## *The Government Deficit*

After the outbreak of war in Europe in 1939 the Chinese government took the view, generally supported by the public, that China would be left to fight alone while attention focused on the European theater of war. It was clear that the Chinese war was becoming part of a worldwide struggle likely to be fought over a considerable period of time, but it was not anticipated that the Japanese would attempt to penetrate the interior in any force. Without regard to the costs in terms of inflation, the government resolved to strengthen the armies of Free China in readiness for embarking on a full-scale counteroffensive at some distant date. Stemming from this policy, a new phase of recruitment was begun in 1940, which proceeded at an annual rate of 500,000 new trainees for the next three years. A large number of additional operational bases were established in the provincial towns, and army officials scoured the countryside in search of suitable men of fighting age. The consequences of this policy were highly inflationary. Since means of transportation in the interior were hopelessly inadequate, the provisioning of troops concentrated near the towns presented a formidable problem and involved the government in heavy expenditures. Since the official army ration of food and clothing exceeded the subsistence standard of living previously enjoyed by the average recruit, the induction of men into the armed forces increased the strain on supplies of consumer goods. Finally, the rural labor supply was disrupted by the recruitment campaign, with subsequent unfavorable effects on rural wages and the volume of agricultural output.

Direct expenditures on the army and on strategically important construction works accounted for 73 per cent of government expenditure in the middle war years compared with a corresponding proportion of 70 per cent in the early period of 1937–1939. Total government spending rose more than three and a half times in the years 1939 to 1941, as against an increase of nearly sixfold in wholesale prices. Until the end of 1941, however, government measures to raise revenues in conformity with increased spending were for the most part unsuccessful. To compensate for the loss of salt revenues, customs duties, and other yields from indirect taxes, the government imposed a number of levies on inland trade that affected a wide range of consumer goods. Direct taxes were also revised by the introduction of an excess profits tax. These changes helped to stabilize tax revenue at about 6 per cent of expenditure during 1940 and 1941, but non-tax revenue fell heavily in 1941. In this year revenue reached a wartime low of

13 per cent of government expenditure compared with 25 per cent in the previous year.

At the end of 1941 the government made two highly significant changes in the tax structure, but favorable results from these changes were not felt in full until 1942. A fundamental weakness of the prewar Chinese tax system was that all indirect taxes were specific rates with yields in accordance with the volume of taxable transactions but not with commodity prices. In September 1941 indirect taxes were levied for the first time on an ad valorem basis, with immediate benefit to revenues. The second important measure grew out of the government's determination to obtain an assured supply of food for the army and to end the procedure by which the government competed on the open market for available supplies of foodstuffs. In June 1941 the right to taxation of land was transferred from the provincial governments to the central government, and the tax was made payable in kind rather than in money. Even in 1941, when the land tax applied to winter crops alone, it represented an enormous saving to the government and was the leading revenue producer. Converted to monetary terms, the land tax contributed about CNC $2,731 million, or 27 per cent of government expenditure, in that year.

The government continued to rely on creation of new currency to finance the deficit (Table 11). In 1940 public subscriptions to bonds

TABLE 11. CHINESE GOVERNMENT EXPENDITURE, REVENUE, AND DEFICIT
(CNC $ million)

| Year | Expenditures[1] | Revenue[2] | Deficit[1] |
|---|---|---|---|
| 1939 | 2,797 | 740 | 2,057 |
| 1940 | 5,288 | 1,325 | 3,963 |
| 1941 | 10,003 | 1,310 | 8,693 |

[1] Based on the data in the statistics of Statistical Department of the Ministry of Finance.

[2] Including the proceeds of bond subscription: 1939, 25 million; 1940, 8 million; and 1941, 127 million.

fell to a wartime low of CNC $8 million. The government ascribed the complete collapse of the bond market to lack of effective promotion, and established a Wartime National Bonds Subscription Committee, headed by Generalissimo Chiang Kai-shek, to conduct a more vigorous selling campaign. In 1941 sales of bonds showed considerable improvement, rising to CNC $127 million. Despite this success, bond proceeds were insignificant when set against the budget deficit, representing less than 2 per cent of the increase in note issue for the year.

### *Bank Credit and the Note Issue*

The steep rise in prices in 1940 brought about a sudden change in the government's attitude toward the extension of credit to private business. In the view of the Chinese populace, private banks were held responsible for the quickening of inflationary trends, although they supplied less than three-tenths of the total credit granted to industry and commerce. Influenced by public opinion, the government decided to abandon the liberal credit policy of the early years and to impose controls on the operations of both government and private banks. Restrictions on banking were introduced in August 1940 and were supplemented by further measures at the end of the year. The two main objectives at this time were to secure a distribution of credit in line with the strategic needs of the economy and to prevent the use of bank funds for speculative ventures. To these ends all banks were directed to devote their resources to financing essential industries, restrictions were placed on the granting of loans secured on commodities, private banks were compelled to maintain reserves equivalent to 20 per cent of their deposits with one of the government banks, and all banks were prohibited from dealing in commodities. These measures were successful in curbing bank lending in the middle war years. The private credit extended by government banks in 1940 was reduced to four-tenths that of 1939, and the increase in private bank credit was also reduced.

The adoption of credit controls affected interest rates throughout Free China. Prior to 1941 the increase in interest rates was moderate. The easy credit policy of the earlier stages of the war actually caused a drop in interest rates in the interior during 1939, when the Chungking market rate stood at 0.9 per cent per month. However, by the end of 1941 the rate had risen to 2.7 per cent per month as a result of growing demand for money generated by the fact that prices were rising at a greater rate than the increase in the supply of funds at the disposal of the market.

As shown in Table 12, the increase in currency issues in 1940 was closely correlated with bank advances to the government. In the following year, however, the new credit restrictions were effective in curtailing the rate of currency expansion. Loans to private enterprise did not expand so rapidly as deposits, and the issue of new notes lagged considerably behind advances to the government.

### *The Foreign Exchange Rate*

Primarily as a result of the Japanese currency warfare, the foreign exchange rate on the Shanghai market underwent in the second half

TABLE 12. GOVERNMENT BANK LOANS AND THE NOTE ISSUE, 1940–1941
(CNC $ million)

| Year | Increase in Deposits[1] | Increase in Private Loans[1] | Advances to Gov't.[2] | Note Issue by Dec.[3] | Increase in Note Issue |
|---|---|---|---|---|---|
| 1940 | 1,377 | 223 | 3,834 | 7,870 | 3,580 |
| 1941 | 4,930 | 294 | 9,443 | 15,100 | 7,230 |

[1] Based on the report of the Joint Board of Administration of Government Banks, 1947.

[2] Based on the Statement of Revenue compiled by the Statistical Department of the Ministry of Finance.

[3] Based on the statistics of Central Bank of China.

of 1939 the steepest rise registered since the beginning of the war. However, apart from a somewhat smaller increase during the first three months of 1940, the exchange rate retained throughout the remainder of 1940 and 1941 a stability that was remarkable in view of the rapid upsurge of internal prices. This stability derived from the uncertainty surrounding the future of other currencies after the outbreak of war in Europe, restrictions placed on the operations of exchange markets overseas, and the moderating influence of stabilization funds.

Despite the assistance given the Sino-British Stabilization Fund by an inflow of funds from Hong Kong and Malaya in October and November 1939, the drain on its reserves was such that early in May 1940 hardly £200,000 remained in the Fund. From the Chinese point of view, it was fortunate that the invasion of Belgium and Holland shook the confidence of Chinese financiers and businessmen in foreign currencies and stimulated a further influx of foreign capital to Shanghai. The demand for foreign exchange abated slightly, while the supply increased greatly. By the end of May, the Fund was able to purchase £1 million at the fixed market rate, and the Chinese government took the opportunity to add U.S. $3 million to its reserves.

This reversal from capital export to capital import continued to assist the Sino-British Fund until a new body was constituted in April 1941. It was estimated that up to the end of 1940 the equivalent of CNC $2 billion in foreign exchange was repatriated from Hong Kong, Malaya, and the Dutch East Indies, where exchange controls were in force. These huge amounts of windfall capital enabled the Fund to hold the exchange rate at between CNC $16.7 and CNC $19.3 per U.S. dollar during the period June 1940–April 1941 (Table 13). The relative strength of CNC frustrated Japanese efforts to drive it out of the foreign exchange market and replace it with Hua Hsing notes, and early in 1941 the Hua Hsing Bank was closed and the Japanese trade dollar withdrawn from circulation.

TABLE 13. THE FOREIGN EXCHANGE RATE AND INTERNAL PRICE LEVELS, 1940–1941

| Period | | Foreign Exchange Rate (CNC per U.S. $1)[1] | Per cent Change in Exchange Rate | Per cent Increase in Prices (All Free China)[2] |
|---|---|---|---|---|
| 1939 | June | 7.80 | — | — |
| | Dec. | 14.47 | 85 | 49 |
| 1940 | June | 18.21 | 26 | 59 |
| | Dec. | 17.76 | −2 | 64 |
| 1941 | June | 19.00 | 7 | 54 |
| | Dec. | 18.93 | negligible | 71 |

[1] Based on table of quotations of U.S. dollar compiled by Economic Research Department of Central Bank of China.

[2] Taken from tables of monthly statistics compiled by Directorate-General of Budgets, Accounts and Statistics.

April 1941 saw the establishment of a new institution, the Stabilization Board of China, to which Great Britain, the United States, and China contributed £5 million, U.S. $50 million, and U.S. $20 million, respectively. The effectiveness of the Board was promoted by a number of measures put into operation by foreign governments. In July 1941, the governments of Great Britain, the United States, and Holland announced the freezing of funds in Chinese and Japanese accounts in banks within their jurisdiction; and in September, Britain and America instructed their Hong Kong and China branch banks to assist the Board through more selective methods of granting foreign exchange to importers in Japanese-surrounded Shanghai and in implementing a system of detailed restrictions on imports. The effects of these measures were to eradicate almost completely speculation in foreign exchange and flight of capital overseas, to reduce black-market transactions in foreign exchange to insignificant proportions, and to stop the seepage of foreign currency into enemy hands. The Board's actions had a large measure of success; the rise in the exchange rate in the latter part of 1941 was negligible, despite the continuation of internal inflation which raised commodity prices in Free China by 71 per cent.

### *The Inflationary Process*

At the beginning of this period a number of circumstances caused a very marked rise in the tempo of inflation in Free China. The most important development was the sharp decline in agricultural production, particularly in Szechwan province, the nerve center of the economy. The chain reaction of increases in prices, consumers' spending, and government spending had now gathered pace. The tightening of the Japanese blockade in Southern and Central China and the depletion of stocks moved to the interior at the outbreak of war aggravated the general commodity shortage. In this connection also, the destruction and dislocation of communications created intractable problems of distribution and added to inflationary pressures on the supply side.

The government deficit was once again dominant in causing inflation. Although the new military recruitment campaign and other additional commitments swelled government expenditures, much of the increase in government spending was a consequence of the rise in prices. Thus the government's procurement efforts, along with other sectors of the community, suffered from the reduction in available supplies, and the real volume of government purchases diminished. In contrast to government spending, the expansion of credit was successfully checked by controls and lost its former potency as an inflationary factor. During 1940 and 1941 the rate of increase in government bank loans to private business was about one-third that in increase in prices. Hence the expansion of the money supply was essentially a response to the budget deficit.

To the excess money demands of the government were added the demands of speculators for industrial raw materials and other investment goods and those of the general public for foodstuffs and other consumer goods suitable for hoarding in order to conserve the value of current assets. Reliable estimates of the magnitude of hoarding of daily necessities do not exist. From the middle of 1940, however, such hoarding took place on a scale possible only in an immature economy which lacked adequate industrial productivity and transportation, in which the government was undecided and unprepared to impose necessary measures to increase revenues commensurate with expenditures and control the distribution of commodities, and in which disruptive private motivations were not restrained in the public interest.

The foreign exchange rate was not significant as an unstabilizing influence at this time. The rate was insulated from the repercussions of internal inflation and the currency warfare of the Japanese by the operations of stabilization funds and fortuitous external events. It was not an important determinant of import prices, which responded mainly to the physical conditions of demand and supply; and, if it weighed at all in the considerations of businessmen at this stage, it probably helped to evoke confidence in the currency.

TABLE 14. INDICATORS OF CHINESE INFLATION, 1940–1941
(Base of all indexes, Dec. 1939 = 100)

| Period | | Government Deficit | Note Issue[1] | Wholesale Prices (All Free China)[2] | Import Prices (Chungking)[3] | Foreign Exchange Rate (CNC per U.S. $1)[4] |
|---|---|---|---|---|---|---|
| 1939 | Dec. | 100 | 100 | 100 | 100 | 100 |
| 1940 | June | 126 | 141 | 159 | 155 | 126 |
| | Dec. | 178 | 183 | 262 | 197 | 123 |
| 1941 | June | 302 | 249 | 403 | 325 | 132 |
| | Dec. | 423 | 352 | 690 | 722 | 131 |

1 Based on the statistics compiled by Central Bank of China.
2 Taken from tables of monthly statistics compiled by Directorate-General of Budget, Accounts and Statistics.
3 Taken from tables of monthly statistics compiled by the Economic Research Department of Central Bank of China.
4 Based on table of quotations of U.S. dollar compiled by the Economic Research Department of Central Bank of China.

It is interesting to note (Table 14) that wholesale prices in Free China increased at almost the same rate in 1941 as in 1940—almost double the rate of advance of 1939, suggesting that there was not further intensification of inflation in the short run following the initial impact of the drop in supply and government recruitment during 1940. This temporary respite, this constant rate of price increase, coincided with a lull in the Japanese offensive, and it lasted until the catastrophe of Pearl Harbor unleashed new inflationary forces on Free China.

## 2. THE FINAL PERIOD OF WAR INFLATION: 1942–1945

### *The Influence of Supply Factors on Prices*

As in the preceding periods of the war, in the years 1942–1945 some of the more marked changes in the tempo of inflation in Free China were directly correlated with supply interruptions caused by enemy action. The occupation of Shanghai by the Japanese shortly after Pearl Harbor deprived Free China of her last remaining contact with the sea and put an end to the smuggling of foreign goods or locally manufactured goods to the interior. A few months later, in May 1942, the Burma Road was sealed off when the Japanese invaded Yunnan from the west. Except for a long and tortuous road outlet through Kansu and Sinkiang to the Soviet border in the northwest, China's sole means of access to the outside world was an air link with Assam. The encirclement was virtually complete; the state of full siege had begun. In 1943 the Japanese concentrated their military attacks in other theaters of war, and, apart from a certain amount of fighting in Hupeh and Honan, the year was comparatively uneventful from a military viewpoint. In the middle of 1944 Chinese and American forces began a major offensive in Yunnan and Burma and gradually thrust back the aggressor beyond the Chinese border. A succession of victories culminated in the liberation of Wanting on the border and the reopening of the Burma Road at the end of January 1945. The situation on the eastern fronts, however, became critical in the autumn of 1944, when the Japanese launched a two-pronged attack on Szechwan. In the north the Japanese pushed steadily westwards through Honan, and in the south they advanced along the railway line from Changsha, through the rich agricultural lands of Hunan into Kwangsi and Kweichow. With the capitulation of the important centers of Kweilin, Ishan, and Tushan on the Kwangsi-Kweichow railway, the whole of the rail communications of the south fell into the possession of the enemy. At the beginning of 1945 the Japanese armies in the south constituted a direct threat to Szechwan. In March they launched a three-front offensive in Honan, Hupeh, and Hunan. However, a strong counteroffensive by the Chinese rolled them back in the south, and the tide of war subsequently flowed in favor of Free China until the unconditional surrender of Japan to the Allies on August 14, 1945.

The closure of the Burma Road and the occupation of Shanghai seriously undermined the economic stability of Free China. Although it is impossible to make an accurate estimate, imports for 1942 were probably around 50 per cent lower than those for 1941. A general loss of confidence in the currency and the expectation of even more acute shortages of foreign goods brought a quickening of price rises in 1942, and import prices considerably more than trebled. In subsequent years the improvement of air services over the hump from Assam to Yunnan led to a slightly improved supply of foreign goods, but in 1944 imports were some 78 per cent below 1941 levels and were only 6 per cent of China's total imports for 1937.

Agricultural supplies were not severely disrupted by military developments until the renewed offensive in Central China in the latter part of 1944, but the trend of food production in 1942 and 1943 was unfavorable. After 1941 the rice crop in the south continued to decline, and it was 28 per cent below prewar in 1943. Although the drop in rice supply was more than counterbalanced by increases in the production of wheat and barley, it remained of inflationary significance since the winter harvests of Honan and Hupeh could not easily be transported to the major consumption centers. Hence in 1942 and 1943 the increasing lag of food supply behind demand resulted mainly from inadequacy of communications rather than from an over-all diminution in production. In 1944 there was an increase in yields from summer crops and a bumper winter harvest which together lifted production for the year to 8 per cent above the prewar level. This compensated for the cutting off of important food-producing areas and means of transportation in the course of the Japanese advance in Central China. Together with the successes of American and Chinese forces in Burma, this development accounts for the fact that wholesale prices rose less in the second half of 1944 than at any time after the early months of 1941. It was not until the opening months of 1945 that price levels began to react violently to the menace of the Japanese offensive. Some indication of the loss of agricultural production stemming from Japanese infiltration of Hunan, Hupeh, and Honan in the closing months of 1944 and early 1945 is given by the fact that the quantity of foodstuffs collected in land tax in 1944–1945 dropped 11 per cent below the previous year's collections.

As regards industrial production, Free China became wholly dependent on local supplies of capital goods and manufactures after the Burma Road was closed in 1942. Production of these commodities was well sustained until 1943, when shortages of raw materials began to prevent full utilization in a number of sectors of industry. In the following year the decline in industrial production became more widespread, being particularly marked in consumer goods. The index of production of consumer goods declined by 9 per cent in 1944, and the output of some important consumer commodities fell even more, e.g., flour by 19 per cent, soap by 33 per cent, and leather by 20 per cent. Industrial production continued to meet only a fraction of the requirements of producers and consumers; and, as shortages of durable goods accumulated over the years, added inflationary potential arose from suppressed demand for these commodities.

These variations in the physical conditions of supply account for some of the discrepancies that are noticeable when price indexes for different categories of commodities over the last four years of the war are studied. Prices of imported goods at Chungking more than doubled immediately after Pearl Harbor and reacted further during the first half of 1942 when the Burma Road was lost. For the remaining war years the supply of foreign goods was limited to government purchases of essential war materials reaching Free China by air, and competition for imported commodities was for the most part eliminated. Hence the index of import prices lagged behind other commodity price indexes. The big jump in prices of home-produced goods between June 1943 and June 1944, as shown in Table 15, was the result of the pressure of excess demand stemming from the government deficit and levies in kind on supplies of agricultural commodities.

TABLE 15. INDEXES OF PRICES IN FREE CHINA, 1942–1945
(Base: December 1941 = 100)

| Period | | Locally Produced Goods (Chungking)[1] | Goods from Other Provinces (Chungking)[1] | Imported Goods (Chungking)[1] | All Commodities (All Free China)[2] |
|---|---|---|---|---|---|
| 1941 | Dec. | 100 | 100 | 100 | 100 |
| 1942 | June | 183 | 256 | 198 | 173 |
| | Dec. | 285 | 541 | 353 | 290 |
| 1943 | June | 452 | 990 | 461 | 613 |
| | Dec. | 938 | 1,524 | 765 | 1,057 |
| 1944 | June | 2,164 | 2,889 | 1,855 | 2,073 |
| | Dec. | 3,001 | 4,677 | 2,931 | 3,220 |
| 1945 | June | 8,663 | 15,290 | 8,610 | 9,547 |
| | Dec. | 8,160 | 11,561 | 6,386 | 10,075 |

[1] Taken from tables of monthly statistics compiled by the Economic Research Department of Central Bank of China.

[2] Taken from tables of monthly statistics compiled by Directorate-General of Budgets, Accounts and Statistics.

However, the influence of supply factors can be detected in the slowing down of price increases of domestic products in the second half of 1944 because of abundant crop yields and in the trebling of prices in early 1945, when most of Hunan was overrun by the enemy. Over the four-year period, prices of locally produced goods at Chungking did not rise so fast as those of commodities obtained from other provinces. The lead of prices of goods from other provinces was a manifestation of the inadequacy of transport systems in the interior. Communications were operated with decreased efficiency as the war continued, and operation was plagued by problems of repair, replacement, lack of fuel, and destruction of facilities by Japanese bombing.

### *The Government Deficit*

After the lavish expenditures on recruitment in 1940 and 1941 the pressure of government spending eased until the latter part of 1944. Military expenses remained the major component of government outlays, and considerable economies were effected in these by the collection of the land tax in kind and compulsory borrowing of agricultural products from the landowners and peasant owners. From the autumn of 1944 until the end of the war, however, government expenditures increased enormously as the Chinese armies in Central China resisted the last desperate onslaught of the Japanese and then gradually assumed the offensive. Military outlays rose from 51 per cent of total expenditure in 1944 to 69 per cent in 1945.

The administrative activities of the government were a further source of increased spending. The number of civil servants increased greatly after 1937, and, in the period under consideration, their ranks were further swelled by new organizations to control prices of daily necessities and carry out other measures of control. At the same time, the government permitted upward revisions in the pay of civil servants to meet the demands of those who had suffered drastic cuts in real income. Administrative and general expenditures of the government consequently rose very steeply toward the end of the war, increasing from 4 per cent of total government spending in 1940 to more than a third during 1941 and 1944. Money expenditure rose so rapidly in the spring of 1945 that the government reached a higher level of money and real expenditure than at any other time during the war.

With the introduction of a number of new tax measures, government revenues showed considerable improvement from the wartime low of 1941. Yields from indirect taxes were improved by the adoption of an ad valorem basis of calculation late in 1941, and further increased by the imposition of a wartime consumption tax collected by customs authorities. This tax replaced internal duties on trade in April 1942. In October 1943 a wartime surtax was imposed on salt, and in March 1944 an additional levy brought the total tax on this commodity to almost 90 per cent of the selling price. Between 1941 and 1944, proceeds from indirect taxes increased forty-nine times, while commodity prices had risen thirty-three times. Revenues from direct taxes also increased appreciably after the central government took over the business tax* from the provincial governments, reaching a peak of about three-eighths of total government revenues in 1943. In the closing years of the war, however, administration of direct taxes weakened, evasion becoming universal; and in 1944 and 1945 these levies dropped to two-eighths of total revenues.†

Non-tax receipts continued to decline relative to other categories of revenue until 1945, when they jumped suddenly to six-sevenths of total government receipts. This increase was reported to be from the revaluation of foreign reserve, and it appears most probably to have included the foreign exchange received from the United States in settlement of the advances made to American military forces in China.

The significance of the wartime fiscal measure in terms of structural changes in the tax system emerges from a comparison of the pattern of government revenues in 1944, the last full year of war, with the prewar period. The principal changes, therefore, were greater emphasis upon the salt tax and the shift toward direct taxes, which were conspicuously absent from the prewar tax system. In the prewar period the salt tax contributed an average of 20 per cent of total revenue—in 1944 almost 60 per cent; direct taxes contributed as much as 22 per cent in 1944, compared to less than 1 per cent before the war. Even so, the main burden of taxation fell on consumers in the form of indirect taxes.

Part of the explanation behind the moderate expansion of the government deficit in 1942 and 1943 (Table 16) lies in the development of these new sources of revenue. However, these measures were secondary in importance to the contribution made by collection of the land tax in kind. It will be recalled that in June 1941 the central government assumed control of the land tax. In July 1942 the government attempted to acquire additional supplies of foodstuffs by compulsory borrowing in kind and by compulsory purchasing. As a result, the quantity of grains collected increased by 150 per cent in 1942–1943.

### *Bank Credit and Currency Creation*

The restrictive measures imposed on the banking system in 1940, although effective at the time, proved inadequate as inflation gathered momentum. Private loans extended by the government banks con-

* A percentage tax on the volume of business transacted by the business establishments and on the actual capital of financial institutions.

† Excluding the profits derived from the revaluation of foreign exchange reserve in the non-tax revenue of 1945.

Table 16. Government Expenditure, Revenue, the Deficit and the Land Tax in Kind, 1941–1945[1] (CNC $ million)

| Year | Government Expenditure | Government Revenue | Government Deficit | Estimated Value of Collections of Land Tax in Kind[2] |
|---|---|---|---|---|
| 1941 | 10,003 | 1,310 | 8,693 | 2,731 |
| 1942 | 24,511 | 5,630 | 18,881 | 19,712 |
| 1943 | 58,816 | 20,403 | 38,413 | 46,446 |
| 1944 | 171,689 | 38,503 | 133,186 | 147,133 |
| 1945 | 2,348,085 | 1,241,389 | 1,106,696 | |

[1] Based on the statements of Revenue and Expenditure compiled by the Statistical Department of the Ministry of Finance; estimated value of collections in kind based on Table 42, Land Tax Collection.

[2] Land tax collections were reported on interyear (e.g. 1941–1942) rather than on a calendar year basis, including purchase and loan in kind.

tinued to increase while the private banks became deeply involved in speculative transactions despite official regulations. In an effort to curtail the activities of the smaller commercial and native banks, the government made an attempt at the end of 1941 to replace the unsecured lending of the private banks with discounting of accepted bills. The practical effects of this policy were negligible, and it was not until February 1942 that the government succeeded indirectly in imposing some measure of restraint on the private banks by tightening controls on the government banks. The government banks were now required to be more selective in granting credit to both industrial borrowers and private banks. Primarily as a result of this policy, the reported loans of the private banks fell from 40 per cent of total credit granted to private enterprise in 1941 to 22 per cent in 1944, although the actual volume of their credit operations may have been appreciably higher than their reported loans.

In February 1942 the government also introduced the practice of checking on the use of loan proceeds to insure that they were being employed by the borrowers for the purposes specified on the loan application. The Joint Board of Administration of Government Banks was made responsible for carrying out this checking procedure, in addition to its function of approving applications for credit. In September 1942 another important banking change was made by the government. The operations of the government banks were finally rationalized by allocating each of them specific lines of banking business, and a great deal of duplication of function was eliminated.

Although these measures contributed to the slowing down of the increase in private loans made by government banks, abuses could not be entirely eliminated. The rapid advance of price levels provided an irresistible temptation for private as well as government banks to use their funds in speculative ventures, and the government became incapable of keeping the distribution of credit in line with the basic defense requirements of the economy.

Interest rates rose steadily throughout the last four years of hostilities. In December 1941 the rate of interest on the fortnightly loans of the native banks was made subject to approval from the Central Bank, and in January 1943 all the private banks were required to submit their interest changes for official authorization. As a result, black-market rates became the ruling rates in the money market, and the government was forced to accept the rise of interest rates as an inevitable concomitant of credit restrictions and inflationary conditions. At the end of the war the market rate in Chungking stood at 5 per cent per fortnight, or 10 per cent per month as compared with a prewar rate of 1 per cent per month.

Restrictions on credit were accompanied by further measures to reduce the pressure of inflation by encouraging savings. The government began to take action to this effect with the introduction of the Thrift and Reconstruction Savings Plan of 1938, but the results were meager. In the winter of 1941 a campaign was launched to boost savings under government programs, and in 1942 government bank deposits nearly doubled as a result. In 1943 savings deposits had risen to 24 per cent of the total deposits of the government banks as against 8 per cent prewar. In view of the fact that the combined amounts of government advances and private credit extended by the government banks in 1943 exceeded the increase of deposits by 340 per cent, the government resorted to compulsory allocation of savings certificates. By this time, however, the value of the currency was depreciating so rapidly that the public resorted to many kinds of evasion to escape obligations under compulsory allocation, and the technique proved ineffective. It was unfortunate that what little was achieved by these methods of encouraging savings was more than counterbalanced by the decline in the fixed deposits after 1939. The ratio of fixed plus savings deposits to total deposits stood at 13 per cent in 1945 compared to 51 per cent in 1939.*

* Savings deposits are those accepted by savings banks or the especially established savings department of commercial banks. They yield compound interest until withdrawn, and usually are in small amounts. Fixed deposits are accepted by ordinary banks for a fixed period of time at simple interest.

During the years 1942 and 1943 the volume of private loans granted by the government banks continued to expand in amount to drain off the increase in deposits, and consequently there was an almost perfect correspondence between advances to the government and the increase in note issue since government banks had to issue new money to meet

TABLE 17. GOVERNMENT BANK LOAN AND THE NOTE ISSUE, 1942–1945
(CNC $ million)

| Year | Increase in Deposits[1] | Increase in Private Loans[2] | Government Advances[2] | Note Issue by Dec.[3] | Increase in Note Issue |
|---|---|---|---|---|---|
| 1942 | 8,865 | 4,511 | 20,081 | 34,400 | 19,300 |
| 1943 | 11,292 | 8,344 | 40,857 | 75,400 | 41,000 |
| 1944 | 64,467 | 13,531 | 140,090 | 189,500 | 114,100 |
| 1945 | 431,616 | 121,661 | 1,043,257 | 1,031,900 | 842,400 |

[1] Based on data compiled by Joint Board of Administration of Government Banks.

[2] Statement of Revenue compiled by Statistical Department of Ministry of Finance.

[3] Based on records of the Central Bank of China.

the government's needs (see Table 17). In 1944 and 1945 the position was reversed as a result of the rapid accumulation of bank deposits by both public and private depositors caused by a higher rate of government spending. In 1945 deposits exceeded private loans by nearly 255 per cent, enabling a fifth of advances to the government to be financed without recourse to the note issue.

## *The Foreign Exchange Rate*

After Pearl Harbor the Japanese took possession of the whole of Shanghai, and the Shanghai foreign exchange market was closed in July 1942. The buying and selling of foreign currencies in Free China was limited to markets in Chungking and Kunming, and the volume of transactions was extremely small following the contraction of international trade. Although the Exchange Stabilization Board of China continued to operate, its quotations of the exchange rate applied mainly to government purchases and its function became nominal after the middle of 1943. Until July 1943 the market rate was CNC $17.8 per U.S. $1, which was lower than the rate quoted by the Board in December 1941, while the market transactions in American currency remained insignificant. From 1943 onwards, the free market rate of exchange (shown in Table 18) recorded changes in the demand and supply of foreign currencies more accurately than the Board rate.

TABLE 18. THE FOREIGN EXCHANGE RATE AND INTERNAL PRICE LEVELS, 1942–1945

| Period | | Free Market Foreign Exchange Rate (CNC per U.S. $1)[1] | Per cent Increase in Foreign Exchange Rate | Per cent Increase in Wholesale Prices (All Free China)[2] |
|---|---|---|---|---|
| 1941 | June | 19 | — | — |
| | Dec. | 18.93 | negligible | 71 |
| 1942 | June | — | — | 73 |
| | Dec. | — | — | 68 |
| 1943 | June | 59 | 311 (relative to 1941) | 112 |
| | Dec. | 84 | 42 | 72 |
| 1944 | June | 192 | 128 | 96 |
| | Dec. | 570 | 197 | 55 |
| 1945 | June | 1,705 | 199 | 196 |
| | Aug. | 2,185 | 28 | 22 |

[1] Based on table of quotations of U.S. dollar compiled by Economic Research Department of Central Bank of China.

[2] Taken from table of Directorate-General of Budget, Accounts and Statistics.

These data suggest that after Pearl Harbor the free market foreign exchange rate was almost suspended. During this period demand for foreign currency was discouraged since imports were unavailable and funds held by Chinese nationals in Great Britain, United States, Holland, and their dependencies were frozen. The sale of U.S. Dollar Savings Certificates and Gold Dollar Bonds, both issued against credit furnished to the Chinese government by the U.S. Treasury, from March 1942 diverted the attention of speculators from foreign currencies. This situation prevailed until the autumn of 1943, when sales of Dollar Certificates and Gold Bonds were discontinued and the spending of American troops became an important source of foreign currency in the free market. Then, the free market exchange rate rose again. In 1944 the government deficit poured funds into the hands of speculators, who, unable to find sufficient outlets for their activities in commodities, turned to foreign currencies. The opening of the Sino-American offensive against the Japanese in Yunnan and Burma strengthened the belief that the war was entering its concluding stages and that normal transactions in foreign exchange would be possible within the foreseeable future. These conditions led to a marked rise in speculative demand for foreign exchange. The market rate nearly trebled in the second half of 1944 as against a 50 per cent increase in price levels, and it continued to climb more steeply than other prices until the end of the war. Even so, the index of the exchange rate over a longer period of time lagged far behind that of the general price level. In August 1945 the exchange rate stood at 600 times prewar, while wholesale prices were 2,455 times the prewar level.

### *Anti-Inflationary Measures*

As early as 1938 the Chinese government passed regulations relating to the control of prices in Free China. However, apart from the highly effective operations of the exchange stabilization funds after 1938 and the partial success of the restrictions imposed on bank credit in 1940, the government did not attack the problem of inflation in earnest until 1942. The various measures then applied had three objectives: to reduce the inflationary impact of the budget deficit, to curb bank lending, and to suppress the rise of prices by direct controls. Some of the measures concerned have been discussed above and are therefore not treated at length at this point.

*Measures to Reduce the Inflationary Impact of the Deficit.* The first efforts of the Chinese government in this direction were aimed at curtailing the growth of the deficit by raising revenues and reducing expenditures. The change from specific to ad valorem rates of indirect taxation, increased duties on the consumption of salt, and the development of income and other direct taxes resulted in a marked improvement in money revenues in the years 1942–1944. The most significant factor limiting the deficit, however, was land taxation, collected in kind and imposed with the express purpose of simultaneously reducing expenditures and securing regular supplies of food for the army. In fact, this was the most important anti-inflationary device employed during the war.

After the crop failure of 1940, government expenditures on food had mounted rapidly and had become the chief cause of the deficit. Through land taxation in kind the government was able to eliminate the bulk of its expenditures on food and to obtain agricultural products adequate to feed the army and provide rations to public servants. This process in turn retarded the growth of the government deficit, thereby restraining the expansion of the money supply by making it unnecessary for the government to bid for these supplies through monetary demand. However, it is evident from the movement of food prices that, in practice, the effects of the land levies were not wholly anti-inflationary. When the land tax was supplemented by compulsory borrowing in kind in 1942 the government share of food supplies increased considerably. The supply of foodstuffs in the market was correspondingly reduced and the rise of prices accelerated, providing a strong incentive to evade the land tax, which in turn increased its costs of collection. Although the introduction of compulsory borrowing of agricultural products in 1942 provoked an upsurge in food prices in 1942, the rise of prices would have been much more violent if the government had attempted to acquire the same amount of products by normal market methods.

Despite the salutary economic effects of the land levies during the war, the longer term social consequences of these measures were highly undesirable. As a class the small landowners and peasant owners already shouldered a heavier burden of taxation than other groups in the community and were least capable of bearing new taxes. The policy caused a great deal of discontent and afforded the Communists an opportunity to spread propaganda and arouse opposition to the established regime.

Government savings programs, including compulsory purchases of CNC Savings Certificates and the sale of U.S. Dollar Savings Certificates, were employed to partially cover the deficit by noninflationary financing. It was unfortunate that the savings thus mobilized were more than offset by the decline in fixed deposits held by the banks. Moreover, the amount of currency withdrawn through sales of gold bonds and dollar savings certificates in 1942 and 1943 was more than replaced by the inflow of national currency from areas occupied by the enemy.

*Restrictions on Bank Credit.* A fair degree of success was achieved in restriction of credit expansion, a primary object of any anti-inflationary program, by enforcing the regulations in 1940 and 1942. Nonetheless, speculative activities of many commercial and native banks continued to be a persistent source of instability throughout the war years.

*Price Controls.* The Chinese government was unable to develop a workable system of price controls, allegedly because it could not surmount the administrative problems involved. The first attempt at price control came in 1938. Late in that year the government had decreed that all prices should be fixed at fair levels by local government authorities in consultation with trade guilds, and that persons engaging in hoarding and speculation would be liable to heavy penalties. The experiment proved completely ineffectual. Many reasons have been given for the failure. Shortages of trained administrative personnel and the lack of co-ordination among the different levels of administration, including the guilds, the local governments, the provincial governments, and the central government; the lack of statistical information on supply and demand and population; the differences in commodity prices resulting from transportation costs and difficulties between the various geographic regions—all were apparent problems. In addition there was general popular antipathy to all forms of control. But perhaps most important of all, the government failed to appreciate the task to which it addressed itself.

The government did not return to the field of direct price controls until the end of 1942, this time with more modest objectives. Price ceilings were imposed in a few of the more important cities and applied to a limited range of daily necessities. The regulations did not stop at the promulgation of legal prices; the government endeavored to enforce them by carrying out physical controls. The principal techniques used in this connection were the so-called "Government Purchases and Sales of Commodities" and limitations on inventories and the use of scarce goods. Purchases and sales related, in the first place, to raw materials and semiprocessed goods, including liquid fuel, coal, coke, newsprint, cotton yarn and cloth, and eventually raw cotton. By bulk buying methods the government was able to ensure the sale of these commodities to producers and wholesalers at official prices. In the case of cotton, the government influenced costs at three levels of production by buying yarn from spinners, bartering it for cloth from weavers, and selling cloth to manufacturers at fixed prices. Eventually the government also became sole buyer of raw cotton. Used in conjunction with limitations on manufacturers' inventories, purchases and sales of these commodities were helpful in damping the price effects of competitive buying by entrepreneurs, in curbing hoarding of producer goods, and in preventing manufacturers from exploiting the public through exorbitant pricing. Bulk buying was also applied to a number of consumer goods—rice, salt, edible oil, and later sugar, matches, and tobacco. However, the efficiency of this system was hampered by some inherent defects. With the exception of rice, the government controlled a large proportion of the available supplies of the goods concerned, but it was unable to supervise effectively the final prices charged by retailers. Surplus supplies of rice remaining after the requirements of the army and civil servants had been met were sold by government agencies to the general public at fixed prices. However, the government supply of rice represented only a small percentage of the total free market supply, and consequently the influence of government selling on the price of this commodity was not great.

The fundamental weakness of price controls in Free China was that the government had neither the adminstrative strength to regulate prices at the retail level nor the ability to prevent dealers from exploiting inflationary conditions. Moreover, there was no way of cutting back consumer demand to the level of market supplies, for rationing of consumer goods presupposed the existence of an intricate administrative organization. As a result, the government's efforts to eliminate hoarding by producers and to hold down production costs in other ways were frustrated at the retail level. Even where controls achieved a modicum of success, price controls affected only a handful of commodities in a few of the larger cities of Szechwan Province and exerted little influence on the general level of prices. In the face of continuous increases in prices despite government controls, a wage freeze, also introduced in December 1942, proved futile.

### *The Inflationary Process*

The outbreak of war in the Pacific and the subsequent closing of the Burma Road threatened Free China with a volatile burst of inflation. In the first six months of 1942 wholesale prices rose by 73 per cent, while the supplies of imports suffered further reductions, perhaps 50 per cent or more. Fortunately the Japanese shifted their best troops to other theaters of war, and their activities did not again become seriously damaging to Free China until the autumn of 1944. Nonetheless, long after the initial impact of Pearl Harbor was felt in the price level, prices continued to rise with a rapidity hitherto unmatched.

The factors underlying the intensification of inflation from mid-1942 to mid-1943 were somewhat different from those operating to accelerate the process during other periods of the war. The government deficit was of less importance in this respect than at any other stage. Following a lull in military activities, the improvement of financial revenues, and economies achieved by the imposition of the land tax and borrowing in kind, the real deficit declined to a low point in 1943, when it was less than half the real deficit for 1941. Bank credit also expanded at a much slower pace than prices. Meanwhile, with the virtual disappearance of privately conducted foreign trade, the exchange rate had little influence upon the inflationary process. Hence the major factors causing inflation in earlier years were not a source of additional pressure in 1942 and 1943.

Three new developments appear to have been mainly responsible for the rapidity of price increases in these years. In the first place, the government's share of total output of consumer goods rose with the introduction of the land tax in 1941 and increased again in the following year when compulsory borrowing in kind was added to the tax. Prices of foodstuffs on the free market, and, hence, wages and the prices of other commodities, responded to the sudden reductions in civilian supplies. Second, the deterioration of communications created a widening gap between demand and market supplies. Perhaps the most important cause of the quickening of inflationary trends in this period, however, was the loss of confidence on the part of the general public in China's ability to survive the onslaughts of the Japanese and the dangers of inflation. China was completely isolated from the outside world. The Japanese armies were strongly

TABLE 19. INDICATORS OF CHINESE INFLATION, 1942–1945[1]
(Base of all indexes: Dec. 1941 = 100)

| Period | | Government Deficit | Note Issue | Wholesale Prices (All Free China) | Import Prices (Chungking) | Foreign Exchange Rate (CNC per U.S. $1) |
|---|---|---|---|---|---|---|
| 1941 | Dec. | 100 | 100 | 100 | 100 | 100 |
| 1942 | June | 155 | 165 | 173 | 198 | 100 |
| | Dec. | 217 | 227 | 290 | 353 | 100 |
| 1943 | June | 316 | 330 | 613 | 460 | 311 |
| | Dec. | 442 | 499 | 1,056 | 765 | 444 |
| 1944 | June | 1,094 | 813 | 2,078 | 1,855 | 1,014 |
| | Dec. | 1,532 | 1,255 | 3,220 | 2,940 | 3,010 |
| 1945 | June | 9,123 | 2,635 | 9,550 | 8,610 | 9,000 |
| | Dec. | 12,772 | 6,834 | 10,075 | 6,380 | 6,455 |

[1] Computed from other tables in the text.

entrenched in Burma and Yunnan and were moving swiftly from victory to victory in the Pacific; and at the time foreign assistance seemed a distant and uncertain prospect. On the domestic front, shortages of every type of commodity existed and prices were trebling annually. In these circumstances it is not surprising that a severe slump in public morale took place. The public showed an increasing disinclination to hold money, leading to an acceleration in the velocity of circulation. Commodity hoarding and speculation became part of the regular business of even the leading financial institutions. To a significant extent, therefore, rapid price increases during 1942 and 1943 reflected the psychological malaise (Table 19).

New developments in the war situation in the middle of 1944 brought about a change in the forces generating inflation. As the

Chinese armies took the offensive in the second half of the year, the deficit increased at twice the rate of the previous six months. In the following year spending assumed huge proportions, with the deficit rising by 378 per cent in the eight months before the end of the war in August. Price levels were cushioned from the impact of the deficit for a time by the very favorable harvests of 1944 and by renewed public confidence brought on by the success of the campaign in Burma. In the latter part of 1944 the increase in prices dropped to half the rate for the first six months of the year. However, prices again gathered upward momentum in 1945, and by August stood 228 per cent above their levels for the previous December. It is worth noting that prices did not advance as rapidly as the deficit in the second half of 1944 and in 1945. The inflationary impact of the deficit was diminished in this period by sales of gold, covering a part of the deficit, and by the consequent revival of optimism. Confidence in the currency strengthened, the velocity of circulation fell, and bank deposits rose significantly. Issue of new currency, which until the middle of 1944 was expanded at more or less the same rate as the deficit, began to lag. Meanwhile, the foreign exchange rate increased very rapidly as speculators once again turned their attentions to foreign currencies. Yet, at the conclusion of the war, the external value of China's currency was much above the internal value (as measured in terms of wholesale prices), and the exchange rate cannot be regarded as an active cause of internal inflation.

Chapter

# 3

# Changes in Income Distribution during the Wartime Inflation in Free China

Because of the lack of basic economic and financial statistics, it is impossible to analyze with any finality the changes in income distribution in China during the wartime inflation. There is some evidence, however, which suggests the directions of change and provides a basis for hazarding certain general conclusions.

Manufacturing output in Free China increased greatly after the Japanese invasion as new industries were established with equipment moved from the coast; agricultural production, too, rose under the stimulus of government encouragement. The index of industrial production prepared by the Ministry of Economic Affairs shows a rise of 86 per cent during the two years 1939–1940, and the index of agricultural output increased by 4 per cent in the crop year of 1939. There was, of course, a sharp decrease in trade with occupied regions, but in most parts of Free China increases in production outweighed the fall in imports; and, at first, the total amount of commodities available for distribution rose. This situation was reversed in 1940 when the disruption of communications with the outside world deprived Free China of imported supplies for China's own industries. At the same time, shortages of manpower in agriculture, resulting from conscription, and subsequent wage increases retarded the further growth of output. Crop production began to decline in 1940, and it averaged about 9 per cent below 1939 during the remainder of the war. Industrial production approximately doubled in the three years 1941–1943 but began to fall in 1944 following increased scarcities of essential materials and rapid increases in wages caused by inflation. From 1941 on, therefore, increases in total production in Free China could not have been very great and were probably outweighed by the loss of imports. Even while production was expanding in the early stages of the war, however, the supply of commodities available to private consumers was quite severely curtailed. Government military and defense expenditures commanded an increasingly large share of total supplies, while total civilian demand continued to increase as a result of inflow of refugees from occupied areas. It follows that average real income per capita started to decline shortly after the beginning of the war. In these circumstances any real gains made by particular groups during the process of inflation must have been balanced by losses in real income by others.

It is clear that the various economic groups experienced uneven fortunes during the period of war inflation. Some of these differences are reflected in the indexes of real returns from various types of economic activity in the six war years prior to 1943, as shown in Table 20.

TABLE 20. VARIATIONS IN REAL RETURNS PER INDIVIDUAL FROM VARIOUS TYPES OF ACTIVITY, CHUNGKING
(1938 = 100)

| Year | Agriculture[1] | Manufactures[2] | Retail[3] | Speculation[4] | U.S. Securities[5] |
|---|---|---|---|---|---|
| 1937 | — | 59 | 105 | 29 | N.A. |
| 1938 | 100 | 100 | 100 | 100 | 100 |
| 1939 | 61 | 106 | 111 | 397 | 180 |
| 1940 | 92 | 85 | 112 | 808 | 512 |
| 1941 | 109 | 71 | 119 | 550 | 1,373 |
| 1942 | 132 | 76 | 120 | 720 | 3,951 |
| 1943 | 124 | 69 | 124 | 263 | 10,260 |

[1] John Lossing Buck, "The Economic Position of Szechwan Farmers," in *Economic Facts,* No. 26, p. 286. Indexes are computed on a three-month basis.

[2, 3] Compiled by Economic Research Institute of Nankai University; profits derived from speculation are excluded.

[4] Based on the data in T. Y. Wu, *The Economics of Price Rises* [in Chinese], pp. 31–40. Real returns refer to profit from hoarding on a three-month basis.

[5] Based on the data in T. Y. Wu, *op. cit.* pp. 31–40.

The real income of the farming community was greatly reduced in 1938 and 1939 by falling food prices following very favorable harvests.*

* This suggests relatively inelastic demand schedules, which appear to be empirically valid because of the highly localized nature of markets in underdeveloped economies.

These returns began to recover in the latter part of 1940 when food prices rose suddenly as a result of bad harvests. The process was once again reversed in 1941 with the introduction of a land tax levied in kind and compulsory borrowing of grains in 1942, and it was aggravated by the acceleration of military conscription, which caused acute shortage of rural labor and led to substantial wage increases.

The relative status of manufacturers was much more favorable than that of farmers in the early years of the war. After the disruption of communications with the coast Free China was forced to become self-sufficient in manufacturing, and people owning machinery and equipment were able to secure large profits by exploiting their semi-monopoly position. Raw material prices and wages rose slowly since agricultural commodities were in abundant supply in 1938 and 1939, while prices of manufactured goods rose rapidly. In Chungking, for example, the wholesale price index for textile goods rose nearly twice as rapidly as the index for foodstuffs in the 1938–1939 period. The situation was reversed in 1940 and 1941 when poor harvests and loss of imports from the coast led to great increases in the prices of raw materials and the costs of labor. It was further affected by the reduction of supply of important imported materials and the decline of armament production associated with increasing difficulties in obtaining supplies of essential materials. Lastly, the purchasing power of the people declined. Throughout the remainder of war inflation, profitability of manufacturing failed to regain its original position. In fact, in 1943 wages seem to have run ahead of prices of manufactured goods but the industrial class still profited by the increase of real value of their plant and equipment. At the end of the war industrialists as a class were securing a larger portion of the real income of Free China than prewar merely by virtue of the extensive development of facilities and the resulting capital gains. But individual industrialists operating on the same scale as prewar and drawing their incomes solely from manufacturing enterprises, as contrasted with commodity or real estate speculation, suffered a relatively greater loss in real income than the farmer.

Speculation abounded in Free China from the time severe price inflation got under way in 1940. The last three columns of Table 20 suggest that professional speculators, as well as retailers who engaged in speculation as a side line, had a greater chance of maintaining their real incomes than either manufacturers or farmers. Traders who succeeded in obtaining supplies of manufactured goods, either produced in the occupied regions or imported from abroad, were assured of monopoly profits. Although the volume of their transactions decreased after the severing of communications with the outside world, great profits could be made on even limited quantities of goods. A new class of businessmen emerged who typically owned means of transportation and worked in company with smugglers who brought in supplies of scarce goods by operating in the no man's land between Free and Occupied China. Most of these individuals conducted their businesses as unregistered firms and successfully evaded income and excess profits taxes. Inflation itself induced speculation rather than investment in industry or agriculture, and the consuming public attempted to hoard commodities to hedge against further depreciation in the value of the currency. When U.S. Dollar Savings Certificates and Gold Dollar Bonds were issued, and deposits redeemable in gold were accepted by the government banks, new avenues for speculation were opened for those holding liquid assets. Monetary gains from these transactions were offset by losses, and, as a class, speculators operating with their own funds could not have increased their relative share of the real national product. Many speculators, however, were able to finance their operations by borrowing from the banks at interest rates well below the rate of increase of commodity price levels. By this means speculators as a group achieved an increase in real income at the expense of the community as a whole.

As in other countries affected by acute inflation in the past, individual and institutional savings in China were almost destroyed. Creditors of all types suffered losses in real income while debtors stood to gain. Holders of government bonds suffered the worst losses. The outstanding amount of all prewar bond issue was CNC $1,270 million, 40 per cent of which was held by the banks and other financial institutions and 60 per cent by individuals or charitable organizations. The market price of government bonds declined in the first years of the war and then, as a result of their continued excessive issue, failed to rise at anything like the speed of commodity price levels. Similarly, the real value of returns on loans dwindled almost to nothing. Shareholders of banks and other financial institutions, the paid-up capital of which totaled about CNC $100 million at the outbreak of war, also suffered severe reductions in real returns. Penalized by an artificially low rate of interest, the banks could scarcely meet their constantly rising expenses; they could not pay dividends in line with commodity price levels. In these conditions, many banks turned to practices which aggravated inflationary pressures and bordered on corruption.

A number of small banks controlled by businessmen used the funds of their depositors to finance speculative operations for their shareholders. Even the leading banks made investments in factories and bought gold and foreign exchange to preserve the value of their assets. Many banks resorted to dubious methods of attracting deposits, one of the most reprehensible consisting of bribing cashiers or accountants employed by the government in return for the deposits of their organizations. By such means private banks were able to participate in profits from speculative transactions by exploiting their depositors, the government, and, on occasion, their own shareholders.

Within the propertied class, therefore, merchants and speculators weathered inflation better than farmers and manufacturers, while holders of bonds or bank shares suffered most. Differential movements

TABLE 21. INDEXES OF REAL SALARIES AND WAGES IN FREE CHINA, 1937–1943
(1937 = 100)

| Year | Civil Servants (Chungking)[1] | Teachers (Chungking)[2] | Servicemen (Chungking)[3] | Laborers[4] | Industrial Workers (Chungking)[5] | Rural Workers (Szechwan)[6] |
|---|---|---|---|---|---|---|
| 1937 | 100 | 100 | 100 | 100 | 100 | 100 |
| 1938 | 77 | 87 | 93 | 143 | 124 | 111 |
| 1939 | 49 | 64 | 64 | 181 | 95 | 122 |
| 1940 | 21 | 32 | 29 | 147 | 76 | 63 |
| 1941 | 16 | 27 | 21 | 91 | 78 | 82 |
| 1942 | 11 | 19 | 10 | 83 | 75 | 75 |
| 1943 | 10 | 17 | 57 | 74 | 69 | 58 |

[1, 2, 3] Based on data in T. Y. Wu, *op. cit.*, pp. 34–36.
[4, 5] Compiled by the Statistical Department of Ministry of Social Affairs.
[6] Compiled by the Department of Agricultural Economics of the University of Nanking.

in real income also occurred within the salaried and wage-earning classes. Salary adjustments lagged much further behind the cost of living than wages. The number of civil servants and servicemen was so large that the government always hesitated to make an upward revision of salaries involving huge increases in government outlays. To offset rises in the cost of living, particular government departments and army units adopted expedients to alleviate hardship. These included such benefits as the granting of special allowances, distribution of daily necessities, and provision of housing—which led to significant differences in real income among various services and ranks.

Table 21 serves to illustrate general trends in the real income of different groups of salary and wage earners during the war years. As early as 1940 inflation had eroded two-thirds of the real incomes of civil servants, teachers, and servicemen. Real wages of industrial and rural workers had fallen by about a third, but those of laborers (i.e., nonfactory, nonrural workers) had risen by nearly a half because of a brisk demand, particularly in the field of transportation. By 1943 the position of salaried workers had deteriorated even further in comparison with other workers, although the real incomes of all employee groups had declined appreciably. Civil servants were reduced to abject poverty and were living on a mere tenth of their prewar real incomes, and teachers and servicemen were not faring much

Table 22. Indexes of the Cost of Living, Money Wages, and Real Wages of Non-Factory Workers in Six Cities of Free China, in Szechwan, April 1944[1]
(Base Jan.–June 1937 = 100)

| Cities | Cost of Living Index | Index of Money Wages of Non-Factory Workers | Index of Real Wages of Non-Factory Workers |
|---|---|---|---|
| Chengtu | 36,937 | 35,950 | 97.2 |
| Loshan | 51,184 | 37,000 | 71.3 |
| Chungking | 36,949 | 24,240 | 65.8 |
| Tzeliutsing | 50,577 | 30,500 | 60.0 |
| Wanhsien | 52,744 | 25,200 | 47.9 |
| Neikiang | 54,886 | 22,280 | 41.6 |

[1] Taken from table in *China Handbook 1937–1945* (New York, 1946), p. 383.

better on less than a fifth of their former real wages. The living standards of laborers and industrial workers had fallen by one-fourth while rural workers in Szechwan province had had their real wages cut in half by the inflation. These figures testify eloquently to the misery inflicted by the process of inflation on the whole class of salaried workers, government employees, and wage earners. Information relating to the behavior of real incomes of salaried workers after 1943 is lacking. According to monthly statistics published by the Ministry of Social Affairs, by April 1944 the index of real wages for industrial workers in Chungking had declined by 59 per cent from its prewar level, and the index for laborers had fallen by 35 per cent.

There were, of course, considerable differences in the movement of real wages among different industries and geographical areas, as Table 22 shows. In April 1944 workers in the tobacco and glass industries of Chungking were earning about 57 per cent of their prewar wages in real terms, but workers in public utilities and in the engineering equipment and printing industries were receiving less than 40 per cent of their former real wages. Interregional differences in wages and living costs were also substantial. Real wages of non-factory workers in Chungking, Wanhsien, and Neikiang were considerably lower than in Chengtu primarily because of the relatively slow increase of money wages in those cities, although in Wanhsien and Neikiang living costs had risen much higher than in other parts of China because of shortages of foodstuffs and housing space. In Loshan the cost of living increases were so much greater than in Chengtu that real wages were higher in Chengtu even though money wages were below those in Loshan.

Despite the fragmentary nature of the information presented above, it is clear that labor's share of the national product diminished during the inflation and that the working classes bore more than a proportionate share of the burden of inflationary financing of the war effort. Inflation weighed most heavily upon the salaried worker, although the damage done to the living standards of peasant labor, and, to a less extent, of laborer and industrial worker, was also very great indeed. Civil servants and teachers emerged from the war as a new depressed class, all the more dangerous politically because of their leftist intellectual leaning. On the other side of the scale, farmers and industrial entrepreneurs may have maintained their shares of the national product. Commercial enterprises of all descriptions, small private banks, and professional speculators were the chief beneficiaries of the inflationary process. A class of nouveaux riches grew up, consisting of people whose wealth was accumulated from a large number of speculative ventures involving the original commitment of small amounts of personal capital rather than from ownership and operation of land, factories, or other means of production. Other groups who fed upon the economic instability of these years included traders who engaged in smuggling scarce goods into Free China from Indo-China, Hong Kong, Burma, or the Japanese-occupied regions; speculators who borrowed money to buy foreign exchange, gold, or commodities; military officers and government officials in the higher ranks who received special allowances, and used their official status to further their business projects, and unscrupulous bankers who defied banking regulations and engaged in the financing of speculation.

Thus inflation in China produced a particularly irresponsible class of war profiteers and reduced most classes, particularly civil servants, teachers, and other salaried employees, to a state of misery far worse than that experienced during the depression of the early 1930's. Public servants and servicemen were demoralized by a degree of poverty extreme even for China and were antagonized by the growth of a wealthy class which had achieved its position by engaging in activities inimical to the general welfare. By its failure to avoid the economic conditions leading to this outcome and its further failure to correct the situation that emerged, the government earned the disaffection of the army and of the administrative services. These conditions led toward the loss of support which eventually brought the downfall of the Nationalist Government and the triumph of Communism in China.

Chapter

4

# Inflation in the Postwar Period

### *The Immediate Postwar Situation*

In the last few months before the end of the war Free China was on the verge of exhaustion. All the savings and marketable possessions of the average consumer had been used in the struggle to subsist. The depredations of tax collectors and soldiers had left the peasants disheartened and embittered, and the list of deserters from the army grew daily. Throughout China the spirit of resistance was being smothered by the relentless inflation. If victory had not come when it did, the economy of Free China would have disintegrated rapidly.

The task of rehabilitation and reconstruction confronting China at the end of the war was of unprecedented magnitude. Some fifty million displaced persons were awaiting return to their former homes. Millions of acres of farm lands had been devastated and lay deserted and unproductive. Internal communications were in a state of disrepair, and in a number of strategic areas of the south many miles of railways had been destroyed. The rehabilitation of refugees, the repair of damage in rural areas, the re-establishment of industries on the coast, and the provision of equipment and raw materials to enable factories to resume production required an astronomical amount of capital resources.

Two major obstacles prevented China from settling down to the task of reconstruction. The Nationalist government found itself unable to reach agreement with the Communists, and the tenor of discussions at the end of 1945 suggested that a compromise would be difficult to achieve. While antagonism and the possibility of resumption of open conflict prevailed, the army was maintained on a wartime basis, and the work of repairing railways and other lines of communications was retarded. On the monetary side, huge military outlays continued to act as a basic source of pressure on commodity prices. Second, repressed demand for local and foreign consumer goods, unsatisfied during the long period of war, came to represent a major force toward economic instability. Speculators, dealers, landlords, corrupt officials, and others who had profited from the national emergency had acquired large holdings of liquid funds. These sums were soon translated into heavy demands for whatever consumer goods were available. No immediate respite from this inflationary pressure could be gained from an inflow of foreign supplies. Some time elapsed before productive capacity in Great Britain and the United States could be readjusted to cope with peacetime needs; and China was only one of a large number of countries suffering from wartime shortages or embarking on ambitious schemes for reconstruction which made demands on the manufacturing output of the major industrial nations.

The Chinese government greatly overrated the stabilizing influence of victory. It was under the impression that the favorable psychological effect of the end of the war, the return to China of the highly productive regions of Manchuria and Formosa, the accumulation of large amounts of gold and foreign exchange, and the revival of foreign trade would all contribute to increases in commodity supplies which would be sufficient to absorb excess spending power in the hands of the public. Since it was thought that there would be an automatic tendency toward stability, the prolongation of wartime controls was considered unnecessary. All controls on prices and the distribution and use of goods were abandoned. Several other considerations prompted this sweeping action. The Chinese retained a traditional preference for a laissez faire economy, and the government hoped by removing controls to regain some of the popularity it had lost through its failure to check inflation during the war. Another consideration that weighed heavily was that foreign opinion was very much in favor of free trade. Foreign businessmen in China, especially Americans and British, took the view that the government was not sufficiently accomplished in techniques of control to apply restrictions efficiently, and that controls on commodity prices and on the movement of goods within China might easily obstruct the flow of international trade. Foreign loans to assist China's reconstruction were being discussed at the time, and the government did not wish to jeopardize its chances of receiving aid by inviting charges of corruption and incompetence in the administration of controls.

Immediately after the war the government optimistically embarked on grandiose schemes to restore government administrative services, to raise living standards of public servants, and to bring relief and reconstruction to areas previously occupied by the Japanese. Meanwhile, military expenditures were maintained at a level sufficient to keep the army at full fighting strength. In the last quarter of 1945 government expenditure in the depreciated currency was very great. Plans for the reconstruction of communications in North China were frustrated by the outbreak of civil war, and provincial trade was never restored to normal. Shipments of cotton and coal from the North were particularly affected by the dislocation of the rail system. Purchases of grain and cloth for the military caused rises in the prices of these commodities, which, in turn, swelled the size of the government deficit. In this way a large part of additional government spending immediately after the war, instead of facilitating the recovery of the economy, simply induced further price rises.

### *Temporary Stability: August–December 1945*

There were prima facie grounds for optimism concerning price trends immediately after the war ended. In the last week of August 1945 prices throughout China fell suddenly. Consumer goods hoarded over the years flooded onto the market and in many instances sold at half price. The ceasefire was a moment of emotional release for the Chinese people, manifested in the temporary break in the price spiral. In Shanghai the price of gold dropped by 90 per cent and in Chungking by 60 per cent, while CNC appreciated by 100 per cent against the U.S. dollar according to the market rate in Chungking. The wholesale price index in Chungking dropped from 179,500 in August to 122,600 in September, and fell again to 118,417 in October. Meanwhile, the Shanghai index fell from 43,200 (in terms of CNC) in August to 34,508 in September. But the downtrend lasted only a short time. Shanghai prices began to mount rapidly after October, and a more gradual ascent in Chungking prices began in November. By December the wholesale price index in Shanghai had risen to 88,544, double the August level.

### *Resumption of Inflation: 1946*

There were several reasons for the early resumption of inflation. The first task of the government in assuming control of the occupied regions was to retire puppet currencies from circulation. Nineteen days after the end of the war the government announced conversion ratios of two hundred Central Reserve Bank (puppet bank in Central China) notes to CNC $1 and of five Federal Reserve Bank (puppet bank in North China) notes to CNC $1. The public was allowed a period of four months in which to complete exchanges, and an upper limit of CNC $50,000 was set to the amount of national currency that could be acquired in this way by any one person. Puppet currency was allowed to remain in circulation as legal tender along with the CNC until the end of the conversion period. The consequences of these arrangements were unfortunate. Puppet currency was greatly undervalued in terms of CNC. According to the August wholesale price indexes of Shanghai and Free China generally, which stood at 8,640,000 and 245,503, respectively, the conversion rate of Central Reserve notes should have been 35 : 1; and according to the indexes of Shanghai (8,640,000) and Chungking (179,500), it should have been 48 : 1. A comparison of the index of wholesale prices for North China (104,868) with that of Free China suggests that Federal Reserve Bank notes should have exchanged for CNC in the ratio 1 : 2. The low conversion rates certainly had the advantage of keeping increases in CNC at a minimum; but, with puppet currency retaining its status as legal tender, it had the overwhelming disadvantage of providing an incentive for people to buy goods with undervalued puppet notes before the conversion period was ended. The arbitrary limit of CNC $50,000 acted in the same direction since people sought to rid themselves of puppet currency in excess of this CNC equivalent. Thus the low rates, the lengthy conversion period, the limit on individual exchanges, and the retention of puppet currency in circulation gave the conversion operation a highly inflationary character.

Other sources of pressure on price levels at the end of 1945 were the accumulated demand for consumer goods and the outflow of capital from the interior in the anticipation that Shanghai would regain its position as China's leading money market. As relations between the Nationalist government and the Communists deteriorated, the flow of funds to Shanghai increased, and the ensuing competition for investment outlets exercised a very considerable inflationary impact.

A substantial amount of a special Manchurian currency* issued by the Central Bank of China in Manchuria after January 1946 also contributed to the inflation. This currency was used for postwar rehabilitation of industry and agriculture in the area controlled by the Nationalist government and also to defray the heavy expenditures of the army sent to Manchuria. While issued for use in that region only,

* For clarity the amount of the Manchurian issue (27.53 billion in 1946, 277.3 billion in 1947, and 3,191.8 billion in July 1948) has been excluded from statistics mentioned elsewhere in this volume.

the notes could be used for remittances into China proper at an initial rate of 11.43 CNC to 1 Manchurian currency. This rate changed later to 10 to 1.

Over and above these forces, however, the budget deficit and the resultant increase in currency placed in circulation remained primary in importance. Wartime conditions had taught the business community to watch these items as reliable indicators of future price trends. Hence the constant expansion of the deficit immediately after the war did much to dispel the renewed feeling of confidence in the currency that followed upon victory. Under these stresses the temporary remission from inflation was soon at an end.

## *The Government Deficit: January 1946—July 1948*

Government expenditure in 1946 increased by 3.2 times while revenue covered only 37 per cent of the expenditure in spite of a large non-tax revenue derived from the proceeds of sales of gold, foreign exchange, and enemy properties. The result was a huge deficit

TABLE 23. GOVERNMENT EXPENDITURE, REVENUE, THE DEFICIT AND THE LAND TAX IN KIND, 1946–1948 (JAN.—JULY)[1]

(CNC $ million)

| Year | Note Issue Outstanding[1] | Government Expenditure[2] | Government Revenue[2] | Government Deficit | Estimated Money Value of Land Tax[3] |
|---|---|---|---|---|---|
| 1945 | 1,031,900 | 2,348,085 | 1,241,389 | 1,106,696 | 188,604 (1945–1946) |
| 1946 | 3,726,100 | 7,574,790 | 2,876,988 | 4,697,802 | 624,675 (1946–1947) |
| 1947 | 33,188,500 | 43,393,895 | 14,064,383 | 29,329,512 | 3,015,899 (1947–1948) |
| 1948 | 374,762,200 | 655,471,087 | 220,905,475 | 434,565,612 | |

[1] Based on statistics compiled by Central Bank of China.

[2] The figures for 1946 and 1947 are based on data in W. Y. Chang, *Money and Finance*. They exclude foreign credits for special projects. Data for 1948 are based on Central Bank records for the first half of that year.

[3] Based on Table 42 of the Land Tax Collection.

asserted by the government to be unavoidable because of the necessity of maintaining a military force strong enough to contain the Communist expansion in Manchuria and China proper and rehabilitating the economy of previously occupied areas. After peace negotiations with the Communists were broken off and civil strife was resumed, military outlays stood at about 60 per cent of total government expenditure in 1946 and 55 per cent in 1947. Administrative expenditure was also increased as a result of monthly adjustments of salaries and wages according to the movement of the cost of living index, forced upon the government by the wide discontent among civil servants. In 1947 expenditure increased to 5.7 times that of 1946 while revenue dropped to 32 per cent of expenditure because non-tax revenue declined as sales of gold discontinued and receipts from sales of exchange and enemy property were reduced. The deficit of 1947 reached nearly 70 per cent of expenditure. There was further financial deterioration in 1948, as military expenditures increased to more than 64 per cent of total government outlay (see Table 23). The government not only continued to resort to direct borrowing from the Central Bank but also had to continue to collect the land tax in kind and to enforce compulsory borrowing of grains, although such policies had proved to be increasingly onerous to the agricultural sector in the war years. However, had the government not continued these policies, monetary expenditures would have been much greater.

### *Attempts to Suppress Inflation: February 1947*

The rapid progress of inflation during 1946 forced the government to reimpose controls in February 1947. Price and wage ceilings were reintroduced despite unfortunate wartime experience with them and in the face of price rises that were twice as rapid as those occurring in 1942 when the previous experiment was made. Currency in circulation was increasing at the rate of 10 per cent per month, and prices in Shanghai were almost doubling every two or three months. Far from improving, the supply position had deteriorated following the restriction on imports after November 1946. There was slight hope that an inflation moving at such a speed could be arrested by the introduction of price ceilings. Nevertheless, an emergency order, announced on February 16, 1947, placed ceilings on the prices of daily necessities (rice and flour, cotton yarn and cloth, fuel, salt, sugar, and edible oil). These were to be strictly enforced in the larger cities, beginning with Shanghai and Nanking, the capital. Wages were to be frozen in accordance with the January cost of living index, and no change in the basic wage rate was to be allowed. Factories were instructed to allocate daily necessities to their employees at the average retail prices prevailing in January. Buying, selling, and hoarding of gold and foreign currencies by private individuals were prohibited. Although the agencies of control and local governments made great efforts to enforce controls with the co-operation of the police, the emergency measures were effective for no longer than one month. At the beginning of April the black market in U.S. dollars revived. This successful defiance of the regulations led to rapid growth of black markets in all commodities, and the government had no choice but to raise ceilings in line with unofficial prices in the middle of April, and to unfreeze wages in May. The monthly increase in Shanghai's wholesale prices was 54 per cent in May, compared with 19 per cent in the month before the emergency order.

### *The Role of the Central Bank*

At the nadir of failure of the government's economic policy, a new governor was appointed to the Central Bank in May 1946, and he attempted to attack the fundamental fiscal causes of inflation. He appealed to the leader of the government, Generalissimo Chiang Kai-shek, and to the Minister of Finance to cut the monthly government deficit in half by raising revenues and reducing expenditures. The Bank agreed to undertake responsibility for financing the remainder of the deficit, preferably by deflationary means such as promotion of sales of bonds, treasury bills, and savings deposits. By this arrangement additions to the inflationary fuel would be reduced by stopping further note issues and by cutting the budget deficit. In view of the manifest failure of all the previous economic and monetary measures, which had been directed at effects, not at causes, such a fundamental departure should have been agreed to by the responsible government leaders. But the exhortations of the governor of the Central Bank were unavailing. The Minister of Finance said that he could not refuse the demands of military expenditures, and his views were tacitly supported by the leader of the government. Thus the government became committed to a policy of supporting the military even at the cost of runaway inflation.

During the discussion on the Central Bank's proposal for attacking the problem of inflation, the Central Bank did its part by issuing two kinds of bonds. One hundred million U.S. dollars worth of bonds were issued in April 1947, subscribed and redeemable on maturity in foreign currency. This issue was followed by an issue of CNC $300 million in treasury bills subscribed and redeemable in CNC but convertible into U.S. dollars at the official rate of exchange. At their outset both issues were quite successful. In four months an amount of U.S. $25,819,550 was surrendered by subscribers to the bonds. The sales of treasury bills in the first two months covered nearly 15 per cent of the monthly deficit. Unfortunately, when the news that the suggestion of the Central Bank was rejected became known to the public, despite the absolute prohibition of black markets in the February emergency order, a black-market exchange rate soon re-emerged.

Holders of foreign currencies were not prepared to forego easy profits from black-market sales by subscribing to the bonds. The sales of treasury bills had to be terminated.

After the failure of these measures the Central Bank no longer pitted its strength against market forces but merely endeavored to cushion their impact. In August 1947 a system of flexible exchange rates, supervised by a Stabilization Fund Committee, was adopted to take the place of the fixed official rate. In the place of price and wage ceilings, controlled distribution of daily necessities to wage and salary earners at relatively low prices was introduced to hold down increases in the cost of living. Restrictions on credit were renewed, the bank rate was raised, and the control of bank credit was transferred from the government to a Loan and Discount Committee composed of banking and business representatives. These measures appear to have been of some benefit in retarding the rise in price levels. In July and August Shanghai wholesale prices rose by 15 per cent and 8 per cent, respectively, in contrast to increases of 54 per cent and 12 per cent in May and June. But government deficit-financed expenditures continued to inundate the market with new currency. Central Bank advances to the government in 1947 were five times those for the previous year, while the note issue increased more than ten times in 1947 compared to three times in 1946, a situation aggravated by a widening gap in the balance of trade accompanying the internal inflation and by a new flight of capital to Hong Kong provoked by Nationalist defeats in the civil war. These conditions led to a decline in the external value of CNC and rising gold prices, both of which reacted unfavorably on internal prices. By December 1947 Shanghai's wholesale prices were nearly fifteen times the level of the previous December, and over the year had risen twice as much as during 1946.

### *The Money Market and Private Credit*

China's monetary system in the postwar period was much less amenable to regulation than during the wartime period. The problem of controlling the Shanghai money market, which resumed operations early in 1946, was very much more complicated than that of supervising the activities of a few centralized financial institutions in Chungking. Shanghai contained a multitude of Chinese and foreign banks, insurance companies, and gold, commodity, and stock markets whose speculative operations accentuated the underlying inflationary trend. The Shanghai money market was closely linked with other financial markets abroad, and there was a constant threat of an outflow of speculative funds, a possibility which could be ignored during the war years, when internal controls and the action taken by a number of allied nations in freezing funds held in Chinese accounts abroad removed the danger of capital flight.

In addition to these general considerations, a number of special features of China's postwar banking system militated against the success of government attempts to control the money market. The Central Bank's sphere of influence was limited to the government banks and to the more responsible private banks. The general standards of banking had deteriorated greatly during the war, many of the small banks having taken the opportunity to abandon approved banking practices and having become deeply involved in speculation. This was a serious problem since the Ministry of Finance had permitted the establishment of a great number of private banks after the war, thereby enlarging the unregulated sector of the money market.

The position of the private banks was strengthened by the unrealistic interest rate policy of the Central Bank. In January 1946 the Central Bank's rediscount rate was fixed at 1.8 per cent monthly; at the same time regulations provided that the rates of the private banks should be submitted to the Central Bank for approval. The approved rate was 8.4 per cent annually, and the private banks were prohibited from offering higher rates than this on their deposits. However, the black-market interest rate was considerably higher than 8.4 per cent at the time, and, despite upward adjustments in the approved rate, the black-market rate remained well in the lead throughout most of the postwar period. Consequently, there was a strong inducement for private banks to offer higher than approved rates on deposits in order to attract funds to finance speculators at profitable black-market rates. The net result was a flow of funds into the unregulated sector of the money market at the expense of those banks which attempted to comply with Central Bank directives, only the government banks and a handful of private banks falling within this category.

These several forces undermined the powers of the Central Bank after 1945. The intrusion of politics into banking affairs also contributed to weaken its position. In 1947, for example, the Board of Joint Administration of the Government Banks refused to raise official interest rates to more realistic levels, a failure directly attributable to the conflicting views between the professional bankers and the executives of the government banks who represented the Kuomintang party. For the same reason the Central Bank was frequently unable to pursue a consistent policy of regulating the money market.

There was thus a fundamental contradiction in the government's postwar banking policies. Its objectives were to keep the over-all amount of credit granted by the banks within bounds while at the same time ensuring a steady flow of credit to essential industries. Inevitably, however, restrictions on the expansion of credit reacted unfavorably on the supply of credit to productive users. Yet there was no way to control the credit operations in the free market. When the potential productive borrowers made complaints, restrictions had to be relaxed, although no effective means could be found to discriminate between productive and speculative end uses of credit.

In line with its optimistic belief that natural economic forces would reverse the process of inflation, the government adopted in early 1946 a policy of credit expansion to stimulate the recovery of industry and trade. (See Table 24.) During the year the loans of the government banks increased at 2.6 times the rate at which the general price level rose. To offset this high rate of monetary expansion the government decided to sell gold, adopting an official price based on free market quotations. From the resumption of sales in March 1946 until the middle of the year this technique seems to have had a steadying influence on price levels. However, in the second half of the year, the rapid growth of the supply of money far overshadowed the effect of gold sales. Recognizing the increased impact of credit expansion by the government banks, the government applied a new set of restrictions on bank lending in September. These regulations were of little consequence in practice, and the credit situation remained inflationary in nature until a total suspension of credit was announced to coincide with the emergency order of February 1947. Gold sales were also abandoned at this date, since the government had at last grasped the fact that, while the money supply continued to increase at an excessive rate, sales of gold did little more than to dissipate precious reserves.

The government embarked on a new line of banking policy shortly after the promulgation of the emergency order. It now took the view that price and wage ceilings could not be held without increases in the output of essential consumer and producer goods, and that such increases in production required an adequate flow of credit. Accordingly, the suspension of credit was lifted. In a new effort to prevent the flow of private bank credit to speculators and profiteers, liberal remortgage and rediscount facilities with the government banks were offered to the private banks making loans to approved borrowers.

A few months later the government sought to arrest the decline of confidence in its currency by tightening credit restrictions. In August 1947 the lending activities of the government banks were limited to five categories of loans embracing only the most essential industries. In December the government banks were prohibited from lending to the private banks, and severe penalties were laid down for infringement of the regulations relating to approved rates of interest. As a final declaration of its intent to control capital flight and to regulate the money market, the government set up a Banking Control Bureau. The establishment of this Bureau signified that the government had abandoned indirect methods of control and had decided to resort to more coercive means. By the beginning of January 1948 prices were doubling every two months and the supply of currency was increasing at about half this rate. Seized with panic, Generalissimo Chiang Kai-shek himself attempted to interfere with the banking system, ordering the total suspension of credit. Since this measure coincided with the Chinese New Year, the traditional date of settlement of debts, it threw the money market into confusion and obstructed bona fide industrial and commercial transactions.

TABLE 24. GOVERNMENT BANK LOANS, DEPOSITS AND INCREASE IN NOTE ISSUE, 1946–1948
(CNC $ million)

| Year | Increase in Deposits[1] | Private Loans[2] | Advances to Gov't.[2] | Increase in Note Issue[3] |
|---|---|---|---|---|
| 1945 | 431,616 | 121,661 | 1,043,257 | 842,400 |
| 1946 | 4,893,940 | 1,073,483 | 5,513,670 | 2,694,200 |
| 1947 | 20,413,953 | 16,119,751 | 27,075,033 | 29,462,400 |
| 1948 (Jan.–June) | 161,101,894 | 156,496,326 | 166,185,674 | 163,332,800 |

[1] Based on the data of the record of Central Bank of China.
[2] Based on the Statement of Revenue compiled by the Statistical Department of Ministry of Finance, published in W. Y. Chang, *op. cit.*, pp. 244–245.
[3] Based on statistics of the Central Bank of China.

For three months the government persisted in its ban on credit. Partly as a result of government action, there was a slight easing of the rate of increase in price levels during February, but the effect was clearly of a temporary nature. With the budget deficit constantly pouring new money into the hands of the public, controls on bank lending failed to curb speculative activities which were now attracting the participation of people in all walks of life (Table 24). Even the Banking Control Bureau was powerless to prevent banks from supplying credit at rates of interest determined by prevailing monetary conditions. Banks conducted underground organizations to cater to the demands of their clients, obscuring their operations by keeping secret accounts.

At the end of March, recognizing the failure of its severe measures, the government revoked the ban on credit. It reverted to a policy of endeavoring to establish some degree of financial stability by operating within the framework of the existing money market. In April 1948 the Central Bank's rate of interest on short-term deposits which had been set in August was raised to the level of prevailing black-market rates. In the same month the Central Bank was made sole fiscal agent of the government in order to prevent the other government banks from using balances on government accounts to finance speculative transactions. The Central Bank also began to sell treasury bills with a currency of one month and a yield of nearly 24 per cent per annum to draw off purchasing power from the general public. The technique of purchasing commodities in advance of production was used more generally by all of the government banks to increase the flow of credit to industry.

These measures were of limited effectiveness in the phase of inflation that had now been reached, and they were offset by the relentless rise in demand for money. Black-market rates of interest soon passed those offered to short-term deposits by the Central Bank, which became unable to hold its own in the competition for funds.

At the end of May 1948 a new cabinet was organized and the Minister of Finance and the Governor of the Central Bank of China were replaced. Open inflation continued. In June and July, Shanghai wholesale prices increased by 260 per cent and 45 per cent, respectively, and the market rate of foreign exchange rose by 98 per cent and 181 per cent, respectively (Table 25). The black-market price of gold trebled, and the supply of currency in circulation doubled during each of those months. These frightening presages of monetary collapse forced the government into the abortive monetary reforms of August 1948.

### *Abortive Monetary Reform and Apparent Stabilization: August 19, 1948*

Throughout 1947 and 1948 the leaders of the financial community had urged the government that retrenchment in government finances was the first step toward restoration of general economic stability.

TABLE 25. THE FOREIGN EXCHANGE RATE AND INTERNAL PRICES (JAN. 1946–JULY 1948)
Price Index 1947 (Jan.–June) = 100

| Period | | Foreign Exchange Rate: Official CNC Rate (per U.S. $)[1] | Foreign Exchange Rate: Market Rate (per U.S. $)[2] | Wholesale Price Index (Shanghai)[3] |
|---|---|---|---|---|
| 1946 | June | 2,020 | 2,665 | 378,217 |
| | Dec. | 3,350 | 6,063 | 681,563 |
| 1947 | March | 12,000 | 14,000 | 1,386,593 |
| | June | 12,000 | 36,826 | 2,905,700 |
| | Sept. | 41,635 | 50,365 | 4,635,700 |
| | Dec. | 77,636 | 149,615 | 10,063,000 |
| 1948 | March | 211,583 | 449,620 | 32,576,900 |
| | June | 1,273,000 | 2,311,250 | 197,690,000 |
| | Aug. | 7,094,625 (Aug. 18) | 8,683,000 (Aug. 9–10) | 558,900,000 (Aug. 19) |

[1] August 1947–May 1948, Stabilization Fund Committee Rate. June–August, 1948 Certificate Rate.

[2] Taken from tables compiled by the Economic Research Department of Central Bank of China.

[3] 1946–1947 based on data compiled by Directorate-General of Budgets, Accounts and Statistics (simple geometric means). 1948 based on data compiled by the Economic Research Department of Central Bank of China (weighted geometric means).

Despite these warnings, the new Minister of Finance proceeded on the assumption that government finances could not be reorganized until general economic stability was achieved. He believed that stability could be restored by a change in the currency standard and that a balanced budget would automatically follow. Accordingly, there was evolved a plan for superseding CNC with a new currency, which received the active support of Generalissimo Chiang Kai-shek. Before this plan was put into effect, financial experts pointed out that, even though the CNC was depreciated, it was at least known and generally accepted by the people, which might not be true of the new issue. Their objections were dismissed on the ground that their ideas were too orthodox for the abnormal circumstances confronting China. The change was made on August 19, 1948. The unit of value was defined as 0.2217 centigram of pure gold, to be represented by a note known as the Gold Yuan. The new notes exchanged at the rate of GY 1 to CNC $3,000,000. A 40 per cent reserve of gold, silver, and foreign exchange was to be maintained against the note issue, which was limited by law to 200,000,000 Gold Yuan. Prices of all commodities were frozen at Gold Yuan equivalents of the levels obtaining on August 19 and could not be altered without the approval of the government authorities. The possession of gold, silver, or foreign exchange was prohibited, and all private holdings were to be surrendered in return for Gold Yuan notes. A series of other measures relating to the improvement of the tax system, controls on credit, reduction of interest rates, and suppression of hoarding accompanied the currency reform. In the three important districts of Shanghai, Tientsin, and Canton specially appointed high ranking officials assumed personal charge of the control system. In Shanghai the government imposed the most rigorous restrictions, enforced by secret police.

For six weeks Shanghai was more or less terrorized into a state of monetary equilibrium. Commodity prices remained at ceiling levels except for perishable goods, and the black market in foreign currencies and gold passed out of existence. Gold, silver, and foreign exchange worth around U.S. $170 million were surrendered to the Central Bank. The government triumphantly proclaimed the success of the reform; but the general public was not deceived by the temporary lull in inflation. Wholesale traders in Shanghai had suspended operations on the announcement of the official fixed prices, shortages were accumulating, and there was no real conviction among the general public that prices would remain steady. While inflation was momentarily suppressed in Shanghai, it became the more violent in the interior of the country, where commodities rose in price immediately upon the exchange decree.

Meanwhile, the government continued to pour money into circulation to finance its expenditures by deficit spending. At the time of the currency reform the Minister of Finance asserted that the budget deficit would be reduced from 70 per cent to 30 per cent of government expenditure. Although the deficit fell to under 50 per cent of expenditure in October, it had again risen to 75 per cent in November. In the latter month the deficit amounted to GY 503 million compared to GY 138 million for September.

Suddenly, in the middle of October, a wave of panic buying in Shanghai forced prices above their fixed ceilings. Retailers withheld their goods from sale rather than sell them at official prices, and even the restaurants refused to do business. In the interior, local government officials, who were either indifferent to the directives of the central government or hesitant to apply them, seized on the rise in Shanghai prices as an excuse to abandon all pretence of enforcing the regulations. By the end of October inflation was once again gathering momentum, and the government had no choice but to abandon its price regulations. The circulation of Gold Yuan was nearly eight times the prescribed maximum limit by the end of October as the result of the issuance of currency to finance military expenditures. Thus the two main safeguards to the value of currency, price and wage stability and restrictions on the supply of currency, were swept away.

The view that the government should not have risked its prestige by gambling on the success of the currency reform plan but should have issued notes of larger denominations to prolong the life of the old currency was current at the time of the reform. It is interesting to observe, however, that if the government could have prevented a further major expansion in the supply of money, it could have made the Gold Yuan freely convertible into bullion, and confidence in the currency might have been restored. The real value of CNC in circulation immediately before the currency reform had fallen so much that the new issue was easily covered by the gold and silver reserves of the Central Bank. In June 1937 the total value of notes in circulation was CNC $1,410 million. By June 1948 the real value of the total money supply had shrunk to U.S. $314 million at the official rate. At this time the Central Bank held a foreign reserve of approximately U.S. $130 million. In addition, foreign currencies, gold and silver surrendered under the currency reform decree, totaled about U.S. $170 million. Thus the Gold Yuan was fully covered by the reserves of the Central Bank and could have been made convertible in practice.

### *American Economic Aid: 1948*

Toward the end of 1947, when the deterioration of political and economic conditions in China was causing grave concern in Washington, the United States Department of State announced its intention of presenting an "Economic Aid Program for China" to Congress. The American government had reiterated the view that China must adopt a comprehensive plan for economic stabilization if she wanted to secure full benefit from foreign aid, and indicated that such action would greatly enhance the prospects for Congressional approval of United States economic assistance to China. Accordingly, in January 1948 the Chinese government announced a ten-point program of reform along lines suggested by the United States. Two pivotal measures provided for reduction of government expenditures and improvement of the tax system; both had been denounced by the Minister of Finance as impracticable when they had been advocated by the Central Bank six months earlier. At this time the tempo of inflation had accelerated and the military situation had worsened. The plan of reorganizing army and civil service was discussed, but the government was reluctant to demobilize servicemen near the fighting front for fear that they would join the Communists. The government also refrained from risking political odium by extensive retrenchments in the public service since its prestige was at low ebb. Hence the program of reform, intended as a condition for American aid, was not put into practice.

The China Aid Act was passed by Congress in January 1948, authorizing grants of U.S. $275 million for the purchase of cotton, petroleum, foodstuffs, construction goods, and other commodities for China. It also provided U.S. $125 million for military aid to be received over a twelve-month period. Many Chinese observers were disappointed at the size of the American grants, believing that assistance should have been on a much larger scale in view of the strategic importance of China. Against this view, it is worth noting that the amount of economic aid given to China was calculated on the basis of the raw material requirements of Chinese industries, the capacity of the transport system to carry goods inland, and the estimated magnitude of the Chinese balance of payments deficit. It is doubtful whether larger shipments of goods to China would have materially alleviated the plight of the Nationalist armies fighting in the north, since means of transportation were inadequate to move what was received. American aid benefited China immediately by increasing the availability of basic commodities such as cotton, fuel, and foodstuffs in a few main cities and by enabling important industries to maintain existing levels of employment. However, American aid failed to stem the tide of inflation.

### *The Collapse of the Currency System*

When price ceilings were abandoned in late October 1948 open inflation once more prevailed. In one week prices increased elevenfold. Never before had prices in China risen with such rapidity. In Manchuria and North China the military situation was deteriorating, and the government's prestige sank to a new low. It now had only 2,000,000 ounces of gold, 25,000,000 ounces of silver, and U.S. $76,000,000 worth of foreign exchange to throw into the battle against inflation. Discussions therefore centered on how best to employ these remaining stocks, for the government had abandoned all hope of controlling inflation directly or by coercion. A decision was made in November to devalue the Gold Yuan by 80 per cent (in terms of gold) and to make it freely convertible into gold.

A few days later the Central Bank announced that depositors who left Gold Yuan notes with the Bank for the period of a year could convert an equal amount of currency into gold coins, or, before these were actually issued, into silver bullion or silver dollars. This device, tantamount to a further devaluation of the Gold Yuan by 50 per cent, reduced it to one-tenth of its August gold value and was designed to protect the Central Bank's gold stocks. However, as the supply of notes in November was more than ten times as great as that in August, even this severe reduction in the value of the Gold Yuan did not enable the Central Bank to undertake free conversion. As the issue continued to rise the Central Bank was threatened with a complete loss of its reserves of specie and bullion.

The public quickly responded to the Central Bank's offer of conversion, and an organized mass of unemployed workers presented notes to obtain gold for resale in the open market. To check the drain on gold, the Minister of Finance ordered that all applications for conversion of notes had to be officially approved and exchanges were restricted to one ounce of gold and forty-nine silver dollars per person every three months. In early December, when application forms were first issued, about 60,000 people gathered in the precincts of the government banks in Shanghai and fought to obtain forms. A serious riot broke out in which dozens of people were killed or injured. The government took the opportunity to suspend convertibility temporarily, and at the end of December put a new scheme into operation. Thereafter the conversion rate was determined on the basis of the Bank of China's quotation of the exchange rate on overseas remittances, which reflected the domestic market price for gold. In short, the Central Bank was now selling gold at the market price and had abandoned its efforts to strengthen the currency by introducing full or partial convertibility.

On January 27, 1949, the Ministry of Finance made a final desperate effort to stave off the approaching collapse of the money market. A short-term bond issue was floated, backed by 2,000,000 ounces of gold, with a maturity of two years and repayable in monthly installments in gold. The selling price was fixed by the Central Bank on the basis of the market price of U.S. dollars. At this stage the Communists were driving southwards, Peiping was threatened, and the general public had lost all confidence in the Nationalist government. By the middle of February the government had succeeded in selling bonds equivalent to only 4,000 ounces of gold. Although the price of these bonds was well below the black-market price for gold, there was practically no demand for them and the issue was withdrawn.

TABLE 26. GOLD YUAN NOTE ISSUE, EXCHANGE RATES, AND WHOLESALE PRICE INDEX, SHANGHAI August 31, 1948–July 31, 1949

| Year and Month | Note Issue: In GY (million)[1] | Note Issue: Converted into CNC ($1,000 billion) | Exchange Rates (U.S. $ per GY): Official Rate | Exchange Rates (U.S. $ per GY): Market Rate[2] | Wholesale Price Index (Shanghai Aug. 1948 = 100; weighted geometric means)[3] |
|---|---|---|---|---|---|
| 1948 | | | | | |
| Aug. 19 | — | 604.0 | — | — | — |
| Aug. 31 | 296.8 | 890.4 | 4 | 4 | 100 |
| Nov. 30 | 3,204.3 | 9,612.9 | 28 | 42 | 1,365 |
| 1949 | | | | | |
| Feb. 28 | 59,663.5 | 178,990.5 | 2,660 | 2,980 | 48,195 Apr. 15 |
| Apr. 25 | 2,037,105.7 | 6,111,317.1 | 205,000 | 813,880 | 112,490 |
| July 31 | 125,124,637.2 | 375,373,911.6 | — | — | — |

[1] Based on statistics of Central Bank of China.

[2] Month-end quotations were used in place of monthly average in GY.

[3] Taken from tables compiled by the Economic Research Department, Central Bank of China.

In the second week of February Generalissimo Chiang Kai-shek resigned, and the gold reserve was removed to Formosa and Amoy. The government of Acting President Li Tsung-jen attempted to use the remaining silver reserve to revert to a silver standard. On February 24 silver was restored as the standard of value, and silver dollars were circulated for the first time since 1935. A minimum reserve of 50 per cent in silver was to be maintained against the issue of notes, and government outlays were to be made in silver dollars. The weakness of this final expedient is demonstrated by the fact that at the going market rate of 320 Gold Yuan to 1 silver dollar outstanding note issues of about GY $60 billion would have required a statutory reserve of 60 million ounces of silver, while the government held actual reserves of only 25 million ounces. Overtures to the United States for a silver loan were rejected. At their peak volume, circulation of silver-dollar notes totaled only $20 million; the public rejected these notes in the same way as they had come to reject the Gold Yuan. By the time the government retreated to Chungking in October 1949 about $25 million silver dollar notes were in circulation and were almost completely withdrawn before the arrival of Communists.

Meanwhile, wholesale prices in Shanghai continued their feverish ascent. In January 1949 prices increased 3.6 times, in February 7.0 times, and in March 4.5 times. The March decline in the rate of increase was caused by a shortage of printed notes. The velocity of circulation of notes increased from 1.60 in October to 17.85 in February, the last month for which calculation is possible. On the eve of the Communists' entry into Shanghai, in May, the exchange rate vis-à-vis U.S. dollars was 40 times what it had been at the end of March. In the same period of time the price of rice had risen 451 times.

The collapse of the Gold Yuan was inherent in the conditions of political and economic instability prevailing in the closing months of 1948. The measures adopted subsequently were similarly doomed to failure, and the succession of futile monetary changes served only to emphasize the weakness of the government. The ultimate rejection of the currency in the concluding stage of inflation was no more than an economic reflection of the impending downfall of the Nationalist government. Table 26 summarizes this process.

Chapter

# 5

# An Analytical Account Of Chinese Inflation, 1937–1949

## 1. Inflation Potential in an Underdeveloped Economy

### *Role of Money in an Underdeveloped Economy, with Special Reference to China before the Sino-Japanese War: The Rural-Urban Dichotomy*

Both monetary flows and the functions which money performs reflect the stage of a country's economic development. In some underdeveloped economies the role of money is restricted by the existence of non-market sectors and by the fragmentation of the economy into isolated economic units. Relatively little specialization of production and little access to distributive and transport facilities may severely limit the flow of goods and productive factors among geographical localities. In this situation money is primarily employed to facilitate exchange within relatively limited geographical areas, and markets tend to be highly localized in nature. At this stage of development in China, characteristic of that country on the eve of the Sino-Japanese war, a proliferation of highly localized markets was not integrated into broader regional or national markets. Sharp discrepancies in conditions of supply, demand, and prices frequently appeared in neighboring areas beyond the reach of modern modes of transport. Surpluses and deficits of food supplies, for example, were reported in markets within a few miles of each other, and resultant price discrepancies were seldom equalized by the movement of goods.*

* See Chang Pei-kang, *Agriculture and Industrialization* (Cambridge, Mass., 1949), pp. 198–199.

The prewar Chinese economy may be broadly described as a dichotomy between an urban sector in which specialization of production had been advanced by the introduction of Western technology and investment and a rural sector which embraced a great number of localized cells of economic activity, oriented toward self-sufficiency and little regional specialization. By 1937 there were important exceptions to this generalization since commercial agricultural crops had been introduced in some areas of the hinterland. In the main, however, this fundamental dichotomy of economic structure persisted. The commercialized areas, in which agricultural production was primarily oriented toward demand in urban centers, were merely outgrowths and extensions of the urban sector itself. The urban or modern sector of the economy, therefore, comprised those areas where production was organized to meet the needs of modern industry and the pattern of consumer demand with which it was associated. Geographically, this sector was located in and near the coastal treaty port cities. In contrast, the greater part of production in the rural sector was oriented toward meeting the needs of small localized markets for family consumption. Such activity was organized around agricultural production, and backward technology did not allow a significant amount of specialization of production by either region or economic unit. Since labor was abundant relative to supplies of land and capital, labor not fully utilized in agricultural activities was devoted to handicraft manufacturing to supply either family or local requirements.

Given this dichotomous structure of economic activity, money performed significantly different roles in the two dominant sectors of the economy. There was little interdependence between these sectors, and hence neither real nor monetary flows between them were quantitatively significant. In the urban sector, input-output relationships were confined largely to this sector itself and to foreign trade. Inputs consisted largely of wage labor more or less permanently committed to the urban sector; raw materials were either imported or brought from the adjacent commercialized agricultural areas, and almost all capital goods were imported. Financial resources, too, came primarily from the urban sector itself or from abroad. Foreign ownership represented about two-thirds of modern industry's capital stock; Chinese entrepreneurs financed their enterprises mainly from commercial and industrial profits, with some assistance from modern Chinese banks whose activities were also concentrated in the urban sector. Although only a small part of total banking resources was devoted to financing industrial investment or even providing working capital to industry, much was used to finance commercial and speculative activities in the larger urban centers, particularly Shanghai. Thus, there was no significant flow of banking resources to the rural sector.

Economic activities in the rural sector, too, had a strong tendency to be oriented toward satisfying needs within this sector itself; in fact, production, distribution, and exchange were focused upon narrow markets within it. Production was oriented toward local requirements of basic necessities such as food and articles of local manufacture. Payments for inputs, to the extent these were not labor of the self-employed peasant, were made to the upper income groups within the sector itself and were predominantly payments to the landlord or gentry class for land rent and credit. Implements for agricultural production as well as the whole range of consumers' goods were primarily of local origin and to the extent they were traded represented payments made to tradesmen within the sector. To the extent that these goods flowed out of local markets, they were distributed largely to nearby markets because of high transport costs over greater distances. Studies of regional exports of rice from areas of South China showed that little reached the large centers of urban concentration. Transportation and distribution channels were inadequate to ship out food in significant quantity.*

### *Role of Money in an Underdeveloped Economy: Interdependence and Intersectoral Relationships*

Although there was a gradual tendency toward economic interdependence between these two basic sectors of the economy, there were persistent obstacles to its growth. By and large, the pull exerted by demand in the urban sector was not great enough to induce significant monetary or real flows. The force of this pull was impeded by lack of development of transport and marketing channels to make interdependence economically feasible. The modern, urban sector, on the other hand, possessed external economies of foreign marketing institutions and access to sea transport, being located in coastal treaty ports. Since these advantages did not extend much beyond the pale of the urban sector itself, most of the raw material, capital, and even consumer requirements of the urban sector were met by production within this sector or by foreign trade. On the supply side, agricultural surpluses in the rural sector were not great because of population pressure on land and backward technology; where they did exist,

* P. K. Chang and C. I. Chang, *The Grain Market in Chekiang Province* (Shanghai, 1940); P. K. Chang, *Food Economy in Kwangsi Province* (Shanghai, 1938).

export to the urban sector was inhibited by costs of transport and marketing (which were high relative to the price at which these goods were supplied from abroad), and by other obstacles. Rural demand for industrial goods from the urban sector was extremely low because of low per capita money incomes in the rural sector, a condition aggravated by highly unequal distribution of income. Thus the demand factor also tended to limit the flow of industrial goods from the urban sector.

In these conditions, intersectoral money and real flows were not of great significance. The major intersectoral flow represented the purchase of agricultural goods for export and raw material use in the urban sector. But even this flow was dependent on the marketing organization furnished by foreign enterprise, and it did not reach far into China's hinterland.* The structure of these facilities prevented much of the flow from being transmitted into income within the rural sector itself. For each export product there was ordinarily one major marketing outlet which was generally able to collect agricultural exports at low supply prices because of its monopsonistic position. Further, much of the purchase price was retained by intermediary supply agencies—traditional traders in the rural sectors. As these groups accumulated monetary wealth, it was transferred back to the urban sector as banking hoards, reducing the effective flow of money between sectors in terms of income dynamics. This process was accelerated in the years before 1935 as silver flowed out of the rural sector in response to the high world price. Thus upper income groups were able to save and transfer money to the urban sector, while the remaining groups spent virtually all of their monetary incomes on consumption.

During the Nationalist government period (1927–1937), government finance failed to induce intersectoral monetary flows. Collection of agricultural taxes was undertaken by the provinces, while the central government based its tax system upon the urban sector of the economy, collecting its revenues from foreign trade and the production of industrial goods.

When the whole of China's prewar rural sector is viewed, it becomes clear that such flows as did take place were not quantitatively significant. They were limited to the areas near the coastal urban sector, export crops not being mobilized from most of the geographical areas of China.

* Chang Pei-kang, *Agriculture and Industrialization* (Cambridge, Mass., 1949), pp. 197–199. R. H. Tawney (editor), *Agrarian China* (Chicago, University of Chicago Press, 1938), pp. 171–175; 179–183.

### *Inflationary Pressures in an Underdeveloped Economy*

Inflationary pressures at a given level of performance may result from new demands upon the current product of an economy, whether such demands arise from increases in government spending, from investment, or from consumer outlays. Inflationary pressures on prices are inevitable unless new spending is offset by any of the following, or a combination of them: decreased spending on the part of one of the other sources of expenditure; increases in taxes or saving; increased output adequate to absorb the new expenditures, plus multiplier effects, at current prices. Essentially, therefore, the question of inflationary pressure is a matter of the expansion of aggregate demand relative to aggregate supply.

Economies respond differently to inflationary stimuli. Similarly, the success of inflation control varies greatly in accordance with the structure of the economy, basic economic propensities, institutional arrangements, and the power of the controlling authority. In an underdeveloped economy, where specific sectors are not closely linked by strong money and real flows, various sectors may show significantly different responses to inflationary pressures.

In an underdeveloped economy an autonomous increase in spending by one of the three spending agencies (consumers, investors, or government) ordinarily reacts upon prices more rapidly and severely in those sectors in which inflationary pressures are released than it does in developed economies. This is true for a number of reasons. In the first place, the marginal and average propensities to consume tend to be higher, and new spending will be reflected primarily in increased demand for consumer goods. Secondly, the supply response to increases in aggregate demand is less elastic than in advanced economies because of fragmentation of the economy into self-contained sectors. Inefficient and oligopsonistic market structures accentuate this rigidity in supply responses. Sectoral fragmentation and low levels of money and real flows among sectors tend to restrict the impact of inflationary pressures to those sectors in which they originate. Thus autonomous increases in government spending, which normally arise in the urban sector of the economy, tend to work themselves out primarily in this sector, since channels through which the spending may be diverted to other sectors are limited. The increase in aggregate of demand tends to be transmitted, if at all, with considerable lag and inefficiency. For the same reason, supply reactions tend to be generated mainly in the urban sector, with considerable leakage to the foreign exchanges. Increased supplies of imports may offset new spending temporarily. Eventually, however, continued new spendings tend to generate balance of payments disequilibrium which reduce the capacity to import. Export goods flow through the urban sector of the economy and thus tend to be significantly affected by costs in this sector. As prices and costs rise, export earnings fall unless frequent exchange rate adjustments are made, and even these fail where inflationary pressures are great. This places very real limits upon the ability of the economy to earn foreign exchange to finance indefinitely expanded supplies of imports.

Inflation control, too, tends to be less effective in underdeveloped economies. In the first place, administration of the tax system is hampered by the problems of economic fragmentation, and it is extremely difficult to significantly offset new spending by greater tax collection. Moreover, taxes are ordinarily indirect in nature and revenues are less responsive to income increases than in developed economies. For administrative reasons also, direct controls of prices and wages are relatively ineffective. Quite apart from the question of the power of the government to enforce such controls over a broad area (which is extremely doubtful in underdeveloped countries), the success of controls in large part depends on the ability to immobilize in some form the redundant income created by new spending. Controls may be described as successful only if they are effective in achieving this objective, which may be accomplished by preventing private spenders from demanding certain categories of current goods and inducing them to purchase government securities, accumulate idle cash, or spend their redundant income on commodities which the authority considers less essential.* If the controls do not succeed in any of these respects, they may be considered ineffective. Lack of effectiveness then may be seen in the development of a black market for goods, in the government's inability to resist pressures for raising the ceiling prices toward black-market levels, or in its grant of discriminatory changes in the interests of special groups.†

But there are differing qualities of effectiveness even if the government is able to hold its ceilings for a shorter or longer period of time. The greatest measure of success results when the government is able to attract redundant incomes into government securities or, to a lesser degree, into savings accounts. In the first case, the government need not borrow from banks to continue its new rate of higher spending; in the second case, it may be able to borrow from banks without necessitating new additions to the money supply. If, on the other

* William Fellner, *A Treatise on War Inflation* (1942), p. 17.

† *Ibid.*, p. 17.

hand, controls induce private spenders merely to accumulate idle funds in the form of cash or current deposits, the government must continue to finance its new level of expenditures by borrowing from banks and adding to the money supply. This process leads to perpetual additions to the accumulations of liquid balances and builds up a supply of volatile funds which may be released at the slightest evidence of weakening of controls. In conditions of rather weak administrative capacity the growth of these balances is almost tantamount to eventual failure of direct controls.

Yet in the conditions of an underdeveloped economy inflation controls, at best, are apt to channel redundant incomes to idle cash balances. As is typical, there has been little experience with exchanging the liquidity of cash or deposits for securities, and experiments with public sales of government bonds have met with little success. Savings are normally held in the form of tangible goods, valuable objects, and, to a lesser extent, in currency. This order of priority would lead to efforts to shift demand from controlled goods to goods which could serve as a store of value. If this were impossible because of supply limitations or comprehensive consumer controls, savings would presumably accumulate in liquid balances held for purposes of conversion to goods at the earliest opportunity. This would pose particularly great problems when controls were relaxed, for example, upon the conclusion of the original emergency, or, if restricted by supply, when new supply sources opened. This latter condition might arise, as it did in China, with the resumption of imports after a blockade.

### *The Inflationary Gap*

The extent to which inflationary tendencies appear in an economy essentially depends on the magnitude of inflationary pressures relative to the success of controls. The problem is that the two are not independent variables, and that the success of control itself depends on the magnitude of inflationary pressures, a variable which has frequently been defined as "the inflationary gap."* When the gap is relatively small, the government, even in an underdeveloped economy, may be able to mop up the addition to disposable income by sale of securities. However, as the gap increases, the consumer may not only be unwilling to convert disposable income to securities, but may also eventually resist the growth of idle balances by greater efforts to convert to goods for hoarding.

All of the foregoing suggests that the inflation potential of an under-

* The inflationary gap may be defined as the excess of disposable income, or ready purchase money, over the supply of goods and services at original or planned prices.

developed economy is much greater than that of a developed economy. In other words, in a backward economy an inflationary gap of say 10 per cent of national income may lead to an inflationary spiral while the same gap might be absorbed in a developed economy by increased output, taxes, and direct controls.

To the extent that the inflationary gap is not offset by controls, taxes, or savings, upward pressures on prices result. In the present discussion let us assume that a new increase in government expenditures for defense has not been offset by any of these devices and that the pressures released are free to increase disposable income in the conditions of an underdeveloped economy.

Where a marked duality in economic structure exists, as in pre-Communist China, new government spending is released primarily in the urban sector of the economy, since increased expenditures for the provisioning of troops—food supplies, clothing, and armaments—tend, in the first instance, to draw upon stocks existing in this sector of the economy. In turn, much of this spending spills over into the foreign-trade sector of the economy, since armaments and other industrially produced goods are not supplied at home. If the expenditure entails the expansion of troops under arms, demand for basic necessities will be increased if the standard of consumption is higher in the armed forces than in civilian life, a situation which frequently exists in underdeveloped countries. Supplies of these necessities will presumably be purchased in relatively large quantities at major markets in the urban sector of the economy, a condition which will result in the development of shortages in these markets as inventories are drawn down in response to government demand. Traders will attempt to replenish inventories by increasing the rates of their purchases of food from the rural sector of the economy and of domestically produced manufactured necessities from the urban sector. Similarly, the government demand for imported goods will be transmitted to foreign suppliers. Given the sluggishness of response in domestic marketing channels and in agricultural production itself, there will be no major leakage of new purchasing power to the rural sector of the economy. Leakage to foreign markets may, however, be significant, creating substantially expanded demand for foreign exchange.

In these conditions, the higher level of government expenditures will, in the first economic period, lead to almost equal expansion of incomes in the urban sector. As a result, disposable income will exceed the value of the total supply of goods and services provided at anticipated prices. Thus a discrepancy arises between disposable income and the values of goods and services supplied (at prices at which suppliers were originally prepared to offer them). This discrepancy will be brought into line by one or several of a variety of possible adjustments:

> A part or all of the goods may be sold at anticipated prices, so that the original supply does not meet the new level of effective demand. In this event, some consumers with disposable income will be forced to save.
>
> Sellers may raise their prices in response to the higher level of demand. This will result in windfall profits to these groups resulting from their falling beneficiary to the difference between what goods were intended to sell for and what they actually do.
>
> Sellers may sell greater amounts than they had planned by drawing upon working inventories of goods intended to replenish their stocks in the next economic period. This will permit a higher level of consumption than would have been achieved in the absence of new government spending and will mitigate price increases.
>
> Consumers may spend less than the disposable income available to them if they find prices rising well beyond their original expectations. This action, which will result in higher rates of voluntary saving, depends in large part on consumer expectations with regard to further price rises, future availability of supplies, and the existing state of time preferences.

The particular combination of these responses which might be expected actually to ensue in a given situation depends primarily upon the state of expectations with regard to further income expansion, supplies of goods, and price rises. If the whole process is expected to continue, consumers will attempt to spend regardless of price rises, and producers will tend to hold their stocks of goods for later sale at higher levels of prices. In the context of a long tradition of deficit financing of emergencies, which was characteristic of modern Chinese fiscal policy, we should expect to find, therefore, the most inflationary of these possible adjustments under way as the level of government expenditures expanded with the onset of war. On all counts, since the inflationary potential of the Chinese economy in mid-1937 was extremely great, extreme caution in expanding the supply of money and aggregate demand was indicated. The economic basis for this conclusion was reinforced by political developments which interfered with supply capacities and further led to an inflationary bias in consumer and producer expectations.

## 2. Application to Inflation in China

The foregoing analysis produces some significant insights into the effects of releasing inflationary pressures in China and the response of the economy under different conditions.

The rather abstract model of inflation in an underdeveloped economy which we have pictured may now be applied to actual conditions in China during the years 1937–1949. It will immediately be apparent that we are describing at least two, and perhaps three, distinct situations.

### *Case A: Inflation during the Early War Years, 1937–1939*

During the period between the outbreak of the war in Shanghai (August 13, 1937) and the retreat of the Nationalist army along the Yangtze from Hankow, the major trading port, to the interior (October 1938), government expenditures were increased mainly to purchase provisions and materials for making ammunition and to transport troops. Most of the purchases were made in the larger cities or from abroad; the expenditure for transportation was distributed over a wide area. Bank credits extended to private enterprises to help finance their removal from coastal ports to the interior were generally small in amount; the proceeds, for the most part, were actually spent on transportation charges and not to increase inventories—partly because transportation was so uncertain and therefore costly.

During this period, inflationary pressures were thus released mainly in the urban sector of the economy; the basic stimulus remained confined to this sector, principally along the coast, and the pressure which was built up was comparatively mild and could be lessened by relatively simple, but costly, economic policies.

The government recognized that the response of the urban sector to inflationary pressures would be largely influenced by the external value of the currency. Accordingly, during the early war years, it undertook to support the exchange rate of the currency through continued supply of foreign exchange to the Shanghai market. This action, which reduced the pace of expansion of the domestic money supply and bolstered general confidence in the currency, mitigated inflationary pressures. Even more important, inflationary pressures were offset by increasing the supply of goods available on domestic markets. The cost, of course, was a considerable leakage of foreign exchange.

Inflationary pressures were relentlessly expanded, however. The government deficit rose 42 per cent in the second half of 1937, and rose another 58 per cent and 30 per cent, respectively, in the first and second halves of 1938. The note issue at the end of 1938 exceeded that of July 1937 by 65 per cent, and the wholesale price index for all of Free China rose 55 per cent in the same period.

Besides the liberal supply of foreign exchange, other factors helping to keep the potentially serious inflation within relatively mild bounds were the comparative shortness of the time involved and the fact that the government left the urban sector before it could compound its effect on the economy by further deficit financing. The effects which might have been expected, according to the model just outlined, remained relatively mild.

Now we find the government moved to Chungking from Hankow, which was in the border area between the urban, modern sector of the economy and the rural sector, not yet blessed with modern industry and modern transportation facilities. In the beginning this move to Chungking appears to have restrained the development of inflation. In terms of the above theoretical analysis and as far as the inflationary process is concerned, the effects of the move can be summarized by stating, first, that the government and the principal consumer groups were brought closer to the supply of basic necessities—in the rural area where they were grown and produced. Several factors combined to endow the move with success insofar as arresting the inflationary process was concerned.

First, the heart of Free China was moved to a rich agricultural area. Szechwan province, for example, where the war capital was located, accounted for about 13 per cent of China's total rice production, and the neighboring province, Hunan, yielded about 15 per cent.

Second, agricultural output in Free China's rice areas in the early years of the war, particularly in Szechwan province, was blessed by abundant harvests. Moreover, the traditional food surplus in the area could not be shipped elsewhere because of war-caused difficulties of interprovincial trade. As a consequence, the price of food in Chungking in December 1937 actually was 10 per cent below the prewar level, and 13 per cent below the level of June of 1938. The deflation in food prices greatly helped the initial stability of the general price level.

Third, communications were improved in this particular part of the rural economy. The newly built Hunan-Kwangsi railway, and the Burma Road, accompanied by the highway network between Szechwan and Hunan and between Kweichow and Yunnan provinces, facilitated the movement of goods between Free China and Hong Kong, Indo-China, and Burma. Thus a minimum supply of foreign goods did continue to flow in to relieve the most acute shortages of certain essential commodities.

Fourth, supplies of many types of goods were attracted into this sector as a result of the exigencies of war—in a rather unique and paradoxical geographical flow of commodities. These commodities were gathered in this sector in anticipation of future price rises. They arrived in time and in sufficient quantities to offset significantly the demand of the millions of refugees who poured into the area. Had it not been for these additional supplies, the influx of refugees, arriving before the establishment of new industries, would have increased demand beyond available supplies and pushed the price level sharply upward.

In terms of the theoretical analysis, a second effect was that the newly created income was distributed primarily among groups whose propensity to consume was relatively low because they were temporarily cut off from supplies of many of the goods which they might have demanded had they remained in the coastal urban sector with access to imported consumer goods.

The relatively low propensity to consume was partially the result of insecurity following upon wartime dislocation and partially due to genuinely patriotic motives. The remoteness of the new wartime locale from the port cities, where there was a keener awareness of the external value (or growing lack of it) of the currency, undoubtedly had some restraining effect upon consumption. Much of the newly created income, therefore, was neutralized from exerting an inflationary force by a strong tendency to hoard. However, the hoards of idle cash were a latent force of inflation which, when later released, gave added impetus to inflation in Free China.

In spite of these stabilizing influences, the money supply in this new subsector of the economy expanded with increasing celerity. The government deficit in 1939 was 124 per cent of that in 1938, and the note issue, which had increased 48 per cent in the previous year, rose by 86 per cent. The price index of whole Free China rose by 67 per cent in 1939.

### *Case AA: Inflation during the War Years, 1940–1945*

As time went on and the relentless expansion of the money supply and income continued, the initial advantages of the move to the rural sector became nullified and inflation became more severe. Moreover, a new urban sector began to evolve here; and, by virtue of its economic infancy and isolation, its resistance to inflationary pressures was slight.

A bad harvest in Szechwan province toward the end of 1939 caused a violent flare-up of inflationary forces. The internal value of the currency in this rural sector had traditionally been measured as much by the price of rice as currency in the coastal sector had traditionally been measured by its external value. The sudden rise in the price of rice brought about an explosive release of inflationary pressures. Oblivious to this, and spurred by the hope for a stronger military position, the government went on pouring out new currency and credit to expand its military establishment, to raise the level of production, and to improve communications. It failed to devise offsets to the increased money supply and new income. Government, industry, and individual consumers all demanded more and more goods and services, while the tightening enemy blockade, the inherently weak industrial foundation in the rural sector, and the people's anticipation of a growing scarcity of goods combined to restrict the effective supply of almost all goods. Because of the cellular fragmentation of this sector and the lack of flow of goods among markets, both demand and supply of whatever goods were available tended to concentrate in the newly expanded cities. While the funds held by buyers were awaiting satisfaction of their demands, they became vehicles for speculative activities. Speculative demand for goods thus was added to the real demand for goods and services, intensifying inflationary pressures. The validity of the inflationary model constructed above became confirmed more with every passing month. New income was created in the nascent urban sector and soon became effective demand for goods and services in this sector. Interestingly, a pattern of greatly varying responses to the inflationary situation developed—as shown by the uneven rise in prices among the interior cities.

In the rural sector the supply response to increasing aggregate demand was even less elastic. Lack of domestic industry, the precedent of little flow of goods because of the traditional self-sufficiency of this area, and fragmentation into self-contained sectors with little interchange between them combined to cause this lack of elasticity. The response of prices to localized spending was severe. A notable example was the wartime experience of Kunming, Yunnan. Before the Nationalist government moved to the interior, the city had a small population with no military concentration, and the average propensity of the residents to consume had been low. When government construction workers (with sharply increased demand) streamed in to work on the Burma Road and the Yunnan-Szechwan Railway and to set up a few factories, the moderately swollen income stream could not be diverted because of Kunming's relative isolation. From then on, the city's price index continued to lead that of all other cities during the entire war period. In the first half of 1942 the local index of wholesale prices was nearly triple, and in 1945 it still was twice, that of Chungking.

In the urban sector, where the bulk of public and private expenditures were released, the supply response to increases in aggregate demand was somewhat more elastic. The expansion of local production and a higher level of flow of goods from outside bolstered supply, and price responses to stepped-up spending were originally comparatively mild. Chungking's experience is pertinent here. In spite of its being the war capital, with a colossal government organization which generated a large volume of spending, its price index always kept below that of Kunming—even though it was above that of other cities. A number of new industries had been established, and the supplies of many other urban centers could be reached by river transport.

The urban centers which had been self-contained because of poor communications and in which only a small increase in public and private spending took place, and also those which had not been self-contained and now had access to transportation but had no market structure that lent itself to speculation, responded least to inflationary pressures. The city of Lanchow in Kansu province in the Northwest was in the former category. Its price indexes were consistently among the lowest in Free China.

Although the urban sector's response to inflation varied among cities, the general rise of prices in the new urban sector pointed to the validity of the hypothesis that the government was unable to contain inflationary pressures by fiscal policy, by anti-inflationary borrowing, and, finally, by efforts to control prices and wages. This is borne out by the history of this period. All these efforts were focused on the new urban sector which had evolved in the interior. Even in this severely limited scope, anti-inflationary policies failed because of the strength of inflationary pressures relative to the capacity of the government to implement controls.

### *Case B: Inflation in the Postwar Period*

The analysis in Section 1 best fits a situation such as existed in China during the postwar period. Shortly after the end of the war the government returned to the coastal region, there to base its power on the more developed urban sector of the economy. The traditionally coastal and urban-minded government authorities relished their return to the more modern and more abundant port cities, abandoning the interior with the new urban sector it had created, and the vast rural resources as if they were of no importance. Partly because of successful Communist efforts to frustrate the government's restoration of communications between the North and South, attempts to integrate the economies of the two regions failed.

As it developed, for a short period the urban sector became almost self-sufficient, with a basic orientation toward world markets. Even raw materials and foodstuffs came to be supplied predominantly from abroad rather than from the Chinese economy itself. In this setting, the government embarked upon a new program of releasing inflationary pressures with little initial thought about restraining their effect on price levels. In the fragmented condition of the economy, these inflationary pressures came to be released almost entirely within the coastal, urban sector, a condition which in turn placed great strain upon the balance of payments since foreign trade became the major avenue by which total supply within the sector could be increased. As it finally developed, the behavior of prices in the coastal sector came to be associated with the state of foreign supply and with abundance (or lack) of foreign exchange.

As time progressed, inflationary responses between the two major domestic sectors grew farther and farther apart. This can be seen from the striking contrast between the high level of prices in the coastal urban markets, and the low level of prices in the interior. The price indexes for September 1947 (the last month for which the wholesale price indexes of major cities were published by the government) gave a clear picture, as shown in Table 27.

TABLE 27. WHOLESALE PRICE INDEX, SEPTEMBER 1947[1]
(Jan.—June 1937 = 100)

| Coastal Cities | Index | Interior Cities | Index |
|---|---|---|---|
| Shanghai | 4,635,700 | Chungking | 2,590,240 |
| Tientsin | 4,574,905 | Changsha | 3,481,400 |
| Tsingtao | 6,304,000 | Lanchow | 3,636,300 |
| Canton | 4,169,327 | Kunming | 2,444,775 |
| Foochow | 4,529,710 | Kweiyang | 1,564,323 |

[1] Source: Based on statistics compiled by Directorate-General of Budgets, Accounts and Statistics.

So far as anti-inflationary policy was concerned, this meant that overt price control measures were destined to fail unless the supply situation could be improved either by the integration of the economy into a working whole or by the provision of almost unlimited access to foreign exchange. Since little was done in regard to the former, anti-inflationary policy in this period became primarily a matter of foreign trade and foreign exchange control.

Foodstuffs furnished one example proving that the supply situation was susceptible of improvement by integrating the economy. During the Pacific War both Occupied China and Free China had kept themselves completely self-sufficient in food supply without importing any grains whatsoever. There was no reason why postwar China could not have done likewise with its domestic production had the government only made an effort to mobilize supplies from the rural sector by improving physical communications to areas of greatest shortage and facilitating better marketing channels. Instead of promoting supplies from within by direct actions, the government extended huge credits to Shanghai rice merchants for rice purchases from the interior. This measure, far from contributing to the integration of the domestic economy, supplied the rice merchants with the funds for speculation—and thus actually encouraged the price rise of rice, instead of halting it.

Meanwhile, government spending rapidly increased the money supply, and inflationary pressures continued to grow. The government's part in this process is shown in Table 28.

TABLE 28. POSTWAR INFLATIONARY PRESSURES GENERATED BY THE GOVERNMENT

| Year | Increase of Government Expenditures | Increase of the Deficit | Increase of the Note Issue |
|---|---|---|---|
| 1946 | 3.2 times | 4.2 times | 3.6 times |
| 1947 | 5.7 times | 6.2 times | 8.9 times |
| 1948[1] | 30.0 times | 30.0 times | 22.4 times |

[1] The rate of increase of expenditures and of the deficit in 1948 is based on figures published for the first half of that year.

The government also failed to take account of the inherent pressure of the purchasing power accumulated during the war years. This force was now being brought into play in the coastal sector, where it was hoped supplies would be plentiful. Thus supply and demand were already badly out of balance, and the addition of the new money could only produce the most inflationary of the alternative responses discussed in Section 1 of this chapter. Supplies of goods were increasingly withheld from the market in anticipation of further price rises; consumers became increasingly unwilling to accumulate monetary savings. Both factors tended to accentuate the velocity of the turnover of money. Sellers had little real opportunity to replenish inventories which had been drawn down by years of wartime demands; and the movement of prices fostered reluctance on the part of merchants to make available what little inventories they had for sale.

All these phenomena first became evident in a few major cities, eventually spreading throughout the urban sector. Inflationary pressures finally seeped through to the entire rural sector, but with varying degrees of intensity according to local conditions of supply and demand. Farmers in the hinterland realized that the decline of the value of the currency was irreversible, and that they would fare better by hoarding their products or by exchanging them for consumer goods. Thus the urban sector was subjected to a new double pressure: the decreasing inflow of foodstuffs and other agricultural raw materials from the commercialized hinterland, and the increasing demand for consumer goods. The lack of foodstuffs brought with it rising prices and wages, and the shortage of raw materials for light industry entailed higher prices for consumer goods turned out by such industry.

Having failed to control prices by measures affecting the dynamics of the domestic economy, the government now had to depend for its price control on the effects of foodstuff and raw materials imports. It attempted to distribute these either at an unrealistically low exchange rate or at controlled prices. This approach is most clearly seen in control of cotton imports after 1946 and rice during 1947 and 1948. The imported food was used mainly to help meet the requirements of the population of some eleven million in the five eastern cities of Shanghai, Tientsin, Peking, Nanking, and Canton, while the cotton imports were to supply about 80 per cent of the cotton industry located in the coastal urban sector.

Although low-priced food and cotton imports somewhat relieved the supply shortage in the urban sector, they also put a damper on prices of domestic production of these commodities. This increased the farmers' preference for hoarding their production, even in the agricultural areas adjacent to the coast, and further aggravated the supply problem in the urban sector. Moreover, the continued excess of imports over exports exhausted China's dwindling reserves of foreign exchange. This eventually forced curtailment of raw material and capital goods imports needed by domestic industries. The net result was the failure of domestic industrial production to restore prewar levels of output.

In this manner the input-output relationships in the urban sector were disorganized, and the flow of goods between the cities and the hinterland also came to a virtual standstill. The economy on which Nationalist power was based became squeezed between monetary expansion on one side and the contraction of the supply of agricultural and industrial products on the other.

Retrospection suggests the conclusion that the government both overestimated the ability of the urban sector to absorb the large additional supplies of money and underestimated the strength and contribution which the rural sector might have made toward the survival of Nationalist China. As it turned out, inflationary pressures could not be smoothly transmitted from the city to the farm, there to be equalized and relieved; instead, they created additional barriers to economic intercourse between the sectors.

The urban sector of the economy, on which the government had hoped to base its power in the postwar period, turned out to be a house of sand in the face of the wind of inflationary finance. The rural sector, meanwhile, tended to return to its age-old state of a self-contained barter economy.

# Part 2

# The Growth of Aggregate Demand

# Introduction

No appropriate policy for financing the war was formulated by the Chinese government after the outbreak of hostilities with Japan in 1937. The increase in military outlay was not offset by a decrease in other expenditures; although the shrinkage of territory entailed a decline in the source of existing taxes, no equitable taxation system was created in the unoccupied areas to offset the loss of taxes from the industrial cities in Japanese hands; faith in government bonds had been destroyed by their excess issue before the war.

From 1937 to 1941 total central government expenditure rose to 500 per cent of the 1937 levels and revenue advanced to 160 per cent, while the corresponding deficit increased to 683 per cent. This trend was reversed between 1941 and 1944—but only temporarily—principally as a result of a land tax levied in kind reinforced by additional government borrowing of grain and the promotion of savings. Government revenue in 1944 stood at 2,938 per cent of the level of 1941 compared to a level of 1,717 per cent in expenditure, while the deficit rose to 15,323 per cent.

Unfortunately, after the end of the war the government not only again failed to balance the budget but even expanded its expenditures further, thus increasing the deficit. In the last quarter of 1945 government expenditure suddenly spurted to 1,547 per cent of that of the preceding quarter. From 1946 on, inflationary pressures necessitated the continued expansion of government expenditures and were in turn aggravated by such expansion. The year-to-year increase in expenditure was 261 per cent in 1946 and 473 per cent in 1947. In contrast, the increase in revenue, raised by 131 per cent in 1946 and 388 per cent in 1947. The resulting deficit, which was 62 per cent of total expenditure in 1946, rose to 67 per cent in 1947. Nearly the entire deficit was met by borrowing from banks.

Aggregate demand for goods and services suddenly spurted after the outbreak of the war in response to the explosive expansion of the money supply. This increase in demand exercised strong inflationary pressures on prices, particularly because of the heavy dependence of government finance on bank borrowing and the primitive state of the economy of China's interior provinces where the output of goods and services could not be increased at short notice.

As the war continued, in the face of rising prices, manufacturers and merchants not only became increasingly reluctant to sell their goods, but also endeavored to convert their cash into commodities. People with available cash also began to speculate in commodities, and landlords were slow to sell the grain they collected as rent. Thus each new wave of price increases caused by government deficits created more money income while it also tended to produce a smaller stream of goods and services made available on the markets. Thus government spending had to assume ever larger proportions to maintain even a relatively low level of real expenditures. This caused government spending itself to become the main engine of inflation. The impact of government fiscal policy upon the level of aggregate demand and, hence, upon inflation will be discussed under the headings of the prewar structure of government finance, war finance, and postwar finance.

Chapter 6

# Prewar Government Finance

### *Weakness of the Prewar Structure*

The origin of China's wartime financial woes can be traced significantly to the country's prewar structure of public finance. As military expenditures in wartime inevitably increase the money supply if deficit financing prevails, the dual problem in war finance, given the military needs, is to avoid an oversupply of money in relation to the output of civilian commodities and services and to distribute the financial burden of the war equitably. While proper fiscal measures alone cannot accomplish these two objectives, they can nevertheless play a key role. Among the necessary conditions for successfully financing war without destroying economic stability are a rational pattern of expenditures, an equitable taxation system, and facilities for direct public borrowing. Unfortunately, none of these elements was present in China's prewar financial structure and none was provided subsequently. Specifically, the government's financial weakness lay in three distinct but related fields: the prewar pattern of government expenditures, reliance on indirect taxation, and mismanagement of the domestic bond market.

The finances of the central government of China were in deficit every year from the time of the founding of the Republic in 1911 to the outbreak of war with Japan in 1937. Until 1927 incessant internal strife produced chaos in government finances, and no budget could be drafted because revenues legally belonging to the central government were retained by local warlords. After the Nationalists came to power in 1927, the central government attempted to enforce its tax claims by direct central collection. In the decade before the outbreak of the war, however, expenditures rose more rapidly than revenues. Between 1928 and 1935 for example, as shown in Table 29, revenues increased by 103 per cent while expenditures rose 156 per cent and the deficit by 379 per cent.

TABLE 29. CENTRAL GOVERNMENT REVENUES AND EXPENDITURES[1]
(CNC $ millions)

| | | | | Deficit Finance[2] | |
|---|---|---|---|---|---|
| Year | Revenue | Expenditure | Deficit | Sales of Bonds and Treasury Bills | Bank Advances |
| 1928–29 | 332 | 412 | 80 | 69 | 11 |
| 1929–30 | 438 | 539 | 101 | 91 | 10 |
| 1930–31 | 497 | 714 | 217 | 193 | 24 |
| 1931–32 | 553 | 683 | 130 | 125 | 5 |
| 1932–33 | 559 | 645 | 86 | 26 | 60 |
| 1933–34 | 622 | 769 | 147 | 88[3] | 59 |
| 1934–35 | 745 | 941 | 196 | 196 | 0 |
| 1935–36 | 674 | 1,057 | 383 | 54 | 329 |

[1] Chia Te-huai, *The Financial History of the Republic of China* (in Chinese; Commercial Press, Shanghai, 1946), p. 16.

[2] It is difficult to obtain the figures of sales of bonds and treasury bills because there were almost no public sales of Government Bonds and bank advances were made on security of bonds which were sold to the banks at varying prices.

[3] Includes CNC $8.3 million American wheat and cotton loan to China.

## *The Prewar Pattern*

In this period, the central government found it necessary to engage in deficit financing because of the disproportionate size of two items of expenditure, military outlays and payments for the services of loans. The history of military expenditure in Republican China places the problem in an illuminating context.

From the first year of the Republic on, the necessity for retrenchment of military expenditures was recognized, but this objective was never actually accomplished despite frequent attempts to effect economies during the next three decades. In 1912 about 900,000 troops were mobilized, and their maintenance required an annual expenditure so large that the heavy burden of bearing the costs prompted an almost unanimous demand for reduction to 500,000 men. In the Reorganization Loan Agreement of 1913, £3 million of the total proceeds of £25 million were allocated to the purpose of disbanding 330,000 superfluous troops. However, the money was spent in other ways and demobilization was postponed.

Although in 1919 the representatives at the Peace and Unity Conference between North and South reported that the number of troops in the country had risen to 1,290,000, a proposal to decrease the army to 500,000 men was rejected.

In 1925, at a military conference representing all of China held in Peking, the representative of the central government reported that the number of troops had further increased to 1,500,000. At this time the central government ordered that the size of detachments in each province should be determined on the basis of the financial capacity of the provincial governments, and that reductions in force should be made according to that principle. Local warlords paid no heed to these directions; and, when the Nationalist government was established in Nanking in the autumn of 1927, the number of troops in the whole of China had grown to 2,000,000.

At the Financial and Economic Conference held in Shanghai in June 1928 the industrialists and bankers in attendance urged that the government demobilize part of the army, divert a portion of military expenditures to reconstruction, and engage former soldiers in productive employment. It was suggested that the total number of troops be limited to fifty divisions totaling about 500,000 men. In 1929 the central government called a conference of the nation's military leaders to discuss concrete measures for demobilization, and it was decided that the army should be reduced to a total of 800,000 men (excluding the navy and the air force). Unfortunately, local military leaders, suspicious of the intentions of the central government, made no effort to comply with the directive. Troops under mobilization combined to number about 2,000,000, and no appreciable economies in military finance were ever effected. The annual military expenditures of the central government from 1928 to 1936 were as shown in Table 30.

The Ministry of Finance emphasized that expenditures reported in the Annual Reports underestimated the actual amounts spent for defense. The central government subsidized military expenditures of local authorities through grants and unrecorded tax allotments, which did not appear as military expenditures. In the period just before the outbreak of the war the central government accounts listed large amounts of unallocated funds; and it is clear that these were employed mainly for defense. The strain which military expendi-

TABLE 30. CENTRAL GOVERNMENT MILITARY EXPENDITURES[1]

| Year | Amount (CNC $ millions) | Per Cent of Total Government Expenditures |
|---|---|---|
| 1928–29 | 210 | 48 |
| 1929–30 | 245 | 45 |
| 1930–31 | 312 | 44 |
| 1931–32 | 304 | 45 |
| 1932–33 | 321 | 49 |
| 1933–34 | 373 | 48 |
| 1934–35 | 368 | 34 |
| 1935–36 | 366 | 34 |
| Average | 312 | 43 |

[1] The figures of 1928–35 were compiled from the data in Chia Te-huai, *op. cit.,* p. 700. Data in the figures 1935–36 were compiled from C. Y. Li, *The Comparative Financial System,* Appendix, [in Chinese].

tures placed upon government finance in the prewar period is not, therefore, adequately reflected in the reported figures.

The Republic of China inherited in 1911 a heavy burden of loan obligations from the Manchu regime, including foreign loans in the amount of CNC $626,000,000, the Boxer Indemnity of CNC $1,870,000,000, and domestic debts of $16,000,000. During the first two decades of the Republic the central government continued to finance a large part of its expenditures by borrowing. Between 1912 and 1926 central government borrowing totaled CNC $500,000,000 in foreign loans and $630,000,000 in domestic loans. Almost two-thirds of these loans were secured on central tax sources, and loans were regularly serviced as the first claim upon revenues from these tax sources. After the Nationalists came to power the government borrowed even more heavily than before. During the period 1927–1934 nearly CNC $1.9 billion worth of domestic bonds and treasury bills was issued, and foreign debts of about CNC $120,000,000 were incurred. By 1934 total outstanding indebtedness was in the vicinity of CNC $2.5 billion which figure excluded CNC $200,000,000 in foreign railway debts and unsecured loans.

From the time the Republic was organized in 1911, successive Republican governments borrowed from the banks by placing domestic bonds or treasury bills with them as security. When loans fell due, the obligations were covered by selling the security at the prevailing price which averaged 40 to 50 per cent below face value. These severe discounts raised interest costs to almost double the nominal yield, and the burden of the national debt was enormously increased. As a result, loan services (Table 31) became a major item of government expenditure second in size to defense outlays.

TABLE 31. CENTRAL GOVERNMENT LOAN SERVICE EXPENDITURES, 1928–1936[1]

| Year | Loan Services (CNC $ millions) | Per Cent of Total Expenditures |
|---|---|---|
| 1928–29 | 160 | 37 |
| 1929–30 | 200 | 37 |
| 1930–31 | 290 | 41 |
| 1931–32 | 270 | 40 |
| 1932–33 | 210 | 31 |
| 1933–34 | 244 | 32 |
| 1934–35 | 356 | 33 |
| 1935–36 | 217 | 20 |
| Average | 243 | 34 |

[1] The figures of 1925–35 were compiled from the data in Chia Te-huai, *op. cit.*, p. 700. Data for 1935–36 are compiled from C. Y. Li, *op. cit.*, Appendix.

In 1932–1933, loan services fell to 31 per cent of total expenditures following a reorganization which in effect reduced the rate of interest the government paid on outstanding domestic indebtedness. However, these costs began to rise again in the following years.

Throughout the two decades prior to the beginning of the Sino-Japanese war an average of 80 per cent of total government spending was devoted to military expenditure and loan services. Most of the remainder was employed to maintain administrative services, leaving almost no funds for public works. Defense and debt service were largely responsible for the prewar deficit financing, thus establishing a strong inflationary bias in government finance. If military expenditure could not be restrained in peacetime, its expansion, with accompanying waste, could be avoided even less readily in war. Moreover, the prewar pattern of expenditures prevented the government from effectively aiding the country's capital formation. In spite of repeated urging by government leaders that economic reconstruction was important, and in spite of the creation of numerous public bodies to tackle this task, the lack of funds prevented any real progress. Thus the potential increase in the supply of goods through economic development, of immeasurable value in retarding or averting inflation, did not come to pass. From the expenditure point of view, the prevailing pattern prevented the government from promoting economic development by financing capital formation. Political and economic obstacles to rational government performance in the expenditure field had much to do with the persistence of stagnant levels of output. Increase in production failed to gather momentum over the first half of the twentieth century, a basic economic fact which must be reckoned as an important factor contributing to the inflation generated in the war years and to the social revolution which it bred.

## *Indirect Taxation*

Shortly after the Republic of China was established, proposals were made to divide tax sources between the central and local governments to replace the former system under which the central government was financed by arbitrary amounts transferred from locally collected revenues. But until the Nationalist government came to power the geographical scope of the authority of the central government was limited, and a large part of the revenues legally belonging to the central government was retained by the local warlords. After 1928 interference of local authorities in the administration of the three most important levies—customs duties, the salt tax, and taxes on commodities—was curtailed. This reform was accomplished with relative ease since the collection of customs duties was confined to the seaports, the salt industry was limited to a few producing areas, and most of the industries paying commodity taxes were located in Shanghai and other coastal cities over which the central authority held sway. In fact, the facility with which those taxes could be collected induced the government to increase them whenever it found itself in financial straits, and distracted the government from devising a more equitable and efficient system of taxation. Table 32 shows the importance of revenues from custom duties, salt imposts, and commodity taxes in the prewar tax structure.

Customs duties on many classes of imported goods, particularly textiles, kerosene, needles, and tobacco; sales taxes on commodities such as home-produced cotton clothing, flour, and matches; and the salt tax were all levies on necessities entering into the daily purchases of lower-income groups. Hence the major prewar taxes were predominantly regressive in nature, and, as they were increased during the thirties, became more and more inequitable. The imposition of direct taxes, to which some thought was given, was impeded by political and economic problems. A plan to establish an income tax

TABLE 32. CENTRAL GOVERNMENT REVENUES FROM MAJOR TAXES, 1928–1936[1]
(CNC $ millions)

| Year | Customs Duty | Salt Tax | Commodity Tax | Cost of Collecting | Net Proceeds from Three Taxes | Per Cent of Total Revenue |
|---|---|---|---|---|---|---|
| 1928–29 | 179 | 30 | — | 10 | 209 | 63 |
| 1929–30 | 275 | 122 | — | 46 | 351 | 80 |
| 1930–31 | 313 | 150 | 53 | 63 | 453 | 91 |
| 1931–32 | 370 | 144 | 89 | 80 | 523 | 95 |
| 1932–33 | 325 | 158 | 79 | 55 | 507 | 91 |
| 1933–34 | 352 | 177 | 104 | 68 | 565 | 91 |
| 1934–35 | 353 | 172 | 108 | 61 | 572 | 77 |
| 1935–36 | 272 | 192 | 115 | 61 | 518 | 77 |

[1] The figures for 1928–35 are compiled from Chia Te-huai, *op. cit.*, pp. 699–700; those for 1935–36 from C. Y. Li, *op. cit.*, Appendix.

system had been considered at the end of the Manchu dynasty, and as early as 1912 an income tax law was actually promulgated. The outbreak of civil war, however, prevented its introduction. When the central government attempted to proceed with the collection of an income tax in 1921, it was forced to abandon its efforts by opposition of the provincial governments and various local guilds. In 1930 the Nationalist government introduced an amended income tax law based on the text of the 1912 regulations. The proposals were again shelved on the recommendations of the Kemmerer Commission, invited by the Chinese government to study problems of financial reform.

Inherently, an income tax system requires an elaborate administrative organization, workable methods of assessment, and some degree of co-operation on the part of taxpayers. China lacked the necessary administrative machinery, and the existing central, provincial, and local government agencies were corrupt and inefficient. As was widely believed at the time, the expense of training and maintaining an army of government officials would have exceeded income tax revenues in the first few years of operation. The technical problems of assessment were also formidable. The accounting methods employed by business enterprises were primitive in the extreme, and the vast majority of the people were illiterate. Furthermore, the Chinese people had good reason to suspect the integrity of tax collectors and to fear interference from the government if they submitted details of their private affairs. Consequently, it would have been useless to rely on statements of income made by individuals. For these reasons, the Kemmerer Commission took the view that it was more desirable to improve methods of collecting the old taxes than to introduce new ones. The government did not return to the idea of levying income taxes until 1936, when an income tax system was announced by which salaries of civil servants and incomes from securities became subject to tax from 1 October. The coverage was gradually to be extended to include all the major classes of income earners, but the outbreak of war in 1937 brought this program to a standstill.

The only direct tax universally applied in China prior to the war was the age-old land tax, which was allocated to the provincial governments in 1928 after customs duty and salt tax had become important sources of central government revenue. Since the amount of tax liability varied according to the quality of land held, classified for this purpose several centuries previously, it was approximate to an income tax. But landholding records had not been revised since the Manchu dynasty, innumerable changes in ownership had occurred, and land areas, yields, and tax liabilities were very seldom in agreement.

Wealthy landowners, in league with corrupt officials, were able to exploit this situation and avoid tax payments, but to the small farmer the tax was a heavy burden. After 1928 the provincial governments made efforts to compile new land records and called on property owners to register their holdings voluntarily. The response was so poor that at the outbreak of war less than half the land in the country had been registered. It was estimated that, if landholdings had been classified according to yields and the records had been completed and brought up to date, the local governments could have trebled their revenues from this source. As it was, the total tax yield from land in 1935 was only about CNC $150,000,000—less than central government revenue from salt.

A thorough overhaul of the land tax before the Japanese invasion would have laid the basis of a comprehensive system of direct taxation; and the development of an income tax, whatever the initial cost involved in building the necessary administrative machinery, would have made government revenues more secure, besides enabling the compilation of valuable statistics and encouraging businessmen to adopt sounder accounting methods. In the absence of income taxes the government was placed in a difficult position when it was deprived of a great part of its revenues from customs duty, salt tax, and commodity tax by the Japanese occupation of the eastern provinces.

The government's excessive reliance on indirect taxes, and its hesitation to apply income taxes, not only resulted in loss of sizeable potential revenue but also demoralized the taxpayers on whom the existing taxes fell. In the absence of an efficient administrative machinery and a long-standing habit of taxpayer co-operation, the efficient collection of direct taxes in wartime became virtually impossible although the only fair and effective method of siphoning off spendable funds and windfall profits would have been a progressive income and profit tax. The lack of a direct income tax meant that much of the rural sector, which plays such a large role in China's economy and on which the government became more and more dependent after its relocation in the interior, was not effectively tapped for revenue. This is true even though the levy of a land tax in kind was imposed in the latter half of the war; this age-old tax did not succeed in taking away the surplus income of many persons and firms in rural areas in a reasonably equitable manner.

### *The Domestic Bond Market*

Before the Nationalist regime, the public had very little confidence in any kind of promissory note issued by the government; even convertible bank notes were looked upon with a certain amount of suspicion and had not attained a very wide circulation. In 1921 CNC $100,000,000 of domestic bonds were issued but only CNC $7,000,000 were sold. In 1914 and 1915 two issues of CNC $24,000,000 each were successfully marketed because of the patriotic support given to the young republic and the government's stratagem of inviting the Foreign Inspector General of Customs to act as Vice Chairman of a newly created National Loans Bureau.

However, the public's enthusiasm for bonds waned rapidly as the financial position of the government deteriorated. Successive bond issues were used to liquidate debts with the government banks, which later sold the bonds on the market at a big discount. By the close of 1920, ten domestic bond issues amounting to CNC $315,000,000 had been floated. Seven of these loans were not specifically secured on items of revenue, and interest and redemption payments were constantly in default.

The need for a reorganization of domestic loans became urgent, and early in 1921 the government adopted a number of proposals for reform put forward by the Bank of China. The Foreign Inspector General of Customs was appointed to the administration of domestic loan services; a sinking fund of CNC $24,000,000, raised from customs surplus and salt, wine, and tobacco taxes, was to be managed by him in conjunction with representatives of the government and of the Peking Bankers' Association; and certain bonds, the market prices of which had fallen absurdly low, were canceled.

This move helped to restore confidence in the bonds, and market prices steadied. Between 1921 and 1926 another seventeen loans were floated with a face value of CNC $310,000,000, bringing the total number of issues to twenty-seven and the outstanding balance in 1926 to CNC $186,000,000. Soon after the Nationalist government consolidated its position in Shanghai in 1927 it proceeded to raise funds by means of short-term loans repayable in monthly installments according to a fixed schedule, with interest coupons also payable monthly. Control of the loan service was entrusted to a new Sinking Fund Committee, on which representatives of the Shanghai Bankers' Association and the Chamber of Commerce replaced the Inspector General of Customs. The first issue, amounting to CNC $30,000,000, was redeemed in 30 months, and the interest paid was 8 per thousand monthly on bonds selling at 20 below par on the market. The public displayed great trust in the new government and was attracted by the high yields on bonds, while banks made handsome profits by buying bonds at a discount and selling them to the public. But the government continued to spend huge sums to build up its military strength, and the ensuing deficit was financed by successive issues of bonds and treasury notes, with disastrous consequences for the loan market.

In addition to the outstanding balance of bond issues of previous governments, amounting to CNC $186,000,000, the Nationalists had raised by the end of 1931 no less than twenty-five internal loans to the face value of CNC $1,108,000,000, the outstanding balance of which was CNC $753,000,000.

The government committed two costly errors in its handling of loan flotations: bonds were given too short a maturity, and interest rates were fixed too high. The financial position deteriorated in the last months of 1931, when the government lost a substantial proportion of customs and salt revenues after the Japanese occupation of Manchuria and incurred heavy expenditures during the local war with Japan in the Chapei district near Shanghai.

By the end of the year it was clear that the government would default on loan service payments—both on its own bonds and on those issued by previous administration—which amounted to approximately CNC $200,000,000 per annum. Early in January 1932 the government intended to impose a moratorium but was dissuaded from this extreme action by the opposition raised in Shanghai banking circles. Finally the bankers agreed to the reduction of the interest on loans and to the extension of the redemption period.

The government offered to allocate to a National Debt Sinking Fund CNC $8,600,000 per month from customs revenue before foreign obligations secured on it were met, and expressed its determination to keep faith with investors by avoiding any further retrogressive changes in loan services. From January 1932 to January 1935 another fifteen loans with a face value of CNC $960,000,000 were floated. At the latter date the outstanding balance of domestic bonds was CNC $1,280,000,000, and the government's annual liability in respect of loan services was CNC $40,000,000 in excess of the maximum consented to four years earlier. By February 1936 the government, finding itself unable to discharge its domestic loan commitments, abandoned its previous undertaking by announcing a second reorganization of the loan services. A compulsory conversion and consolidation loan of CNC $1,460,000,000 was issued to retire the outstanding balance of CNC $1,280,000,000 on the existing thirty-three issues, the balance of the new loan being used to meet the government deficit for 1936. The bonds were divided into five kinds of 12, 15, 18, 21, and 24 years' maturity according to the redemption periods of the old issues. The nominal interest rate on bonds was lowered, and monthly installment repayments were abolished.

The confidence of the public had been shaken considerably by the first reorganization of the loan services in 1932, as is indicated by the increase in the annual redemption yield from 20.6 per cent in 1928 to 27.7 per cent in 1932. However, the Manchurian incident and the Sino-Japanese hostilities in the early 1930's discouraged investment in domestic industry, an effect that was strengthened by the world depression and an appreciation in the external value of the Chinese dollar. The lack of alternative investment outlets reacted favorably on the market for government securities, the index of bond prices rose steadily, and, by 1935, the average annual redemption yield had fallen to 15.9 per cent. The second reorganization came as a profound shock to the market, and the price of bonds rapidly declined, as shown in Table 33.

Most of the bond issues were absorbed by the banks, which were embarrassed by the fall in market prices. It was estimated in February 1936 that the 28 principal banks held CNC $400,000,000 of bonds as investments and another CNC $250,000,000 as part of their reserves against the note issue, making a total of CNC $650,000,000 of bonds valued at market prices. Converting this sum to face values, CNC $900,000,000 of bonds or two-thirds of the total issue were in the possession of the banks. The decline in market prices, by reducing the liquidity of the banks and by seriously undermining the value of their assets, prevented them from lending much support to further government issues.

TABLE 33. BOND QUOTATIONS BEFORE AND AFTER THE 1936 REORGANIZATION[1]

| 6 Per Cent (per annum) Consolidation Bonds Secured on Customs Revenue | Quotations (CNC $ per hundred) | |
|---|---|---|
| | Immediately before Reorganization February 1936 | June 1936 |
| Twelve-year bonds | 76.46 | 63.80 |
| Fifteen-year bonds | 71.33 | 61.15 |
| Eighteen-year bonds | 64.26 | 57.75 |
| Twenty-one-year bonds | 61.00 | 57.60 |
| Twenty-four-year bonds | 61.00 | 57.65 |

[1] Price quotations from *Bankers' Weekly,* June 1936.

The banks took up the bonds at sizable discounts and used them mainly as reserves against note issues. This practice not only raised the effective cost of money to the government, thus increasing the share of loan service charges in the budget, but also failed to accustom both the public to subscribing to government bonds and the banks to purchasing bonds that could not be used as reserve for note issue. Furthermore, while the government indulged in borrowing as an easy source of cash, it was blind to the progressive deterioration of its credit, mainly caused by the frequent refunding and reorganization operations. When the war came, this prewar policy soon proved to have been shortsighted. The public scarcely responded to bond sale drives, which failed not only to raise money when needed but also to sop up inflationary cash from the spending stream.

Chapter

7

# Government War Finance and Expenditure

## 1. The Budget

### ***Principles of War Finance***

At the outbreak of war the Chinese government, which for two and a half decades had barely sustained itself by borrowing, was presented with the task of financing preparations for resisting a formidable military power. Huge sums were required to equip and maintain fighting units, to construct roads and railways in the interior, to transplant industries of the coast to inland centers, and, in general, to mobilize the resources of unoccupied China for the purposes of war. Moreover, with the government's financial requirements growing daily, it lost the greater part of its revenues from salt tax, customs duty, and commodity taxes as a result of the invasion of North China and the subsequent occupation of the central and southern coastal areas. With the incidents of the early thirties as a reminder of the imperialist ambitions of the Japanese, perhaps it should have been foreseen that the subjugation of the coast or a blockade of the major ports would deprive the government of much of its revenues. Once the war had started, there was little hope of developing alternative sources of revenue in the interior. The taxable capacity of the inland provinces was extremely limited because of the general poverty of the peasant farmers and the lack of developed secondary industries; and there was no capital market for the government to exploit as it had the Shanghai market in prewar days. In these circumstances of dwindling revenues and mounting expenditure, the most serious financial crisis the Nationalist government had yet experienced arose.

There was a sharp divergence of views on the appropriate financial policy China should pursue during the period of war emergency.

Most economists, arguing that China should follow the precedent of the Western nations during World War I, recommended three main financial measures to enable the government to pay for the war while maintaining reasonable economic stability.* First, this group believed that a war profits tax should be imposed to capture windfall profits resulting from wartime conditions. It was argued that the excess demand generated by government expenditures would particularly benefit manufacturers, merchants, and speculators, who were in a position to take advantage of rising price levels. Moreover, the coastal blockade had severely interrupted the inflow of imported goods and had closed normal outlets for exportable raw materials. Hence the prices of raw materials formerly exported would decline while those of manufactures would rise, a dual process promising windfall profits for Chinese manufacturers. For instance, textile supplies from overseas would be seriously restricted, and the export of raw cotton would come to a standstill. It was therefore strongly recommended that an excess profits tax should be introduced to offset the loss of revenues from salt tax, customs duties, and commodity taxes, to counteract the regressive effects of inflation on the distribution of incomes, and to tax the windfall gains of industries temporarily favored by the special conditions of war.

Secondly, the economists had specific policy recommendations concerning the bond market. Since bond issues were the only means of financing the government deficit, and inflationary conditions were developing, it was suggested that the redemption prices of bonds should be adjusted according to the index of gold prices or the cost of living index. The need to maintain the confidence of the public in bonds was paramount, and the best way to do this was to eliminate the possibility of capital loss through inflation. It was also realized that Shanghai, the center of the bond market, might be occupied by the enemy, and the government was advised to begin selling bonds in the interior. The propertied classes had never been interested in this form of investment, and economists thought that it would be necessary to force them to take up bonds by making subscriptions compulsory.

Finally, in order to supplement the government's foreign exchange reserves, it was suggested that people be compelled to relinquish their holdings of gold, silver, silver dollars, and foreign currencies in exchange for Chinese currency. A premium of 10 per cent should be paid on silver and silver dollars exchanged by the public, and a

* *Bankers' Weekly*, Shanghai, No. 41, Oct. 19, 1937.

premium of 20 to 50 per cent should be paid on gold. Further, the public should be persuaded to transfer their deposits with foreign banks to Chinese banks and to recall liquid assets held abroad.

The official view of the financial measures appropriate to a war economy was very different from that outlined above. It was in sympathy with arguments concerning the adverse effects of increases in taxation on the efficiency of production, adding that taxation of war profits would be beset with technical difficulties of assessment and would damage public morale since businessmen would regard such a scheme as untoward interference in their private affairs. The compulsory allocation of bonds or surrender of gold, silver, and foreign exchange holdings would also be considered authoritarian and would lower the government's prestige in the eyes of the public. For these reasons, any new financial impositions would weaken the spirit of resistance and were to be avoided. Finally, the official view was that, although some taxation adjustments might have to be made to allow for changing conditions, the correct way of meeting the government deficit was to raise foreign loans and to sell bonds to the banks who could increase their note issues.

Thus the economists believed that the modern, and, for China, novel, techniques should be used to provide the government with the means of financing a total war, while the heads of the government insisted that the traditional methods of deficit finance, external and internal borrowing, were the only ones applicable in the backward political and social conditions of China. The recommendations of the economists were sound, but they should have been tempered by considerations of political expedience. The government appreciated the difficulties of introducing new and unpopular measures and therefore remained conservative, using its traditional financial techniques.

In the first months of the war the feeling of loyalty to the government was so intense that nobody dared challenge its financial plans. The leaders of the government considered that it would be unwise to bring the weaknesses of government finances to the notice of the people for fear of adversely affecting public morale. Moreover, two further reasons for the lack of appropriate fiscal policies emerge from an ex post facto analysis. First, the government leaders responsible for war finance lacked a clear view of the potential magnitude of required military expenditures. Second, they long nurtured the belief that the government could cope with any financial difficulty that might arise. The upshot of these views was an increasing budget deficit and the consequent rapid expansion of aggregate demand. These grave consequences of the government's indifference to financial problems and its failure to develop new sources of revenue and to exercise a reasonable degree of budget control are clearly illustrated in Table 34.

TABLE 34. GOVERNMENT EXPENDITURE AND REVENUE, 1936–1945[1]
(CNC $ millions)

| Year | Budgeted Expenditure | Actual Expenditure | Revenue | Deficit (Surplus) |
|---|---|---|---|---|
| 1936–37 | — | 1,894 | 1,972 | (78) |
| 1937–38 | 1,001 | 2,091 | 815 | 1,276 |
| 1938[2] | 856 | 1,169 | 315 | 854 |
| 1939 | 1,705 | 2,797 | 740 | 2,057 |
| 1940 | 2,488 | 5,288 | 1,325 | 3,963 |
| 1941 | 4,610 | 10,003 | 1,310 | 8,693 |
| 1942 | 17,311 | 24,511 | 5,630 | 18,881 |
| 1943 | 36,236 | 58,816 | 20,403 | 38,413 |
| 1944 | 79,501 | 171,689 | 38,503 | 133,186 |
| 1945 | 263,844 | 2,348,085 | 1,241,389 | 1,106,696 |

[1] The figures for the years 1936–37 and 1945 were compiled from W. Y. Chang, *op. cit.,* pp. 140–144. The unused balance of the new consolidation loan in 1936 accounted for the small surplus for 1936–37. The figures for the years 1937–44 were compiled from the data in the statistics of the Statistical Department of the Ministry of Finance and the Directorate-General of Budget, Accounts and Statistics, published in Part III of *The Public Finance Year Book,* pp. 129–150.

[2] July–December only. In 1938 the government accounts were converted from a financial to a calendar year basis.

### *Budgetary Disequilibrium*

At the very beginning of the war military costs were disregarded as the country rose to resist the aggressor. But toward the end of 1938, when the government retreated to the Southwest, China had already lost a great deal of territory from which much of the government's revenue was formerly derived, and a long war of attrition appeared certain. This was the time for a re-examination of the pattern of expenditures, to make sure that they would henceforth be in accord with the then available resources, and to reduce or eliminate the budget deficit. The fact that the government at this time had already left the urban sector behind would have made this task all the easier. As a result of the expansionary policies followed between 1935 and 1937, prices in the urban sectors had been rising and inflation was already under way. In contrast, inflationary trends in the interior rural provinces were as yet weak, and a government program of austerity and budget balance could have been enforced. But expenditures were not curtailed. Instead, they were further expanded while at the same time revenues were not increased. Naturally, the budgetary disequilibrium mounted steadily.

## 2. The Growth of Government Expenditures: 1937–1945

There was a conflict between the necessary and the possible. While expenditures could not be pushed much beyond the economic resources of the unoccupied areas without creating inflationary conditions, the government actually embarked on a dual policy of armed resistance and simultaneous economic reconstruction. Between 1940 and 1945 the armed forces nearly doubled in size; development projects were carried on at very high economic costs to satisfy both military and civilian demands; and the number of administrative agencies and

Table 35. Central Government Expenditures, 1937–1945
(in percentage)

| Item | 1937–38 | 2nd Half 1938 | 1939 | 1940 | 1941 | 1942 | 1943 | 1944 | 1945 |
|---|---|---|---|---|---|---|---|---|---|
| Military[1] | 66 | 60 | 66 | 78 | 51 | 48 | 49 | 51 | 69 |
| Development[2] | 8 | 12 | 13 | 11 | 10 | 10 | 8 | 12 | 11 |
| Loan service[3] | 18 | 21 | 16 | 7 | 5 | 6 | 6 | 3 | 1 |
| Administrative and general | 8 | 7 | 5 | 4 | 34 | 36 | 37 | 34 | 19 |
| Total | 100 | 100 | 100 | 100 | 100 | 100 | 100 | 100 | 100 |

[1] The percentage of military expenditure, including "emergency expenditure," was compiled from the data compiled by the Statistical Department of the Ministry of Finance and the Directorate-General of Budget, Accounts and Statistics. Military expenditure included three items: defense expenses, defense construction, and combat and emergency expenditure, the figures of which for 1939–43 were estimates based on the figures of 1944 and 1945.

[2] Development expenditure included construction and emergency expenditures, but excluded administrative expenses. Yearly percentages have been compiled from the data compiled by the Statistical Department of the Ministry of Finance.

[3] Data for loan service expenditure are based on the Statement of Government Expenditures 1937–1945 compiled by the Statistical Department of the Ministry of Finance. A higher percentage for 1941 and 1942 was published by various authors, but no obvious reason can be found which would account for the increase in these two years.

employees multiplied rapidly. No system of priorities was set up to program the various activities. This haphazard and unplanned stimulation of the economy resulted in considerable waste.

During the war years military expenditure always ranked first, and the development expenditure and the loan service ranked next until 1940. After 1941 the expenses incurred in collecting the land tax in kind, the improvement made in the treatment of civil servants, and the compensation given to the local governments for their transference of land tax to the central government raised the expenditure for administrative and general purposes. Reliable estimates of the composition of Chinese government expenditures during the war years are lacking. The budget estimates were of little practical value as no allowance was made for the unexpected price increases, and no official statistics of actual expenditures were published. Furthermore, "emergency" expenditures, accounting for one-fifth to two-fifths of total expenditures in the last years of the war, were not included in the published budget. Consequently, given the fragmentary data available, only an approximate estimate of the percentages of different items of expenditure can be made, as shown in Table 35.

### *Military*

During the first years of the war the government's military expenditures were moderate. The sudden transition to a state of war at the end of 1937 led to a sharp rise in the importance of military spending, from 36 per cent of total government expenditures in 1935–1936 to 66 per cent of the total in 1937–1938. In spite of the loss of the northern and central coastal districts and the consequent immobilization of large numbers of Chinese troops who were cut off by the enemy, military expenses were still maintained at the same level in 1939. Allowing for a 50 per cent increase in prices in Free China during the first two years of the war, in real terms military expenses in 1939 were only about half the magnitude of those in 1937–1938.

In 1940 a new phase of expansion in the scale of military preparations began. Generalissimo Chiang Kai-shek launched an ambitious long-term program for resistance, which, as it turned out, was predicated on a dangerously over-optimistic estimate of the economic strength of Free China. Numerous new field commands were established, which led to a rapid growth of administrative units whose functions overlapped, and local recruitment was stepped up in order to achieve the largest possible army. No reliable records of army strength were compiled, but the armed forces appear to have increased in size from about 2.5 million men in 1940 to nearly 4.5 million in 1941. The nominal size of the army early in 1944 was 5.7 million, but this is considered to overstate the actual size by 25 per cent.

The drive to create a mammoth army inevitably involved the government in huge expenditures, and in the year of 1940 military outlay rose to 78 per cent of total expenditure. From 1941 the government was able to effect some economies in the provisioning of the army by the levy of land tax in kind and an additional borrowing in kind from the taxpayers. Eighty-eight per cent of the grains collected were supplied to the army. This accounted for the decline of military expenditure during 1941 and 1944. However, the expenses incurred in collecting grains ranged between 12 and 14 per cent of government expenditure during 1941 and 1943. Thus, if these expenses were added to the military expenditures, the latter would already stand at approximately 60 per cent. In 1944 an attempt was made to reduce military expenditures by reorganizing the army, and by restricting its size to an upper limit of 4.5 million men. Military expenses in 1945 did not register any of the economies envisaged in the government's schemes for retrenchment, and reached the very high proportion of 69 per cent of government expenditure.

There was an element of futility in the government's policy of strengthening the army by numerical increase alone. With the increase in size went a decrease in efficiency. The new recruits, drawn from the southern provinces, lacked the fighting traditions of the men of the North, who, in the past, had formed the backbone of China's armies. Lacking also were the generalship and coordination required to maneuver 5 million men effectively. The very magnitude of the army was an almost insuperable obstacle to operational efficiency. Moreover, and this was the most irrational aspect of the expansion of the army from a military point of view, the supply of equipment for the troops could not keep pace with their numerical increase. The inadequacy of equipment had been a noticeable defect of the Chinese army even in peacetime, and during the war it was accentuated by the loss of foreign and domestic supplies of military materials. For these reasons the rapid expansion of the army could not be justified on military grounds, and much of the huge sums expended on the army was dissipated to no purpose.

Certain features of the inflationary impact of the government's military policy are particularly worthy of mention. The 2–2½ million men recruited between 1940 and 1944 were gathered from outlying regions and concentrated in units near the larger provincial towns where the headquarters of the various field commands were located. Such a massing of population in comparatively small areas added enormously to the pressure of excess demand in the cities and created problems of transportation which were only partially overcome at great cost to the government. The more remote farming districts maintained barter economies and were to a large extent insulated from inflationary disturbances.

The difficulty of supplying the requirements of the troops was enhanced by the fact that army rations of foodstuffs and clothing provided a higher standard of living than the subsistence level which most recruits were accustomed to in their normal occupations. Each soldier was allowed a daily ration of 25 ounces of rice (or 26 ounces of flour), one ounce of peanuts, one ounce of meat, half an ounce of salt, one-fifth of an ounce of beans, nine-tenths of an ounce of vegetable oil, ten ounces of vegetables, and 21.3 ounces of fuel. The clothing ration was one suit of summer and one of winter uniform per year plus two suits of underclothing. These rations were lavish compared with normal standards of living in China, and, consequently, the rise in military demands for consumer goods as recruitment progressed from 1940 onwards exerted a powerful inflationary influence on price levels in provincial centers. In addition to encouraging inflation from the side of demand, excessive recruitment also adversely affected supply by causing a shortage of rural labor. This was partly the reason for the lowered output of argricultural products in Free China from 1940–1943 and for the rapid increase of wages of farm workers. Both of these developments contributed to rises in food and raw material prices, particularly in Szechwan Province.

The Chinese government, at very great cost in terms of inflation, built up an army the numerical strength of which belied its real powers of resistance. The improvidence of this policy was clearly demonstrated in the second half of 1944, when the Chinese army showed signs of disintegration before the renewed offensive of the Japanese and the continuation of China's whole war effort was threatened.

### *Development*

Three main types of development projects were carried out by the Chinese government: economic reconstruction, mainly concerned with the development of manufacturing and mining industries in the interior; rural reconstruction, consisting of irrigation works and other projects connected with agriculture and forestry; and communications, including the building and repair of railways and highways and the extension of telecommunications. The relative importance of these items in total development expenditures is indicated by the figures in Table 36.

TABLE 36. PERCENTAGES OF DEVELOPMENT EXPENDITURES[1]

| | 1937–38 | 1939 | 1940 | 1941 | 1942 | 1943 | 1944 |
|---|---|---|---|---|---|---|---|
| Economic | 62 | 33 | 16 | 22 | 21 | 15 | 13 |
| Rural | 4 | 2 | 4 | 6 | 6 | 8 | 7 |
| Communications | 34 | 65 | 80 | 72 | 73 | 65 | 73 |
| Development of Northwest | | | | | | 12 | 7 |
| Total Development | 100 | 100 | 100 | 100 | 100 | 100 | 100 |

[1] Percentages were computed from the construction expenditures compiled by the Statistical Department of the Ministry of Finance.

Total development expenditures rose rapidly in the early stages of the war, increasing from 8 per cent of total expenditure in 1937 to 13 per cent in 1939. During this period large sums were spent in order to move machinery and plants from threatened areas and to equip mining and manufacturing enterprises, and to lay the foundation of a communications system inland with the ultimate objective of opening transport routes with Indo-China and Burma. Thus economic reconstruction and communications occupied well over a third of the total government expenditures in the early period of the war. From 1940 until the end of the war, because of the difficulty of obtaining equipment and materials, work on civil industrial projects and communications slowed down and real volume of all construction activity declined. From 1943, in view of the danger of the enemy's further advance in Southeast Free China, the government paid more attention to the development of the northwest provinces, and special appropriations were made for this purpose.

### *Loan Services*

Despite the loss of the greater part of customs revenue and salt tax, on which foreign and domestic loans were secured, loan services continued to be paid according to schedule during the first year of war. In September 1938, however, interest and redemption payments on foreign loans secured on salt revenue were discontinued; and in January 1939 loan services on foreign obligations secured on customs revenue were likewise suspended owing to the loss of a large part of customs revenue. The suspension of foreign debt services saved the government about 40 per cent of its annual bill for interest and redemption, and between 1937 and 1940 loan services fell from 18 per cent to 7 per cent of total government expenditures. Services on domestic loans were maintained with the idea of encouraging the market to absorb further government issues.

Apart from Liberty Bonds issued immediately after the outbreak of war, government efforts to raise loans from the general public failed dismally, and the government banks became the only major bond holders. While over-all government expenditures moved upwards in accordance with inflationary trends, liabilities with respect to services on past loans remained fixed in money terms. This development, while superficially advantageous to government finance, served in the long run only to undermine the confidence of the bondholders, who became increasingly reluctant to participate in future issues. In the short run, however, loan service payments tended to become a diminishing portion of total government expenditures, an effect that was only partly counteracted by the increase in the total volume of bonds outstanding with successive new issues during the war. Thus, in the period 1940–1943, loan services remained near 6 per cent of total government expenditure, and, in the last two years of the war, fell to as little as 3 and 1 per cent of the total.

### *Administrative and General Expenditures*

In the first three years of the war departmental expenses and general expenditures (subsidies, pensions, payments to relief funds, etc.) became less important in the over-all picture of government outlays. The normal administrative structure of government was dislocated by the hasty retreat inland; the various departments had not yet been able to reform and recruit new staffs; and the loss of tax receipts, while striking a heavy blow at government revenues, reduced the administrative costs of tax collections. In 1940 administrative and general expenditures amounted to only 4 per cent of total expenditure, compared with 8 per cent in 1937. However, from 1941 government expenditures in this category rapidly increased, because of the additional expenses involved in collecting the new land tax in kind and in compensating the provincial and hsien (county) governments for loss of revenues when the central government took possession of the total yield from land tax in 1942 (Table 37).

Administrative expenditures, growing further in importance in 1943, accounted for 37 per cent of total government outlay because the costs of food collection increased. In 1944 a sweeping revision of the wages and salaries paid to public servants, whose incomes throughout the war had lagged farther and farther behind the cost of living, was forced on the government by unmistakable signs of disaffection among its employees. Departmental expenses also increased.

The government's refusal to compensate civil servants for their

TABLE 37. PERCENTAGES OF TOTAL ADMINISTRATIVE EXPENDITURE[1]

| | 1941 | 1942 | 1943 | 1944 |
|---|---|---|---|---|
| Departmental | 5.4 | 7.9 | 5.5 | 8.9 |
| Food collection | 14.6 | 12.3 | 14.5 | 8.1 |
| Grants to Provincial and County Governments | 2.3 | 7.5 | 5.8 | 3.7 |
| Civil servants' allowance (Central Government) | 0.7 | 2.2 | 2.3 | — |
| Other | 1.1 | 6.1 | 8.9 | 13.4 |
| Total administrative and general | 34 | 36 | 37 | 34 |

[1] These percentages were computed from the data in the Statement of Expenditure compiled by the Statistical Department of the Ministry of Finance. The grand total percentages of the table were based on Table 35.

loss of real income during the inflation kept down administrative expenditures to artificially low levels, with serious damage to departmental efficiency in the later stages of the war. Immediately after the outbreak of hostilities a large number of experienced businessmen, technical experts, and intellectuals offered their services to the government to aid the national cause. The recruitment of these men was followed by a noticeable improvement in the efficiency of government administration, but this effect was soon destroyed by the fall in the living standards of government personnel, which bred laxity and corruption.

It has been estimated that the real incomes of civil servants declined, on the average, by 85 per cent in the period 1937–1943, although they were compensated with rations of rice. At the same time, the number of public servants mounted rapidly as the government evolved new wartime functions, such as the collection of the land tax in kind and the establishment of price and other economic controls. It is estimated that the number of government employees, including those engaged on construction works, rose from 8,000 prewar to about 200,000 in March 1945. There is little doubt that the public service had swollen in size over the war years, as is suggested by the government's statement in March 1945 that to effect economies in administration 21,027 persons were removed from the government's payroll at one stroke. Public service pay was too meager to attract men of high caliber, and most of the new recruits were of poor quality.

In these circumstances many unsatisfactory practices developed: officials held several posts concurrently and used their authority to install members of their families in government positions; and many participated in business transactions connected with their official duties. The government may have saved itself a large volume of additional administrative expenses by neglecting to provide reasonable salaries to its employees, but, in the process, its administrative organizations became inefficient and corrupt.

### *Extra-Budgetary Expenditures*

After Pearl Harbor an American military mission and a contingent of American forces were sent to China. The Chinese government met part of their living expenses, such as for food and housing, and undertook some construction projects on their behalf. It spent a total of about CNC $10,000,000,000 on this account between September 1942 and February 1944. From 1944 onwards, all expenses of American forces were advanced by the Chinese government in national currency; and up to the end of the war these advances totaled CNC $200,000,000,000, which was nearly a third of Chinese military expenditures from January 1944 to August 1945. The expenditures for American forces in China were debited to a suspense account not appearing in the official budget, and therefore constituted an extra expenditure.

## 3. The Behavior of Revenue

Strenuous efforts were made by the government to increase its revenue in order to offset the substantial reduction in receipts that resulted from territorial contraction from its former three revenue mainstays—customs duties, the salt tax, and commodity taxes. The income tax was extended to business enterprises; and a progressive company tax, an excess profits tax, and an inheritance tax were introduced. The stamp tax rate was raised. Commodity taxes, customs duties, and the salt tax were placed on an ad valorem basis in lieu of the former flat rates. A wartime consumption tax was created. Government monopolies of salt, sugar, tobacco, and matches were attempted. Levy of the land tax in kind, together with compulsory borrowing of grains, also made substantial contributions. However, collections of direct taxes were far from satisfactory. Although they accounted for as much as 27 per cent of government receipts (excluding land tax) in 1942, their share declined to 25.1 per cent in 1943 and 19.7 per cent in 1944. The consumption tax as adopted by the government had certain serious defects of its own. State monopolies of selected commodities also proved to be unrewarding.

In the revenue pattern that emerged the salt tax stood out as the most important revenue producer, while the land tax, together with the forced grain loans, ranked second. As a whole, the tax structure was not able to raise sufficient revenue for the government or to mop up the excess disposable income generated by deficit financing. It failed to live up to the wartime demands placed upon it, mostly because it had not been strengthened in more normal times. The ineffectiveness of new measures and the earlier failure to undertake basic reform were particularly evident in the rural provinces of Free China to which the government, because of their remoteness, had pre-

TABLE 38. GOVERNMENT REVENUES DURING EACH YEAR: 1937–1945[1]
(CNC $ millions)

| | Tax Revenue | | Non-Tax Revenue | | Sales of Bonds | | |
|---|---|---|---|---|---|---|---|
| Year | Amount | Percentage | Amount | Percentage | Amount | Percentage | Total Revenue |
| 1937–38 | 451 | 55.2 | 108 | 13.4 | 256 | 31.4 | 815 |
| 1938 (2nd half) | 211 | 67.1 | 85 | 27.2 | 18 | 5.7 | 315 |
| 1939 | 483 | 65.3 | 232 | 31.9 | 25 | 3.8 | 740 |
| 1940 | 267 | 20.1 | 1,050 | 79.3 | 8 | 0.6 | 1,325 |
| 1941 | 666 | 50.8 | 517 | 39.5 | 127 | 9.7 | 1,310 |
| 1942 | 4,163 | 73.9 | 1,104 | 19.6 | 363 | 6.5 | 5,630 |
| 1943 | 15,326 | 75.2 | 1,191 | 5.8 | 3,886 | 19.0 | 20,403 |
| 1944 | 34,651 | 90.8 | 1,863 | 4.9 | 1,989 | 5.3 | 38,503 |
| 1945 | 102,253 | 8.2 | 1,076,313 | 86.8 | 62,823 | 5.0 | 1,241,389 |

[1] Based on the data of the Statement of Revenue compiled by the Statistical Department of the Ministry of Finance, published in *The Public Finance Year Book* (1948), pp. 129–150. Figures for Non-Tax Revenues for 1945 are based on data provided in W. Y. Chang, *op. cit.*, pp. 140–145.

viously paid but scant attention. Even when the fundamental step was taken to change the land tax from a monetary impost to a levy in kind, the opportunity to make its incidence more equitable and the collection more productive was missed.

As proceeds from indirect taxes shrank, non-tax receipts became increasingly important in the total revenue picture (Table 38). The principal items of non-tax revenue were proceeds from sales of gold, foreign exchange, and other assets (which cannot be excluded from revenue since the separate details are not available), surpluses of public authority undertakings, and contributions and donations to central government funds. In 1940 non-tax receipts amounted to more than three-quarters of the government's total income, mainly because of the increase in the amount of foreign exchange sold. Between 1940 and 1944 their relative importance declined. In 1945, however, they were again responsible for more than four-fifths of total revenue; and the profit derived from the revaluation of foreign exchange received from the United States government in payment of China's advances to the American military forces in China was reported to account for the increase of non-tax revenue and for the small percentage of tax receipts in the total revenue.

### *Indirect Taxes*

*Customs Duties.* With the swift advance of the Japanese occupation forces, revenues from customs, salt, and commodity taxes were rapidly lost to the government. Sixty-five per cent of customs duties fell into Japanese hands by 1938, and about 90 per cent by 1941. By that time exports had virtually ceased, and what little was imported came by road from Indo-China, Burma, and India. To offset this loss, a new wartime consumption tax was introduced.

*Wartime Consumption Tax.* Early in the war the provincial governments had begun to levy various kinds of transit duties on commodity shipments within areas under their jurisdiction; and, with the entry of the central government into this field of taxation, all the old evils of "Likin," under which a shipment was often taxed several times during its progress to its destination, were revived. In April 1942 the central government introduced an ad valorem wartime consumption tax to supersede both its own interport duties and provincial transit taxes. The tax rates were 5 per cent on most daily necessities, 10 per cent for less essential commodities, 15 per cent for semi-luxuries, and 25 per cent for luxury goods. The tax was collected by the Customs Administration along with customs duties, many new inland customs stations being established for this purpose. The dutiable value of the goods subject to tax was taken as the landed costs for imports. For domestic products, their average market prices in the preceding month were used. The nature of this tax is not dissimilar to a commodity tax, which tends to be shifted to ultimate consumers without giving proper weight to the latter's ability to pay. As inflationary forces were under way, the government came to realize that an unimpeded movement of goods was necessary and desirable. As a result, while its collection proved to be extremely lucrative, the tax was abolished in January 1945.

*Salt Tax.* Salt revenue was reduced by more than one-half when the Japanese occupied the four salt-producing provinces on the coast (Hopeh, Shantung, Kiangsu, and Kwangtung) late in 1938, after which time the government attempted to develop alternative sources of supply in Western China in order to restore the tax yield from salt production. Together with customs and commodity taxes, the salt tax was calculated on an ad valorem basis from September 1941 onwards. In October 1943 a wartime surtax on salt was imposed at the rate of CNC $300 per picul (equivalent to 133⅓ pounds), and in March 1944 an additional surtax of CNC $1,000 per picul was levied. The new impositions of these two surtaxes increased the price of salt to consumers by over 25 per cent. The salt tax accounted for 60 per cent of revenue from indirect taxation in 1944, compared with 40 per cent in the previous year. While this tax was most outstandingly productive of revenue, it weighed heavily upon the minimum subsistence of the lower income groups.

*Commodity Tax.* The commodity taxes were not placed on an ad valorem basis until September 1941, a fact which partly accounts for the diminishing receipts prior to this time in spite of the rise of prices. Except for this move the commodity taxes underwent little change during the war. Only beverages and sugar were added to the list of taxable commodities, which included rolled tobacco, cotton yarn, matches, flour, wine, cured tobacco leaf, barbed wire, and cement.

### *State Monopolies*

In its effort to raise revenue, the national government took note of the success of the state monopolies of salt and camphor in Japan in raising revenue during the Sino-Japanese and Russo-Japanese wars. As a result of a comprehensive study of the subject in May 1941, monopolies in the distribution of salt, sugar, tobacco, and matches were put into effect in 1942.

It is interesting to follow the line of reasoning used by the proponents of state monopolies. The argument was that the government could obtain assured revenues from state distribution of these commodities and that the widespread tax evasion practiced under the system of private marketing could be eliminated. In actual operation the state monopoly would be more productive of revenue than commodity taxes since the government would also be able to secure the profits previously accruing to middlemen. At the same time, speculative activities of merchants would no longer be a factor contributing to price increases. It was also suggested that under state monopolies certain inequitable features inherent in the flat rate of a specific tax, such as the disproportionately heavy burden it imposes on low price articles of inferior quality as compared with better quality goods of the same commodity class, could be avoided. Finally, it was argued that the government would always be at liberty to blame changed conditions of supply and demand for rises in the prices of the monopolized goods, and so could parry some of the objections invariably raised to increases in tax rates.

The success of any state monopoly in raising revenue without the government's losing popularity with the public is dependent on a number of factors. The government must control production and distribution of the commodities involved; those in charge must have broad business experience, which cannot be acquired in a short period; and the prices of monopoly goods must be prevented from rising to exorbitant levels. In China the experiment in state monopoly was doomed from the start. The government was compelled to limit the scope of its regulation of the four industries by lack of administrative machinery and personnel. It established control over the production of sugar, and it took delivery of a small part of the salt output; but the production and distribution of tobacco and matches remained entirely in private hands.

Thus, apart from sugar, the "monopolies" of the Chinese government were not monopolies in any accepted sense of the word; even in the sugar industry, state enterprise did not extend beyond the stage of production. Since producers of the commodities concerned paid the government the difference between the official ex-factory purchase price and the government selling price, in all respects the state "monopolies" were identical in effect to purchase taxes. Retail prices were fixed at the discretion of individual merchants; and it was this fact that, over a period, led to the failure of state monopolies as a means of augmenting public revenue. With prices uncontrolled at the retail level, any attempt by the government to increase its monopoly margin on the ex-factory prices of salt, sugar, tobacco, and matches was reflected in higher prices to consumers, and the government immediately incurred the displeasure of the general public.

Even with such a restricted degree of state monopoly, the government was continually beset by difficulties on all sides. The revenue from the four monopolies rose as the currency depreciated, but it did not increase in real terms. The expense of operating the monopolies amounted to 60 per cent of receipts in the initial stages. This heavy ratio of expenses, the rise in the price of sugar, and the inflationary effect of government borrowing from the banks for the purchase of monopoly goods together gave rise to a three-pronged attack on the government for its administration of the monopolies. Alarmed at the public opprobrium attaching to its policies, the government suspended the state sugar monopoly in the middle of 1944, and later in

TABLE 39. GOVERNMENT REVENUES FROM INDIRECT TAXES, 1937–1945[1]
(CNC $ millions)

| Year | Customs Duty | Salt Tax[2] | Commodity Tax | Wartime Consumption Tax | Total Indirect Tax | Percentage of Total Tax Revenue |
|---|---|---|---|---|---|---|
| 1937–38 | 239 | 141 | 47 | — | 427 | 94.9 |
| 1938 (2nd half) | 128 | 47 | 25 | — | 200 | 94.8 |
| 1939 | 346 | 61 | 44 | — | 451 | 93.4 |
| 1940 | 38 | 80 | 72 | — | 190 | 71.6 |
| 1941 | 15 | 296 | 189 | — | 500 | 75.2 |
| 1942 | 160 | 1,180 | 783 | 399 | 2,522 | 60.6 |
| 1943 | 377 | 3,026 | 3,335 | 718 | 7,456 | 48.7 |
| 1944 | 494 | 14,528 | 7,576 | 1,838 | 24,436 | 70.2 |
| 1945 | 3,321 | 53,507 | 24,372 | 304 | 81,504 | 79.6 |

[1] The figures of this table are based on the Statement of Revenue compiled by the Statistical Department of the Ministry of Finance.

[2] Revenue from monopoly of salt is included in Salt Tax column and that from the monopoly of matches, sugar, and tobacco included in Commodity Tax figures.

the year the other monopolies were replaced by the old commodity tax. Thus, instead of being able to raise the yield from these sources by the introduction of the so-called monopolies, its growing unpopularity with the public prevented the government from making justifiable increases in monopoly margins.

The role of indirect taxes in the government's wartime finances is reflected in Table 39. When the government adopted ad valorem rates in 1941, yields from indirect taxes began to regain their previous importance as a source of revenue.

### *Direct Taxes*

As noted in a preceding section, the Chinese government placed little reliance on direct taxes in the prewar period. However, the loss of revenue from indirect taxes was so severe that a number of direct taxes were put into operation. In August 1938 the scope of income taxation, which had commenced in 1936 and 1937 with levies on the salaries of civil servants and on earnings from equity investment, was broadened to include the income of business enterprises. A progressive company tax was introduced, graded not according to the absolute level of earnings but according to the ratio of profits to nominal capital employed. The rate of tax ranged from 3 per cent on company income of 5–10 per cent on total capital to 20 per cent on earnings amounting to 70 per cent of capital or more, and was levied at these rates on the entire income. In October 1938 an excess profits tax and a levy on house rents and income from lease of property were added although actual operation was delayed until September 1939.

As in the case of the company tax, the rates of these taxes varied with the ratio of income to capital invested, but they were not levied on the entire income, progressive rates being applied on separate income brackets instead. The lowest rate of excess profits tax was 10 per cent on profits ranging between 20 and 25 per cent of capital; it increased to 50 per cent on profits of over 60 per cent of capital. Levies on incomes from house rents or property leases were somewhat heavier, starting from a rate of 10 per cent on returns of 15–20 per cent of the assessed value of the property. The burden of the company and excess profit taxes can be gaged from the figures in Table 40 showing the tax liabilities at different levels of income of a company with CNC $10,000 capital investment.

TABLE 40. INCOME TAXES AS PERCENTAGES OF INCOME

| | Rate of Return on Invested Capital of | Company Tax | | Excess Profits Tax | | | Total Tax |
|---|---|---|---|---|---|---|---|
| Income (dollars) | $10,000 (per cent) | (per cent) Rate | Actual Tax (dollars) | Rate (per cent) | Actual Tax (dollars) | Total Tax (dollars) | (per cent of income) |
| 1,100 | 11 | 4 | 44 | 0 | 0 | 44 | 4.0 |
| 2,100 | 21 | 8 | 168 | 10 | 10 | 178 | 8.5 |
| 3,100 | 31 | 12 | 372 | 20 | 145 | 517 | 16.7 |
| 4,100 | 41 | 14 | 574 | 30 | 355 | 929 | 22.9 |
| 5,100 | 51 | 16 | 816 | 40 | 665 | 1,481 | 29.0 |
| 6,100 | 61 | 18 | 1,098 | 50 | 1,075 | 2,173 | 35.6 |

Thus the tax on business enterprises varied from 4 per cent in the lower brackets to 36 per cent in the higher brackets. On income ranging upwards from 60 per cent of capital the total tax rate gradually approached 50 per cent of income.

In addition to the above direct taxes, an inheritance tax also came into operation in mid-1940. Because of both a lack of efficient methods of checking the value of estates in probate and universal evasion, it made no appreciable contribution to government income prior to 1943.

Finally, the stamp tax and the so-called business tax were transferred from the provincial authorities to the central government. Control of the stamp tax reverted to the central government in June 1940, after which the rate was increased. The business tax, taken over by the central government in 1942, comprised two types of levy: a capital tax of 4 per cent per annum on banks, pawnshops, and insurance companies, and a turnover tax of 3 per cent on all other business organizations. When it was administered by the provincial governments, the business tax yielded an average annual revenue of CNC $160 million; under the central government revenue from this source increased greatly after 1942 owing to the rise of the general price level. No further important revisions of direct taxes were made during the war. Direct taxes were yielding an average of about a fifth of government revenue between 1942–1945 compared with a negligible prewar contribution.

In its attempt to employ these fiscal devices the government encountered all the difficulties of administration and assessment that in 1930 had deterred the Kemmerer Commission from advising in favor of the introduction of direct taxes. When the government began to levy the company and excess profits taxes, it copied the Western technique of self-assessment. Business enterprises were required to complete a detailed statement of income supported by balance sheet, profit and loss accounts, and other documentary evidence of their activities; and the local tax bureau, after checking the authenticity of the declaration, calculated the amount of tax payable. In practice, it quickly developed that in an illiterate population few businessmen were capable of completing the official forms; and the majority rendered false returns not only to avoid tax but also as a matter of principle, to prevent the disclosure of their private affairs to government officials.

Speculators and war profiteers falsified their returns and kept forged accounts to satisfy the authorities. Businesses employing systematic accounting were so rare that with the majority of firms accurate assessment of income and tax liability was impossible. In 1944 the self-assessment method was abolished for businesses not maintaining complete accounts, and the tax bureau was entrusted with the computation of income and tax liability on the basis of the record of previous years, corrected for price changes. The assessment was then referred to the local Chamber of Commerce and trade guilds for scrutiny and adjustment. The adoption of this procedure, however, did not solve the intractable problems of assessment, since tax officials were largely untrained and inexpert in the basic techniques of financial appraisal.

The administration of both the income tax and the excess profits tax was made unusually complex by their reference to the rate of return on invested capital and by the price inflation. The estimation of profit, a difficult matter in the best of circumstances, becomes far more complicated under conditions of inflation. Since depreciation allowances failed to reflect the steeply rising replacement costs, strict enforcement of the Chinese tax legislation would have been extremely unjust. Partly for this reason, the law was not enforced to the letter, and, in the light of the general failure to enforce the rate of return provisions of the law, the income tax came to be assessed as a progressive levy on total net profit.

The proportion of total business income actually reached by the tax must have been extremely small, and it shrank rapidly toward the end of the war. As inflation intensified, tax evasion became more prevalent. Hoarding became the most profitable form of enterprise, and there was a decrease in the number of registered firms paying tax. Between 1942 and 1945 proceeds from direct taxes fell from 5 per cent to below 1 per cent of government expenditures. Whereas at their peak in 1943 revenues from this source were CNC $35 million in prewar dollars, in the last year of the war the comparable figure was about CNC $10 million.

## *The Land Tax in Kind*

Of all the fiscal measures adopted during the war the most immediately effective was the collection of the land tax in kind. In 1940 the harvest of Szechwan province, the most fertile rice-producing area in Free China, was unusually poor. When the government attempted to buy rice for the army at official prices, the landowners withheld their produce and the rice merchants began to operate a black market. Only a very small quantity of rice reached the normal markets, and prices rose steeply. The price of rice in Szechwan in June 1941 was more than thirty times that of September 1940, and there was a corresponding upward movement in commodity prices generally. Accordingly, a Financial Conference was convened in June 1941, and the following measures were approved:

> The land tax, which had been relinquished to the provinces in 1928, was to be surrendered to the central government, which would subsidize the local governments to compensate for their loss of revenue.

> Beginning the second half of 1941, all land tax was to be paid in kind. The tax rate was fixed at one-fifth of a picul (one picul equals 2.91 bushels) of unhusked rice for every dollar of land tax levied before the war. In regions where little or no rice was produced the land tax in kind was to be collected in wheat, sorghum, barley, or other foodstuffs. In areas where the tax was excessive relative to crop yields a certain proportion to be determined by representatives of the central government could be paid in money.

This change in the land tax restored the ancient practice of payment in kind, which had ceased to be imposed in 1436 during the Ming Dynasty. Five hundred years later, in 1936, the revenues of the provinces from the land were budgeted as 36 per cent of all local government revenue, and exceeded central government revenue from commodity taxes. In 1941–1942 the estimated yield in kind from the territory still under the authority of the Chinese government amounted to about 70 million bushels, and an estimated additional amount of CNC $45,000,000 was to be received in money. However, since the collection of grain was insufficient to meet the government's military and civil commitments, in July 1942 it was decided to acquire from landowners an additional amount of foodstuffs, equal to the land tax, by compulsory purchase. The purchase price was to be the average of market prices for the previous thirty days, and 30 per cent of the payment was to be made in cash, the rest in Food Treasury Notes.

Both the principal of the Notes and one-fifth of the interest could be used by the farmer in part payment of the land tax after the lapse of one year. The notes were ultimately redeemable in kind. Owing to the widespread corruption amongst public officials, some payments in cash did not reach the farmers; and, because the Treasury Notes were in units of (piculs of) rice and were not freely accepted in market transactions, many small taxpayers were forced to discount their notes to the big landholders. Finally, in July 1943, the government abandoned the attempt to make direct cash purchases from the farmers, and a system of outright borrowing in kind was introduced in all provinces. Under this new scheme the government promised to repay farmers in kind in installments beginning five years from the date of the loan.

The above measures were relatively successful, mainly because the land tax system was well established and the farmers had long ago resigned themselves to meeting their tax commitments. The large quantity of food collected gave the army an assured supply and provided an appreciable proportion of the needs of civil servants and metropolitan workers. Moreover, the reduction in the government's direct outlay on foodstuffs greatly damped the rate of increase in the note issue as the market value of the produce accumulated by the government was far greater than the total of collection expenses and compensatory payments to the local governments. The expenses incurred by the Ministry of Food in the collection of grain, although small in the percentage of money value of food collected when prices rose, were high in the percentage of the government expenditure. In addition, the central government had undertaken to reimburse the land tax to the provincial and hsien authorities. The costs of collection were greatly increased by the deteriorated state of the roads during the war and the lack of adequate storage space in provincial centers. Dishonest collectors enriched themselves by understating the amount received, adulteration, and making fictitious reports of road and river accidents. Since the loss of grain due to these factors may have been as high as 5 per cent of the total amount collected, the figures in Tables 41 and 42 tend to overstate the volume at the government's disposal. It must also be admitted that, had it not been for this measure, the expenditure for 1941–42 and 1942–43 would have been greater by about 30 and 80 per cent, respectively, and that for 1943–44 and 1944–45 would have been about 80 and 85 per cent higher.

While the government's levies on landowners did go a long way toward solving the problem of provisioning the army, they were most onerous to individual farmers. Some owners paid more than the nominal rates of tax on their properties because the antiquated assessment rolls, unrevised for centuries, were no longer accurate and equitable. Following its imposition of the land tax in kind the government had announced its intention to reassess the land, but it was so anxious to begin collections that no revision was ever effected, and existing inequities were aggravated, particularly in the case of small landowners, since they were responsible for transporting their produce to the nearest collection center at their own expense and for making good any losses of grain in transit. Standard methods of grading agricultural products and uniform weights and measures were lacking. If the tax collector objected to the quality and quantity of grain paid in, the farmer was obliged to travel back and forth between his property and the tax center until the official was satisfied. While other classes of the community were exempt from direct taxes or else could avoid taxation with comparative ease, peasant owners found their tax and loan liabilities increasing from year to year with little possibility of evasion. Naturally many farmers thought that they were being called upon to make much larger sacrifices of real income in the

TABLE 41. GOVERNMENT REVENUES FROM DIRECT TAXES, 1937–1945[1]
(CNC $ millions)

| Year | Income Tax | Excess Profits Tax | Inherit-ance Tax | Stamp Tax | Business Tax | Land Tax[2] | Total Direct Tax | Percent-age of Total Tax Revenue | Percent-age, Excluding Land Tax |
|---|---|---|---|---|---|---|---|---|---|
| 1937–38 | 19 | | | 5 | | | 24 | 5.1 | |
| 1938 (2nd half) | 8 | | | 3 | | | 11 | 5.2 | |
| 1939 | 27 | | | 5 | | | 32 | 6.6 | |
| 1940 | 44 | 25 | [3] | 7 | | | 76 | 28.4 | |
| 1941 | 80 | 70 | | 16 | | | 166 | 24.8 | |
| 1942 | 197 | 291 | 1 | 26 | 610 | 516 | 1,641 | 39.4 | 27.0 |
| 1943 | 761 | 884 | 15 | 355 | 1,842 | 4,013 | 7,870 | 51.3 | 25.1 |
| 1944 | 1,445 | 1,189 | 50 | 1,063 | 3,076 | 3,392 | 10,215 | 29.8 | 19.7 |
| 1945 | 2,009 | 1,833 | 111 | 3,140 | 7,330 | 6,326 | 20,749 | 20.4 | 16.1 |

[1] Based on the data in the Statement of Revenue, compiled by the Statistical Department of the Ministry of Finance.

[2] The land tax, as discussed in the following section, was not collected as an income tax although it is similar to it, and it did not represent its whole picture because the compulsory purchase and loan in kind did not appear on the revenue account.

[3] Tax revenue negligible in these years.

national cause than were other sections of the community, and the government became increasingly unpopular among the agrarian

TABLE 42. LAND TAX COLLECTION 1941–1945[1]
(in 1,000 bushels)

| Fiscal Year | Kind | By Tax | By Purchase | By Loan | Total Collection | Supply to Army |
|---|---|---|---|---|---|---|
| 1941–42 | Rice (husked) | 38,416.0 | | | 38,416.0 | 26,397.0 |
| | Wheat | 9,201.7 | | | 9,201.7 | 43,817.6 |
| 1942–43 | Rice | 45,957.1 | 41,355.6 | | 87,312.7 | 29,288.1 |
| | Wheat | 20,120.9 | 14,173.5 | | 34,294.4 | 32,248.8 |
| 1943–44 | Rice | 46,248.0 | 18,145.9 | 22,773.6 | 87,167.5 | 27,456.0 |
| | Wheat | 19,650.0 | 5,376.0 | 6,912.7 | 31,938.7 | 34,705.5 |
| 1944–45 | Rice | 36,941.3 | | 40,492.7 | 77,434.0 | 23,196.3 |
| | Wheat | 16,736.4 | | 11,006.4 | 27,742.8 | 23,308.4 |

| Fiscal Year | Kind | Production[2] | Collection in Per Cent of Production | Estimated Money Values of Collection in Kind (CNC $ millions)[3] | Cost of Collection (CNC $ millions)[3] |
|---|---|---|---|---|---|
| 1941–42 | Rice | 783,000 | 4.90 | 2,731 | 1,458 |
| | Wheat | 408,000 | 1.87 | | |
| 1942–43 | Rice | 793,000 | 11.01 | 19,712 | 3,040 |
| | Wheat | 610,000 | 5.62 | | |
| 1943–44 | Rice | 567,000 | 15.37 | 46,446 | 8,590 |
| | Wheat | 579,000 | 5.51 | | |
| 1944–45 | Rice | 948,000 | 8.16 | 147,133 | 13,869 |
| | Wheat | 722,000 | 3.84 | | |

[1] The figures for 1941–42 are based on data published in the Statistical Abstract of the Republic of China, 1947; those for 1942–45, together with the figures of supply to army, on data published in the Abstract of Facts on Finance and Money, compiled by the Ministry of Finance.

[2] Based on Table 63.

[3] The approximate money value was calculated from the average market prices of husked rice (34 per cent higher than unhusked rice): with the price of wheat at 80 per cent of rice price; 1941–42, CNC $180 per picul (2.91 bushels); 1942–43, CNC $400; 1943–44, CNC $1,200; and 1944–45, CNC $4,300. Land tax was included in the money value. The cost of collection is based on data from a Statement of Expenditure compiled by the Statistical Department of the Ministry of Finance.

classes. Thus the long term political and social effects to a large degree outweighed the immediate advantage of securing low cost food for the army.

## 4. The Impact of Foreign Aid

Foreign assistance, although an important feature of China's wartime economy, was received mainly in the form of military supplies. Two Soviet credits equivalent to a total of U.S. $250 million were extended to China in the form of ammunition, trucks, and other supplies. Four United States Export-Import Bank loans totaling U.S. $120 million were used for the purchase of trucks, gasoline, rolling stock and other railway equipment, and basic industrial equipment and materials. The United Kingdom also extended two similar Export Credit Loans to China amounting to £3 million. These loans had little salutary influence on the budget deficit.

On the other hand, two other series of foreign loans were primarily anti-inflationary in their effect. The Stabilization Fund Loan of £ sterling 5 million from the United Kingdom in 1939 had as its objective the maintenance of the external value of Chinese currency; Chinese currency thus withdrawn from the market and credited to non-tax revenue through the sale of sterling helped to reduce the deficits slightly. This also applies in part to the United States Treasury Credit of U.S. $500 million, a portion of which was used during the war. The operations of these credits will be discussed in greater detail in Part 4, on Anti-Inflationary Policies. A complete list of the wartime foreign loans is presented in Table 43.

## 5. Deficit Finance

As discussed above, the relentless expansion of expenditure and the failure to increase revenue pari passu set the stage for deficit financing. By 1945 (Table 44) the deficit had grown to more than 80 per cent of the government's total expenditure, a most eloquent indicator of economic collapse.

Immediately after the outbreak of the war in 1937 an issue of National Liberty Bonds amounting to CNC $400 million at par value was brought out by the government. Compared with previous issues, the bonds carried a lower rate of interest and had a longer maturity. It was hoped that the public, out of patriotism, would subscribe to it enthusiastically. However, the then falling bond market, which was further depressed by the war, made sale of these bonds extremely difficult; the banks, already overburdened with government script, were reluctant to increase their holdings. It was only through the government's urgent and earnest appeal and the people's initial patriotism that about one-half of the issue was finally sold. Even so, this proved to be the largest sale recorded by any single domestic issue in the long history of Chinese government loan operations;

TABLE 43. WARTIME FOREIGN CREDITS
(in thousands)

| Year | Credits | Amount | Use of Credits |
|---|---|---|---|
| 1938 | 1st Soviet Credit | U.S. $50,000 | To purchase war supplies |
| | 2nd Soviet Credit | U.S. $50,000 | To purchase war supplies |
| 1939 | 1st U.S. Import Export Bank Credit | U.S. $25,000 | To purchase war supplies |
| | 3rd Soviet Credit | U.S. $150,000 | To purchase war supplies |
| | British Stabilization Loan | £ 5,000 | To stabilize currency |
| | British Export Credit | £ 3,047 | To purchase war supplies |
| 1940 | 2nd U.S. Import Export Bank Credit | U.S. $20,000 | To purchase war supplies |
| | 3rd U.S. Import Export Bank Credit | U.S. $25,000 | To purchase war supplies |
| 1941 | 4th U.S. Import Export Bank Credit | U.S. $50,000 | To purchase war supplies |
| | British Export Credit[1] | £ 50,000 | To purchase war supplies and to be used as security for domestic loans |
| 1942 | U.S. Treasury Credit | U.S. $500,000 | To strengthen currency reserves and for flotation of domestic loan and issuance of certificates |
| | Total..... | U.S. $870,000<br>£ sterling 58,047 | |

[1] Only £8,163,576 was actually drawn. Based on the data in the Statement of Revenue compiled by the Statistical Department of the Ministry of Finance.

subsequent public subcriptions were no longer attended with comparable success.

Two large issues totaling more than CNC $1,400 million were later offered for sale in 1938. About three-fifths of the entire amount were set in terms of various foreign currencies, a device adopted to attract the people's gold and foreign currency holdings and overseas Chinese subscriptions; but subscription came to less than 4 per cent. The second issue, totaling CNC $500 million, received no public response at all and was handed to the government banks as security against advances to the government. This marked the beginning of the

TABLE 44. DEFICIT FINANCE DURING THE WAR[1]
(CNC $ millions)

| Year | Deficit or (Surplus) | Bank Advances to Government | Increase in Note Issue |
|---|---|---|---|
| 1936–37 | (78) | 0 | 0 |
| 1937–38 | 1,276 | 1,194 | 397 |
| 1938 (2nd half) | 854 | 854 | 666 |
| 1939 | 2,057 | 2,310 | 1,982 |
| 1940 | 3,963 | 3,834 | 3,580 |
| 1941 | 8,693 | 9,443 | 7,266 |
| 1942 | 18,881 | 20,081 | 19,227 |
| 1943 | 38,413 | 40,857 | 41,019 |
| 1944 | 133,186 | 140,090 | 114,082 |
| 1945 | 1,106,696 | 1,043,257 | 842,471 |

[1] The figures of deficit are based on Table 34. The increase in Bank Advances to Government are based on the data of the Statement of Revenue, compiled by the Statistical Department of the Ministry of Finance.

banks' practice in making advances to the government against bonds irrespective of their marketability, a practice that was to be repeated year after year.

Another public issue was offered by the government in 1940, the bonds being in terms of foreign currencies and sold either for foreign currencies and gold or for CNC at a fixed rate. Intended as a safeguard of their value, this feature was offered as a special attraction to subscribers. The issue also met with failure, for the public, mindful of the repeated reorganizations of loan services in the past, and in the light of the unbridled bond issues, was not convinced of the government's credit worthiness.

In 1941 the government, concluding that lack of public support for bonds was the result of ineffectual promotion, established the Wartime National Bonds Subscription Commission headed by Generalissimo Chiang Kai-shek, with branches in each of the provinces directed by the chairmen of the provincial governments. Despite the activities of the Commission, total subscriptions for 1941 were little more than 5 per cent of the total bond issue, which amounted to CNC $2,400 million.

In 1942 the government devised another means of obtaining funds from reluctant investors—compulsory allocation of bonds. Owners of real estate, businessmen, merchants, and professional men were required to buy specified amounts varying with the size of their incomes. Objections were raised by the provincial governments, which pointed to the many obstacles to enforcing such a measure in rural areas, and the allocation was limited to urban districts only. Individuals possessing either personal property or an annual income of CNC $250,000 to CNC $1,000,000 were assigned bonds equivalent to 5 per cent of their income. The allocation was increased to 8 per cent in the property (or income) range of CNC $1,000,000 to $2,000,000; 10 per cent in the range of CNC $2,000,000 to $3,000,000; and rose by 5 per cent for every CNC $2 million dollars of property or income above CNC $3 million until the maximum reached 50 per cent.

Initially, this scheme appeared to be a success as the loan proceeds received in 1943 rose to 6.6 per cent of total government expenditure compared with only about 1.5 per cent in the previous year. But lack of adequate assessment of personal and corporate income and of property values—which had already resulted in the failure of direct taxes—precluded an equitable allocation of subscription quotas; and a large part of the quotas was filled by the provincial and municipal governments from their own public funds, and therefore paid by public bodies. Finally, in 1944, the original enthusiasm in loan promotion having spent itself, the local governments having reached the limit of their financial resources, and the public making increasing complaints about the inequity of allocations and resorting to a variety of stratagems to avoid compulsory assignments, subscriptions declined to 1.3 per cent of government expenditures.

The various loans floated by the Chinese government in 1937–1944 were as shown in Table 45.

Except for the relatively negligible proceeds from sales of bonds, amounting to 5 per cent of cumulative deficit for the 1937–1945 period, the government deficit was financed from bank advances which caused a continuous rise of the note issue. During the first years of the war the government issued bonds to the banks as collateral; but after the sole right of note issue was conferred on the Central Bank of China at the beginning of 1942, the formality of lodging bonds with the bank was dropped and advances were henceforth covered by treasury bills.

The relative importance of bank advances as against noninflationary borrowing and financing out of taxes and other revenue may now be

TABLE 45. WARTIME BOND ISSUES[1]

| Year | Loan | Nominal Issue (000) | Public Subscriptions (000) |
|---|---|---|---|
| 1937 | National Liberty Bonds | CNC $ 500,000 | |
| | Kwangsi Currency Readjustment Loan | CNC $ 17,000 | CNC $ 256,184 |
| 1938 | National Defense Loan | CNC $ 500,000 | |
| | Gold Loan | C.G.U. 100,000[2] | |
| | Relief Loan | £ Stg. 10,000 | |
| | | U.S. $ 50,000 | |
| | | CNC $ 30,000 | 18,402 |
| 1939 | Military Supply Loan | CNC $ 600,000 | |
| | Reconstruction Loan | CNC $ 600,000 | 24,812 |
| 1940 | Military Supply Loan | CNC $ 1,200,000 | |
| | Reconstruction Gold Loan | £ Stg. 10,000 | |
| | | U.S. $ 50,000 | 7,615 |
| 1941 | Military Supply Loan | CNC $ 1,200,000 | |
| | Reconstruction Loan | CNC $ 1,200,000 | 127,290 |
| 1942 | Allied Victory American Gold Loan | U.S. $ 100,000 | |
| | Allied Victory Loan | CNC $ 1,000,000 | 362,720 |
| 1943 | Allied Victory Loan | CNC $ 3,000,000 | 3,886,167 |
| | Readjustment Loan (of Provincial Loans) | CNC $ 175,000 | |
| 1944 | Allied Victory Loan | CNC $ 5,000,000 | 1,988,900 |
| 1945 | | | 62,823,335 |
| | Total | CNC $15,022,000 | $69,495,425 |
| | | £ Stg. 20,000 | |
| | | U.S. $ 200,000 | |
| | | C.G.U. 100,000[2] | |

[1] Wartime Bond Issues were published in China Handbook, 1937–1945, p. 209. The figures of Public Subscriptions were based on the data of the Statement of Revenue compiled by the Statistical Department of the Ministry of Finance.

[2] C.G.U. Customs Gold Unit; one C.G.U. equals CNC $20.

seen as a whole in the summary of government receipts and outgo for the entire war period (1937–1945) presented in Table 46. This synopsis reveals that 50.1 per cent of wartime expenditure was financed by inflationary borrowing while only 6 per cent was financed by taxation. This sheds a most illuminating light on the plight of China's wartime finance.

TABLE 46. TABULATION OF GOVERNMENT DEFICIT FINANCING (1937–1945, CNC $)

| | |
|---|---|
| Total wartime expenditure (unit: million) | 2,626,343 |
| Tax revenue | 158,471 |
| Non-tax revenue | 1,082,463 |
| Noninflationary borrowing | 69,495 |
| Inflationary borrowing | 1,315,914 |

Chapter

8

# Postwar Government Finance

## 1. The Budget

### *Principles of the Postwar Finance*

China's national finances were perilously close to complete collapse when the war ended. It was critically necessary for the government to give serious consideration to the dangers of an acutely inflationary situation, and to adopt strong measures to balance the budget and to prevent further monetary expansion. Unfortunately, the leaders of the government welcomed the victory as an automatic solution to the problem of inflation. The government would control the wealth of both Manchuria and Formosa, as well as valuable assets in the form of enemy property in areas formerly occupied by the enemy.

Besides, the successful conclusion of the war had raised China's status in international affairs, and had temporarily unified the Chinese people under the Nationalist government. It was maintained that these circumstances in themselves constituted an adequate invisible reserve against the note issue: that such abundant assets not only would provide backing for the existing volume of currency in circulation, but could also render harmless further increases in the note issue up to several hundred per cent. This tremendous over-optimism provided the basis for unrealistic postwar fiscal policies of the Nationalist government, which, in the hour of victory, advanced China on the road to economic disintegration and political disaster.

At the end of July 1945, immediately before the cessation of hostilities, the note issue of Free China stood at CNC $462,327 million backed by the unused portion of American Treasury credit, a second substantial credit with the United States in respect of Chinese government expenditures on behalf of American forces, and foreign exchange, gold, and silver held by the Central Bank of China. These reserves represented a ratio of U.S. $1 for every CNC $538 of notes outstanding. At the end of December 1945 the note issue had jumped to CNC $1,031,900 million or CNC $1,200 for every U.S. $1 held in reserve. Circulating in the former Japanese-occupied regions were CRB $4,199,300 million of Central Reserve Notes and FRB $142,000 million of Federal Reserve Notes, which were issued by banks of the Japanese-occupied regions and backed respectively by enemy property valued at U.S. $400 million (i.e., Central Reserve $10,498 per U.S. $1) in Central China and Shanghai and U.S. $20 million (i.e., Federal Reserve $7,100 per U.S. $1) in North China.

Taking the CNC and the puppet notes together, the situation as to reserves was not irreparable, and currency reorganization would not have been impossible to effect if the central government had been able to achieve a balanced budget. The fulfillment of this last condition presented no insuperable obstacles. Immediately after the victory the pressure on price levels temporarily eased as commodities hoarded during the war years were released onto the market. This lull in inflation offered definite scope for economies in government expenditure. At the same time the recovery of coastal areas in which the major industrial and mercantile centers were located promised an increase in revenue from customs duties and the salt and commodity taxes approaching prewar levels. But, in order to exploit fully this opportunity of attaining financial equilibrium, the government should have put into operation a plan for rapid demobilization, a course then advocated by all political parties.

In January 1946 a program for peacetime reconstruction was adopted by the Political Consultative Conference, which was attended by representatives of the government, the Communists, and other minority political parties. The resolution contained three articles dealing with fiscal and monetary reforms:

> Government receipts and expenditures were to be published, and the use of domestic and foreign loans was to be supervised by an independent committee of leading citizens. An orthodox system of budget control was to be introduced, public expenditure curtailed, and a balanced budget achieved. Central government finances were to be segregated from provincial government finances. Along with these measures should go a reduction in the note issue and stabilization of the monetary system.
>
> Tax reforms were necessary. Illegal taxes imposed by local government officials and other forms of extortion practiced on the general public were

to be eliminated, the numerous agencies for tax collection were to be amalgamated under a single central government administration, and the procedure of tax collection was to be simplified. Provision was also made for development of income and capital taxes.

Private capital funds which had taken refuge in foreign countries, or had been frozen by the national government, should be commandeered and used to balance the budget.

Two articles relating to the reduction in the size of armies were as follows:

The government should demobilize all units in excess of a total of 90 divisions, and the Communist Party all units in excess of 18 divisions. The demobilization should begin immediately and proceed at the monthly rate of approximately one-twelfth of the total number to be demobilized.

During the six months subsequent to the first year of demobilization the Nationalist divisions were to be further reduced to 50 and the Communist divisions to 10, making a total of 60 divisions, which were to be organized into 20 armies.

These resolutions adopted by the political parties reflected the unanimous demands of businessmen, who realized that unless far-reaching reforms were made inflation would continue and fiscal and monetary improvement would be impossible.

However, the leaders of the national government failed to appreciate the gravity of the economic situation, and the various government agencies, in the aggregate, continued to spend beyond the income of the government. No effective effort was made to offset the resulting expansion of the money supply by income taxes or by encouraging savings. Also not fully appreciated in their effects were the circumstances in which the reoccupied areas were found: low levels of output, distrust of managed money because of the inflation left behind by the Japanese, and monetary hoards concealed during the war but now being injected into the spending stream.

Upon the removal of psychological and physical restraints which had been imposed by war, this vast monetary overhang itself, accompanied by the people's anxiety to get rid of the puppet government's notes, increased demand for goods significantly. This called for deflationary policies. Instead, government expenditures, revenues, and borrowing policies once again were carried on with apparent unconcern about their effect on aggregate demand. The effects of surplus disposable income, generated by fiscal policies, were not nullified or mitigated, and the situation deteriorated until China's monetary structure collapsed.

### *Government Expenditure*

The budgeted expenditure for 1945 was CNC $263,800 million, but actual outlay during the year proved to be nearly nine times the estimate, or $2,348,000 million. Sixty per cent of this enormous outlay was spent after victory during August to December. In 1946 provision was made in the budget for an expenditure of CNC $2,524,900 million; but by the end of May CNC $1,500,000 million had already been spent, and for the whole year actual expenditure reached CNC $7,574,790 million, almost three times the original estimate and 2.9 times the wartime aggregate.

TABLE 47. CENTRAL GOVERNMENT EXPENDITURE, REVENUE, AND DEFICIT, 1945–48[1]
(CNC $ millions)

| Year | Expenditure | Increase | Revenue | Increase | Deficit |
|---|---|---|---|---|---|
| 1945 | 2,348,085 | | 1,241,389 | | 1,106,696 |
| 1946 | 7,574,790 | 3.2 times | 2,876,988 | 2.3 times | 4,697,802 |
| 1947 | 43,393,895 | 5.7 times | 14,064,383 | 4.9 times | 29,329,512 |
| 1948 (Jan.–July) | 655,471,087 | — times | 220,905,475 | — times | 434,565,612 |

[1] The figures of expenditures and revenue for 1946–1947 are based on data from W. Y. Chang, *op. cit.*, p. 243; those for Jan.–July 1948 on the amount of payments and receipts for the Treasury's account made by the Central Bank.

During the war government expenditure was chiefly for defense, but after the victory huge sums were spent for rehabilitation and reconstruction in addition to the expenses of the campaign against the Communists. Expenditures increased tremendously as the range of government activities and the unit cost of its operations rose with the intensification of inflation. Expenditure for 1947 was nearly six times that for 1946, and the budgeted amount for the first half of 1948 was CNC $96,000,000 million, which was more than double the actual outlays for the whole of the previous year. Up to the end of July 1948, one month before the change in the currency standard, actual expenditure totaled CNC $655,471,087 million, or close to seven times the estimate.

Government revenues increased also during the postwar period, but as they continued to fall far short of expenditure the deficit grew to astronomical proportions (Table 47).

Details of the composition of government expenditures during the postwar years are not readily available from one single source. Table 48, showing the percentages of each item in total expenditure for 1946 and the first half year of 1947 and 1948, has been synthesized from different reports.

TABLE 48. ESTIMATED COMPOSITION OF CENTRAL GOVERNMENT EXPENDITURES, 1946–1948[1]
(in per cent of total)

| Expenditure | Average 1941–44 | 1946 | 1947 | 1948[2] |
|---|---|---|---|---|
| 1. Defense expenditure | 60 | 59.9 | 54.8 | 68.5 |
| Military | 50 | 53.6 | 48.4 | 64.1 |
| Cost of food collection | 10 | 6.3 | 6.4 | 4.4 |
| 2. Loan service | 5 | 0.6 | 1.2 | 2.6 |
| 3. Development | 10 | 11.0 | 14.3 | 5.2 |
| 4. Administrative and general expenditure | 25 | 28.5 | 29.7 | 23.7 |
| Departmental | 7 | 13.2 | 17.8 | 13.7 |
| Subsidies to provincial governments | 5 | 6.4 | 6.4 | 7.2 |
| Civil servants' allowance | 2 | — | — | — |
| Rehabilitation and relief | — | 8.0 | 4.9 | — |
| Other | 11 | 0.9 | 0.6 | 2.8 |
| Grand Total | 100% | 100% | 100% | 100% |

[1] Military and Development Expenditure based on statistics compiled by the Statistical Department of the Ministry of Finance and Directory-General of Budget, Accounts and Statistics. Other expenditures based on the Statement of Expenditure and Revenue compiled by the Statistical Department of the Ministry of Finance.

[2] 1948 is for half year, January–July.

## *Military Expenditure*

The budget estimates for 1946 cut back military expenditure to only 43 per cent of total government expenditure, a reduction almost to the prewar proportion of military to total spending. The government claimed that it planned to reduce military expenses at this stage, as is indicated by a statement made by the Prime Minister on March 8, 1946:

> During the war, because we had to fight for victory, the government found it absolutely impossible to reduce the number of soldiers. Exhaustion of the government's financial resources was unavoidable, and every possible source of additional finance for the military was explored. However, now that war is ended military expenditure must be rigorously

> reduced. At the Military Conference held recently the government decided to reduce the size of the army from 253 divisions to 90 divisions. When this has been accomplished the government's burden will be lighter, but it will take time to carry out this decision. There will be a very hard period ahead, requiring great effort. At the same time the government will provide a certain amount of money for the disbandment of troops.

Shortly after this speech was delivered negotiations between the Nationalists and the Communists broke down, armed conflict began in a number of localities, and the government once again turned its attention to mobilization. The government continued to maintain the wartime strength of the army of from 4 1/2 to 5 million men, and the whole of the CNC $1,095,000 million allocated in the 1946 budget to military purposes was expended in five months. According to an official pronouncement of the Minister of Finance, actual military outlays for 1946 amounted to 60 per cent of total government expenditure. As the war spread in subsequent years, military spending became an even larger proportion of total expenditure, rising to 68.5 per cent in the first half of 1948.

### *Rehabilitation and Relief*

The greater part of the increase in government expenditures in the final quarter of 1945 was attributable to the expenses of rehabilitating occupied areas, which included the costs of reestablishing the Chinese administration in the formerly occupied regions, of repatriating enemy soldiers, of taking over and operating Japanese enterprises, and of confiscating other enemy property. These items together involved the government in expenditures amounting to CNC $500,000 million, which was 65 per cent of total expenditure during the last three months of 1945 and more than 20 per cent of the total for the year. Government officials entrusted with the task of rehabilitation spent lavishly, free from the restraint of a planned budget since there was no provision in the original estimates for expenditures of this description. In 1946 and 1947 another new expenditure was the operation cost of the UNRRA program. These two items cost 8.0 and 4.9 per cent of total spending. Although they represented a smaller component of government outlay after 1945, nevertheless it was an additional burden at a time when government finances were already overstrained.

### *Administrative Expenditures*

As noted previously, the proliferation of central government departments during the war years led to a substantial increase in the number of civil servants, and at the end of the war 200,000 persons were reported to be listed on the central government payroll. Because of serious discontent among public servants at the low level of wages and salaries, the government introduced a system by which earnings were adjusted quarterly with reference to the cost of living index, but not necessarily in accordance with the full amount of the rise in this index. Early in 1947 adjustments were switched to a monthly basis; in April 1948 increases were automatically granted to the full amount of the rise in living costs.

Very big increases in money wages and salaries resulted from the application of the various methods of adjustment. For instance, the government's payroll increased by CNC $125,000 million per month in the period April–August 1947, by CNC $85,200 million per month in September–December 1947, and by CNC $871,800 million per month in January–April 1948. This measure, though perhaps necessary to maintain the morale of the civil servants, helped to perpetuate an automatic upward wage-price spiral. Consequently, administrative and departmental expenditure became increasingly important in total government spending, accounting for 17.8 per cent of the total during the year of 1947 and 13.7 per cent in the first half of 1948.

## 2. The Behavior of Revenue

### *Failure to Expand Revenue*

Immediately after the war the government planned to restore its revenues by improving both the indirect and direct tax systems and by disposing of enemy property. As was indicated by a statement made by the Prime Minister in March 1946, the government believed that sales of enemy property would yield large revenues, but the sums realized fell far below expectations. Non-tax revenues were temporarily augmented by proceeds from sales of gold and foreign exchange, but as reserves were run down and it became difficult to dispose of enemy property these revenues declined. The yield from indirect taxes failed to keep pace with rising price levels, and the government was unable to improve and extend direct taxes because of the exigencies of inflation and a semi-war economy. Consequently, government revenues, after recovering encouragingly in 1946, lagged increasingly behind the rise in the price level and in government spending (Table 49).

Shortly after the end of the war the Ministry of Finance announced three important objectives of tax policy: (1) Tax revenues were to be

Table 49. Government Revenues in the Postwar Period[1]
(CNC $ millions)

| Year | Tax Revenue Indirect | Direct | Total | Non-Tax Revenue | Sales of Bonds | Total Revenue | Revenue as Per Cent of Expenditure |
|---|---|---|---|---|---|---|---|
| 1945 | 81,504 | 20,749 | 102,253 | 1,076,313 | 62,823 | 1,241,389 | 52.8 |
| 1946 | 961,450 | 256,191 | 1,217,641 | 1,657,333 | 2,014 | 2,876,988 | 38.0 |
| 1947 | 7,133,910 | 2,012,129 | 9,146,039 | 4,330,000 | 588,344 | 14,064,383 | 32.4 |
| 1948 | N.A. | N.A. | N.A. | N.A. | — | 220,905,745 | 34.8 |

[1] The figures of Tax Revenue and Sales of Bonds for 1946, excluding foreign credit for specific projects, are based on data compiled by the Statistical Department of the Directorate-General of Budgets, Accounts and Statistics. The figures of Non-Tax Revenue of 1946–47, and Tax Revenue for 1947, and Sales of Bonds for 1947, are based on data in W. Y. Chang, p. 244. The figure of Revenue for 1948 (Jan.–July) is based on the record of the Central Bank on government receipts but cannot be considered as an exact figure of the total revenue.

restored to prewar level in real value. (2) Allowance was to be made for the rising price level in fixing tax rates and in deciding on methods of assessment. (3) Consideration was to be given to the use of taxation as a means of securing a more equitable distribution of income.

At first sight, the restoration of revenue from customs duty and the salt and commodity taxes to prewar level in real value appeared easy enough, but all three objectives were contingent on the development of a sound system of tax collection. This last had been neglected, and the tax administration had become particularly inefficient because the hardships inflicted on government employees by the inflation had caused a serious deterioration in the quality of their services. Thorough administrative reforms should have preceded the introduction of new tax schemes and were a prerequisite for the success of efforts to restore yields from indirect taxes to prewar standards.

Customs duties had ad valorem rates calculated on wholesale prices at the port of entry, and unit yields automatically followed price fluctuations. Salt and commodity taxes were also on an ad valorem basis, but unit yields lagged considerably behind the general level of prices. Salt prices were fixed by the government, with an element of self-righteousness, much lower than general price levels, which were often twice as high as salt. Commodity taxes were based on average market prices for the previous three months. In a period of rapid inflation there was a growing discrepancy between the average price level for tax purposes and current market prices. In 1947, for instance, when prices were doubling every three months, the liability under the commodity tax was a third less than it would have been if the tax had been calculated on current market prices. In these circumstances the government was unable to achieve its initial objective of restoring indirect tax yields to prewar levels. In 1946 the real yield from these levies was 41 per cent of prewar, and in 1947 it fell to 34 per cent of prewar.

The situation with regard to direct taxes was slightly more favorable, and their percentage in the total tax revenue increased in 1946. However, the direct tax system was still inefficient. Poor methods of assessment and lack of adequately trained personnel created opportunities for evasion and caused lengthy delays before the government came into possession of its due receipts. One example will suffice to illustrate the loss of real revenue to the government arising from cumbersome administrative techniques. The income tax liability of a particular firm in Shanghai for 1945 was assessed by the Tax Bureau at CNC $60,000 million; but the assessment of the guild amounted to only CNC $13,000 million. After long negotiations between the Tax Bureau and the Chamber of Commerce the tax authorities reduced their claim to CNC $45,000 million. The firm refused to recognize this assessment, and, pleading special circumstances of hardship, actually paid only CNC $4,500 million in tax at the end of 1946. Meanwhile, commodity prices had risen ninefold, reducing the real value of the tax the government received to CNC $500 million, or 1.1 per cent of its original claim value.

The government made a number of attempts to remedy the defects in direct taxation but with little success. Under a regulation announced early in 1946 the system of self-assessment of tax liability was retained and profit-making enterprises were bound to declare their taxable incomes one month after the close of the financial (i.e., calendar) year. But tax payments were not made until the Tax Bureau had checked the authenticity of the declarations and notified the taxpayers of their liabilities. The personal income tax returns of professional men were first approved by their respective guilds and then passed on to the Tax Bureau for assessment. The Bureau was empowered to investigate the accounts of 5–10 per cent of all firms each year to ensure that returns had not been falsified. A further regulation promulgated early in 1947 provided for the payment of a provisional tax in advance of the final assessment of liability made by the Tax Bureau. Firms and private individuals subject to income tax were required to pay the provisional tax calculated by the Tax Bureau on the income disclosed in the taxpayers' returns.

These measures were in some degree effective. Real revenue from direct taxes declined by 13 per cent during 1947, much less than the drop of 18 per cent in real yield of indirect taxes. But direct tax receipts still lagged badly behind rising income and price levels, and in January 1948 the government finally resorted to a scheme for prepayment of income taxes. By the middle of April taxpayers were to pay in advance six times the amount paid in 1947, the advance payment to be deducted from their total tax liability for the year when final assessment was made. So rapid was the pace of inflation at this stage that in the second half of 1948 the government was compelled to levy a further prepayment equal to forty times the installment paid in April, or 240 times the total tax paid for 1947.

The changing importance of the different types of taxes as sources of government income is reflected in Table 50, which compares the postwar composition of tax revenues with previous years:

TABLE 50. THE PERCENTAGE COMPOSITION OF GOVERNMENT TAX REVENUES[1]

| | 1936–37 | 1945 | 1946 | 1947 |
|---|---|---|---|---|
| Customs duty | 47.8 | 4.1 | 25.9 | 26.9 |
| Salt tax | 25.8 | 52.7 | 19.1 | 13.9 |
| Commodity tax | 25.8 | 23.0 | 34.0 | 36.9 |
| Total indirect tax | 99.4 | 79.8 | 79.0 | 77.7 |
| Direct tax | 0.6 | 20.2 | 21.0 | 22.3 |
| Total Tax | 100.0% | 100.0% | 100.0% | 100.0% |

[1] This percentage was computed from the data of the Statement of Revenue compiled by the Directorate-General of Budgets, Accounts and Statistics (unpublished) for 1946 and 1st half year of 1947.

It is worth noting that the Nationalist Government committed a serious error in continuing to collect the land tax and compulsory loans from the peasants after the war ended. The peasant landholders had supplied the government's demand for produce in the belief that the special burdens imposed on them would be removed as soon as victory was won. The government itself had originally announced at the end of 1945 that taxpayers in previously occupied areas would be exempted from the land tax in 1945–1946 and those in unoccupied districts in 1946–1947. Shortly afterwards this scheme was modified and landowners in unoccupied regions were required to make tax and loan contributions in kind, although the rates were cut by half. At the Finance Conference of July 1946, in view of the imminence of a full-scale campaign against the Communists, the government again altered its decision and prolonged the life of these much criticized levies at the full rates. By this action the government saved about 8 per cent of 1945 expenditure and 8.2 per cent and 7 per cent for 1946 and 1947 respectively, as shown in Table 51. However, the central government agreed to pay the local provincial and hsien governments 70 per cent of the market value of these contributions in kind in lieu of returning to them the prerogative to levy the land tax.

TABLE 51. LAND TAX COLLECTION, 1945–1948[1]

Collection in Kind (in bushels)

| Crop Year | | By Tax | By Loan | By Purchase | Total | Estimate of Money Value of Land Tax in Kind (in million CNC) |
|---|---|---|---|---|---|---|
| 1945–46 | Rice | 11,899,102 | 13,236,602 | | 25,135,704 | 188,604 |
| | Wheat | 2,817,627 | 1,311,428 | | 4,129,055 | |
| 1946–47 | Rice | 25,501,156 | 11,897,148 | | 37,398,304 | 624,675 |
| | Wheat | 2,907,967 | 1,553,809 | | 4,441,776 | |
| 1947–48 | Rice | 5,417,250 | | 12,300,250 | 17,717,500 | 3,015,899 |
| | Wheat | 637,162 | | 1,953,377 | 2,572,539 | |

[1] The figures for land taxation in kind are compiled from the data in the Abstract of Facts on Finance and Money compiled by the Ministry of Finance. Monetary value was calculated from the price index for food in Shanghai compiled by the Central Bank. Rice prices were: 1945–46, CNC $19,300 per picul (2.91 bushels); 1946–47, CNC $44,390; 1947–48, CNC $443,800. The purchase price was calculated at half of the market prices. The price of wheat was 80 per cent of rice price.

Again, the government revived conscription, which, as in the war years, caused a shortage of rural labor and raised farm production costs. Farming communities remained in semi-isolation from the coast since lines of communication destroyed in the process of war had not been restored, and inland prices of essential materials and manufactured consumer goods rose prohibitively. With the rise in costs and prices the land tax and compulsory loans became increasingly onerous to the peasants, who believed that their grievances had a common origin in the discriminatory and oppressive policies of the government toward the agricultural sector of the population.

### *The Disposal of Enemy and Puppet Property*

In the 1946 budget, proceeds from sales of enemy property were estimated at CNC $620,000 million, equal to a third of total estimated revenue and only slightly less than the estimated yield from taxation. There was a gap of CNC $680,000 million between budget expenditure and revenue which the government repeatedly emphasized would be filled by additional receipts from sale of alien property. Enemy and puppet property was believed to have a total market value of CNC $1,200,000 million, or U.S. $600 million at the prevailing exchange rate. Of this total, commodities and raw materials accounted for 26 per cent; factories 37 per cent; real estate 11 per cent; gold, silver, and jewelry, 14 per cent; wharves and warehouses 8 per cent; and sundry items 4 per cent.

Had the government carried out its idea of selling these properties in line with the program decided upon by the Political Consultative Conference, the objective of balancing the budget might have been reached. Such sales would not only have produced sizeable amounts in government revenue but would also have removed significant sums of cash and credit from the aggregate demand, thus restraining inflationary pressures. But it proved as difficult to decide between the various disposal schemes as it was to balance expenditures with revenues.

The most valuable and most readily marketable assets were the Japanese cotton mills in China; these were converted into a government-owned enterprise. Wharves and warehouses were given to the government-owned China Merchant Steamship Company; a large portion of the commodity stocks was transferred to the Department of Defense; inventories of raw materials were taken over by state-owned factories; and gold and silver were given to the Central Bank of China. Thus a large part of enemy assets was retained by the government or its subsidiary enterprises. By the end of 1946 CNC $500,000 million had been received from sales of enemy assets to the public. This was four-fifths of the original estimate in money value, and probably about one-third in real value since wholesale prices had more than doubled during the year. Moreover, these sales covered only 6.6 per cent of actual expenditure for the year instead of almost 25 per cent as estimated in the budget.

In the budget of 1947 sale of enemy assets was expected to net CNC $800,000 million, which was 8.5 per cent of estimated total expenditure. Although about CNC $900,000 million was received during the year, this was a mere 2 per cent of actual expenditure. When inflation accelerated in the early months of 1947 the Central Bank strongly recommended that the government sell factories, warehouses, and wharves. A Planning Committee for disposal was established, but it debated the question of the appropriate formula for disposing of these assets for nearly a year without arriving at a decision. In the spring of 1948 the government allocated to the Central Bank two-thirds of ex-alien textile mills, valued at U.S. $200 million, and all the wharves and warehouses in its possession, valued at U.S. $100 million, to be sold to create resources against the note issue. However, by this time political and economic conditions were extremely unstable and there was little demand from private investors for fixed capital assets. Even had these assets been disposed of by the Central Bank of China, inflationary pressures would thereby have been alleviated but slightly.

Another source of revenue considered promising by the Ministry of Finance was the sale of surplus stores accumulated by American Forces in the Pacific Islands, which the Chinese government had purchased at the cut rate of 17 per cent of original cost. The total amount of surplus property available for purchase was estimated at U.S. $500,000,000, but actual deliveries were appreciably lower—only U.S. $370,000,000. In the budget of 1947 the government expected to realize CNC $1,120,000 million from sales of surplus goods, equaling 12 per cent of anticipated expenditure. Actual proceeds from sales amounted to CNC $1,191,000 million, about 2.7 per cent of actual expenditure. At least half of the property was transferred to government departments lacking their own sources of revenue; and the total recorded receipts from public sales after two years was only 36 per cent of the value of goods delivered to the Chinese government.

Sales of gold and foreign exchange were the third major source of the government's non-tax revenues. Since open market operations in gold and the government's foreign exchange policy are dealt with in a later chapter, they need only be mentioned briefly here. Heavy sales of gold and foreign exchange, together with disposals of enemy assets, lifted non-tax revenues to 30 per cent above receipts from taxation for 1946. Gold sales and foreign exchange, amounting to U.S. $512 million netted approximately CNC $1,200 million or about 15 per cent of expenditure. Early in 1947 sales of gold were discontinued and sales of foreign exchange were reduced; in that year the sale of such assets equivalent to U.S. $260 millions withdrew about CNC $3,129,000 million or 7.2 per cent of expenditures.

The significant point which emerges from the preceding discussion is that during the period the government depended to an uncommonly large extent on non-tax revenues—particularly the sale of assets, a practice which could not be repeated indefinitely and which the government could ill afford. In particular, the gold and foreign exchange which were so liberally sold could have been used to undertake a necessary basic currency reform. Without a firm over-all policy to reach financial stability, such sales only dissipated the resources of China and weakened the potential capacity of the government to survive.

It is generally admitted that immediately after regaining control of the whole of China the government should have overhauled its tax structure, using its experiences in war finance to advantage. Instead of adopting a broad tax structure to support a significant share of public expenditures, however, the government chose to adhere to the old pattern of indirect taxation which for twenty years had proven inadequate. Failure to reorganize the tax structure to curb the expansion of aggregate demand was one of the basic causes of the persistence of inflationary pressures in the postwar period.

## 3. Deficit Financing

In May 1947 the Central Bank made a final attempt to induce the government to reorganize its finances and place them on a sound basis. The Governor of the Central Bank was of the opinion that unless budgetary reforms were immediately effected inflation would become uncontrollable. He appealed to Generalissimo Chiang Kai-shek to limit the government's monthly drawings on the Central Bank to a prescribed amount, which the bank would endeavor to obtain without resorting to further issues of notes.

Behind this approach of the Central Bank lay the hope that if the government could achieve a reasonable degree of financial stability China would be able to obtain assistance from the United States in carrying out monetary reforms. At this time the deficit was running at the rate of about CNC $1,500,000 million per month. The bank suggested a limit of CNC $1,000,000 million per month, which the bank would finance from savings deposits and proceeds of sales of U.S. dollar bonds and short-term treasury bills. The balance of the deficit was to be covered by the Ministry of Finance through the increase of tax revenue or reduction of expenditure.

The proposal was examined at a number of meetings which included Generalissimo Chiang Kai-shek, the Prime Minister, the Minister of Finance, the Directorate-General of Budgets, Accounts and Statistics, and the Governor of the Central Bank. The sole opposition it aroused came from the Minister of Finance, who insisted that budget control was impossible as long as prices continued on an increasingly rapid upward trend and he was not in a position to refuse the demands of military expenditure. His views were tacitly supported by the leader of the government. As a result, the plan to deal with a fundamental cause of inflation was shelved.

In anticipation of the adoption of its plan, the Central Bank made a strenuous effort to acquire funds for advances to the government without increasing the note issue while the scheme for budget reform was still being discussed at a succession of conferences. It offered for public subscription U.S. dollar bonds to the value of U.S. $100 million, purchasable in foreign exchange and redeemable in U.S. dollars. It also offered short-term treasury bills to the equivalent of U.S. $300 million redeemable in national currency according to the prevailing official U.S. dollar exchange rate. Although public reaction was favorable when these issues first appeared in April, as soon as it became generally known that the government did not intend to scale down its borrowing from the banks and new notes again flooded the market, the black-market rate of exchange rose far above the official quotation, prices increased, and purchases of bonds and treasury bills rapidly dwindled. When the subscription was closed in August 1947, dollar bond subscriptions totaled only U.S. $25,819,550, about a quarter of the amount called for, the main purchasers being the leading commercial banks and cotton mills.

This was the first time that significant voluntary sales were obtained since the issue of National Liberty Bonds at the beginning of the war. In time of inflation these foreign holdings were their most valuable assets. Unfortunately, fiscal developments soon led to the breach of government's obligation to pay loan services in foreign currency and the bonds became worthless. This brazen breaking of confidence was not forgotten by the subscribers. Sales of treasury bills amounted to CNC $514,225 million, the equivalent of U.S. $30,834,680, in the period April–December 1947, and further sales in the first quarter of 1948 netted CNC $3,355,516 million, equivalent to U.S. $11,635,660. After March the treasury bills in the present form, because of the rise in the exchange rate, were replaced by a new short-term treasury bill issued in Chinese currency and marketed at a heavy discount. The response to this issue was extremely poor. The proceeds of sales of bonds amounted to about 4.3 per cent of total revenue.

From 1947 onwards the government deficit was almost wholly financed by increases in the note issue. At the end of 1947 the government's credit requirements became so great that the banks were forced to cease providing accommodation to private undertakings, and increases in the note issue had their origin solely in the government's credit demands (Table 52).

TABLE 52. GOVERNMENT DEFICIT, BANK ADVANCES, AND INCREASES IN NOTE ISSUE, 1946–1948[1]

| Year | Deficit (CNC $ millions) | Bank Advances to the Government (CNC $ millions) | Increases in Note Issue (CNC $ millions) |
|---|---|---|---|
| 1946 | 4,697,802 | 4,697,802 | 2,694,200 |
| 1947 | 29,329,512 | 29,329,512 | 29,462,400 |
| 1948 (Jan.–July) | 434,565,612 | 434,565,612 | 341,573,700 |

[1] The government deficit is based on Table 23 and the figures of government advances and note issue are based on the record of the Central Bank of China.

A summary of the total picture of inflationary government finance in the postwar period (1946–July, 1948) is presented in Table 52A.

TABLE 52A. POSTWAR GOVERNMENT EXPENDITURE (CNC $ millions)

| | |
|---|---|
| Postwar government expenditure | 708,787,857 |
| Taxes and other revenue | 237,256,758 |
| Noninflationary borrowing | 590,358 |
| Inflationary borrowing | 469,717,622 |

Although foreign credits totaling U.S. $130 million were obtained, they were specified for the purchase of ships, equipment, and raw materials; and no proceeds in Chinese currency could be produced to reduce the deficit. With minor exceptions the pattern of finance presented here shows a close parallel to the tragic wartime experience shown earlier. Apparently it was difficult either to learn from the past or to have the courage to put a lesson, however well learned, to profitable use.

## 4. EFFORTS TO REDUCE THE LEVEL OF GOVERNMENT DEFICIT FINANCING: 1948

In August 1948, when the monetary standard was changed to "Gold Yuan" (GY), the Ministry of Finance published an estimate of government expenditure and revenue for the next twelve months. The figures gave the impression that a miraculous improvement in the budget would be achieved. With no change in political and economic circumstances, the deficit was to be reduced from 70 per cent to 30 per cent of expenditure. Expenditure and revenue were respectively estimated at GY 3,600 million (equivalent to CNC $10,800,000,000 million) and GY 2,460 million (or CNC $7,380,000,000 million). Whereas expenditure for the year August 1948–July 1949 was 16.5 times the rate of spending in the last seven months of 1948, revenue was put at no less than thirty-three times the rate of collections for the same period.

The ability of the government to limit expenditure to the planned amount was contingent on the success of price and wage controls. When ceiling price and wage schemes broke down completely in November 1948, it was impossible to confine spending within the prescribed limits. The estimates of the Ministry of Finance were equally unrealistic on the revenue side. Planned revenues comprised GY 480 million from customs duties, GY 700 million from commodity taxes, GY 360 million from direct taxes, GY 220 million from the salt tax, GY 200 million from miscellaneous taxes and profits from government-owned enterprises, and GY 400 million in proceeds of sales of American surplus property and former enemy assets. Since the readily saleable items of U.S. surplus stores and enemy property had already been marketed by the government, the estimate of receipts from these sources was, to say the least, optimistic. It was also naively optimistic to envisage a restoration of real revenues from taxes to prewar levels.

Revenue from customs duties was lagging badly owing to reduction in the volume of imports occasioned by shortages of foreign exchange and the limited volume of exports. Similarly, receipts from commodity taxes were affected by the decline in factory output and sales due to the distortions of inflation; and the salt tax was an inefficient means of raising revenue since the official price for purposes of tax rating remained unwarrantedly low. The yield from direct taxes could not be augmented, and evasion became increasingly prevalent.

The government planned to meet the deficit partly out of proceeds from sales of goods received from the United States under the E.C.A. program of April 1948 and partly by issuing Gold Yuan bonds. So far as sales of goods were concerned, since there was a considerable delay before commodities ordered in America could be procured and shipped to China, receipts fell far short of the government's anticipations. Public confidence in bonds had been destroyed some years previously, as indicated by the repeated failures of the Central Bank to sell bonds and treasury bills, and the Gold Yuan bond issue fared no better than its predecessors. These considerations make it difficult to understand the basis of the government's belief that the deficit could be offset without resort to unsound financial practices.

Figures for expenditure and revenue in the months September to December 1948 (Table 53) show that, apart from October when the deficit fell to 49 per cent of expenditure, the currency reform of August could not check the growing imbalance in government finances.

TABLE 53. GOVERNMENT REVENUES AND EXPENDITURES: SEPTEMBER–DECEMBER, 1948[1]

| Month | Expenditure | Revenue | Deficit, Per Cent of Expenditure |
|---|---|---|---|
| Sept. | GY 343,414,000 | GY 108,854,000 | 69 |
| Oct. | GY 282,833,000 | GY 145,090,000 | 49 |
| Nov. | GY 674,944,000 | GY 172,410,000 | 75 |
| Dec. | GY 2,649,609,000 | GY 446,747,000 | 83 |

[1] These figures are based on records of the Central Bank of China.

When the Gold Yuan system began to collapse in early November 1948, the government was unable to make any forward estimate of either expenditure or revenue. After the fall of Peking and Tientsin to the Communists the authority of the central government was undermined and the provincial governments issued their own bank notes redeemable in silver dollars and retained revenues properly belonging to the central government. At the end of February 1949 the government announced that customs duty was to be collected in Customs Units (1 Customs Unit equaled U.S. $0.40) or their equivalent in Gold Yuan, and that commodity taxes were to be levied in kind or its equivalent in Gold Yuan at the prices prevailing on the date of collection. The armed services were to be paid in silver dollars, or the equivalent in Gold Yuan. In March, because of difficulties encountered in attempting to levy the commodity taxes in kind, a new Tax Unit equal to 1/100 ounce of gold was devised to be used as the basis for calculating all tax liabilities other than customs duties. These measures proved pointless in the disintegrating economy of Nationalist China and contributed to the depreciation of the Gold Yuan. Two months later, when the government withdrew from Nanking to Canton, completely discredited in political and economic affairs, no financial policy could alter the fundamental insecurity of its position.

No report on the government's revenue and expenditure was published during the chaotic period when the Nationalist government moved from Nanking to Canton. After the government had temporarily settled in Canton the silver standard was readopted. Expenditures for the second half of 1949 were reported at 255,846,154 silver dollars; revenue at 31,738,420 silver dollars or 12 % of expenditures. The deficit had to be met with gold, silver, and foreign exchange since bank notes no longer enjoyed the people's acceptance.

Chapter

# 9

# The Money Market and Private Credit

## 1. The Money Market, Private Credit, and the Level of Aggregate Demand

The preceding chapter has outlined how the tremendous increase of disposable money income in China, resulting from the large and rising volume of government expenditures and the inadequate tax program, constituted a major factor in the increase of aggregate demand. This chapter will deal with the second major stimulus to aggregate demand, namely, the expansion of private credit.

Before the war, credit facilities in the interior of China were exceedingly poor while there was a heavy concentration of financial resources and institutions in the Treaty Ports. Thus, when the tide of war turned against China and it was necessary to fall back upon the interior for continued resistance, a liberal credit policy was adopted by the government to facilitate the relocation of industry from the coast and to stimulate the establishment of new enterprises and the production and movement of goods in the interior. Credit was made available to finance industry's moving costs, new enterprises, and purchases of finished goods and other materials for shipment to the interior. The immediate impact of this policy was to increase the aggregate supply of goods in Free China and, at the same time, to hold inflationary pressures to moderate dimensions.

However, toward the end of 1939 the supply of capital goods and raw materials in interior China had dried up as a result of the enemy blockade and the unresponsiveness of the region's primitive productive apparatus to external stimuli. Specific shortages developed. The liberal credit given to industry, by which the government had expected to increase the supply of goods, now merely helped competitors to bid up prices against each other; and the additional money supply was not accompanied by an increase in the real output of goods. Meanwhile, the merchants' expectation of rising prices stimulated their quest for credit with which to buy and hoard goods. Thus less credit was available for productive purposes and more for speculation, the latter being more lucrative as it was free from the perplexing problems which beset all productive endeavors and as the interest rate was actually below the rate of increase of some of the prices.

Not even rural credit remained immune from the temptation of speculation. It was quite common for officers of credit cooperatives, which they had themselves set up in a haphazard manner, to retain for brief periods such money as passed through their hands to finance speculative ventures before passing it on again to members requiring funds. As inflation gathered momentum, the speculative fever spread to the entire community and virtually everyone was seeking credit for a quick turn of profit.

When the coastal banking institutions, which were unsound in the first place, were transplanted and superimposed on the primitive credit structure of the interior, the result was a less than perfect fusion, and the end-product left much to be desired. The weakness of the banking structure had much to do with the difficulties encountered by the government in its efforts to control the volume and flow of credit.

Although each of the government banks was entrusted with certain special functions, the demarcation of their responsibilities was indistinct and there was considerable interbank competition for business. For example, with the exception of the Central Bank of China, all government banks extended rural loans in spite of the existence of the Farmers' Bank. Conversely, the Farmers' Bank also made industrial and commercial loans and operated a foreign exchange business. The many local commercial and native banks, most of which had small capital and deposit accounts only, depended for their operations on short-term funds from two sources: short-term deposits attracted by high interest rates, and remittance funds between cities and their surrounding provinces. The most striking feature of the short-term deposit system was the custom in a number of the major cities of Szechwan Province to make "fortnight loans." Deposits were accepted for a period of two weeks, and loans were made with these funds at high interest rates for the same length of time. This short-term deposit and loan system, practiced principally by the native banks, but also employed by the commercial banks, was a significant vehicle for speculators when the pace of inflation increased.

Not only had the people in the interior never developed a habit of saving through banking institutions; the continuous depreciation of the currency actively discouraged such saving. Moreover, the undeveloped banking institutions of the interior were not able to absorb and mobilize such savings as still existed. Consequently, the investments and speculations fed by bank credit found no counterpart in new savings within the banking system. The growing volume of bank deposits which accompanied the general credit expansion represented active balances and were readily introduced into circulation. Uncontrolled by the government, when not actively encouraged by it, the expansion of private bank credit (i.e., excluding bank advances to the government) accordingly exerted an increasingly potent influence on aggregate demand.

The worst features of the wartime credit expansion were magnified in the postwar period. As the war ended, instead of carrying out the much needed banking reform, government policy aimed at the restoration of the prewar status quo. Even this proved to be impossible because of the general deterioration of banking standards, the indiscriminate growth of commercial and native banks, especially at the country's financial center, Shanghai, and speculative excesses carried over from the war period. The government's spasmodic attempts to tighten credit proved completely futile; indeed the expansion of credit accelerated. Toward the end of our period, private credit expansion rivaled deficit financing as the prime mover of the rampant inflation. The greater part of the responsibility fell on the government banks.

## 2. The Money Market and Private Credit in the Prewar Period

### *The Growth of Independent and Self-Regulating Money Markets*

The Chinese banking system grew up, not like a tree having one trunk and many branches, but like a grove of trees with new ones growing up at intervals. During the process of this growth the competition between different groups and within each group made integration most difficult. Consequently, up to the time of the Sino-Japanese war in 1937 China had not developed a unified banking system.

Banking activities in China, such as remittance and exchange, which began about the thirteenth century, were conducted by private money-dealers. From these origins evolved the native banks known in modern times, which are partnerships formed by members of a family, or clan, or a group of friends, with unlimited responsibility guaranteed by the partners. With the establishment of the Treaty Ports, foreign banks made their appearance. The first one was opened in Shanghai in 1857; later, banks were established by each of the treaty nations in the different ports. The native banks, besides their original functions, began to act as intermediaries between the foreign banks and Chinese merchants. As agents for the various financial institutions of the Treaty Ports, the native banks of the interior came to provide a vital link between the town and village communities of the inland and the cities of the coast. Thus the foreign and native banks complemented each other's activities.

However, the Chinese business world was not satisfied with this state of affairs, and, for reasons of prestige, a bank along the lines of a modern Western bank was set up in 1897, the first of a number which were to appear during the next few years. Although their resources could not compete with those of the foreign banks, and their adaptability to, and experience in, the type of business conducted by the native banks could not compare with those of the latter, the modern banks emerged as a new banking force by virtue of their business acumen and the patriotic support of the Chinese business community. So the native, foreign, and modern Chinese banks settled down side by side, each having its own specialized facilities while fulfilling many of the functions of the others, and the Chinese banking structure took shape.

The primary functions of the native banks were to accept deposits and to extend short-term credit to Chinese merchants and firms against personal guarantees. For the most part they confined their activities to the local markets which they served. Their resources were current account deposits, interbank deposits, and call loans from the foreign and modern banks. The foreign banks financed most of China's overseas trade, supplied credit to foreign industries in China, and extended call loans to the native banks. Their resources of Chinese funds were plentiful since they could always purchase Chinese currency with foreign exchange, and also because, before the advent of the Central Bank of China in 1928, they handled foreign loan flotations of the Chinese government and acted as custodians of customs duties, salt tax, and railway revenues, pledged as security for loans.

The modern Chinese banks supplied credit to central and local government bodies and to the larger Chinese industries whose credit requirements could not be fully satisfied by native banks and whose business methods were regarded by the foreign banks as unreliable according to Western standards. They financed a certain amount of inland trade by accepting checks drawn on native banks in the interior, by providing the latter with short-term loans, and by maintaining current account deposits with native institutions. When the Chinese government began to issue securities, the modern Chinese banks became the most important sellers of bonds as well as the most consistent supporters of the bond market. As time went by, their resources gradually expanded through increase in their note circulation, which enabled them to accumulate silver dollars in the early years, and through an increasing volume of government and private deposits.

A major defect of the Chinese banking structure as depicted above was already apparent long before the war. The growth of an organized discount market was prevented by the domination of the short-term credit market by the native banks. The modern Chinese banks, along with the foreign banks, helped to finance the short-term operations of the native banks, but this type of business involved a large element of risk due to the native banks' custom of granting overdrafts to their clients without requiring collateral security. The modern banks had no desire to extend, or even continue, their credit operations on this uncertain basis; but they did not want to refuse accommodation to the native banks or to raise interest charges on loans to them for fear of losing business to the foreign banks. Instead, they established a rediscount market in 1936 and made efforts to encourage dealings in properly secured bills, in the hope of eliminating the inefficient practices of the native banks and of gaining control over the supply of credit by varying rediscount rates.

These attempts were unsuccessful because of the public's aversion to the new system, which seemed unnecessarily formal and cumbersome, and the obstructive attitude of the native banks, which believed that the modern banks were planning to infiltrate their traditional sphere of activity. The failure to develop a strong discount market must also be attributed to the fact that the three government banks would not pledge their combined support to the project, nor would any one of them individually assume the risk of carrying out the function of rediscount. If the government banks had shown their readiness to back a rediscount market, the psychological effect would probably have been such that over a period a flourishing bill market would have grown. As it was, the unsecured loans of the native banks remained the principal form of short-term commercial credit.

### *The Failure to Develop a Central Banking System*

It may seem strange that China did not develop a central banking system in spite of the founding of two government banks early in the century and the establishment of the Central Bank of China in 1928 with the specific purpose of carrying out the functions of a central bank. There were several reasons for this lack of progress.

The chronic deficit in Chinese government finance, dating from the establishment of the Republic in 1912, dominated policy toward the banks for more than three decades. The government, therefore, viewed official banks more as appendages to its fiscal operations than as institutions whose business was to support and regulate the money markets. The year 1906 witnessed the birth of the first government bank, the Hu-pu (Board of Revenue) Bank, which was reconstituted two years later as the Ta Ching Bank. Its charter granted it sole right of note issue and made it the government fiscal agency. Yet at the same time a second government bank, the Bank of Communications, was given a similar charter on the recommendation of the Board of Posts and Communications. In 1912 the Ta Ching Bank was reorganized under a new charter as the Bank of China; but the Bank of Communications was also granted a new charter, leaving the position as regards the note issue and fiscal agency as unsatisfactory as before. In 1916 the Shanghai Branch of the Bank of China resisted a government instruction to suspend the redemption of notes and to freeze deposits, designed to divert the banks' cash reserves to government uses. The Bank of Communications, on the other hand, acted according to the directive.

After this, public support for the Bank of China increased and its deposits and note issue rose accordingly. But in spite of its enhanced prestige, which gave the Bank of China an opportunity to assume banking leadership, it was prevented from doing so by the powerful political backing afforded the Bank of Communications. In 1928 the government approached the Bank of China and offered to raise it to the position of a central bank on the condition that the government receive a controlling interest. If government finances had been in a sound state at the time, the Bank would undoubtedly have acceded to the request, and would have been able, on the basis of its long experience in banking affairs and its public standing, to embark on the work of a central bank.

As it was, the Bank, aware that it would lose its only protection against excessive government borrowing if it relinquished its independent status, declined the government proposal. The Bank agreed to make a loan to the Government to be used as capital for a central bank, which was then formally constituted as the Central Bank of China. Thus the chance to build a central bank on the solid foundations of the Bank of China was discarded; and the new Central Bank had to pass through the lengthy process of developing the normal facilities of a trading bank before it had either the experience or the prestige to attempt monetary management.

The two government banks were further prevented from developing some of the essential functions of a central bank by the government's indiscriminate granting of the right to issue notes to a large number of other banks. From the very beginning, the foreign banks had circulated their own notes, but it was not until World War I that the modern commercial and provincial government banks began to issue a considerable quantity of notes.

When the war severed China from foreign sources of finance, which for many years had been the principal means of financing the government deficit, the government turned its attention to the modern Chinese banks, using the right of note issue to bargain for loans or overdrafts. Many modern commercial banks were given authority to issue notes in anticipation of their future aid to the government, while at the same time the government banks were threatened with the revocation of their charters or the withdrawal of government support in the event of a bank run if they refused to comply with official demands for credit. The notes issued by the foreign banks reached a maximum of eleven different varieties in 1914; and in 1927 those circulated by the modern commercial banks also totaled eleven kinds. The provincial government banks, which numbered 28 in 1927, issued several different kinds of notes redeemable in small copper or silver coins or in local silver dollars.

Through the years several private commercial banks were deprived of the right of issue when they failed to honor their notes. The silver reserves of the provincial banks were often drained by compulsory loans to the local warlords, and most of their notes became irredeemable and depreciated. Sound notes issued by the two government banks could not be kept in circulation in competition with debased currency, a typical instance of Gresham's Law, and their use was greatly restricted.

With the creation of the Central Bank of China in 1928, the Bank of China and the Bank of Communications expressed their readiness to forego their right to issue notes and to withdraw these from circulation as soon as the government had repaid the outstanding balance of their advances, amounting to CNC $100 million, or no less than 42 per cent of their combined note circulation. The government, however, could not liquidate its debts with the two banks; nor was it willing to consent to the loss of two sources of money supply. Thus, no change was made in the situation and the banks continued to issue notes as before.

Various associations were formed by the Shanghai banks to discharge specific co-ordinating functions, but none of these was strong enough to exercise banking leadership. The Foreign Bankers' Association, the Shanghai (modern) Bankers' Association, and the Shanghai Native Bankers' Association, which supervised the business methods of their respective members, were established early in the century. During the Sino-Japanese hostilities at Shanghai in 1932, the Chinese banks found themselves in the midst of a liquidity crisis and were unable to meet their commitments by selling their investments because of a drastic fall in the value of real estate, which was considered at this time the best investment in the banks' portfolios. Joint Reserve Boards were separately organized by the Shanghai Bankers' Association and the Shanghai Native Bankers' Association to provide the members in need with cash on the security of their illiquid assets.

After the emergency had passed, the Boards remained in operation and administered the clearing institutions of their member banks, namely, the Shanghai Native Banks Clearing Association and the Shanghai Clearing House. The two clearing houses were amalgamated for a short period in 1935, but this attempt at co-operation did not succeed, and the modern and native banks remained self-contained groups. While some progress was made toward self-regulation, no joint organization for the formulation of banking policy was ever formed, and, in the absence of a powerful central bank, the activities of the three different groups of banks could not be co-ordinated to serve community interests.

In 1935 China took the first step toward the formation of a central banking system when she adopted measures recommended by certain foreign advisors, including Sir Frederick Lieth Ross, for far-reaching monetary reforms. The notes of the Central Bank of China, the Bank of China, and the Bank of Communications were recognized as the nation's legal tender, and the issues of the commercial and provincial banks were retired. However, since the government was still unable to repay its outstanding debts to the Bank of China and the Bank of Communications, the suggestion that the note issue should be concentrated in one central banking authority was not adopted before the war.

In 1936 the notes of the Farmers' Bank were made acceptable as legal tender by government order. The 1935 plan contemplated further important changes in the Chinese banking structure. A pivotal clause of the new draft charter for the Central Bank stipulated that the government was not to hold more than 40 per cent of the Bank's capital stock, the remainder to be distributed as follows: private banks

35 per cent, private citizens 20 per cent, and provincial and municipal governments 5 per cent. Eight out of seventeen directors and five out of nine supervisors were to be elected from among private shareholders. This clause, aimed to ensure independence for the Central Bank, failed to gain acceptance at the highest level of government, ratification of the charter was blocked, and no decisive action was taken prior to the war. The draft charter also envisaged that, like the Federal Reserve Bank and the Bank of England, the Central Bank would undertake the function of rediscount, hoping in this way to exercise some control over the money market and the supply of credit, and would be entrusted with the legal reserves of the commercial banks against deposits. Owing to the delay in reorganizing the banking system in accordance with this new conception of the role of the Central Bank of China, these recommendations were unfortunately never put into effect.

Thus at the outbreak of the war in 1937 the Central Bank of China was still struggling for recognition in a banking community dominated by the old and well-established Bank of China and Bank of Communications, and was without the necessary prestige to exercise moral leadership. The right of note issue was shared with these two banks as well as the Farmers' Bank. Since the volume of transactions in the discount market was small, the Central Bank could not significantly influence the supply of credit by manipulating the rediscount rate. It was unable even to conduct open market operations in bonds. The government-bond market, which had taken a long time to develop, was upset by repeated reorganizations of the loan services after 1927; and private investors sought other outlets for their funds, notably in foreign security markets and real estate.

Unable to attract public subscriptions, the government sold the bonds to the banks at prices lower than those ruling in the market. Although the banks received considerably more than 10 per cent yield on these bonds, their resources were drained by the undertaking. Consequently, the government and private banks were unwilling to lower their cash reserve ratios or to further restrict the volume of their private business in order to purchase bonds from the Central Bank. The Central Bank was equally impotent in the foreign exchange market. As a result of the currency reforms of 1935, the control of foreign exchange transactions was transferred from the foreign banks to the Central Bank of China. At the same time the government announced that there would be no limit on sales of foreign exchange by the Central Bank. The Bank was forced to sell foreign exchange at the market rate according to the demands of the other banks, and it could not control supply when conditions warranted.

A final impediment to central banking was that the board of the Central Bank of China was dominated by government nominees, and sound financial principles could not be maintained against considerations of political expediency. On the eve of the war against Japan, therefore, the Central Bank of China was incapable of exercising effective monetary management, a condition which proved to be an outstanding weakness of the financial system of Free China during the long years of military struggle.

### *The Concentration of Banking Activities in Shanghai*

One of the most significant structural features of the Chinese banking system was the concentration of the money market in Shanghai. Originally there were three money markets, Shanghai in South China, Tientsin in North China, and Hankow in Central China, which shared a common background in the increasing activities of the foreign banks, the expansion of foreign trade, and the political stability of foreign settlements. They grew in the same pattern. There was the foreign exchange market in which the various banks quoted both the telegraphic transfer and demand selling rates and the buying rates for four- and six-month bills of exchange and documentary bills. The exchange rates quoted morning and afternoon by the Hong Kong and Shanghai Banking Corporation, a British organization regarded as the leading foreign exchange bank, served as a standard of reference for the rest of the market. There was the native money market under the Native Bank Association quoting internal rates of exchange on domestic remittances and quoting interest rates on interbank deposits and loans, call loans from the foreign banks, overdrafts and fixed loans, and current and fixed deposits. Two kinds of paper money were used: the bank notes issued by the modern Chinese and foreign banks, and the cash orders of the native banks. In Shanghai there were also two stock exchanges, one dealing in foreign securities and the other in domestic securities.

After the establishment of the Republic in 1911, Peking, then the capital of China, enjoyed a short period of prosperity and made a bid to emerge as a rival money market. This attempt was short-lived owing to political instability and over-borrowing by the government at very high rates of interest which undermined the normal functioning of the market. The surrender of their settlements in Tientsin and Hankow by the defeated Central Powers at the end of the First

World War, followed by the return of the British settlement in Hankow, reduced the international importance of these two cities and gave more prominence to Shanghai.

Both foreign and Chinese businessmen regarded this city as offering the greatest protection for trade, and believed that the Western powers would hold this economically strategic position to the last. The persistent civil war in the interior drove more and more Chinese and their wealth to Shanghai, and even the Chinese banks kept their cash reserves there to escape the threat of seizure by warlords. The establishment of the national capital in Nanking in 1928, only 250 miles away from Shanghai, less than a quarter of the distance between Shanghai and Peking, also had the effect of drawing more financial activities to the Shanghai market. Indicative of the growth of the Shanghai money market was the increase in the volume of transactions in the Clearing House from CNC $2,200 million in 1933, its first year of its organization, to $5,800 million in 1936. The silver resources of all the Shanghai banks, native, modern, and foreign, including reserves against note issues, totaled only $47 million in 1917. By 1935 they had advanced to a figure of $330 million, which was estimated to be more than one-half of the total banking reserves of China. When silver stocks held in Tientsin were at their peak (sometime before 1935), the amount was less than a quarter of its figure, while stocks in Hankow were less than one-half of the Tientsin figure.

The opinion was widely held in China that the growth of the Chinese banks in the Treaty Ports, particularly in Shanghai, was a primary obstacle to the development of an integrated banking system regulated by a central bank and free from foreign influence. It was argued that, from the very beginning, the modern Chinese banks had followed the lead of the long-established and experienced foreign banks, and that, lacking the compulsion to formulate their own policies, Chinese bankers did not develop the qualities of initiative and independent thinking that would have enabled them to make a more imaginative contribution to the solution of China's financial problems during the war years. Again, it was believed that the central government had little hope of promoting banking reforms since the foreign banks in Shanghai were outside its jurisdiction. For instance, if the government had resolved to proceed with its plans for strengthening the Central Bank at the time of the currency reforms of 1935, it could not have compelled the foreign banks of Shanghai to comply with the measures contemplated, such as the deposit of cash reserves with the Central Bank. There had grown up and been accepted by both the government and the public the tradition that the Chinese and foreign banks should receive equal treatment. Consequently, the Chinese banks were not required to carry out genuine reforms that were unacceptable to the foreign banks.

This view of the adverse effects of the foreign settlements on the Chinese banking organism contains a large element of truth, but, in all fairness, we must take into account certain aspects of foreign influence which were favorable. It is doubtful whether the modern Chinese banks could have survived the first years of growth if they had not been sheltered against some of the predatory warlords. In the absence of foreign settlements, the development of Chinese banking beyond the native bank stage might have had to await the coming of a much more stable and enlightened political regime than had been experienced before the 1930's. Moreover, the modern Chinese banks could not have achieved an efficiency unrivaled by any other form of Chinese business enterprise if they had not patterned their internal organization and operational techniques on the Western model with the assistance of the foreign banks.

Clearly, some of the major defects of the Chinese banks—their concentration in Shanghai and their lack of independence in thought and vision—were not derived so much from their common origin in the international settlements as from their continuing need for protection because of the political immaturity of China. The advent of the Nationalist government did not entirely change the view of the banks that their location in Shanghai might mitigate against any unreasonable credit demands the government might raise; and, although the modern banks desired to extend their business into the interior, where they could operate without competition from the foreign banks, they were not prepared to take the risk in the absence of legal checks to local government borrowing. Even in Shanghai itself the banks were not entirely free from central government interference, as is illustrated by the following incident.

On March 28, 1935, the government acquired a controlling interest in the Bank of China and the Bank of Communications. The government originally held CNC $5 million of the capital stock of the Bank of China out of a total of $25 million. The private shareholders of the Bank of China were compelled to issue another $15 million new shares which the government purchased with a promissory note. Similar tactics were used by the government to acquire a majority interest in the Bank of Communications. Since the shareholders of the two banks were perfectly satisfied with the progress achieved under private management, they would not have yielded to the government except under extreme duress. Occurrences of this description shook public confidence in the modern banking system and made the banks themselves unwilling to venture beyond the comparatively safe precincts of Shanghai.

For several reasons, then, the private banks remained attracted to Shanghai and in 1937 were scarcely fitted to assume the responsibility of guiding China through the difficult years of war inflation. When the coastal cities fell to the hands of the Japanese and the government retreated to areas in which there was no organized banking system, there was no way of transferring the personnel and resources of the modern banks to the interior; and the rudimentary credit facilities existing there were no substitute for the well-developed institutions of Shanghai.

### *The Deficiency of Credit in the Interior*

The establishment of the Republic in 1911 marked a turning point in the fortunes of the rural sector of the economy. The continuing civil war which ensued devastated large sections of the rural areas, prompting a withdrawal of the propertied class to the safety of the Treaty Ports, and causing a drop in the price of land which destroyed a large part of the assets of the farming communities. The old credit system was faced with destruction, but no new system was created to take its place. Although some of the modern banks extended credit to farmers, this was a drop in the ocean compared to their real needs.

The old native credit system of the interior commonly comprised four kinds of credit machinery: the native banks in the larger cities, the commercial firms which extended purchase credit to the small traders and farmers of the towns, the pawnshops scattered throughout the larger communities, and the individual money lenders in the villages. As poverty spread through the countryside after 1911, the native banks found their deposits falling and debts accumulating, and, short of credit accommodation from the modern banks, lapsed into a state of acute insolvency. The commercial firms no longer provided adequate purchase credit because they could not obtain sufficient accommodation from the native banks. The pawnshops, besides being affected by the universal credit shortage, found the articles pledged to them deteriorating in quality and the disposal of unredeemed pledges increasingly difficult. They curtailed their business, and appraised the value of articles so rigidly that only a very small loan could be obtained by the pawner. Credit institutions could not lend freely because they lacked the resources; and individuals could not borrow because they could offer no acceptable security as assurance for loans as the price of land had dropped to such an extent that it was no longer considered a safe collateral. Thus primary producers were deprived of the credit facilities which had served them tolerably well in the past.

Two events of the early 1930's contributed toward a further worsening in the rural situation. The emigration of the wealthy landowners to the coast after 1911 had imposed a drain on the silver reserves of rural financial institutions which would have been much more severe if the outflow of funds involved had not been offset by a normal surplus in the interior's "balance of trade" with the coast. However, when world food prices reached a low point in 1931, China was flooded with imports of cheap foreign produce which induced a decline in internal agricultural prices. The surplus in the interior's "balance of trade" with the coast turned into a chronic deficit; and from then on, the inland was rapidly drained of its silver reserves. Increases in the export price of silver in 1933 and 1934 aggravated this trend since it became profitable for Chinese merchants to accumulate silver in the interior and sell it overseas.

The second adverse development was the temporary suspension of the Shanghai money market at the outbreak of the Sino-Japanese hostilities in August 1932, when the banks ceased all trading operations for a week and chaotic conditions persisted for some time. At the end of the year the native banks in the rural sector, which were in grave financial straits, seized the opportunity to refuse repayment of debts they owed to the native banks of Shanghai on the ground that they were unable to recover loans granted to commercial enterprises, farmers, and traders in the interior. This failure to observe the traditional custom of settling accounts at the end of the Chinese year made the Shanghai money market reluctant to finance native banks of the interior, almost severing the vital credit link between country and coast. Thus the alienation of the Shanghai banks coupled with the exhaustion of the silver stocks of the interior severely weakened the remaining foundations of the old credit system.

### *The Retarded Growth of Savings Deposits*

The age-long habit of the people of hoarding gold and silver and investing in land reflected their lack of confidence in the banks. Before the establishment of modern banks the main source of deposits for the native banks was government revenues. Besides public funds, the native banks had deposits by the merchants; however, the latter did not deposit their funds for safekeeping but primarily to be able to overdraw their accounts when necessary. There were few idle deposits under those conditions.

The foreign banks were able to attract short-term deposits from wealthy Chinese in the Treaty Ports, but it took the Chinese modern banks a long time to build up their credit to the point where their short-term deposits became sizable. Long-term deposits never reached comparable size.

Though a few banks had accepted savings deposits before the establishment of the Republic in 1912, the amounts they attracted were small. Beginning in the 1920's the modern banks began to promote savings by adopting Western methods, and eventually the native banks followed suit. Even the government banks began to compete for savings. Special savings banks and savings societies were organized. By 1933, savings had climbed to 9.5 per cent of total deposits of all Chinese banks in China; no information is available covering savings deposits in foreign banks. At the end of 1937 government banks held about CNC $190 million in savings deposits, including Post and Savings Bank deposits; this was 9 per cent of total deposits, while demand deposits were 60 per cent and time deposits were 31 per cent of the total at the time. It is probably safe to assume that total savings deposits in that year were less than 10 per cent of total bank deposits.

However, all banks had their main offices or branches in the large cities and maintained few branches in the interior. A large sector of the people therefore lacked effective savings facilities. Although the Chinese post office accepted savings and set up a special banking department to serve this purpose, lack of trained staff limited the service to a relatively few branch post offices.

What progress was made in the promotion of savings was due in part to high interest rates averaging about 10 per cent per annum, and in part to the growth of public confidence in the modern Chinese banks. Had the government been able to provide more facilities in the interior and in rural areas, the bank-savings habit might have been better developed. But the government neglected the promotion of savings, the banks focused their attention on the large cities, and the warlords, controlling their provincial banking institutions, abused their power by arbitrarily stopping redemption of bank notes or imposing moratoria on the payment of deposits. Thus, when the government wished to attract popular savings to withdraw purchasing power during the war years, it found too late that people had not learned to save in banks.

## 3. The Role of the Money Market in the Expansion of Aggregate Demand: 1937–1940

After the Japanese invasion had begun, the government tried to speed the evacuation of public and private industry from the coast to the interior, to stimulate the growth of enterprises already established inland, and to increase the flow to Western China of commodities imported from abroad or produced in occupied regions by extending liberal credit accommodation through the government banks to manufacturers and merchants.

When the Sino-Japanese hostilities reached Shanghai, the banking center of China, in August 1937 a moratorium was declared by the government in order to check a run on the banks caused by the general uneasiness. The intent was to limit the withdrawal of cash from current accounts. The moratorium succeeded in averting a panic in the Shanghai money market, but at the same time affected the money market in the interior unfavorably. In the first place, because of the moratorium, the interior could no longer obtain funds from the Shanghai banks which had been its only outside source of credit. Secondly, there were no alternative banking facilities in the interior. As a consequence, the government initiated a most liberal private credit policy for the interior. Unfortunately, this was done without much forethought of effective credit control or concern for the eventual need to neutralize the expansionary effect upon aggregate demand.

Under this policy the government banks were instructed to organize a Joint Loan and Discount Committee, with its head office in Shanghai and branches in leading commercial centers, to cater to the credit need of the interior by making joint loans to which all the government banks would contribute. The Committee was made responsible for ensuring a plentiful supply of credit to basic defense industries and other enterprises of strategic importance, but it dealt only with government bank loans in excess of CNC $500,000, which it was empowered to approve or reject. Since inland trade was almost at a standstill because of the inactivity of the Shanghai money market, and very few commercial bills could be found in the market, all the actual lending of the Committee took the form of industrial and commercial loans.

As is shown in Table 54, the supply of credit to industry and commerce increased greatly in the first years of the war as a result of the government's liberal credit policy. The outstanding balance of industrial and commercial loans advanced from CNC $2,220 million at 1937 year-end to CNC $3,592 million at the end of 1939. This was an increase of 40 per cent in money value, and, allowing for price increases in the interim, of about 19 per cent in real value. The rise of CNC $1,092 million in total private credit during 1939 amounted to 47 per cent of advances to the government in the same year. Thus in the early stages of inflation the expansion of credit to the private sector of the economy was an important factor in generating increases in income. But a reversal of government credit policy toward the end of 1940 slowed down the expansion of private credit considerably, and advances to the government rose much more rapidly than private credit.

The government banks were responsible for the greater part of the private credit expansion in the interior; and in the three years to the close of 1940 their loans rose from 65 per cent to 68 per cent of total credit granted to private enterprise by all the modern banks. Meanwhile, commercial and provincial bank loans declined from 33 per cent to 26 per cent of the total. However, the Joint Loan and Discount Committee was unable to obtain concerted action from the government banks, and was superseded in September 1939 by a Joint Board of Administration of the Government Banks, presided over by Generalissimo Chiang Kai-shek.

Despite the government's endeavors to stimulate the flow of credit to farmers, the supply of rural credit was only 5 per cent of total private credit in 1940. In April 1938 the government introduced a plan to increase the note circulation of the provincial banks in the country towns in order to extend the scope of their operations. In the belief that notes of small denominations were more likely to remain in circulation than the larger denominations in farming districts, where average income levels were extremely low, the government decided to allow the provincial banks to obtain CNC $1 notes and subsidiary coin notes from the government banks. The notes were to be issued to the provincial banks in the form of a loan, 50 per cent of which was to be secured on farm or manufactured products, agricultural bills, or deeds to factory buildings. The banks were then to extend credit to local manufacturers or farmers out of these sums. However, since there were few factories or warehouses in the interior, and agricultural bills were seldom used, the provincial banks were unable to provide securities for such a loan and the scheme ended in failure.

In June 1938 an Agricultural Credit Administration was organized with capital partly subscribed by the government and partly by the banks. Its main functions were to buy and sell produce on behalf of the government and to promote the growth of rural financial institutions. It was thought that consumer and producer co-operative societies in the interior could act as the basic credit distributors. However, the amount of funds initially supplied by the government banks for this project was very limited, and further action had to be taken toward the close of 1939 to make more credit available in the rural districts. The government banks were directed to devote a larger

TABLE 54. GOVERNMENT, COMMERCIAL, AND PROVINCIAL BANK CREDIT, 1937–1945

(CNC $ millions)

| | Outstanding Balance of Industrial and Commercial Credit | | | | | | Outstanding Balance of Rural Credits[1] | | Outstanding Balance of Total Private Credit |
|---|---|---|---|---|---|---|---|---|---|
| | Government Banks[1] | | Commercial and Provincial Banks[2] | | Total | | | | |
| Year | Amount | Percentage | Amount | Percentage | Amount | Percentage | Amount | Percentage | Amount |
| 1937 | 1,471 | 65.3 | 749 | 33.2 | 2,220 | 98.5 | 35 | 1.5 | 2,255 |
| 1938 | 1,696 | 64.8 | 851 | 32.6 | 2,547 | 97.4 | 67 | 2.6 | 2,614 |
| 1939 | 2,578 | 69.6 | 1,014 | 27.4 | 3,592 | 97.0 | 114 | 3.0 | 3,706 |
| 1940 | 2,801 | 68.1 | 1,102 | 26.8 | 3,903 | 94.9 | 211 | 5.1 | 4,114 |
| 1941 | 3,095 | 55.3 | 2,029 | 36.4 | 5,124 | 91.7 | 465 | 8.3 | 5,589 |
| 1942 | 7,606 | 67.0 | 3,111 | 27.0 | 10,717 | 94.0 | 685 | 6.0 | 11,402 |
| 1943 | 15,950 | 70.0 | 5,140 | 22.6 | 21,090 | 92.6 | 1,678 | 7.4 | 22,758 |
| 1944 | 29,481 | 72.9 | 8,227 | 20.4 | 37,708 | 93.3 | 2,715 | 6.7 | 40,423 |
| 1945 | 151,142 | 87.6 | 16,201 | 9.4 | 167,343 | 97.0 | 5,126 | 3.0 | 172,469 |

| Year | Increase of Total Private Credit | Government Advances[3] | Total Credit Increase | Increase in all Bank Deposits[4] | Deposit Increase as Per Cent of Credit Increase[4] |
|---|---|---|---|---|---|
| 1937–38 | — | 1,195 | — | — | — |
| 1938 | 357 | 854 | 1,211 | 847 | 70.0 |
| 1939 | 1,092 | 2,310 | 3,402 | 1,905 | 56.0 |
| 1940 | 408 | 3,834 | 4,242 | 1,777 | 41.8 |
| 1941 | 1,475 | 9,443 | 10,918 | 5,979 | 54.7 |
| 1942 | 5,813 | 20,081 | 25,894 | 9,146 | 35.3 |
| 1943 | 11,356 | 40,857 | 52,213 | 12,784 | 24.5 |
| 1944 | 17,665 | 140,090 | 157,755 | 69,614 | 44.1 |
| 1945 | 132,046 | 1,043,257 | 1,175,303 | 432,543 | 36.8 |

[1] Based on the data of the report compiled by the Joint Board of Administration of Government Banks, including credits to public enterprises and some non-profit working organizations and government agencies.

[2] Based on the data in W. Y. Chang, *op. cit.*, p. 164.

[3] Based on the Statement of Revenue compiled by the Statistical Department of the Ministry of Finance.

[4] Government Bank deposits are based on the report of the Joint Board of Administration; Commercial and Provincial Bank deposits on W. Y. Chang, *op. cit.*, p. 164.

proportion of their funds to financing primary production in Szechwan province as the strength of the resistance effort was to a large extent contingent on the fuller exploitation of its fertile lands and rich natural resources. The banks were also instructed to distribute their funds as evenly as possible over the other provinces, to simplify the procedure for granting loans, and to raise the amount of individual accommodation. Unfortunately, funds for agricultural credit were spread over such a large area that they could not have influenced production very significantly even if every cent of the sums involved had actually reached the farmer. In practice, most of the co-operative societies were organized in haste by landowners or party members designated by the local branches of the Kuomintang. In some cases bank loans were used for purchasing agricultural products for personal gain in anticipation of further shortages and price increases. This speculative activity set a bad example for farmers, who immediately followed suit by hoarding their produce instead of using loans to raise output.

Thus, in the early stages of the war, the government's easy credit policy was far more successful in the new urban centers on which it based its authority and power than in the more remote agricultural communities. Since modern banking institutions had not been developed before the war in the agricultural areas of the interior, which, in addition, suffered from poor transport facilities, the impetus to inflation generated by credit expansion was felt in the first instance largely in the urban centers only, except, of course, for the effects of secondary income expansion. Even in the new urban centers there were only moderate price increases, accompanied by some rise of the interest rates, until 1940, since the public was still willing to hold liquid assets and to maintain its bank deposits in a not too active state. The annual increase of deposits, which had fallen soon after the Japanese invasion, more than doubled in 1939 to reach 56 per cent of the total expansion of government and private credit. At the same time, Chungking was still receiving locally produced and imported goods from Shanghai, while production in the interior also registered some increase. As a result of all these factors, prices did not rise in proportion to the increase in the money supply, and the full impact of the credit expansion on price levels was not yet felt.

## 4. Private Credit and the Expansion of Aggregate Demand: 1940–1945

Financial and monetary stability in Free China deteriorated rapidly after the middle of 1940, when a severe crop failure in Szechwan province caused a sudden spurt in food prices. Anticipating all-round increases in wholesale prices, many city businessmen immediately attempted to accumulate stocks of raw materials and the farm population began to hoard produce. These reactions to poor harvests precipitated a sharp rise of the general price level. The easy credit policy of the private banks was popularly held responsible for the upward movement in prices, even though they supplied only one-fourth of total bank loans to private enterprise at this time.

For the first time the government now imposed restrictions on private bank credit operations. The quantitative and qualitative control measures introduced proved temporarily successful in checking the expansion of bank advances in the closing months of 1940. The annual rate of increase in industrial and commercial credit extended by the government banks dropped from 50 per cent in 1939 to 9 per cent in 1940 principally because advances to public enterprises and organizations were curtailed. During the same period the rate of expansion of credit by commercial banks also declined from 19 per cent to only 9 per cent.

In 1941, however, commercial bank credit again began to increase with great rapidity. Although the accelerated credit expansion was partly an unavoidable result of the rising general price level, a more important reason was found in the increase in the banks' credit to their own subsidiary enterprises. The banks' direct participation in business was increased in order to enhance their profits to meet the rising costs of administrative overhead and to protect the real value of their capital and reserves. In a few instances the objective was purely speculative. The government's attempt to restrict private bank loans to enterprises producing essential goods for defense and supplying daily necessities met with no success.

Government bank credit to the private sector resumed its steep rate of increase during 1942, mainly because of an increase in credit demands from private business. It involved the granting of larger loans to public enterprises such as the salt administration and the government commodity supply agencies with a view to stabilizing prices by raising production.

Beginning in 1943 the government banks were no longer able to resist demands for advances from public organizations as the flow of appropriations to the latter had become more irregular. In fact, much of the private credit extended by government banks at this time was equivalent to government appropriations. The government banks now also assumed the responsibility for essential business loans, a function which had been deserted by the commercial banks, which were now devoting their funds to their own enterprises. However, except for the Central Bank of China, the government banks also owned all manner of enterprises. Their business holdings had developed from their original mission to promote industries for which private funds were unavailable; but gradually their direct participation, in part through the financing of inventories in inflationary times, became indistinguishable from speculation. The increasingly close relationship between the banks and their enterprises caused the latter to depend increasingly on their mother banks for credits.

The government attempted to rationalize the extension of private credit by delimiting spheres of credits as between the government banks. But the inherent weakness of the national banking structure, coupled with pressures exercised by the various public bodies, defeated all attempts to delimit the banks' spheres of activity or to curb credit expansion.

Throughout the war, government banks were the main source of industrial and commercial credit loans to both public and private enterprises and non-profit organizations. Government credit for these purposes rose from CNC $2,801 million to CNC $151,142 million from 1940 to 1945, compared to a rise in commercial and provincial bank credit from CNC $1,102 million to CNC $16,201 million. The latter represented 39.3 per cent of the government credit in 1940 and only 10 per cent in 1945. The government itself, then, was the primary contributor to the increase in aggregate demand, both through its inflationary deficit financing and through its unchecked expansion of private credit.

Beginning in 1942, according to published statistics, expansion of private credit by the commercial and provincial banks was relatively slower than that of the government banks. But these statistics do not show the full picture as some credits were omitted from the banks' books in order to avoid additional government interference with their flourishing fortnight loans and other types of black-market credit operations. An estimate made in 1942 places the call deposits of the native banks at about 66 per cent of their total deposits; 96 per cent of their total advances were short-term commercial loans. These figures strongly suggest that credit and its source were both of a short-term nature, primarily suited only to speculative purposes.

While private credit and advances to government grew, the government failed to find any solution to the rural credit problem despite the expedients adopted soon after the retreat into the interior and the attempted concentration of all rural banking business in the Farmers' Bank in 1942. As a measure of the growing deficiency of credit outside the main urban centers, it is significant that the volume of rural loans declined from 8.3 per cent of total private credit in 1941 to 3.0 per cent in 1945. Lack of banking facilities and inadequate means of communication remained intractable obstacles to progress in this sphere of banking.

Unfortunately, the fundamental weakness of wartime finance remained: the overwhelming volume of bank advances to the government. In 1942 government advances were increasing at 3–1/2 times the rate of private credit expansion; by 1945 they were rising at 8 times the rate of increase in private credit.

The attempt to restrict private credit, therefore, seems inconsequential when set against the overwhelming increase in the money supply emanating from government deficit spending.

## 5. The Impact of Wartime Credit Expansion on Aggregate Demand

The preceding review points out quite clearly the role of credit expansion and the government's part in it as the wartime inflation ran its course. From the end of 1937 to the end of 1945 the outstanding balance of total private credits rose from CNC $2,255 million to CNC $172,469 million, representing an expansion of CNC $170,212 million, which was counterbalanced by an increase of fixed deposits and savings deposits in government banks of CNC $60,109 million (Table 55). No complete statistics on fixed and savings deposits in the commercial and provincial banks are available. In all probability,

Table 55. Government Bank, Commercial and Provincial Bank Deposits, 1937–1945
(CNC $ millions)

| | Government Bank Deposits | | | | Commercial and Provincial Banks—All Deposits | Total Deposits—All Banks |
|---|---|---|---|---|---|---|
| Year | Current | Fixed | Savings | Total | | |
| 1937 | 1,318 | 685 | 188 | 2,191 | 1,115 | 3,306 |
| 1938 | 1,808 | 928 | 251 | 2,987 | 1,166 | 4,153 |
| 1939 | 2,408 | 1,906 | 312 | 4,626 | 1,433 | 6,059 |
| 1940 | 3,297 | 2,172 | 533 | 6,002 | 1,884 | 7,836 |
| 1941 | 6,446 | 3,382 | 1,104 | 10,932 | 2,833 | 13,815 |
| 1942 | 15,039 | 1,782 | 2,976 | 19,797 | 3,164 | 22,961 |
| 1943 | 22,811 | 891 | 7,387 | 31,089 | 4,656 | 35,745 |
| 1944 | 78,887 | 1,213 | 15,456 | 95,556 | 9,803 | 105,359 |
| 1945 | 466,190 | 5,289 | 55,693 | 527,172 | 10,740 | 537,912 |

however, non-demand deposits registered very little increase during this period in view of the predominance of their short-term funds and speculative use of bank deposits. Since certain other bank loans were not recorded, these opposing factors may be disregarded, and the banks' wartime contribution to the increase of money supply estimated to total nearly CNC $110,000 million (CNC $170,202 million minus CNC $60,109 million).

Comparing this estimated net credit expansion with the wartime deficit financing of CNC $1,314,941 million, one cannot fail to notice the overwhelming role played by the government borrowing in the increase in money supply. The government's role was even more important than these figures suggest inasmuch as CNC $149,671 million of the CNC $165,123 million increase in industrial and commercial loan accounts originated from the government banks, and the greater part of the increase in rural credit could be traced to the same source. Moreover, as mentioned earlier, some of the loans were extended to government agencies which had received insufficient budget appropriations. Thus, insofar as this was true, the government merely shifted a part of the financing of its operations from deficit financing through the budget, that is to say, by direct bank advances to the Ministry of Finance, to individual borrowing from the banks by its agencies. The government was not only the source of deficit financing but also, through its individual organs, an additional borrower from the banking system in the course of the latter's ordinary banking operations and, through the government banks, the major supplier of credit to the non-governmental borrowers.

## 6. Private Credit and the Expansion of Aggregate Demand in the Postwar Period

### *The Money Market*

After the victory over Japan one of the chief factors which had shaped the development of the Chinese banking system ceased to be operative. The treaty nations relinquished their extraterritorial rights, and the international settlements in Shanghai were abolished. Here was a golden opportunity for China, fresh from the bitter experience of financial mismanagement during the war years, to reorientate her monetary and fiscal policies and to remedy some of the more malignant defects in her banking system. Unfortunately, the government continued spending at a phenomenally high rate, concentrating its efforts on trying to stabilize directly the internal price levels and the foreign exchange rates, to the neglect of long overdue banking reforms.

The government hoped to gain support for its financial policies from the existing monetary institutions by restoring the Shanghai money market to its former position of leadership. The foreign banks reopened, as head offices of the government banks were moved back from Chungking. The latter continued to handle commercial business, and to act as fiscal agencies for the government and as bankers for government enterprises. No attempt was made to stamp out the unsound practices developed in the wartime inflation.

During the war the money market in the occupied area had become morally and legally uncontrolled after the withdrawal of the government banks and the leading modern banks to Chungking. When the foreign banks closed down, Western banking methods and procedures gradually disappeared, and there was a prolific growth of new banks, the number of modern and native banks almost doubling between 1938 and 1945. The market was dominated by the activities of speculators, who, at the beginning, dealt in foreign exchange, gold, and foreign commodities, and later turned their attention to Chinese securities, which increased in number from about 40 listed on the stock exchange in 1937 to 199 in 1945. At the same time, as noted earlier, the banks in Free China also engaged in operations of a dubious nature. The government banks began to participate directly in industry and favored their subsidiaries with special credit facilities; many banks became deeply involved in speculative transactions. When the attempt was made to restore the prewar status in Shanghai, these wartime malpractices, accompanied by the general lowering of banking standards, contributed to the instability of the money market.

Further developments now tended to weaken the authority of the Central Bank in the money market. In the first place, although the Central Bank through the Board of Joint Administration could regulate the three other government banks to some extent, the operations of the commercial banks remained largely outside its control. As a result of the government's postwar policy to encourage the growth of commercial banks, the size of the unregulated portion of the money market was increased. To be sure, immediately after the cessation of hostilities 74 modern banks and 92 native banks in Shanghai were suspended for having collaborated with the puppet Japanese government; but during the next two years the number of modern banks in Shanghai again rose from 71 to 145, and that of native banks from 48 to 78. With meager capital resources at their disposal and very low deposits, the new banking concerns tried to cover their increasing overhead expenses by making short-term loans at the black-market rate of interest. They were used by their customers as a source of funds for speculative operations. Skyrocketing prices made the purchase and resale of commodities, gold, and American or Hong Kong dollars increasingly profitable; and people endeavored to borrow to the limit from the private banks or individual moneylenders for a day or only a few days in order to widen their speculative activities. The demand of the public for this type of day-to-day advances from private banks or individual lenders became so great that the amount of normal credit accommodation for industry and commerce was severely reduced.

The money market was further disturbed by the growing intrusion of politics into banking and business. Under one-party rule it is inevitable that the party should try to extend its dominance into every part of the economy. Also, the representatives or appointees of the party inevitably find that their acts and opinions carry a psychological impact above and beyond their outright consequence. Anticipating the promulgation of China's new constitution after the war, which among other things would end the payment of party expenses from public funds, the leader of the party encouraged Kuomintang members to occupy leading positions in banking and to operate industrial and commercial enterprises financed with party funds. It was only natural that the party appointees managing these industrial and commercial enterprises, in their zeal to produce large profits, tended to rely more on cheap and easy credit from government banks than on gradual expansion and more traditional business methods. The result, likewise inevitable, was a conflict between the views of the professional bankers and the party views. This conflict, though persistently minimized by the government and party leaders, seriously impeded the smooth management of the money market by the Central Bank.

Thus the war and postwar years saw the rapid growth of large numbers of new commercial banks that had developed financial techniques suitable for the exploitation of an inflationary situation but not much concerned with community responsibilities. The Central Bank's powers of control were weakened both by this diversification of the money market and by the government's close surveillance of Central Bank policies, which made the other banks suspicious of its intentions. Moreover, the hostility with which the government was viewed because of its failure to combat inflation lowered its prestige to such an extent that it was unable to secure the voluntary co-operation of the private banks. These factors partly explain why, in 1948, the money market became uncontrollable, either by the Central Bank or the government, and reverted to a state of chaos resembling that in Shanghai in the closing months of the war.

### *Private Credit Becomes the Major Factor in the Growth of Aggregate Demand*

When the occupied areas were liberated, large amounts of capital were required by the government and by private industries on the coast to replace obsolete or damaged equipment and to build up inventories of raw materials, supplies of which had been cut off since Pearl Harbor. Because of their lack of resources, the commercial banks were powerless to assist in meeting these needs. Although their total deposits at the end of 1945 were 9.5 times the prewar level, the real value at 1937 prices was only 0.4 per cent of the prewar value of deposits. The three government banks, however, had fared better—their deposits were 10 per cent of the prewar figure in 1937 dollars—and they had access to the resources of the Central Bank, which could increase its advances by printing more notes. Industry and commerce were almost entirely dependent on the government banks for credit supplies in the first months after the war. As government banks exercised little discrimination in extending rehabilitation loans to industry, the government directed in January 1946 that loans of this description should not be approved until the Ministry of Economic Affairs had established the bona fide nature of the enterprise concerned. Nevertheless, the government continued to sponsor large loans to merchants for the purpose of increasing market supplies of specific commodities. Commodity credits began with the loans to Shanghai merchants to enable them to procure rice from the interior. It was hoped that this would halt the rise in food prices in coastal districts. Many similar loans followed for the purchase of important commodities such as silk cocoons, tea, salt, wheat, and tobacco leaf and other raw materials. The government also attempted to facilitate the process of rural reconstruction by means of loans and technical assistance.

In order to reduce the strain on the government banks in the task of re-establishing normal conditions of production and trade, the Central Bank took steps in May 1946 to recruit the resources of the commercial banks. At least 50 per cent of commercial bank loans were to be granted to agricultural, manufacturing, and mining enterprises, to merchants distributing daily necessities, or to exporters. In addition, groups of commercial banks were invited to provide loan funds for allocation by the Central Bank to merchants and industrialists, on the understanding that up to 70 per cent of the joint loan contracts of the commercial banks could be rediscounted or remortgaged with the government banks. This represented a noticeable relaxation of the controls introduced in 1942, under which access to such facilities by the commercial banks had been greatly restricted.

However, the commercial banks were still permitted to make unsecured loans in the form of overdrafts. Consequently, little enthusiasm was shown for this proposal of the Central Bank, and the commercial banks continued to reserve their resources for the use of their regular customers. The responsibility for satisfying the more essential credit requirements of the community remained with the government banks. As a result, private credit by government banks expanded rapidly from CNC $151 billion in 1945 to CNC $1,224.6 billion in 1946. By the end of 1946 total credit extended by the commercial banks, estimated at CNC $353 billion, was no more than 28.8 per cent of the amount loaned by all the government banks to the private sector (Table 56).

Some of the credit expansion by government banks would not have been necessary if the economic conditions of the country had been more favorable. Sources of private credit might have been fostered through the repatriation of domestic capital from abroad, the inflow of foreign capital following the resumption of operations by foreign banks, and domestic capital within the country seeking investment. Industrial rehabilitation could have been adequately financed had reasonable economic stability prevailed—particularly in Shanghai, the traditional financial center of China.

Given the unavailability of the above sources of capital, domestic credit expansion was resorted to by the financial and banking authorities, who hoped to increase production through credit expansion and to stabilize prices through increasing production. However, the inflationary impact of the rapidly expanding flow of government expenditure, once felt by the people, could not be overcome by credit expansion.

On the contrary, once the business community became generally aware of the profit possibilities offered by cheap credit from government banks and the rising prices, increasing reliance on these virtually automatic profits psychologically precluded any reduction in the rate of credit expansion. The accelerated rate of credit expansion merely aggravated the general inflationary spiral without any visibly beneficial effect on output.

Thus, while government banks increased their private credit eightfold in 1946, the price level increased 7 times. Again, in the following year, in spite of the government's "tight" credit policy, private credit

TABLE 56. GOVERNMENT AND COMMERCIAL BANKS, CREDIT TO PRIVATE SECTOR, AND GOVERNMENT, 1946–1948
(CNC $ millions)

| | Outstanding Balance of Industrial and Commercial Credit | | | | | | | | | |
|---|---|---|---|---|---|---|---|---|---|
| | Government Banks[1] | | Commercial and Provincial Banks[3] | | | | | | |
| Year | Amount | Percentage of Total | Shanghai 60 Per Cent of All Cities | Other Cities 40 Per Cent | All Cities | Percentage of Total | Total Industrial and Commercial Credit | Outstanding Balance of Rural Credit[5] | Grand Total—Outstanding Balance of Private Credit |
| 1945 | 151,142 | 90.3 | — | — | 16,201 | 9.7 | 167,343 | 5,126 | 172,469 |
| 1946 | 1,224,625 | 77.8 | 211,877 | 141,251 | 353,128 | 22.2 | 1,577,753 | 49,528 | 1,627,281 |
| 1947 | 17,344,376 | 76.0 | 3,279,024 | 2,186,016 | 5,465,040 | 24.0 | 22,809,416 | 624,667 | 23,434,083 |
| 1948 (Jan.–June) | 173,840,702 | 89.0 | 12,842,784 | 8,561,856 | 21,404,639 | 11.0 | 195,245,341 | 6,000,000 | 201,245,341 |

| Year | Increase of Total Private Credit | Increase of Bank Advances to Government[2] | Total Credit Increase | Increase in All Bank Deposits[4] | Deposit Increase Per Cent of Credit Increase |
|---|---|---|---|---|---|
| 1945 | 132,046 | 1,043,257 | 1,175,303 | 432,553 | 36.8 |
| 1946 | 1,454,812 | 5,513,670 | 6,968,482 | 5,381,555 | 77.2 |
| 1947 | 21,806,802 | 27,075,033 | 48,881,835 | 24,436,006 | 50.1 |
| 1948 (Jan.–June) | 177,811,258 | 166,185,674 | 343,996,942 | 184,109,984 | 53.5 |

[1] Based on the report of Central Bank of China, including four government banks, Central Trust, Post Savings Bank, and Central Co-operative Bank.

[2] Year 1945 based on the Statement of Revenue compiled by the Statistical Department of the Ministry of Finance, years 1946 and 1947 based on the data in W. Y. Chang, *op. cit.*, p. 244; year 1948 based on the data of the report of Central Bank of China.

[3] The figure for 1945, including all commercial and provincial banks, is based on W. Y. Chang, *op. cit.*, p. 164; for years 1946–48, the column entitled "Shanghai" is based on the statistics compiled by the Auditing Department of Central Bank of China; amounts for other cities are estimated as two-thirds of that of Shanghai.

[4] Based on statistics compiled by Auditing Department of Central Bank of China.

[5] 1945–47 based on data of report compiled by Board of Joint Administration of Government Banks; 1948 figure was the amount of allocation by the Board.

increased 14 times and the general price index in Shanghai multiplied 14.7 times. By the first half of 1948 the volume of private credit expansion had reached a level comparable to that of bank advances to the government. Deficit financing and the expansion of private credit were now equally important in generating inflation.

While the expansion of private credit may have helped to increase production in 1946, several adverse factors more than annulled these potential deflationary effects. A strong wave of capital flight followed the promulgation of the government's Emergency Measure of 1947, which attempted to restrict the black market in foreign exchange. Reduced availability of foreign exchange entailed a gradual tightening of imported raw materials and equipment. Interest rates and labor costs rose, while the widespread hoarding of goods for speculation caused shortages even of domestic goods. The purchasing power of the poorer classes declined. Communist disturbances affected the entire scene. As a result of these factors, industries were forced to curtail output. Early in 1948, for example, the cotton textile industry curtailed its operating hours by 20 per cent; about half of the tobacco industry suspended operations; the cement industry reduced its output; the rubber industry decreased production to less than two-thirds of the previous period; 50 out of 124 cosmetic manufacturing enterprises suspended operations. The supposedly beneficial effects of liberal credit expansion on productive enterprises anticipated by the government were thus wholly nullified by the inflationary pressures generated by the government deficit financing, political instability, and the foreign exchange stringency.

Another strong inflationary influence was the low ratio of fixed and savings deposits to current deposits, which is shown in Table 57. Moreover, only slightly more than one-half of total new credit led to bank deposits of any kind (Table 56). This was brought about mainly by the need for currency on the part of the community at large. While bank credits in most Western countries create approximately equivalent amounts of deposits, this was not so in China because banking facilities were only accessible to residents and businesses in the larger cities. The higher prices rose, the more people needed currency—and the more currency was required by industrial and commercial paymasters. As restrictions on commodity speculations and black-market operations in gold and foreign exchange tightened, such transactions were increasingly carried on in currency outside the banks.

Inflation in China was thus aggravated not only by the expansion of credit itself, but also by increased velocity of circulation, demonstrated by the shift from deposits to currency. Borrowers from government

TABLE 57. GOVERNMENT, COMMERCIAL, AND PROVINCIAL BANK DEPOSITS[1]
(CNC $ millions)

| Year | Government Bank Deposits | | | | Commercial and Provincial Bank Deposits | | | Total Deposits All Banks |
|---|---|---|---|---|---|---|---|---|
| | Current | Fixed | Savings | Total | Current | Fixed | Total | |
| 1945 | 466,190 | 5,289 | 55,693 | 527,172 | — | — | 9,448 | 536,620 |
| 1946 | 5,028,773 | 19,747 | 372,592 | 5,421,112 | 426,721 | 70,342 | 497,063 | 5,918,175 |
| 1947 | 23,894,000 | 442,741 | 1,498,396 | 25,835,137 | 3,883,059 | 635,985 | 4,519,044 | 30,354,181 |
| 1948 (Jan.–June) | 179,384,000 | 1,745,000 | 5,808,000 | 186,937,000 | 23,187,340 | 4,339,825 | 27,527,165 | 214,464,165 |

[1] Based on statistics compiled by Auditing Department of Central Bank of China.

banks were more prone to withdraw their credits in cash than borrowers from commercial banks, a result of the former's attempt to withdraw funds from the authorities' supervision. The demand for currency reached such proportions that the bank note printing efforts of Chinese printing companies and the supply of bank notes from abroad were outpaced by corresponding demands—which was one of the reasons for the currency reform of August 1948.

Against the rising wave of credit expansion and the accompanying increasing velocity of circulation which fed the inflationary process, the half-hearted attempts of qualitative credit control proved completely ineffective. Speculative use of credit predominated, and a constant clamor for more credit prevented any serious quantitative restriction for any length of time. Such deflationary effects as might have been expected from expanding production, which was the government's assumption in credit expansion, were either illusory or nullified because bank loans ostensibly for productive purposes were shunted to speculation while the propensity to save out of the rising income had fallen to a negligible magnitude. In the circumstances, other measures of monetary and economic control which failed to touch the core of the problem of inflation—deficit spending and credit expansion—could not have been expected to be successful and were, indeed, utterly without effect.

Chapter

# 10

# Aggregate Supply

## 1. Supply Conditions before 1937

### *Domestic Production*

Several paradoxical developments were noticeable in the economy of prewar China: the backwardness of agricultural production along with the growing habit of consuming and using imported modern manufactured goods; the concentration of light modern industry in the coastal Treaty Ports with apparent disregard for their sources of raw materials and the market of their products, both of which were predominantly in the interior; emphasis on railway construction in a relatively small coastal area, with hardly any mileage built in the much larger area of the country's interior, and a simultaneous lack of other modern transportation facilities in interior regions. Other noticeable factors were the neglect of flood control and irrigation in spite of China's dependence on agriculture; the lack of active export promotion despite the strong need for imports; and the failure to develop heavy industry despite the large-scale defense expenditures. All this helped to set the stage for frequent shortages of food and agricultural staples and the consequent need for emergency imports. Furthermore, the interior depended on the Treaty Ports for its manufactured consumption goods; all heavy industrial goods had to be imported; all heavy ammunitions and war equipment, and most minor strategic materials, likewise, were imported; the trade balance was chronically adverse; distribution of goods was difficult, slow, and costly.

Foreign investment and overseas Chinese remittances filled the foreign trade gap in peacetime and permitted a higher level of imports than China's exports earned. The Treaty Ports, which imported foreign capital goods and raw materials whenever these were locally unavailable or too expensive to be procured domestically, in turn supplied the minimum demand of the interior for manufactures. In peacetime the loss of time and efficiency resulting from a distribution system which blended the modern and the primitive into an inharmonious whole was relatively unimportant.

When the war broke out, the weaknesses of the existing pattern of production, distribution, and foreign trade made themselves immediately and painfully felt in all sectors of the economy of Free China. Supplies from abroad and Occupied China were reduced. Modern communications and transportation facilities contracted as the territory under the government's control shrank and growing shares of supplies for the civilian sector were channeled into military uses. On the other hand, aggregate consumption was increased by the influx into Free China of large numbers of refugees and the rising incomes of certain occupational groups in sudden demand, such as transportation workers.

At first it was considered feasible to increase withdrawals from inventories and to stimulate new production by a liberal credit expansion. But with the tightening of the enemy blockade and the rise in prices threatening and curtailing production, bottlenecks appeared in the form of scarcities in essential materials and capital goods. There was no effort to allocate available supply rationally. Increases in raw material prices and failure to resist pressure for increased benefits and labor wages, resulting from the inflationary pressures, more than nullified any possible benefits of the credit expansion; and the hoped-for rise of production failed to occur.

After the war the government attempted to increase over-all supply and relieve local shortages by encouraging imports and the flow of internal trade. These measures were thought to have more promise of quick results than an increase in domestic production. But before long the prewar pattern of production and foreign trade had reemerged, and the government's measures soon proved to be ineffective in the face of mounting inflation in spite of the fact that China was now reunified.

Given the basic weaknesses in China's economic structure as described above, the immediate postwar problem was not how to promote a rapid increase in supply but how to utilize the country's existing supplies of resources in more economical and efficient ways. What actually happened to aggregate supply during China's wartime and postwar inflation is described in this chapter.

Throughout the first half of the twentieth century, China remained primarily agricultural country with four-fifths of her population employed in the rural sector of the country dependent on farming. In spite of a long history of agriculture, primitive farming methods still prevailed. The productivity of the average farmer was so low that he was left with very little after meeting his obligations and his subsistence needs. The subsistence economy of Chinese agriculture rendered it impossible to create capital for industrial development or the improvement of agriculture itself. Estimates suggest that agriculture and related activities produced more than two-thirds of the nation's prewar output and that almost three-fourths of manufacturing was done by handicraft methods.

Natural conditions and time-tested techniques of production influenced the pattern of agricultural output in different parts of the country. Notable geographical specializations in agriculture included wheat in Northern China, rice in Southern China, and cotton in the area north of the Yellow River.

Industrial development was strongly influenced by foreign investments and extra-territoriality, factors which led to the narrow concentration of modern industry in a few Treaty Ports. Once these conditions existed, concentration was further accentuated by the pressure of external economies provided by the availability of complementary industries, markets, trading facilities, and banks in these areas. Chinese-owned industry followed foreign enterprises to these cities as Chinese entrepreneurs and workers sought security from the political and military disturbances of the interior.

Had peace and order prevailed over the country after the overthrow of the Manchu dynasty, the government might have used more of its financial resources to improve agriculture, and a better climate might have been created to attract domestic capital to develop industry in the interior. Throughout the Republic era, however, the contrary situation prevailed. Even after the establishment of the Nationalist government, civil wars occurred intermittently. The treasury was exhausted by the large expenditures for military purposes, and only a small fraction of the budget was devoted to economic construction; such Chinese entrepreneurs as existed, following the flight of capital, were drawn from the interior to the Treaty Ports.

Before the outbreak of the war with Japan, Chinese production showed symptoms of stagnation in all lines of activity. These conditions were characterized by the inability to achieve self-sufficiency in food or in raw materials for clothing; the backwardness of manufacturing industry; the condition of coal mining, electricity, and petroleum production; and the lack of basic industry.

During prewar years China produced approximately 7 billion bushels of food—about 60 per cent in main food staples such as rice and wheat, and the remaining 40 per cent consisting of miscellaneous cereals such as kaoliang, barley, millet, and corn. Rice is the common diet for southern Chinese, wheat flour provides the favorite food for the northern Chinese, and the coarser cereals are used as subsidiary food. Between 1931 and 1937 the average yearly production of unhusked rice was 2.6 billion bushels (equal to 1.7 billion bushels of husked rice); and that of wheat, 1.2 billion bushels. Taking an average daily requirement of husked rice or wheat flour at 1.33 pounds for each person, the production of main food crops was able to supply the needs of 55 per cent of 454 million people. If the people could have been encouraged to eat rice and flour of a lesser fineness, the total supply of the main staples would have been 70 per cent of consumption requirements, and, with the supplement of subsidiary food crops, the total demand for foodstuffs could just barely have been met by domestic production.

However, droughts and insect blights frequently reduced production significantly below the average. Transportation was inadequate to bring the surplus of certain areas to relieve the needs of deficit areas. More than 70 per cent of the flour mills were located in seaports, such as Shanghai, Tientsin, and Tsingtao, and had easier access to the supply of foreign wheat. After the loss of Manchuria to Japan the supply of miscellaneous cereals to Northern China was reduced; and between 1931 and 1937 China had to import husked rice and wheat (including flour) at the average annual rate of 41 million bushels and 29 million bushels, respectively, representing 2.5 per cent and 2.4 per cent of the domestic production of rice and wheat.

The basic garments worn by the common people throughout the country, from gowns, jackets, and trousers to hats, shoes, and stockings, now as then, are all made of cotton cloth. So cotton production ranks with the production of food crops in importance as a basic agricultural necessity. According to incomplete statistics, the yearly average of cotton production between 1931 and 1937 was about 3.6 million bales. Assuming 80 per cent of spindles in full operation and a cotton consumption rate of 1 pound per spindle in a 20-hour day during a 26-day month, and assuming the minimum requirements for hand-spinning, padding for clothes, and bedquilts to be about 0.66 pound per person (970,000 bales in total), the yearly shortage was estimated at about 880,000 bales. Moreover, China was short of cotton of long staple. Taking the annual average of 1931–1937, China imported about 600,000 bales of raw cotton annually as well as substantial amounts of cotton yarn and cloth. In the decade before the war, therefore, Chinese agriculture failed to provide adequate supplies of basic necessities in the form of foodstuffs and raw material fibers for clothing. There seemed to be no immediate prospect for improvement.

During that decade China's manufacturing industry was still in the very first stages of development. It continued to be dominated by light consumer goods, and no significant heavy industrial base existed except in the Japanese puppet state of Manchukuo. The greater part of manufactured goods was produced by handicraft methods. Modern industrial development was organized and financed with foreign capital, principally Japanese and British, and was located almost exclusively in Treaty Ports and their adjoining districts.

Cotton textile, flour milling, tobacco, and matches were the four major industries which had been most developed before 1937. Cotton textile manufacturing was by far the most important from the standpoint of volume and value of production. In 1936 there were 5,200,000 spindles and 58,000 looms in China proper, and the yearly production of yarn was sufficient for a cloth production of 6.4 yards per person. About 89 per cent of the spindles were located in the east coast provinces—50 per cent in Shanghai, and more than 22 per cent in Tientsin and Tsingtao.

In 1936 there were 94 modern flour mills in China proper, 50 per cent of which were located in Shanghai and about 30 per cent in other cities along the coast. Most of the mills were Chinese-owned. Few of them had been in full operation since 1931 because of the growth of the Japanese flour milling industry in Manchuria, which had been the largest customer, and because of the competition of cheap foreign flour.

More than 90 per cent of the cigarette manufacturing industry was located in coastal cities, particularly in Shanghai. Foreign-owned factories produced 70 per cent, and Chinese-owned factories 30 per cent. The only industry which was evenly distributed throughout the country and which was mostly Chinese-owned was the match industry. Its producing capacity exceeded consumption requirements.

Numerous new industries, all on a small scale and concentrated in Shanghai, were developed prior to 1936; these included cement, paper making, enamel, soap, glass, canning, cosmetics, and hosiery.

The growth of manufacturing output was confined to a few industries with small needs for capital and with a large consumer market ready at hand. Even in these few lines the Chinese-owned factories were not only outpaced by the foreign-owned plants, which had available to them more capital and more modern techniques, but also were more subject to competition from imported goods of similar category.

Thus development of industry in the interior appeared unattractive to Chinese entrepreneurs.

Coal, electricity, and petroleum, the basic sources of power for industrial development, were produced in prewar China in small quantities, and their production was not well located. The location of the principal coal mines in China proper bore no relation to the largest coal reserves or to the market demands of industry, a condition resulting from the development of coal mining along railway lines, most of the railways being built with foreign loans within the sphere of influence of each investing country. Total coal production in China proper during 1936 was 22.25 million metric tons, 60 per cent of which was produced in Hopeh, Shantung, and Honan Provinces, while the two provinces of Shansi and Shensi, with 80 per cent of China's coal deposits, produced only 13.7 per cent. In the lower Yangtze valley and southeast coast provinces, where industry was concentrated and the density of population high, coal production was only 17.2 per cent of the total.

The prewar installed capacity of power plants was only 652,000 kilowatts in China proper. Five coastal provinces possessed 92 per cent of the installed capacity. Shanghai alone had 263,000 kilowatts of potential capacity; and 92 per cent of the total capacity was concentrated in areas representing only 13.3 per cent of Chinese territory if we include Manchuria, Mongolia, Tibet, and Sinkiang. Because of this uneven distribution, 86.7 per cent of China, with 64.8 per cent of the population, was deprived of electricity.

China produced only 200,000 gallons of petroleum annually in the distant northwest provinces, an output achieved without modern refining equipment.

Iron and steel, the backbone of an industrial economy, were produced in prewar China proper only in insignificant amounts.

In 1936 China proper had 21 furnaces producing 50,000 tons of steel and 150,000 tons of pig iron annually; and numerous small native iron smelters, chiefly in the northern and western provinces, produced annually about 50,000 tons. Although there were more than one thousand machine shops and foundries in different cities, most of them were poorly capitalized and equipped. The small number of workshops which could produce a wide variety of simpler types of machinery could not be considered engineering shops by Western standards.

Shortly before 1937 several Chinese chemical plants were brought into being, producing sulphuric acid, nitric acid, caustic soda, and soda ash. There were six acid plants and two electro-chemical plants of comparatively large size and fifteen small acid plants, the larger ones all located in seaport cities, such as Shanghai, Tientsin, and Canton except for one in Kwangsi province. Production was scarcely able to satisfy the demand of the few light industries. The chemical industry could hardly be considered initiated.

In view of the Japanese war threat, the government planned to build up a few heavy industries in the south and west of China. Included in the program were two steel plants, one plant each for refining tungsten and making synthetic nitrogen, and a few machinery works to manufacture airplane engines, generators, and machine tools. Factories to make tubes, cables, telephones, and miscellaneous generating equipment were also blueprinted. The facilities were to be located east of the Canton-Hankow railway. However, when the war broke out, nothing had progressed beyond the planning stage except that the building which was to house the steel plant was partially complete and one small electrical goods factory was nearly complete.

The failure to strengthen the mining and industrial base to furnish minimum defense needs seriously weakened China's war potential. The concentration of industrial capacity in a few areas and the dependence on imports for vital supplies, coupled with the early loss, through enemy occupation and the effectively crippling blockade, of what modern industrial potential China did have at the beginning of the war, hampered early resistance no less than the long fight for survival.

### *Distribution*

The lack of modern transportation facilities greatly hampered the countrywide distribution of agricultural products to consumers and of raw materials to manufacturers. It caused peculiar problems, such as the simultaneous shortage and oversupply of foodstuffs in different parts of the country and the import of industrial raw materials from abroad at cheaper costs than similar materials from domestic sources.

In many parts of the country commerce was still carried by junks, handcarts, pack animals, and human carriers—transportation which appears cheap per day but is expensive per mile; farmers seldom took their goods more than thirty miles to markets, and Chinese markets were highly localized. One survey showed that prior to 1937 most agricultural production was consumed near its point of production, being sold locally, 49 per cent in nearby villages, and 29 per cent in towns or cities of the same district. Only 3 per cent, produced by areas accessible to railway and steamship transport, was marketed in more remote places.

Internal waterways have furnished the principal means of distribution in China for centuries. An extensive system was built up, and even remote villages are still reached by some types of boats during the wet seasons. But this mode of transportation is little adapted either to the needs of modern industries or to warfare. The Yellow River, for example, the great stream of North China, is not navigable for steamships; the Yangtze and the Si-kiang, two main west-east river systems in South China, are navigable only a limited distance by steamship; the balance of the main rivers and their tributaries are usable only for small shallow-draft boats.

After the loss of 3,726 miles of railways in Manchuria in 1932, the railway mileage in China proper was only 11,035 miles in 1937, serving a territory of 2.3 million square miles. More than a third of the remaining tracks were located in the three coastal provinces of Hopeh, Kiangsu, and Kwangtung. The plateau and mountain country of West China was untouched by railways except for the Haiphong (Indo-China)-Kunming line.

Only about 56,000 miles of highways had been built in China proper before the war, and about four-fifths of this mileage was in the eastern part of the country.

The slow development of modern distribution organizations with modern management was a direct consequence of the lack of modern transportation facilities. Since the long journeys and heavy freight transportation costs to the interior tied up large amounts of working capital, and the primitive transport means made insurance protection excessively costly, few merchants could build up modern distribution systems of any size.

In prewar times the foreign importers of kerosene, dyes and fertilizers, and tobacco had a relatively modern and efficient distribution system through their Chinese agents. The demand for these commodities was extensive and constant, and grew in proportion to the extension of the distribution system. The monopolistic nature of the firms selling these commodities and the financial strength of the foreign importers and manufacturers were important factors in the success of these ventures. For the opposite reasons, no such distribution systems were ever developed in other lines by Chinese merchants. Most of the Chinese distributors were poorly capitalized, and consequently failed to achieve an even distribution of their products and thus lower the prices of basic agricultural and manufactured goods.

### *Imports*

After China was opened to foreign trade, tariffs on both imports and exports were fixed by treaty. The basis was a duty of 5 per cent ad valorem, imposed on values agreed upon between the trading parties. Other than this nominal duty, no restriction was placed on China's foreign trade by the Manchu government, on the theory that foreign trade was a foreign matter and should therefore be let alone. The doctrine of free trade which prevailed in Europe in the middle of the nineteenth century was also introduced into China at that time, and was accepted by the government in relation to foreign trade as being in line with the existing policy.

As a result, the government never showed much desire to reduce imports or to promote exports in spite of the chronic imbalance of trade. It was only after the establishment of the Nationalist government that China regained tariff autonomy from the treaty nations. From that time the government gradually endeavored to reduce imports of luxury goods and to use tariffs to protect domestic industries. However, the previous government's laissez faire policy of some ninety years' standing and the long existence of treaty tariff limitations were never fully thrown off, and the foreign trade structure continued to bear their imprint.

In the first place, China had had a long period of adverse trade balances. During the 72 years from 1864, when customs returns were first published, to 1936, a favorable trade balance appeared in only 6 years. By 1936 the trade deficit had accumulated to CNC $12,260 million, equivalent to U.S. 3,678 million at the conversion rate of 30 U.S. cents per CNC $1.00.

Luckily, foreign loans, foreign investment, and overseas Chinese remittances balanced this deficit; in fact, a similar amount was added to real consumption in China. However, the foreign origin of this addition made it subject to foreign influences: the world depression which began in 1929 reduced overseas Chinese remittances; the Manchurian Incident in 1931 and the resulting political uncertainty in China discouraged foreign investments. The combination of these factors resulted in such heavy drains of China's accumulated gold and silver reserves to meet the adverse balance of trade between 1931 and 1935 that the foundations of the national economy were nearly undermined. The currency devaluation of 1935 and the gradual improvement in domestic production partly corrected this condition; but in 1936 the foreign trade deficit still was about 14 per cent of total imports and was only offset by overseas Chinese remittances and, in a smaller measure, by export of silver.

Second, a paradoxical structure of foreign trade existed. Some basic agricultural products and raw materials actually flowed both ways. Between 1931 and 1936, for instance, imports of rice averaged about 46 million bushels annually, while exports averaged 5.5 million bushels. China imported wheat and flour in an average volume of 30 million bushels annually during those years, while exports averaged 4 million bushels. An even more pronounced two-way flow existed in cotton during the same period: imports averaged about 600,000 bales annually, contrasted with exports of more than 120,000 bales. Tobacco leaf also was traded both ways, although in a lesser degree.

It is paradoxical enough for China, a primarily agricultural country with extensive farming, to import large quantities of agricultural goods. It is even stranger that the country exported a lesser amount of the goods it needed to import. The reasons for the movements were mainly the lack of modern transportation facilities, concentration of manufacturing in port cities, and failure of the domestic producers to improve the quality of their products and to adopt uniform standards.

As mentioned in a previous section, many areas with food deficits had to import supplementary supplies from abroad because they were unable to use surpluses in nearby areas; thus Kwantung Province imported rice from abroad fairly regularly. Shanghai, Tientsin, Tsingtao, and other port cities normally preferred to import cotton and wheat, not only because c.i.f. prices of these commodities from abroad were sometimes lower but also because the grade of similar domestic supplies was often lower and usually unpredictable and deliveries were uncertain.

Coal was another commodity which moved both in and out of the country simultaneously. Between 1934 and 1936 average annual coal exports ran to 700,000 metric tons while imports were at the level of 800,000 metric tons. Coal, although it is one of China's most abundant mineral resources, was not always available for economical or dependable domestic delivery to the power plants and factories located along the southeast China coast, particularly Shanghai. Domestic producers were unable to develop a reliable market for their coal at home. Therefore, they looked for customers abroad.

Third, the growth of foreign trade was slow. Imports increased 176.85 per cent between 1912 and 1930, exports 141.5 per cent, and total foreign trade 161.31 per cent. Failure of agriculture to improve the quality and quantity of its output, lack of transportation facilities, concentration of industries in the coastal cities, existence of the treaty tariffs, lack of uniform grades and standards of commodities, and absence of a well-organized domestic distribution system all contributed to the slow growth of foreign trade. The loss of Manchuria also set China back in her foreign trade, exports from Manchuria at one time having accounted for one-third of those of all China, while imports into Manchuria were as high as one-fifth of total Chinese imports. Exports of China in 1932 were 50 per cent under those of 1930; imports contracted about 15 per cent in the same two years.

Fourth, creation of a domestic base of industry was obstructed by the types of imports. While imports gradually declined as a per cent of gross domestic output (Table 58), they increased in absolute value. Heading the list of imports were textiles, foodstuffs, tobacco, dyes, and timber—primarily consumer goods. Machinery, tools, and metal manufactures, on the other hand, became one of the first ten import items only in 1933. They comprised 2.5 per cent of the total value of imports, increasing subsequently to 2.9 per cent, 4.7 per cent, and 6.0 per cent, respectively, in the next three years.

TABLE 58. PERCENTAGE OF IMPORTS IN THE TOTAL VALUE OF GROSS DOMESTIC OUTPUT, 1931–1936[1]

| Year | Per Cent |
|---|---|
| 1931 | 14.2 |
| 1932 | 9.9 |
| 1933 | 9.3 |
| 1934 | 8.3 |
| 1935 | 6.0 |
| 1936 | 4.8 |

[1] Based on the data in Ou Pao-san, *National Income of China* [in Chinese], p. 19, 1947.

The main reason for China's adverse balance of trade was thus found in the requirements of the urban sector, particularly the port cities, of foodstuffs, agricultural raw materials, and other consumption goods. Foreign trade, as a consequence, was concentrated in a few port cities. Meanwhile, because the imports were largely consumed by the urban sector, they contributed little to the development of the economy as a whole. Hence the ability of the interior regions to create an exportable surplus of goods remained low, and they failed to add significantly to the total level of supply. The narrow concentration of foreign trade and supply routes in the coastal sector also limited the usefulness of imported goods as an anti-inflationary measure during and after the war.

## 2. SUPPLY CONDITIONS DURING THE WAR

### *Domestic Production*

China plunged into war with a modern power under the false impression that since she had vast territory, rich resources, and unlimited manpower she could sustain herself in a prolonged war of attrition. When the Chinese army retreated from Shanghai and its surrounding area after a three-month battle, and this most important supply center was lost, the government leaders were gravely concerned with the insufficient supply of defense materials and essential commodities. Presuming that the enemy would overrun North China and the coast provinces, and stop at a line east of the Canton-Hankow railway, China hoped that fourteen provinces* with a population of 170,000,000 would remain free. But it was anticipated that Hunan, Hupeh, and Kiangsi could not be entirely held for China and, in addition, the southern part of Kwangtung might not be held. In a normal crop year these provinces were self-sufficient in food supplies to a varying degree, but, because of inadequate transportation, they could not provide for a large concentration of troops or a sudden increase of refugees; and modern industry was almost nonexistent in the area because of its narrow concentration in the Treaty Port cities—which had already been lost. The percentage of production of main agricultural products and certain types of manufactured goods in the area just defined compared to total prewar production is shown in Table 59.

The 14 provinces named include only half of Kiangsi, Honan, and Hupeh and a small portion of Kwangtung. Theoretically the rice production shown in the table, which was half of total production, should have been sufficient to feed the population of Free China, estimated to be about 37 per cent of the total. Szechwan province, where the war capital was to be established, was the richest rice producing area, and a greater concentration of population could seemingly have been supported. However, transportation within the province and between Szechwan and adjoining provinces and the limited production of cotton in Southwest China posed an almost insoluble problem of how to feed and clothe both the army and the civilians.

In attempting to build up industry in Free China when the war began in North China, the government dismantled the machinery in the arsenals for removal to West China. Private industry around Shanghai was urged to move its equipment to the West. But owing to the quick retreat from Shanghai, only 146 units of privately owned factories with 14,600 tons of equipment and 2,500 skilled workers were moved away. During the lull after the fall of Nanking and before the retreat from Hankow, more time was available for removal of factory equipment from Hankow. Fifty thousand spindles owned

* Shensi, Kansu, Ninghsia, Chinghai, Szechwan, Yunnan, Kweichow, Hunan, Hupeh, Honan, Kiangsi, Kwangsi, Sikang, and Sinkiang.

TABLE 59. AGRICULTURAL AND INDUSTRIAL PRODUCTION IN FREE CHINA

Agricultural Production[1]

| 1931–37 Average Production | | Per Cent of Total Production (China proper) |
|---|---|---|
| Rice (husked) | 800,000,000 bushels | 50 |
| Wheat | 500,000,000 bushels | 40 |
| Cotton | 650,000 bales | 18 |
| Tobacco | 510,000 tons | 71 |

Industrial Production[2]

| 1936 Production | | Per Cent of Total Production | |
|---|---|---|---|
| Cotton yarn | 29,700 bales | 1.2 | (2.5 million bales) |
| Wheat flour | 70,000,000 pounds | 2.3 | (3 billion pounds) |
| Pig iron | 48,000 tons | 32.0 | (150,000 tons) |
| Steel | 1,000 tons | 2.0 | (50,000 tons) |
| Coal | 4,553,400 tons | 20.4 | (22.25 million tons) |
| Cement | 100,000 barrels | 17.5 | (5.7 million barrels) |
| Paper | 470 tons | — | |
| Sulphuric acid | 216 tons | 0.35 | (60,450 tons) |

[1] Estimates are based on data of *China Handbook, 1937–45* (New York, 1946); area including Ninghsia, Chinghai, Kansu, Shensi, Honan, Hupeh, Szechwan, Yunnan, Kweichow, Hunan, Kiangsi, Chekiang, Fukien, Kwangtung, Kwangsi. Fifty per cent of reduction is made on the rice production of Hunan and Kiangsi and two-thirds of reduction on that of Kwangtung. Same percentage of reduction is made on the cotton production of Honan and that of Hupeh, Hunan, and Kiangsi, respectively.

[2] Taken from S. H. Tan's *China's Economy during 1937–47* [in Chinese], (1948); area limited west of Peking-Hankow and Canton-Hankow Railways.

by cotton textile factories in Hankow and another 50,000 spindles dismantled from a cotton mill in Honan were shipped to Chungking. Also, a part of the equipment of the government-owned Hanyang Iron Works and the Yangtze Engineering Works at Hankow and the mining equipment of Foo Chun mines (Sino-British enterprise in Honan) were removed and sent to Chungking. This small quantity of equipment later turned out to be the foundation of the textile, coal, and steel industry in Free China. At the time of the fall of Ichang, when river communication between Chungking and Hankow and Changsha was cut off, altogether 120,000 tons of equipment and more than 600 manufacturing units had been moved to Free China, most of which were located in two provinces, Szechwan and Hunan, with a small portion shipped to Shensi. These are classified in Table 60.

TABLE 60. CAPITAL EQUIPMENT IN FREE CHINA[1]

| | | |
|---|---|---|
| Equipment for mining | 8 | mines |
| Equipment for metallurgy | 2 | plants |
| Equipment for machinery | 230 | factories |
| Equipment for electrical goods | 41 | factories |
| Equipment for chemical production | 62 | factories |
| Equipment for cotton textiles | 115 | factories |
| Equipment for food processing | 54 | factories |
| Equipment for production of educational supplies | 81 | factories |
| Others | 54 | |
| Total Units | 647 | |

[1] Based on Report of Ministry of Economic Affairs.

In addition, the National Resources Commission secured new supplies of machinery from abroad before the close of the Indo-China railroad line. Both government and private enterprise brought in a total of 10,000 skilled workers. Upon this fragile foundation the industry in Free China had to be built.

The government at first attempted to build up a few industrial bases in Free China in accordance with the availability of natural resources. The National Resources Commission was entrusted with the task of developing the heavy manufacturing and mining industries, while every assistance given to private enterprise was mainly devoted to the development of light industry. However, many difficulties prevented fulfillment of the government plan.

The most serious obstacle was the shortage of electric power. In 1938 only 35,509 kw of electric power capacity, equivalent to 5.4 per cent of the prewar total supply, was located in Free China. Despite the great efforts to transport the existing equipment of small power plants in Hunan and Hupeh Provinces to Szechwan, the National Resources Commission managed to increase the generating capacity by only 27,899 kw. It is obvious that this small supply of electricity was not sufficient to satisfy the demands of industry. In some cases it was insufficient for existing operating needs.

Another obstacle was the difficulty of developing complementarity among the various components of industry, particularly heavy industry. The most striking example was that of iron and steel. Twenty-four furnaces were installed, either by private enterprises or by the National Resources Commission, twenty of which were placed in operation. Fourteen were for the production of steel; of these, four each had 10-ton capacity and the others, 3 1/2-ton or 1-ton capacity. Ten blast furnaces for the production of pig iron were installed, including one 100-ton furnace, one 50-ton furnace, and one 30-ton furnace, the rest being 15-ton, 10-ton, or 5-ton. In addition, there were numerous native smelters which could produce nearly as much as the modern blast furnaces did. Thus the capacity for producing pig iron greatly exceeded the capacity to use it in steel production or for iron working. Meanwhile, the demand for steel could not be met adequately. Table 61 demonstrates how the supply of iron was abruptly decreased. The annual average of imports of iron ingots and steel during 1934–1937 in China proper had amounted to 165,000 tons, which was three times the production of iron and steel in 1944, as shown. This illustrates how inadequate was the output level of strategic materials in wartime.

TABLE 61. IRON AND STEEL PRODUCTION IN FREE CHINA, 1940–1944[1]
(Unit: tons)

| Year | Iron | Steel |
|---|---|---|
| 1940 | 49,500 | 1,650 |
| 1941 | 70,000 | 2,212 |
| 1942 | 105,600 | 3,300 |
| 1943 | 77,000 | 7,480 |
| 1944 | 44,150 | 15,697 |

[1] Based on data in Statistical Abstract of China compiled by Directorate-General of Budgets, Accounts and Statistics, 1948.

Insufficient supplies of raw materials also produced serious bottlenecks, a fact well illustrated by the difficulties of the machinery-making industry. This industry had the largest number of workshops in operation in Free China: 181 in 1940, and 900 in 1944, most of which were on a small scale. Not more than a dozen of them were well equipped and able to produce industrial and machine-making machines. The National Resources Commission operated 6 machine-making factories. Nearly all of the machine shops received orders from the government arsenals to supply small arms, and were originally in full operation; but when the stock of essential materials such as tool steel, alloy and special steels was exhausted, and no new supply could be imported, production had to be curtailed. Many small machine shops were closed, while the larger ones, because of the shortage of some raw materials, could carry out orders to make machinery only for the light industries.

The difficulty of obtaining raw materials was also striking in the textile industry, which had always been vital to the economy of Free China. Even though demand was great and a ready market existed, production lagged. This was because of an inadequate supply of cotton due to transportation difficulties from the producing centers of the Northwest; so only small production took place in the Southwest.

In spite of the many difficulties, limited achievements were made. By 1942 the production of coal was increased by 35 per cent over 1936; wheat flour 160 per cent; cement 2 times; sulphuric acid 2.8 times; paper 6 times. Also, several new industries were developed. The Yumen oil field in Kansu province was developed by the National Resources Commission, producing 2,000,000 gallons of crude oil annually and 36,000 gallons of lubricating oil. The production of alcohol reached 7,000,000 gallons. Three electrical equipment factories operated by the National Resources Commission produced copper and iron wire, radio receiving and transmitting tubes, and insulators.

The difficulties in obtaining scarce but strategic production goods increased as the war went on. The arsenals were unable even to produce sufficient small arms for the army. At the end of 1944 a War Production Board was established under Sino-American joint management. The United States government rendered assistance in procuring scarce materials and shipped them to China by air. But industries not directly essential to the war effort could not enjoy this benefit and experienced a slump until the end of the war.

In the later stages of inflation during the war years, price levels were focused on two major items of supply. They were the cotton industry and the production of food. This acute focusing was given impetus because of the stagnation of diversified industries and reduction of purchasing power to a bare subsistence level. On the eve of the war, there were only 30,000 spindles and 320 looms in Southwestern and Northwestern China, about 0.6 per cent of the total number of spindles and looms in China proper. In the most populated area, Szechwan province, the seat of the National government, there was no cotton textile industry at all. When the newly arrived machinery was placed in operation, supplemented by locally made hand-spinning frames, there were 232,294 spindles in Southwestern China and 71,872 spindles in Northwestern China.

Before the war the supplying of Southwestern China's clothing requirements depended completely upon imported cotton yarn and cotton piece goods, and the need of fostering cotton farming had not been deemed necessary. In Szechwan province only 340,000 acres of a total of 14.6 million acres of cultivated land were used for cotton growing, while in Yunnan only 39,000 acres out of 4.1 million acres were so used. After the government's retreat to Chungking it made great efforts to extend the cotton growing acreage and to introduce American cotton seeds; but the farmers were not enthusiastic about cotton farming, not only because it was an unfamiliar crop but also because it was more profitable to grow rice. The price of rice was higher than cotton during the first few war years. When more spindles came into operation, but the shipment of cotton from Shensi was handicapped by the limitation of transportation, the shortage of cotton became increasingly acute. Yet from Table 62 it can be seen that production of raw cotton expanded very slowly up to 1943, while even the 1944 output was substantially below the average of 1940–1943.

TABLE 62. RAW COTTON AND COTTON YARN PRODUCTION IN FREE CHINA, 1940–1944

| Year | Raw Cotton[1] (bales) | Cotton Yarn[2] (bales) |
|---|---|---|
| 1931–37 | 650,000 | 29,700 (1936) |
| 1940 | 900,000 | 48,916 |
| 1941 | 820,000 | 88,994 |
| 1942 | 660,000 | 102,536 |
| 1943 | 870,000 | 127,913 |
| 1944 | 770,000 | 121,021 |

[1] See Footnote 1, Table 59.
[2] Statistics of Ministry of Economic Affairs.

Less than 40 per cent of this limited output was harvested in Szechwan and Yunnan, the remainder coming from Shensi and Honan. When the enemy penetrated into Honan in 1944, cotton supply for the mills in Free China was abruptly reduced. Yet only slight improvements in transportation were made between Chungking and its major source of cotton, Shensi.

On the basis of the low level of cloth consumption in the prewar years, amounting to 4 yards per capita, and on the assumption that the population in the five provinces of Southwestern China (Szechwan, Yunnan, Sikang, Kweichow, and Kwangsi) was about 100 million, an annual supply of 341,000 bales of cotton yarn would have been required. Production in Free China, however, did not exceed a maximum of 130,000 bales. Although various control measures were attempted to increase the supply, the situation became so desperate just before the end of the war that cotton textiles had to be flown in from the United States.

In retrospect these trends suggest that industry cannot be developed without providing the external economics of a whole range of supporting facilities, raw material supplies, and transport.

Had it not been for relatively adequate food supplies, the economic life of Free China could have been strangled by the Japanese blockade and the morale of the people would not have been maintained. Fortunately, Southwestern China always had been rich in food production, and with the exception of bad harvests in 1940, it suffered no serious famine. In addition, from 1941 onwards the government took measures to increase food production and the acreage under cultivation by extending winter ploughing, utilizing fallow fields, reducing the acreage under less essential crops, and encouraging the planting of ordinary rice instead of glutinous rice. Steps were also taken to introduce improved rice varieties and improved wheat seeds and to promote double-cropping in rice areas. Among the more basic improvements was the erection of irrigation projects. As a result of the various government efforts, total production of rice and wheat (Table 63) remained sufficient in spite of considerable year-to-year fluctuations.

TABLE 63. PRODUCTION OF BASIC FOOD CROPS IN FREE CHINA: 1939–1944[1]

| Year | Rice (husked) Production (1,000 bushels) | Wheat Production (1,000 bushels) | Total Bushels |
|---|---|---|---|
| 1939 | 915,000 | 576,000 | 1,491,000 |
| 1940 | 760,000 | 585,000 | 1,345,000 |
| 1941 | 780,000 | 410,000 | 1,190,000 |
| 1942 | 790,000 | 610,000 | 1,400,000 |
| 1943 | 570,000 | 580,000 | 1,150,000 |
| 1944 | 950,000 | 722,000 | 1,672,000 |

[1] See Footnote 1, Table 59.

### *Distribution*

Japan's war strategy was to drive the Chinese Nationalist forces into the interior and cut off military and civilian supplies at the coastal supply points. To frustrate the Japanese strategy of strangulation, China attempted to complete the Hunan-Kwangsi railway in the Southwest, in order to establish rail connection with Indo-China. The Yunnan-Burma highway, commonly known as the Burma Road, was also built; the Yunnan-Burma railway was planned but not begun. The highway from Kansu to Sinkiang and thence to the Soviet border was improved. To connect the war capital, Chungking, with the international supply routes both in the Southwest and in the Northwest, a railway between Szechwan and Yunnan was started, and the highway from Szechwan to Yunnan and from Szechwan to Shensi and Kansu was improved.

After the Japanese capture in 1939 of Nanning, capital of Kwangsi, followed by the stationing of Japanese troops in North Indo-China in 1940, the Indo-China supply route became unusable. The route from Sinkiang to the Soviet border was of limited capacity because of the small quantity of available vehicles and constant operation difficulties. Only a small amount of goods had been brought in over the Burma Road before it was closed by the Japanese invasion of Burma. All ports along the Chinese coast were blockaded. By also blocking navigation on the Yangtze River and the Si-kiang, on which much of the flow of supplies into the interior had previously taken place, the Japanese made the blockade nearly fully effective.

Highway transportation became increasingly difficult as automotive parts, fuels, and tires ran out. Work on the Yunnan-Szechwan railway was discontinued because of a lack of materials and equipment. Air supply was the only remaining possibility of bringing in goods from abroad.

Internal communications were inadequate but were being improved. Free China had less than 600 miles of railroad trackage; but about 5,000 miles of existing roads were reconditioned and 8,000 miles were newly built. Shipping routes were extended by improving navigation on the upper reaches of the Yangtze River, the Si-kiang, and several smaller rivers. Towing stations with mechanical pulling devices at river rapids were established; the construction of wooden boats was encouraged with government credit. All of the native transportation means were pressed into service, including carts drawn by men and animals, human carriers, pack animals, junks, rafts, and shallow-draft steamers. Stage transportation, the ancient way of transporting goods, was resumed and systematized under the National Stage Transportation Administration. But the maximum annual volume of freight ever carried by the Stage Transportation Administration did not exceed 200,000 tons. Even adding the carrying capacity of provincial and private stage lines, the estimated total did not account for more than one million tons per year.

Automotive vehicles in service numbered only 12,000; because of this small number and the inadequacy of replacement parts and fuels, the movement of goods under the Highway Transportation Administration reached 350,000 tons only in one year.

These small tonnages were insufficient to effect adequate distribution of military and civilian supplies. The progressive deterioration of the transportation system in turn brought about higher prices. Illustrating the high cost of transportation are the steamship freight rate from Shanghai to Haiphong (Indo-China), which was 5.7 cents per ton mile, and highway transportation from Kunming to Chungking, which was CNC $1.16 per ton mile, or about 20 times as much. And what took four days to transport by truck took three weeks by stage.

As transportation difficulties required an ever-increasing investment of working capital in the movement of goods, merchants gradually withdrew from intercity commerce; those who continued operating raised their prices not only by the amount of transportation charges but also by the high interest rate they had to pay for the lengthening periods of transit. This situation, inevitably worsening as inflationary pressures increased, led directly to the organization of several governmental bodies which were to deal with the procurement and sale of daily necessities at equitable prices. Such commodities included grains, cotton and cotton textiles, coal and fuels, papers, edible oils, and salt which had already been under government control. However, the government's distribution organs, operating in only a few important urban centers, did not alleviate the maldistribution and shortage of supplies elsewhere.

### *Imports*

From 1942 onward, foreign trade to Free China was almost completely blockaded. In Occupied China, although there was still a flow of trade with Japan, there were no goods available for export because of the shortage of material in Japan. Therefore there was also a complete stoppage of imports. This situation was a great test of how far Chinese economic life could be maintained under complete blockade, as it had been thought that neither Free nor Occupied China could live without foreign trade. The greatest problems arising from the loss of foreign trade are briefly summarized here.

The lowest living standard could not be maintained. Requirements for food and clothing, the two most important needs, could not be satisfied. Shortage of foodstuffs was felt more acutely in Occupied China than in Free China, but in the latter clothing material was much more scarce. The next most important item was kerosene, for which there was a big demand in the interior for lighting because electric power was lacking. When the import of kerosene was reduced, candles made from foreign materials replaced it; when the supply of candles was short, Chinese oil was used instead.

Communications and transport could not be maintained efficiently. All the equipment and parts for railways, road transport, shipping, and telecommunications depended on foreign supply. As materials for replacement and spare parts became unobtainable, efficiency was progressively reduced; and, had the war lasted any longer, there might have been a complete breakdown of transport. This deficiency affected both economic conditions and the ability to wage war in Free China.

Normal industrial production could not be maintained. When the supply of metals, metal manufactures, and chemical materials was short, most factories in Free China had to reduce production and others closed. Since only a very small supply of strategically important materials was shipped from Japan, similar conditions prevailed in Occupied China.

The loss of foreign trade had unfavorable repercussions upon popular morale. When trade stopped, and the people anticipated a shortage of supplies from abroad and possibly eventual starvation of import commodities, they hoarded their existing stocks—at first of domestic products which were possible substitutes for foreign imports, and then of general domestic products. The result was a general shortage of commodities, increasing prices, and accelerated depreciation of the currency.

All these factors accelerated inflation in Free China. In effect, the loss of trade forced on China the problem of survival without any of the advantages which modern technology and strategic supplies might have contributed to an effective and economic use of the resources of her underdeveloped areas.

### *Total Supply*

While supply limitations were not the most basic cause of inflation during the war years in Free China, the failure of output to respond to the stimuli of expanding aggregate demand accentuated the primary forces producing inflation. Aggregate demand was swollen by the influx of population into Free China and more especially by the expansion of monetary income as the means of payment were relentlessly multiplied. It is clear that the total supply of all goods and services provided to the private sector fell, but the decline showed significant differences among various categories of output. Supplies of basic agricultural foodstuffs were somewhat erratic, averaging 10 per cent below 1939 for the war years 1940–1944. Supplies of clothing were far below the prewar average for all China. Factory-produced consumer goods, too, showed considerable variation from year to year, and in 1944 were 10 per cent below the 1938 level and 62 per cent below the 1939 output. It should be borne in mind that these output levels were substantially below the average for prewar China as a whole since the area that became Free China was the least developed region in China proper in 1937. The total supply situation was further worsened by the loss of imports which as late as the decade before the war had added greatly to supplies of consumer goods of many kinds, particularly basic necessities. Distribution problems, aggravated by deteriorating transport facilities, intensified supply shortages in heavily populated areas—the cities and military camps, where inflation proceeded most rapidly.

## 3. Supply Conditions in the Postwar Period

### *Domestic Production*

At the time of victory the whole nation was overwhelmed by the prospect of unification and peace, the recovery of the lost territories of Manchuria and Formosa, and the gaining of control over Japanese industries in China proper. China's economy had been split into five segregated areas before the war—the Nationalist area, the semi-autonomous warlord areas, the Communist area, the Japanese-occupied territories, and the foreign settlements.

Those in control of the economy of the Communist area opposed to the interests of those in control of the Nationalist area, each isolated from the other; and the resources of Manchuria and Formosa had been completely channeled to the benefit of the Japanese economy. The concentration of foreign industry in the Treaty Ports had produced a change in economic control to the detriment not only of China's internal development but also of the progress of her infant industries. When the war ended it was believed that this sad situation of a fragmented economy would come to an end, that the four areas of production would be integrated, and that easily perceptible results would follow to relieve China's economic hardships within a short time. It was thought both by the government and by the public that Manchuria's large production of miscellaneous cereals would reduce the food deficiency in China proper; its iron and steel would make China self-sufficient; its paper and paper-pulp industries and those of Formosa and the sugar industry of Formosa would make China independent of foreign imports of paper and sugar.

It was also thought that the industrial productivity of Manchuria and Formosa, when incorporated with that of China proper, would enormously increase China's industrial output. The large number of cotton spindles and looms owned by the Japanese in China, when handed over to the Chinese, would make the cotton textile industry there subject to complete domestic control and would meet home demand for some years to come. When Communist hostility to the Nationalist government ceased, the destruction of communication lines would end and the coal and cotton produced in North China could then be brought to the South. It can easily be imagined that the economy would have been greatly strengthened had internal peace and security been realized. Production might have been increased to a level many times higher than the prewar level and imports could have been reduced to a minimum—which would have contributed inestimably to halting the inflation.

Unfortunately, the negotiations with Soviet Russia over the peaceful transfer of Manchuria were not crowned with success, and fighting there between the Communists and the Nationalist Army started following the withdrawal of the Soviet army, which had destroyed or removed important equipment in all industries. The coal mines taken over and operated there by the Nationalist government barely met the demand of local public utilities and individual consumers. Food for the army on the Manchurian front had to be brought from China proper, and thousands of factories around Mukden lay idle. Many plants in Formosa, damaged by bombing, could not be repaired on account of the lack of local funds and foreign exchange to purchase machinery and parts from abroad because the government's financial resources continued to be utilized for military expenditure. Within ten months after the end of the war fighting between the Communists and the Nationalists spread from Manchuria to Northern China. The two most important trunk lines, the Tientsin-Pukow and the Peiping-Hankow railways, linking North and South China, could not be repaired because of continued Communist sabotage. It was difficult to ship the surplus coal and cotton of North China to the South, and to ship manufactured goods from the South to the North. The fruits of victory were barren, and the disintegration of the economic structure was hastened.

In order to strengthen its position, the Nationalist government felt it necessary to import more goods to halt rising prices and to check inflation. The effect of the flood of foreign manufactured goods was immediately felt by the domestic light industries, which had mushroomed in the occupied coastal area after Pearl Harbor to take advantage of the complete stoppage of imports. A more serious impact was felt by the uneconomical small industrial plants which had been established in Free China and which employed improvised methods. The large quantities of cotton, rice, and flour, imported either by government purchases or by UNRRA shipments, dislocated the price structure of local agricultural products and thereby hampered the natural recovery of the rural economy.

Within eighteen months after the end of the war the government reserves of foreign exchange had dwindled away and imports had to be gradually reduced. The fact that raw materials required by manufacturers could not be imported in sufficient quantities cut down production. The relatively low prices of agricultural products, as compared with the prices of manufactured goods which were forced up by the low production, not only reduced the income of the farmers, thus leaving them very little money for improvements, but also discouraged their incentive to increase production.

As a result of Japanese efforts, peak production was reached in many industries in Manchuria during 1943. Some of the output and capacity data are outlined in Table 64.

TABLE 64. ANNUAL OUTPUT OF MANCHURIAN INDUSTRY IN THE PEAK YEAR, 1943[1]

(In thousand metric tons unless otherwise specified)

| | | | |
|---|---|---|---|
| Pig iron | 1,700 | Cement | 1,800† |
| Steel | 500 | Chemical fertilizer | 33† |
| Lead | 10* | Paper pulp | 133* |
| Zinc | 7* | Paper | 122* |
| Copper | 3* | Automobiles | 2,800§ |
| Aluminum | 8* | Rolling Stock: | |
| Magnesium | 0.4* | Engines | 90‖ |
| Coal | 25,700† | Passenger cars | 130‖ |
| Electric power | 1,708,000‡ | Freight cars | 2,400‖ |

* Annual capacity.
† Data for 1944.
‡ Kilowatts of installed capacity.
§ Number of cars.
‖ Annual capacity in number of units.

[1] Data of Northeastern Economic Commission of the Chinese government.

In addition to the items listed, 1,200 training planes and 1,000 airplane engines were produced during the war by the Mukden Aircraft Company. For heavy industrial equipment the largest factory was the Manchuria Engineering Works, which produced vehicles, iron towers, bridges, shapes, cast-iron pipes, boilers, radiators, and other machinery. During the war a new machine tool plant was built in Mukden, and a heavy industrial machinery plant was erected in the vicinity of Dairen. In addition to the tabulated manufacturing capacity for rolling stock, the shops of the South Manchurian Railways Works had a combined capacity for the assembly and repair of 1,100 engines, 2,000 passenger cars, and 11,400 freight cars. There were several hundred smaller factories manufacturing machinery and parts. The textile industry was equipped with 560,000 spindles and 20,000 looms. All these and other industrial establishments constituted a most impressive array of industrial power which could have been immensely helpful in relieving China's postwar shortage of goods and in furnishing a foundation for the country's long-range industrial development. Although there was some dislocation of production in 1944 as a result of American bombing raids, particularly in the iron and steel and aircraft manufacturing industries, Manchuria's industrial power was largely intact on the eve of V-J Day.

Moreover, in 1944 Manchuria produced 3,549,000 tons of soybeans, which should have been sufficient to make up the deficiency of edible oil in China proper and to give China an income of foreign exchange in the amount of U.S. $60 to $90 million a year (more than 80 per cent of the soybeans and soybean products being produced for export). Out of 15,681,000 tons of food production in 1944 it was estimated that China would be able to draw 700,000 to 1,000,000 tons of grain to relieve the chronic shortage of food in North China. It was thought that the large supply of lumber, with 144 mills capable of producing 4 million cubic meters of lumber, would replace a large part of the foreign lumber on which China proper used to depend.

The foregoing account of Manchuria's industrial and agricultural potential indicates what a disastrous blow it was to Manchuria to suffer the removal of major industrial equipment by the Soviet Occupation Army and further extensive destruction by the Chinese Communists. During the negotiations between the Soviet Occupation Army leader and the Chinese representative over the withdrawal of the Soviet army and the transfer of Manchuria to the Chinese government, the Soviet army forced the Japanese president of the Manchurian Heavy Industry Company to sign a document to the effect that all of the Company's industries had worked for the Japanese Kwantung Army. Immediately after obtaining this document, which was used to justify the claim that these industries belonged to Russia as war booty, the Soviet army seized the industries controlled by the Company and removed all the vital equipment of the major industries. As a result of the failure of Sino-Soviet negotiations, the Soviet army withdrew from many places before the Chinese army could arrive, and the Chinese Communists looted plants and mines and committed much destruction.

The decrease in the percentage of the production capacity of different industries caused by the removal of equipment is shown in Table 65.

TABLE 65. ESTIMATED DECLINE IN PRODUCTION CAPACITY[1]

| | | | |
|---|---|---|---|
| Electric power generating | 60% | Cement | 54% |
| Steel and iron | 60–100% | Non-ferrous metals | 50–100% |
| Coal | 80% | Textiles | 50% |
| Machinery making | 68% | Pulp and paper | 80% |
| Liquid fuel | 90% | Food industry | 50% |
| Chemical industry | 33% | Radio, telephone and telegraph equipment | 30% |

[1] Based on Report of Northeastern Economic Commission of the Chinese government.

As soon as the Soviet army withdrew from Manchuria most of the areas except those along the South Manchurian Railway line south of Changchun were infiltrated by Chinese Communists and were prevented from being taken over by the Nationalist government. Only 1,677 miles of railway out of a total mileage of 6,980, with rolling stock totaling 808 locomotives, 658 coaches, and 7,917 freight cars, were placed under the control of the Nationalist government. In 1945 the Japanese had operated 2,403 locomotives, 3,049 coaches, and 39,523 freight cars. The seven coal mines controlled by the government produced only about 250,000 tons monthly in 1946 compared with a monthly production of 1,150,000 tons in 1944. The capacity of electric power plants was reduced to 650,000 kw from 1,708,000 kw. In 1946, as only a part of the old stocks of materials was left, the production of pig iron was only 46,000 tons and that of steel 70,000 tons. Only 175,000 cotton spindles out of 560,000 were in condition to be operated. What was left in the machine shops was limited to taking care of repair work for railway rolling stocks and coal mines.

Agricultural land under cultivation within Nationalist territory was 17.3 million acres out of a total of 49.4 million acres, and 6.09 million tons of grains were collected from the Nationalist controlled areas, representing 38 per cent of the 1944 production of Manchuria. It was estimated that food production was short by 50,000 tons for meeting local requirements, since a large percentage of food crops had to be requisitioned to feed the increasing number of Nationalist troops sent to Manchuria; and supply for local consumption became acutely deficient. There was a surplus of 300,000 tons of soybeans and other vegetable oils or seeds available for export, but, on account of transportation difficulties, only 60,000 tons were collected and exported by the government in 1946.

Except for sporadic guerilla warfare, there was little large-scale fighting in North China during Japanese occupation. With the intention of utilizing the mining and agricultural resources of this region to bolster the war effort of the home government and the Kwantung Army in Manchuria, Japan invested 984,300,000 yen in the coal and iron industries and in the production of cotton and salt. Indeed, these four items were then, as now, the most important export products of North China. Coal production in 1942 reached the peak of 25,000,000 tons, an increase of 9,000,000 tons over the prewar level. The Shih Ching Shan Iron Works in the suburbs of Peking were completed and began to produce pig iron from 1939; rails were laid to the iron mines to facilitate the shipment of iron ore to Japan. Two iron works in Shansi Province were improved and their producing capacity was increased. According to incomplete statistics, the combined production of pig iron from these three iron works was just under 100,000 tons a year.

Japan's plan of increasing cotton crops failed, partly because of the low price fixed for government purchase and the higher price of grains and partly because of guerilla activities. Cotton production in Hopeh, Shantung, Shansi, and North Honan fell to less than 50 per cent of the prewar crop. Salt production was more than doubled. The Japanese also strengthened the cotton industry in North China by increasing the number of spindles in Tientsin and replacing the spindles and looms of the Tsingtao textile mills, which had been destroyed by Nationalist troops at the outbreak of the war, 1937. The number of spindles and looms in these two places totaled 730,000 and 15,700, respectively, the former being 28 per cent of the total in China proper. In Tientsin several new industrial plants of moderate size were established, producing chemicals, iron and steel, refined oil, machinery, and other goods.

As guerilla warfare progressed, the Communists succeeded in penetrating into the interior in North China and even in extending their activities along the railway lines. Postwar rehabilitation of the trunk lines in North China was subject to constant disruption from the Communists, whose sabotage destroyed both rolling stock and rails. In view of the impossibility of continuing repair work, the Nationalist government abandoned its hope of restoring communications in North China and concentrated its attention on the regions south of the Yangtze River. The Communist sabotage forced the coal mines along the railway lines in North China to reduce production or to close down, since their products could not be shipped out. If the Kailan mine, the largest coal producer, had not been located near Tientsin and safe from interruption, power plants and many industries in the coastal cities, as well as coastal shipping, would have been paralyzed. Coal production in North China was reduced to 7,700,000 tons in 1946 and 7,000,000 tons in 1947, less than one-third of the production during Japanese occupation, of which three-fifths were produced by the Kailan coal mine.

The cotton industry in the South was unable to obtain supplies of cotton from North China, where there was a surplus. The cities in the North were short of food because no grains were shipped from Manchuria and no rice was sent from the South. Internal strife not only reduced mining and agricultural production in North China and affected industrial production in South China but also prevented the distribution of supplies throughout China.

The most important factors contributing to postwar production were the gaining of control of Japanese-owned industries in China proper and Formosa and aid from the United Nations Relief and Rehabilitation Administration.

Although Japan handed over to China 917 factories, including cotton textile, chemical, machinery making, electrical manufacturing, tobacco, food processing, printing, and other plants, and 29 mines and 9 power plants, most of those enterprises had previously belonged to Chinese owners and had been transferred to Japanese hands for one reason or another. Only the cotton textile mills and electrical manufacturing plants had been established by the Japanese, the former having been built before the war and the latter during the war. The reason for Japan's lack of enthusiasm in making new investments in South China, estimated to be only 248,800,000 yen (one-quarter of that invested in North China), was her plan of ultimately abandoning control of South China when peace was negotiated. Her investments were therefore confined to restoring the damage caused by war and to establishing means of reducing imports of consumer goods.

The most important and most valuable property surrendered by the Japanese was the cotton textile mills, which had 1,120,000 cotton spindles and 17,500 looms in Shanghai and 730,000 spindles and 15,700 looms in Tientsin and Tsingtao, a total of 1,850,000 spindles and 33,200 looms as against 2,900,000 spindles and 28,000 looms owned by

Chinese. The mills, after being taken over, were entrusted to the management of the China Textile Development Corporation, a government organization. More than 70 per cent of their spindles were in operation in 1947. The electrical manufacturing plants were taken over by the National Resources Commission and integrated into its general plan of developing the electrical manufacturing industry.

The industries in Formosa which made the greatest contribution to China's economy were those of sugar and paper making. The sugar mills, possessing a total annual production capacity of 1.4 million tons, were seriously damaged by American bombing. Efforts were made to rehabilitate the damaged plants, and production was increased from 86,000 tons annually immediately after the war to 260,000 tons in 1947 and to 600,000 tons in 1948. Before the war China had imported sugar from abroad in the amount of between 200,000 tons and 300,000 tons annually. This need was replaced by Formosan sugar. The paper making industry in Formosa, which had a capacity of producing 74,000 tons of paper, paper pulp, and paper strawboard annually, was also damaged by wartime bombing. Along with the progress of rehabilitation, production was increased from 10,000 tons in 1946 to 20,000 tons in 1947 and 1948. China planned to expand the Formosan paper industry in order to manufacture newsprint and thus to reduce its dependence on imports, this being a large item in China's total imports.

The aid given by the United Nations Relief and Rehabilitation Administration greatly contributed to the rehabilitation of agriculture and the production of cotton textiles and coal. During the war, damage and destruction to agriculture were widespread, and the rural economy deteriorated greatly in both occupied and unoccupied areas. Land adjacent to the fighting zones was deserted for quite a long time, and millions of acres lay fallow. Farm animals were either slaughtered for food or requisitioned for transportation by enemy troops. Even farm implements were taken away by the enemy for their metal content. The government's action in opening the southern dyke of the Yellow River at Huayuank'ou, Honan, in order to throw an obstacle in the path of the enemy advance, caused the flooding of more than three million acres of rich land and left several million peasants homeless.

The conscription of farmers for labor by the Japanese army involved a great number of farm workers. In many places where fighting occurred or the Japanese army was stationed maintenance work on river and sea levees was neglected and millions of acres were inundated. During the war years food production in China proper suffered a decline of 5 per cent from the prewar average. Cotton production was reduced to less than one-half of that in prewar years. Again, the Japanese carried out a plan to destroy the Chinese silk industry by demolishing buildings and equipment of silk filatures and compelling the people to uproot mulberry trees to the extent of one-half of the acreage.

Under the aid program of UNRRA nearly one million persons were resettled in their farmlands; a little more than 4,600 miles of dykes and a few hundred miles of river and sea levees were built or repaired; fertilizers and seeds were distributed to the farmers. These undertakings expedited the return of agricultural production to normal proportions. The 1947 production of husked rice in China proper reached 1,800,000,000 bushels, or about 6 per cent higher than the prewar 1931–37 average, and that of wheat in the same area reached 1,230,000,000 bushels, or 3 per cent higher than the prewar average. Cotton production was restored to more than 2,400,000 bales in the same year, which was 33 per cent less than the prewar. During 1946 and 1947 UNRRA imported 633,900 bales of cotton, 26.5 per cent of the total cotton imports to China, which not only relieved the shortage of the cotton supply from North China to the Shanghai mills, caused by the disruption of transportation, but also eased the difficulty of manufacturers in obtaining foreign exchange allocations from the government. A number of small power units were allocated to coal mines, thus facilitating their early rehabilitation.

At the end of the war China was like a starving person wanting to get every kind of commodity necessary for relief, rehabilitation, and general consumption. The government authorities, intending to halt the inflation by increasing the supply of goods, adopted a liberal policy on imports. American army surplus properties, including equipment and consumer goods, were bought both by the government and private firms and sold at low prices on the market. The poor people could even afford to enjoy foreign fruits and canned goods which they formerly considered luxuries. Moreover, merchants were quick to seize the opportunity for profits by importing a great variety of consumer and luxury goods. Thus foreign goods flooded all the big cities and were sold at cheap prices. The impact of these supplies during mid-1946 had adverse effects upon domestic industries, particularly those which had been built up in the interior during the war with but small capital and poor equipment and had already lost local markets as a result of the relocation of population. It was reported that 80 per cent of the 1,100 plants in the interior, mostly in Chungking and Kunming, were forced out of operation.

The revival of many industries in Shanghai was hampered by the competition of foreign goods. Those which were affected the most were the metal, paper, pharmaceutical, cement, caustic soda, condensed milk, tobacco, and the knitting and hosiery industries. After the Shanghai Industry Federation appealed to the government for help in the latter part of 1946, large loans were granted to industries by the government banks at low interest rates, and the privilege of foreign exchange at the official rate, which was lower than the market rate, was liberally extended to manufacturers to aid them in the purchase of imported raw materials. However, the manufacturers sold their products at a price based upon that of raw materials imported at the foreign exchange price if bought at market rates, and thus made greater profits as the difference between the official rate and the market rate became increasingly wider. The granting of foreign exchange at the official rate was, on the whole, a great help to domestic industry.

It is ironical that the large imports of rice, wheat, wheat flour, and cotton, which were intended to relieve the distress of the people suffering from shortage of food and clothing and to slow down the rise of prices, held down the prices of indigenous agricultural products and discouraged increases of domestic production. The import of rice and wheat (including flour) by UNRRA and others amounted to 716,000 bushels and 3,860,000 bushels, respectively, in 1946, and 1,910,000 bushels and 1,300,000 bushels, respectively, in 1947. The UNRRA and commercial imports of cotton totaled 1,600,000 bales in 1946 and 787,000 bales in 1947. Such large imports of the most essential necessities kept the prices of agricultural products exceptionally low in comparison with those of manufactured goods. In the commodity price index, foodstuffs ranked the lowest and textiles next throughout 1946 and 1947. The distortion of the normal relative price relationship between agricultural products and industrial goods naturally upset the equilibrium between costs and prices in agricultural products.

The depressing effect of the large volume of imports on domestic production was more lasting and more serious than government leaders appreciated. While the policy of encouraging imports relieved many shortages that had built up during the war, when foreign trade limitations existed, its long-run effects were not desirable. However, since industrial and commercial importers were making good profits on their imports, they brought effective pressure on the government whenever quantitative or qualitative import restrictions were proposed. As a result, the few restrictions which were imposed not only did not go far enough to protect domestic production but even encouraged additional imports to be made to anticipate tightening of regulations.

Had selective import controls, restricting the inflow of consumer goods and encouraging that of producer goods, been imposed in the critical period of 1946, when chances for progress toward stability were best, they might have had good effects.

From 1942 to the end of the war, speculation in commodities was widespread. Not only did the propertied classes employ their surplus money in speculative investments, but entrepreneurs too, instead of increasing production, diverted their capital to hoarding both producer goods and consumer goods in anticipation of price rises. This resulted in increasing shortages and higher costs of raw materials, which again depressed production. The trend of speculation halted momentarily after the end of the war. At one time entrepreneurs were enthusiastic in investing in industry in view of the expected postwar demand for goods. Machinery ordered abroad during the war was brought in, and new orders were sent out. However, as soon as the inflation became acute and the government emergency measures of February 1947 announced a scale of of ceiling prices, the trend was reversed and the following phenomena developed.

The prices of all commodities rose without interruption, and no fall in prices ever occurred. Therefore, everybody was inclined to get rid of his money and buy goods in anticipation of further price rises.

The government banks adopted a policy of cheap money, and the market rate of interest lagged behind the rises in commodity prices, thus enabling speculators to make profits from hoarded goods purchased with bank credit.

Restrictions on imports became more and more rigid as government foreign reserves dwindled, resulting in a growing scarcity of imported raw materials and an increasing difficulty of replacement. It was generally believed that the hoarding of foreign raw materials was the surest way to make a profit.

The longer the goods were held, the larger the profit would be. As a result, many people hoarded raw materials; and certain materials essential to industry, such as steel, iron and other metals, machinery parts, cotton, and timber became difficult to obtain in the market.

Because of the increasing scramble for raw materials by manufacturers who did not have sufficient working capital to stockpile such materials to keep the machines in production, prices of raw materials rose much higher than those of manufactured goods.

Because of the increase in wage rates, the cost of manufacturing became progressively higher, and it was more profitable to hoard raw materials or to hold the existing stock of manufactured products than to produce new goods.

The government was at last compelled to restrict banking credit because it found that cheap money only fostered speculative activities without making any contribution to production. On the other hand, manufacturers had more plausible grounds to justify a cutback in production and a reduction in payrolls since they could be assured of making profits from the rising prices of inventories.

The farmers became reluctant to buy high-priced consumer goods which were less essential, preferring to reduce their standard of living so that there would be no need for them to dispose of their products. This created difficulties for industry because of the reduction of the farmers' demand and the decrease in the volume of domestic raw materials available for sale on the market.

When inflation reached an acute stage, speculation became widespread. Not only did the manufacturers hoard raw materials but the general public also scrambled for them for hoarding! Meanwhile, manufacturers who had been able to increase inventories by offering a high rate of interest to attract money began to lose deposits and to meet a new competition for raw materials from individual speculators.

Finally, the government was obliged to give assistance to essential industries with credits and raw materials, accompanied by government price fixing for manufactured products. At the same time greater preference was given to government enterprises because they were more easily controlled. As a result, private enterprise gradually lost its independence of operation and incentive to increase productivity and government enterprises were placed in a dominant position.

As the government began to control the selling price of manufactured goods, it also had to control the cost of production, that is, the buying price of raw materials and the scale of wages. Wage control involved the control of a few basic factors such as the price of food, clothing, and shelter. Because the earning power of the farmers was extremely sensitive to the relative price of controlled commodities, they chose to grow crops which commanded either relatively higher prices or uncontrolled prices. Consequently, the production of essential commodities which were subject to rigid controls tended to decline, and that of less essential ones which were not under rigid control or left free tended to increase.

From the postwar production record, as shown in Table 66, it can be seen that agricultural production showed signs of gradual recovery as the result of the termination of war and the resettlement of dis-

TABLE 66. PRODUCTION IN POSTWAR PERIOD

| Agricultural Production | 1931–37 Average | 1946 | 1947 | 1948 |
|---|---|---|---|---|
| Rice (1,000 bushels) | 1,700,000 | 1,710,000 | 1,800,000 | — |
| Wheat (1,000 bushels) | 1,200,000 | 1,360,000 | 1,230,000 | — |
| Cotton (bales) | 3,600,000 | 2,134,000 | 2,410,000 | 2,300,000 |
| Tobacco (metric tons) | 659,000 | 618,650 | 606,200 | — |
| **Industrial Production** | **1936** | **1946** | **1947** | |
| Coal (metric tons) | 22,250,000 | 18,408,000 | 19,487,000 | — |
| Steel (metric tons) | 50,000 | 15,700 | 63,000 | — |
| Iron (metric tons) | 150,000 | 81,000 | 85,000 | — |
| Cotton yarn (bales) | 2,500,000 | 2,582,000 | 1,400,000 | (Jan.–June) |
| Wheat flour (1,000 pounds) | 3,000,000 | 3,782,359 | N.A. | — |
| Cement (1,000 barrels) | 5,700,000 | 2,047,269 | 3,268,398 | (Jan.–Aug.) |
| Paper (tons) | — | 62,361 | 28,062 | (Jan.–June) |
| Sulphuric acid (tons) | 60,450 | 7,205 | 3,963 | (Jan.–June) |

placed peasants; and that industry made a little progress in 1946 followed by a decline which set in in 1947.

The factors listed in the preceding paragraphs effectively diminished the incentives and even the possibilities of carrying on production in existing establishments, and certainly did not encourage the creation of new ones. As the fiscal situation gradually got out of hand after the latter part of 1947, many factors intimately associated with inflation itself reacted more and more unfavorably upon production for exchange, until the output of nonagricultural goods came to a virtual standstill. At the same time, cotton producers in North China, who already were finding it difficult to carry their output to the textile industry centers, were confronted with competition by foreign imports.

Only in 1946, therefore, was production for the market in any way an independent variable which could have been manipulated to combat inflation. By 1947 production was almost entirely subject to inflationary influences, and little could be done to increase the former without first breaking the latter.

## *Distribution*

As soon as the foreign supply routes were reopened after the war, emphasis was placed on steamships and railways as the principal means of transportation, while highway transportation was neglected and stage transportation fell into disuse. The first cargo vessel to enter Shanghai after the war carried relief supplies from the United Nations Relief and Rehabilitation Administration (UNRRA); it was soon followed by other ships of different flags carrying commercial cargoes anxiously awaited by the merchants and UNRRA relief cargoes needed by the government. Since all of these early shipments came to Shanghai, severe port congestion soon developed. It was aggravated by war damage to warehouses and go-downs, reduction of berthing space pending the removal of sunken ships, and the inadequacy of transshipment facilities. Now that Treaty Port privileges for foreign bottoms to engage in inland and coastal shipping were limited to one port of discharge, the load of subsequent transshipment could not be adequately handled by the seriously depleted domestic shipping.

The world shortage of supplies at the end of the war also prevented an import level comparable to prewar. Import tonnage clearing through all Chinese ports in 1946 was only 26 per cent of that in 1936. However, as Chinese private shipping was rebuilt to reach 1,200,000 tons in 1949, and the government-purchased fleet and UNRRA's own shipping became more plentiful, the inland and coastal tonnage increased through 1947 and 1948.

Rehabilitation of the railroads was the first problem which needed to be solved to effect efficient internal distribution. About 1,500 miles of track, 13 per cent of the total prewar mileage, had been dismantled by the Japanese or destroyed by war action, and another 1,300 miles had been severely damaged. A great number of bridges were wrecked, much of the rolling stock was war-damaged, and roadbeds and rails were in need of heavy maintenance. Substantial contributions of railway supplies of all kinds by UNRRA permitted the rehabilitation to proceed apace. Because of Communist disturbances in North China, the Nationalist government determined to concentrate the rebuilding effort to Central and South China, and by 1947 the lines in those regions were virtually all operable. The over-all picture was less rosy: because of the obstacles to rehabilitation in North China, the temporary character of repairs in the central and southern parts of the country, and the lack of rolling stock, freight traffic on all lines controlled by the Nationalist government in 1946 was 31 per cent of the 1935 volume and had risen to only 48 per cent a year later. The flow of coal and cotton from North to South and that of rice and manufactured goods from South to North were particularly affected.

Compared to the war years, distribution in the postwar period was much improved. Shipping and railway traffic replaced the costly highway transportation and the cumbersome distribution by stage transport; foreign supply routes could again be utilized without interference; and shortages of any commodity could be met by imports—all of which should have helped to hold inflation in check. Unfortunately, however, the rapid rise of prices caused by increasing governmental expenditure and the expansion of credit strongly motivated the people to hoard commodities. The advantages of better distribution, being more than offset by the decline in the flow of trade, failed to exert a beneficial effect on aggregate supply.

### *Imports*

After foreign trade had been resumed with the promulgation of relaxed regulations, effective from March 1946 imports began to rise as shown in Table 67. Before the regulations were modified at the end of October to tighten up on imports because the foreign exchange reserve was decreasing, the aggregate of imports had reached U.S. $440,000,000. Total imports for 1946 were U.S. $560,579,822, and total exports were $148,878,808. The adverse balance of trade was U.S. $411,701,014, with a monthly average of $34,308,418. The table shows monthly imports in 1946:

TABLE 67. CHINA'S FOREIGN TRADE BY MONTHS, 1946
(in U.S. dollars)

| 1946 | Imports | Exports | Ratio of Imports to Exports |
|---|---|---|---|
| Jan. | 7,363,425 | 4,339,553 | 1.70 |
| Feb. | 8,192,710 | 2,238,981 | 3.66 |
| March | 21,137,235 | 4,543,189 | 4.65 |
| April | 46,212,424 | 3,709,308 | 12.46 |
| May | 44,319,478 | 9,703,007 | 4.57 |
| June | 67,740,081 | 8,909,892 | 7.60 |
| July | 54,560,933 | 14,922,206 | 3.66 |
| Aug. | 56,135,822 | 24,674,267 | 2.28 |
| Sept. | 72,766,459 | 19,987,408 | 3.64 |
| Oct. | 68,056,580 | 12,405,277 | 5.49 |
| Nov. | 67,427,095 | 21,391,332 | 3.15 |
| Dec. | 46,471,520 | 22,004,388 | 2.11 |

Leading import commodities were, in order of importance: cotton, gasoline, fuel oil, vehicles, paper, chemicals, wool and woolen goods, tobacco. The most striking feature was the large quantities of foodstuffs (including powdered milk, canned goods, oranges, sea foods) and cigarettes, and the large variety of miscellaneous goods imported. Table 68 shows the percentage commodity composition of total imports in 1946, with comparative figures for the prewar year of 1936:

TABLE 68. COMPARISON OF PRINCIPAL IMPORTS

| Commodity | Per Cent of Total Imports 1946 | 1936 |
|---|---|---|
| Cotton | 22.2 | 3.9 |
| Oil | 9.7 | 9.2 |
| Metals | 5.1 | 11.5 |
| Machinery and tools | 2.9 | 6.4 |
| Paper and paper pulp | 6.3 | 6.1 |
| Chemicals and pharmaceuticals | 6.3 | 5.5 |
| Wool and woolen goods | 5.0 | 3.1 |
| Cereals and flour | 2.6 | 5.2 |
| Dyestuffs, paints, varnishes | 4.1 | 4.4 |
| Vehicles, ships, and boats | 6.5 | 5.6 |
| Metal manufactures | 3.4 | 5.0 |
| Tobacco leaf | 3.0 | 1.9 |
| Timber | 1.7 | 3.0 |
| Ramie and ramie goods | 1.1 | 1.9 |
| Others | 20.1 | 27.3 |
| Total | 100.0 | 100.0 |

Postwar imports were excessive for many reasons. Surplus purchasing power accumulated by the people during the war not only was not contracted after the war ended but was increased by large postwar government disbursements in taking over and rehabilitating occupied territories. New purchasing power was pouring into the market. Buyers were scrambling for any kind of imports for which early delivery could be promised because good profits could be made if the goods reached China quickly. Import and export firms sprang up like mushrooms in Shanghai. The abnormal price level for imports had not undergone any readjustment. After 1940 prices for imported goods far exceeded those for domestic products, and they jumped to a level quite beyond reason after Pearl Harbor. On V-J Day in August 1945 in Free China the general price index in the city of Chungking for foreign commodities was (1937, Jan.–June = 100) 6,607. This was 2½ times the index for local products. In Occupied China, the price index for Shanghai was (1937, Jan.–June = 100) 9,740.

In terms of index numbers, metals were nine times dearer than food, and chemicals twice as dear as food, because they were of purely foreign origin and because their prices were not based on the price at the place of production but on what the people would pay for them. This situation produced an extremely irrational price structure. Because the supply of foreign goods could not immediately satisfy the long-standing demand, the public still believed that foreign goods must be high-priced. At the same time the government fixed the exchange rate far below the price level. According to the index for the exchange rate, the official rate was one-fifth of the commodity price index for the whole country and one-quarter of the price index for Shanghai. Because of this overvaluation of Chinese currency and the continued high price level for imported commodities, easy profits could be made on any kind of commodity imported. Thus many goods were imported not to satisfy real demand but to bring large profits.

Internal trade had not returned to normal. After the war the demand for agricultural goods from coastal regions could be more easily satisfied by imported goods, because imported goods of standard quality could be delivered punctually in large quantities, while the rural areas of China's interior had not been rehabilitated from the effects of the war and interior communications had not returned to normal.

At the time of victory the inflationary crisis had reached the stage of an almost complete breakdown. The business community believed that the government should continue its austere war economy, that the people should postpone replenishing consumer goods, and that even the rehabilitation and reconstruction programs should be carefully planned to avoid additional inflation.

It was also believed that the trade figures for 1938 (i.e., imports at U.S. $250 million and an adverse trade balance of U.S. $90 million) would be the best criterion on which the government could work to fix the limit for imports. The figure of imports in 1938 not only represented a volume of goods which the government could afford to pay for but also was one that could be absorbed by the whole of China. Moreover, if relief supplies coming from UNRRA were added to the 1938 import figure, the total would be more than double the 1936 import figure. Unfortunately, the government was much more concerned with increasing supplies of goods from abroad than with curbing the expansion of purchasing power. It had no plan to coordinate UNRRA supplies with other imports. After large reserves of foreign exchange had been spent and large quantities of relief goods had been handed out, inflation was still rampant; and the change in the government's trade policy could not succeed because inflationary cause and effect would bind its hands and put it in a position where it could not attain the object it wished.

In retrospect, it appears that during the postwar period because of accumulated shortages and redundant purchasing power, no encouragement of imports by the government was necessary. What was needed—and not supplied—was a rational plan, equitably enforced, to allocate limited foreign exchange resources among almost unlimited varieties of demand for consumers' and capital goods.

# Part 3

# Anti-Inflationary Policy

# Introduction

Early in the war the government sought to bring about the mobilization of resources for defense by public spending and credit expansion. No thought was given to the inflationary effects of this approach or how they might be controlled. Official awareness of the problem began toward the end of 1939, when the price index moved upward with increasing steepness. After that time the government reacted to every wave of price increases either with new price controls or with restrictions on credit. Central control agencies and subsidiary organs were established and successively reorganized many times. But, although these organs could, on occasion, check the symptoms of inflation temporarily, they were helpless before the steady injection of new purchasing power into the market.

After Pearl Harbor, when aggregate supply and demand began to be in open imbalance, Generalissimo Chiang Kai-shek himself assumed the responsibility for carrying out the anti-inflationary policies—but to no avail. Measures aiming at the effects of inflation were manifestly useless so long as the underlying causes were not corrected. The government itself had unleashed a dynamic growth of demand by continuing inflationary deficit financing and relentless expansion of credit. Unless this primary cause of inflation was removed, the endless array of control measures not only did not halt the symptoms of rising prices and rampant speculation but also advertised the government's apparent inability to cope with the crisis. The lack of adequate administrative machinery and personnel and the inflation-induced moral weakness of the officials in charge of the various control programs further contributed to the ineffectiveness of the controls.

In retrospect, the many attempts to break the inflationary spiral appear to have been a search for a panacea. The government pursued a policy of dealing with inflationary symptoms and ignored the underlying causes with unbelievable consistency—in fact, until the complete collapse of the economy.

Chapter

# 11

# Fiscal and Monetary Policies

## 1. Fiscal Policy

During the war period, 1937–1945, governmental expenditures totaled CNC $2,626,343 million. The fact that only CNC $158,470 million, or 6.0 per cent, of this amount was raised through taxes is dramatic evidence of the extent of the government's failure to use its fiscal powers to relieve inflationary pressures. Two factors made it evident that China needed a vigorous tax policy right from the start of the war in order to absorb the surplus purchasing power of her citizenry. One was that the total mobilization of the country's economy for a modern war was bound to create an unprecedented flow of income to individuals; the other was that, under the then prevailing conditions of the underdeveloped economy, mobilization was bound to create real scarcities as distinct from artificial or temporary shortages, thus building up discrepancies between supply and demand sooner than in countries more advanced economically. A vigorous tax policy was the only practical way to stop inflation.

As if the backwardness of the economy of Free China were not enough of a problem, during the period of wartime stress first priority had to be given to the removal of equipment and goods from the areas being occupied and to the installation and utilization of the equipment. Commercial and industrial buildings also had to be erected quickly, as well as housing for government employees and refugees streaming into Free China's interior, a condition which exerted a severe upward pressure on the wage level of transportation and construction workers. The second phase in the progress of inflation was marked by increased retail trade brought about by the rising level of consumption of these workers and by the population influx.

Higher military and civilian demand as well as inflationary pressures pushed food prices up, ushering in the third phase of inflation—inflation on the farm. The farmers' money income rose and laborers and small merchants began acquiring larger purchasing power while the government was pumping money into the economic stream. The fourth inflationary phase began when people with large incomes utilized an increasing portion of their funds for speculation.

In the early period of the war, therefore, the government's spending injected more money into the income stream flowing to low-income groups than into that going to industries and business firms. Only as inflation gathered momentum was the situation reversed. However, since the farmers, workers, and small businessmen seldom kept books, their income could be ascertained and reached only with utmost difficulty. Even the larger business firms and industries lacked a standardized accounting system. In these circumstances, the taxable income of all brackets could have been reached and the disposable money income of all individuals and businessmen could have been limited only with a skillfully planned taxation system.

But unfortunately, in the management of its war finance, the government never seriously attempted to balance expenditures with tax revenues. Nor did it institute effective measures intended to reduce the disposable money supply of individuals and businessmen. No drastic taxation reform was favorably considered.

The old tax structure was only nominally enlarged by imposing a tax on the lease and sale of property, by installing an inheritance tax, and by levying an excess profits tax in addition to the tax levied on earnings of business firms and salaries and other emoluments of individuals. Heavy reliance on indirect taxes was continued, particularly the salt tax. The scope of collection of direct taxes was enlarged, but it neither effectively reached the income of individuals and business firms nor was it able to capture the windfall profits of war profiteers. The inadequacy of the tax structure is illustrated by the fact that only 2.1 per cent of wartime revenues were derived from direct taxes (excluding the land tax).

The levy of the land tax in kind and the compulsory borrowing of grains from rural taxpayers were effective in reducing their level of monetary expenditure. But this form of levy was motivated by the need to supply the military with food, and not by an intent to curtail the disposable money income of the agricultural classes. Uncorrected were all the injustices of collection arising from the antiquated system of the land tax, and new injustices were added: the cost (imposed on the taxpayer) of shipping the grain to the collection depot, the lack of standardized grades of grain, and the absence of uniform units of measure.

The end of the war brought a new opportunity for a sweeping reform of the taxation system. The enhanced prestige of the government and its stronger central authority now placed it in a favorable position to do what it should have done but did not do during the war: find new sources of revenue to balance the budget. But once more the government chose to rely mostly on indirect taxes; the direct taxation system was not improved. Not even the land tax in kind was changed, in spite of its manifest defects and the many complaints from the taxpayers.

And the budget deficit continued to mount. Between 1937 and 1949 the government made no attempt to combat inflation by bringing the level of expenditures in line with revenues. This conclusion is inescapable from an analysis of the fiscal policy and management in those years. The level of expenditures was dictated by the demands of military and administrative spenders who pushed aside considerations of financial stability. The relationship between government expenditure and inflationary pressures had not been critically recognized or earnestly acted upon.

Yet the real value of expenditures fell constantly as a consequence of inflationary finance. As will be shown in the following section, the government neither chose to utilize the most potent weapon in its hands to curb inflation—tax policy—nor did it utilize effectively another weapon of some promise—monetary policy.

## 2. Wartime Anti-Inflationary Monetary Policies

Having failed to attack the basic causes of inflation, and having neglected to use fiscal measures to reduce inflationary pressures, the government's main anti-inflationary efforts lay in the monetary field. But in this area too its efforts lacked success because of many handicaps.

The Central Bank of China was not the sole source which supplied money to the community. The other government banks, which before 1942 had the right of issuing money and always had a large amount of deposits, were in a position to compete with the Central Bank of China. No central banking body existed which could coordinate in harmonious cooperation the activities of private banks. Most of these, particularly the local banks, tended to operate independently, even to the extent of frequently evading government regulations whenever these conflicted with the banks' own interests.

The lack of co-operation of the commercial and native banks with government efforts was largely due to the partial, sporadic, and inconsistent nature of the regulations. Indeed, the government's enforcement of whatever measures were enacted at any time rose and fell with the apparent severity of the increase in inflation.

The banks were also unable to serve the government in mopping up excessive purchasing power of the public either by attracting savings or by selling bonds. The habit of bank-saving had not been developed in the people; the banking system had not developed adequate facilities to serve potential savings account holders. And the bond market had long been mismanaged by the government. As the value of money rapidly depreciated, it became increasingly difficult to induce people to save or to buy government bonds.

The government's anti-inflationary efforts in the monetary field thus remained sterile.

### *Control of Private Credit*

Throughout the war the government's principal credit control device was the screening of bank loans to the private sector. Loans by government banks were passed upon by the Joint Board of Administration of the Government Banks, and restrictions on loans by private commercial banks were also directed. But public and private enterprises as well as other influential groups, neglecting the credit needs of increasing production, constantly brought pressure on the Joint Board whenever it showed reluctance in approving credit applications. And even though the commercial and native banks showed a reduction in recorded credits extended, actually their loans appeared not to have shrunk in any significant degree because many of these banks furnished abundant credit to their own subsidiaries, and some were even engaged in clandestine (unrecorded) lending operations.

Despite sporadic and temporary effects, in the long run the government's credit control efforts failed to alleviate inflationary pressures significantly.

In mid-1940 a severe crop failure in Szechwan Province caused a sudden jump in prices, accentuated by the strong latent inflationary forces. The credit policy of the private commercial banks was blamed for the price rise. On August 7, 1940, a regulation relating to the control of the modern commercial banks was issued in which the following provisions were laid down: banking advances were to be confined to defense industries, developmental projects, and rural cooperative concerns for increasing production and facilitating the movement of goods; loans secured on commodities were to be made only to genuine merchants; no new loans were to be granted on daily necessities; the banks were prohibited from trading in commodities on their own account or on behalf of their customers; and banks were required to maintain reserves equivalent to 20 per cent of their total deposits in one of the government banks. At the same time, the government banks were instructed by the Joint Board of Administration to apportion more credit to manufacturing and mining, and to curtail commercial advances. In order to curb speculation in daily necessities, which had spread alarmingly in 1940, an amendment of December 7th, again applying to the commercial banks, further stipulated that: the mortgagor of any commodity had to be a bona fide member of a merchant guild; the period of a mortgage loan might not exceed three months; no individual mortgage loan was to exceed 5 per cent of the total volume of mortgage loans made by the bank; and one renewal was allowed on mortgage loans, but only if the collateral were real estate, factory plant, buildings, or commodities other than daily necessities.

These measures were successful in checking the expansion of private advances in the closing months of 1940. The annual increase over previous year in industrial and commercial loans extended by the government banks dropped from 392 per cent in 1939 to 25.3 per cent in 1940. But the annual increase over previous year of commercial bank loans began to increase with great rapidity, although there was no appreciable rise in government bank credit until 1942 (Table 69). To a large extent an increasingly rapid rate of credit expansion was inevitable owing to the rise in general price levels.

The regulation contained no restriction on unsecured credits. Since most credits extended by native banks and in a lesser degree by commercial banks were unsecured, a credit loophole thus remained for these banks. The commercial and native banks also placed more emphasis on collateral security and on the borrowers' standing than on the purpose of the credits. Moreover, no agricultural, industrial, or commercial paper representing the productive or distributive process had been developed, a lack which made it most difficult for the government to ascertain whether the final use of credits was in conformity with the regulation.

Attempting to plug the loophole of unrestricted unsecured loans, the government in December 1941 promulgated the following regulations: An unsecured personal loan was limited to CNC $2,000, and was to be granted only if such a loan was essential to the maintenance of livelihood. An unsecured loan for commercial purposes was not to exceed CNC $5,000, and was to be granted only to the bona fide members of those merchant guilds which agreed to assume responsi-

TABLE 69. ANNUAL PERCENTAGE INCREASE IN INDUSTRIAL AND COMMERCIAL CREDIT

| | Increase of Private Credit of Government Banks[1] | | Increase of Private Credit of Commercial and Provincial Banks[2] | | Increase of Rural Credits[1] | | Increase in Advance to the Government[1] | Increase in Price Levels[3] |
|---|---|---|---|---|---|---|---|---|
| Year | Amount | Percentage Increase over Previous Year | Amount | Percentage Increase over Previous Year | Amount | Percentage Increase over Previous Year | Percentage of Annual Increase | Percentage of Annual Increase |
| 1938 | 225 | — | 102 | — | 32 | — | 143 | 27 |
| 1939 | 882 | 392 | 163 | 160 | 47 | 147 | 59 | 68 |
| 1940 | 223 | 25.3 | 88 | 54 | 97 | 206 | 66 | 133 |
| 1941 | 294 | 131 | 927 | 1,052 | 254 | 262 | 146 | 153 |
| 1942 | 4,511 | 1534 | 1,083 | 117 | 220 | 87 | 113 | 201 |
| 1943 | 8,344 | 184 | 2,029 | 187 | 993 | 451 | 104 | 222 |
| 1944 | 13,531 | 162 | 3,087 | 152 | 1,037 | 103 | 243 | 244 |
| 1945 | 121,661 | 899 | 7,974 | 258 | 2,411 | 233 | 645 | 278 |

[1] Based on the Report of the Joint Board of Administration of Government Banks, 1947.

[2] Based on data in W. Y. Chang, *op. cit.*, p. 164.

[3] Based on Monthly Statistics compiled by the Directorate-General of Budgets, Accounts and Statistics.

bility for the character of their members, for the proper use of loan funds, and for the repayment of the loan on the due date. No single unsecured loan was to exceed 5 per cent of total unsecured loans made by the bank, and the aggregate sum of unsecured loans was not to exceed 50 per cent of the banks' total advances. The term of an unsecured loan was limited to three months, and an unsecured loan could be renewed only once for a period of three months.

At this time the government also sought to curtail the amount of deposits obtained by the native banks. A major source of credit in the interior was the unsecured loans of the native banks, which obtained deposits from the public and from some of the smaller commercial banks for a two-week period on the long-established call markets in Chungking and other major cities in Szechwan Province. The government issued an order directing the native banks to discontinue the practice of accepting fortnightly deposits, and to replace fortnightly call loans by the discounting of accepted bills. The only results were that the native banks offered black-market rates of interest to obtain short-term deposits and a great number of forms and papers were created to pass as bills; the character of loans did not change in the slightest degree. According to a survey made in 1940, 88 per cent of the advances made by local commercial banks and 99 per cent of those made by native banks were commercial loans providing the bulk of the working funds of speculators.*

It was not until 1942 that, with the introduction of new measures, the government welded the diverse restrictions on private credit into an integrated system of control. In February of that year steps were taken to limit further the volume of government bank lending. Emphasis was laid on channeling credit into essential enterprises, such as irrigation works and other developmental projects, which would produce additions to output within a year and did not involve excessive capital outlays. As a general principle, accommodations were to be granted only to defense industries and related enterprises, and to producers and merchants engaging in the production and distribution of daily necessities. Loans for any other purpose were prohibited; and it was understood that rediscount and remortgage loans to commercial or native banks were included in the nonessential category. Projected loans in excess of CNC $1 million were subject to the approval of the Joint Administration, and a procedure was adopted to guard against the misuse of loan funds. Prospective borrowers

* Based on Y. J. Kang's article on "The Development and Control of Commercial and Native Banks," Economic Reconstruction Quarterly [in Chinese] No. 1, July, 1942 (Chungking).

were required to furnish details of the output, sales, and financial position of the business for which the loan was desired, which were then checked by the officers of the bank concerned. If accommodation was granted, the borrower was obliged to render a monthly return to the bank on the use of loan funds, and the banks, in turn, forwarded a monthly report of their operations to the Joint Administration.

Later in the year the government introduced measures to strengthen the position of the Central Bank and to rationalize government bank lending activity. At the beginning of the war the reluctance of the banks, excepting the Central Bank of China, to move their headquarters to Chungking led to the assumption of banking leadership by the Central Bank. In the early years the Central Bank financed the government and provided credit to strategic industries in the interior almost singlehanded; and there was a general demand that the Bank's position should be fortified by its being granted sole right of note issue. When this was eventually done, on July 1, 1942, one of the most glaring historical defects of the Chinese banking system was eliminated. The right of government fiscal agency was still shared by all the government banks. Two months later the various lines of banking business were divided among the government banks. Henceforth the Bank of China was to handle all financial transactions related to internal or foreign trade; the Bank of Communications was to deal with all business bearing on transportation, communication, industry, and mining; and all rural financing was transferred to the Farmers' Bank. The Central Bank, besides handling loans to the government and its administrative agencies, was given the responsibility of providing credit to the other banks, enabling it to develop the central bank function of a bankers' bank. The Central Bank was also to assist the Finance Minister in forming monetary policy and in supervising the operations of the money market.

With the addition of new control measures the government achieved a large degree of success in its efforts to curtail the amount of credit made available to the private sector of the economy by private commercial and native banks. The controls imposed on commercial bank lending in 1940 and 1941 and a ban on government bank lending to commercial banks in 1942 were reflected in the comparatively low rates of increase in commercial bank loans during the second half of the war. In the period 1942–1945 commercial bank loans expanded at one-half of the increase in price levels, and commercial bank credit fell from 36 per cent of total private credit in 1941 to 9.4 per cent in 1945. It must be admitted, however, that one reason for the marked decline in the commercial and provincial banks' share of industrial and commercial business was that in the last two years of the war they devoted an increasing proportion of their funds to their own speculative enterprises, which had become far more profitable than ordinary bank lending. This factor partly accounts also for the more rapid rate of expansion in government bank credit, since the government banks were forced to assume responsibility for the essential business deserted by the commercial banks. Even so, total private loans of the government banks increased at less than 10 per cent the speed of prices until after the war, at the end of 1945, when the government encouraged a massive expansion of credit for the purposes of rehabilitation and reconstruction.

In one respect, however, the government failed, in that it was unable to effect even a partial solution of the rural credit problem despite the number of expedients adopted soon after the retreat into the interior and the concentration of all rural banking business in the Farmers' Bank in 1942. As a measure of the growing deficiency of credit outside the main urban centers, it is significant that the volume of rural loans declined from 8.3 per cent of total private credit in 1941 to 3.0 per cent in 1945. The lack of facilities and adequate means of communication remained intractable obstacles to progress in this sphere of banking.

Unfortunately, the fundamental weakness of wartime finance remained: The overwhelming volume of bank advances to the government rose at a rate of about 3.4 times the increase of private credit in 1942 and 7.8 times the increase in 1945. The restrictions on private credit, therefore, seem inconsequential when set against the fantastic increase in the money supply emanating from government deficit spending.

### *Attempts to Control Interest Rates*

The policy of the Chinese government with respect to interest rates, deviating from the policy followed in Western countries in wartime, was not to keep rates low and thus keep charges on the government debt low. Rather, interest rate policy in China was motivated in one direction by a desire to curb inflation, and influenced in the other direction by pressures of industrial groups alleging that high rates would curb production.

Toward the end of 1940 prices and interest rates both began to rise steeply; but it was generally known at the time that the rise of prices was the cause and the rise of interest rates the effect—and not vice versa. The effect of interest rates on production was exaggerated by the industrial pressure groups; bank interest was such a small fraction of the cost of production that the volume of output would hardly be affected by actual or anticipated changes in its rate.

It is possible that the government's interest rate policy had some beneficial effect for psychological reasons in early wartime; but the potency of other economic and market trends soon nullified its effects, and it was a failure.

In the organized markets of Free China there were five groups of interest rates: those of the Central Bank, the government banks, the modern commercial banks, the native banks, and the pawnshops. The loan and deposit rates of the Central Bank, which were the lowest in the market, were followed closely by the government banks, which were controlled by the Joint Board of Administration. The rates of the commercial and native banks were higher than those of the government banks, and the spread between their deposit and loan rates was also larger. The special fortnightly loan and deposit rates of the native banks in the major cities of Szechwan Province were higher than the commercial bank rates. The rates of pawnshops were higher than those of the native banks. In Szechwan Province the fortnightly rate in Chungking and other major cities was taken as the market rate for non-institutional credit operations; in other provinces of Free China the native bank rate was considered to be the market rate.

Prior to 1941 the increase in interest rates was moderate. After the outbreak of war the fortnightly rate in Chungking rose to 1.6 per cent per month from the previous rate of 1.0 per cent; and rates in other parts of the interior varied from 1.4 per cent to 1.5 per cent per month. However, the easy terms of credit offered by the Central Bank, in consonance with the government's policy of encouraging the growth of industry in the interior, caused a fall in interest rates; and in the middle months of 1939 the Chungking market rate declined to 0.9 per cent. In 1940 commodity shortages became acute, competition for industrial raw materials intensified, and the liberal credit policy was abandoned in favor of controls. Interest rates, along with other prices, were forced up, and in the latter part of 1941 the Chungking market rate stood at 2.7 per cent per month.

In conjunction with the measures to abolish the unsound lending practices of the native banks in December 1941, the government tried to control the fortnightly interest rate on native bank loans, subjecting it to the approval of the Central Bank. A market rate of 2.9 per cent, considerably higher than the approved rate, immediately arose in Chungking. In January 1943 the associations of the modern and native banks in the various cities were required to fix their interest rates in accordance with those of the Central Bank, with an allowance for local conditions, and to submit them to the Central Bank for approval. Despite this regulation, market rates rose, and in Chungking ranged between the limits of 3.4 per cent and 10.0 per cent in 1943, and 7.0 per cent and 9.3 per cent in 1944. Market rates per month were considerably higher in Northwest China, the most excessive rate of 15.0 per cent existing in Sian in August 1944. Throughout 1943 and 1945 the Central Bank's rate on monthly discount loans remained fixed at 2.1 per cent.

The annual averages of monthly market rates in five large cities of Free China during the war are shown in Table 70.

TABLE 70. ANNUAL AVERAGE OF MARKET INTEREST PERCENTAGE RATES PER MONTH: 1937–1945[1]

| Year | Chungking | Kweiyang (Kweichow) | Kunming (Yunnan) | Sian (Shensi) | Lanchow (Kansu) |
|---|---|---|---|---|---|
| 1937 | 1.0 | 1.5 | 1.1 | 1.4 | 1.3 |
| 1938 | 1.2 | 1.5 | 1.0 | 1.4 | 1.1 |
| 1939 | 1.3 | 1.9 | 1.8 | 1.9 | 1.4 |
| 1940 | 1.5 | 2.5 | 2.4 | 2.5 | 2.7 |
| 1941 | 1.9 | 3.0 | 2.9 | 5.2 | 3.7 |
| 1942 | 2.8 | 3.4 | 3.4 | 5.8 | 6.0 |
| 1943 | 6.0 | 3.8 | 4.0 | 8.2 | 10.1 |
| 1944 | 9.3 | 6.0 | 10.0 | 9.1 | 10.5 |
| 1945 | 10.1 | 15.0 | 12.5 | 12.0 | 10.5 |

[1] Taken from Abstract of Statistics compiled by the Directorate-General of Budgets, Accounts and Statistics, 1947–1948.

The comparatively low interest rates obtaining in Chungking during the first five years of the war were due to the close supervision of the money market by officers of the government. But by 1943 the relentless rise in prices had induced a huge demand for credit, much of which went unsatisfied because of the government banks' policy of restraint in granting loans. Since many manufacturing firms and commercial enterprises accepted deposits at market rates of interest to meet their credit requirements, the banks were forced to raise interest rates to attract new deposits. Some banks offered high rates on deposits to government organizations, and on occasions even tendered commissions to public servants in charge of banking funds in exchange for the deposits of their departments. Interest rates in Chungking could no longer be held in check against these pressures, and shortly before victory in 1945 the market rate reached 12 per cent per month. In such uncontrollable conditions, the Central Bank hesitated to raise its own rates for fear that they would soon reach the levels of market rates. Consequently, although its facilities for cheap money were exploited to the full by the other government banks and commercial banks, there was no infallible way of ensuring that the latter used Central Bank funds for productive purposes alone.

Fortunately, the expansion of private credit by the government banks, which by 1945 were providing 94 per cent of total private credit granted by the modern banks, was kept within bounds by the policy of direct controls instituted by the government in 1942. To a very small extent, the steep rise in interest rates was one of the less favorable consequences of this policy; but, in the main, it was the inevitable concomitant of excess demand for money in a period of inflation.

### *Attempts to Increase Bank Savings*

In the early war years the government, aware of the necessity of increasing deposits and of keeping the increase in new money as low as possible, launched a number of savings schemes. In the latter part of 1938 a Thrift and Reconstruction Savings Deposits and Savings Certificates Scheme was put into operation. Interest on savings deposits varied from 8 per cent to 12 per cent per annum, and the minimum period of a deposit was three years. The certificates were issued in denominations from CNC $5 to $10,000, and repayment by installments began after a period of six months. A lottery savings scheme was also introduced under which people who deposited money in savings accounts were to receive tickets in a lottery, to be drawn at least a year later, in lieu of interest payments. The public's reaction to these inducements to saving was not enthusiastic, and the total of savings under these schemes was small—CNC $15 million in 1939, and CNC $125 million in 1940. In September 1941 the government endeavored to inject new life into the Thrift and Reconstruction Savings Scheme by presenting it to the public as part of the nationwide war effort. A national committee was organized, with a branch in each province, a sub-branch in each county, and a promotion group in each village.

The public's response was moderately favorable, and savings under this scheme nearly trebled in 1942. However, the rate of savings was still considered unsatisfactory, ordinary savings and deposits under government savings schemes amounting to little more than one-twentieth of total government bank credit; and in 1944 the government resorted to compulsory allocation of savings certificates. Each county and village was given an allocation of savings certificates entitled "County and Village Public Welfare Savings," and the local government was made responsible for their sale. The goal of the subscription was set at CNC $22,900 million for 1944, but less than a quarter of this sum was secured; and the local governments, rather than the public, were the main subscribers (Table 71).

TABLE 71. TOTAL NOMINAL SAVINGS IN THE GOVERNMENT BANKS[1]
(CNC $ millions)

| Year | Ordinary Savings | Government Savings Schemes | Total Savings | Sales of U.S. $ Certificates and Gold Savings Deposits | Combined Total | Percentage Ratio of Savings to Total Deposits |
|---|---|---|---|---|---|---|
| 1940 | 403 | 125 | 528 | 5 | 533 | 8 |
| 1941 | 600 | 498 | 1,098 | 6 | 1,104 | 10 |
| 1942 | 1,094 | 1,436 | 2,530 | 446 | 2,976 | 15 |
| 1943 | 2,938 | 2,539 | 5,477 | 1,910 | 7,387 | 24 |
| 1944 | 6,425 | 4,989 | 11,414 | 4,042 | 15,456 | 16 |
| 1945 | 34,039 | 11,698 | 45,737 | 9,956 | 55,693 | 11 |

1 Based on Report of Joint Board of Administration of Government Banks, 1947.

Included in the Chinese government's estimates of savings were proceeds in CNC from sales of U.S. $100 million Savings Certificates, issued in April 1942 and secured by the proceeds of the United States Treasury Credit of 1942 amounting to U.S. $500 million, and Gold Savings Deposits Certificates, issued at the end of 1944, redeemable with gold to be purchased from the United States with the proceeds of the same credit.

Both these certificates could be purchased with CNC and were redeemable after one year. The Dollar Savings Certificates were sold at a conversion rate of CNC $20 to U.S. $1, which compared to the black market rate of CNC $40 to U.S. $1 in the first half of 1942 and CNC $30 to U.S. $1 in the second half of the same year. The conversion rates of the Gold Savings Deposits were set at half the market price of gold. In addition to these attractive conversion rates, sales were more in the nature of investments than savings, the transaction involved being identical to forward buying of foreign exchange and specie. The Chinese public was quick to take advantage of opportunities to make profitable investments, and in 1944 proceeds from sales of Gold Savings Deposit Certificates amounted to 26 per cent of total savings.

The government's drive for savings was not effective as a means of combating inflation. At no time after 1937 did the volume of savings, including proceeds from sales of certificates, amount to more than 9 per cent of the total outstanding loans of the government banks; and in 1945 it amounted to a mere 4 per cent of total loans. Furthermore, the increase in savings after 1939 was more than offset by the decline in fixed deposits of the government banks. The combined ratio of fixed deposits and savings to total deposits dropped from 47 per cent in 1939 to 11 per cent in 1945 (Table 72), reflecting the growing reluctance of the general public to hold money. Thus the savings campaign, although moderately successful considering the negligible level of savings in China before the war, did not approach the scale that was necessary to counter the inflationary impact of the expansion of private loans and government advances.

TABLE 72. SELECTED CHINESE BANKING INDICATORS, 1937–1945

| | Government Banks | | | Commercial and Provincial Banks |
|---|---|---|---|---|
| Year | Ratio Fixed Deposits and Savings to Total Deposits | Ratio Private Loans to Total Deposits | Ratio Total Loans to Total Deposits | Ratio Total Loans to Total Deposits |
| 1937 | 40 | 67 | 96 | 67 |
| 1938 | 39 | 59 | 110 | 73 |
| 1939 | 47 | 58 | 110 | 71 |
| 1940 | 45 | 50 | 114 | 60 |
| 1941 | 41 | 32 | 118 | 70 |
| 1942 | 24 | 42 | 143 | 98 |
| 1943 | 27 | 57 | 188 | 110 |
| 1944 | 17 | 34 | 180 | 84 |
| 1945 | 11 | 29 | 230 | 151 |

## *Sales of Bonds to the Public*

The government almost abandoned its effort to sell bonds to the public after its indifferent success in issuing National Liberty Bonds in 1937. But in March 1941 bond sales efforts were renewed; a Wartime National Bond Subscription Commission was established, and an intensive promotion by the central, provincial, and municipal administrations was undertaken.

Actual sales in 1941 covered 1.5 per cent of the deficit for the year. Small as this amount was, it relieved inflationary pressures by that much.

Compulsory allocation was the government's next step. With the purchase of bonds remaining voluntary in rural districts, subscription by assignment was resorted to in cities. To rich merchants, professionals, landowners, and owners of improved real estate the government assigned certain amounts of war bonds in proportion to their incomes. This brought about an improvement in bond sales, raising such financing from 1.9 per cent of the deficit in 1942 to 10 per cent in 1943.

However, the central and local authorities failed to create a systematic method of appraising properties and ascertaining the amount of individual incomes; instead, assessments were made in an improvised manner. In most instances, public bodies were allocated a lump sum for further allocation to business firms and individuals in their jurisdiction. This system precluded equity and faced increasing resistance. Proceeds from bond sales dropped to 1.5 per cent of the deficit in 1944 and 5.7 per cent in 1945—even after a part of the subscriptions was made by local governments and public organizations themselves.

Recorded bond sales in 1942 and 1943 include the issue of U.S. $100 million Bonds of 1942, which was secured by the proceeds of $500 million of the United States Treasury Credit of that year. Because the issue's redemption period was ten years, public subscriptions at first were unenthusiastic in spite of the low conversion rate between CNC and U.S. dollars: CNC $20 to U.S. $1, compared to the average market rate of about CNC $35 to U.S. $1 in 1942 and about CNC $64 to U.S. $1 in 1943. The full issue was finally sold, at less than the expected amount, by allocation to different local governments.

### *Gold Sales*

After the Chinese government had obtained the Treasury Credit of U.S. $500 million from the United States, many suggestions about the use of the proceeds were voiced in China.

The cutting off of all communication lines precluded bringing in goods from abroad. The relatively low value of foreign exchange compared with commodities and gold strongly suggested the desirability of employing the loan to purchase gold; but views on how to utilize the gold differed.

One proposal was to sell a modified gold certificate to the public. It was to be sold at the current market price of gold, and could either be held as savings or negotiated freely at the market value of gold. It was not to be redeemable until after the war. Issuance of the certificates and control of the gold backing was to be under a trustee board composed of representatives of the Bankers' Association, chambers of commerce, and the government. The intent was for the certificates to absorb a part of the excess purchasing power without dissipating the gold. A contrary view held that the public would not welcome a modified gold certificate which was not to be redeemed in gold and that the certificate would have no immediately anti-inflationary effect.

Government leaders finally decided to sell gold to the public, in addition to issuing Dollar Savings Certificates and Dollar Bonds, and to use another $200 million for the purchase of gold in the United States, to be shipped to China for sale, the balance to be drawn later. The Farmers' Bank was placed in charge of the sale of gold in November of 1943. Before long, however, the government found it most difficult to fix the selling price of the gold. On the one hand, the government's interest demanded the adjustment of the selling price whenever the market price of gold rose. But on the other hand, the upward revisions invited criticism that the government led the rise of prices. As a result of such criticism, upward revisions of the selling price lagged, and there resulted a considerable spread between the official and the market prices, which in turn greatly benefited the profiteers. In an effort to overcome this situation, purchasers of gold were required to buy so-called Village Public Welfare Savings to the extent of 10 per cent of their gold acquisitions; this requirement was soon raised to 20 per cent.

Gold sales were discontinued in November 1944, after $17 million of gold from the United States and a small quantity of gold held by the Central Bank of China had been disposed of. About one million ounces of gold were thus sold. Delay of gold shipment from the United States accounted for the discontinuation.

## 3. Postwar Anti-Inflationary Monetary Policies

### *Renewal of Gold Sales*

Early in 1946 the Central Bank was again instructed by the government to sell gold with the purpose of neutralizing increases in consumer purchasing power arising out of the budget deficit. This technique had proved a failure during the war years because the supply of money had increased too fast to be appreciably influenced by sales of the limited amount of gold available. Despite the unfavorable wartime experience, the government believed that the gold which the United

States government had agreed to ship to China and which was held by the Central Bank, equivalent to approximately U.S. $200 million, could now be used as an effective weapon against inflation. To avoid the previous mistake in rate policy, the Central Bank's official quotations of gold now moved with the market price. The former method of making direct sales to the public of a quantity of gold specified in advance was replaced with sales of undisclosed amounts through the Central Bank's agents.

When gold sales were resumed on March 8, 1946, the market price of gold had been increasing rapidly for two months and was more than double its immediate postwar level. Shortly before the Japanese defeat the puppet Central Reserve Bank in Shanghai sold Gold Savings Certificates, redeemable in gold after a lapse of one month, as a means of countering inflation. The price of the certificates started at CNC $780,000 per tael (one tael nearly equal to one ounce) in May 1945, and finished up at CNC $7,000,000 per tael in August. In the latter month the price of gold in Free China (Chungking) reached a peak of CNC $230,000 per tael. After victory the price of gold all over China fell heavily and remained in the region of CNC $70,000 to $80,000 per tael until the beginning of January 1946. Because of the increasing amount of speculative activity involving gold, the Shanghai market price of gold jumped from CNC $84,000 on January 12 to CNC $185,000 at the end of February. The Central Bank quoted a price of CNC $165,000 per tael when it resumed selling; and its heavy sales, which, as reported, from the beginning of March to the end of May equaled one-fifth of the private banks' total deposits, exercised a steadying influence on prices. In June, however, the Shanghai market price was forced up to $200,000 per tael by an increase in gold prices inland, especially in Northern China, where civil war had broken out. During the next seven months the Shanghai price continued to ascend steeply as a result of a combination of factors, the chief of which were the depreciation of the official exchange rate against the U.S. dollar in August, the influx of refugee capital from the interior, much of which was dissipated in gold speculation, and, most important of all, the cumulative decline in the internal value of the currency stemming from excessive advances to the government. The demand for gold increased, and the Central Bank was unable to check rises in the market price by raising the quantity sold. By February 1, 1947, the price of gold had reached CNC $407,000 per tael, and ten days later stood at CNC $960,000. In view of the drain on the Central Bank's gold reserves, which had been reduced by 60 per cent or 3,300,000 ounces since the initial sales eleven months earlier, the government decided to suspend the gold policy on February 17. Thus the policy was in effect for less than one year.

### *Experiments in Credit Control*

The economic precepts of the Chinese government were rudely shaken by developments in 1946. Credit policy vacillated between easy money and restriction; and, when the policy was restrictive, qualitative and quantitative controls alternated.

In order to decrease the private commercial banks' ability to expand credit, attempts were made to reduce their credit base by prohibiting government banks from depositing funds with them and by offering the private commercial banks higher interest rates on their deposits with government banks to induce them to deposit funds with the latter. But these measures failed to attack the monetary sources of inflation.

By August 1946, when Shanghai prices were almost three times their January levels, it was considered in political circles that the over-expansion of government bank credit to the private sector had become the immediate cause of inflationary trends. In September 1946 the government, influenced by this opinion, suddenly decided to restrict government bank lending by temporarily suspending credit other than loans to salt merchants, documentary credit, and loans approved by the Joint Administration of the Government Banks. Mortgage and unsecured loans were banned. Yet at the end of the year the government acceded to the request of the business community for large-scale production loans to relieve the financial burdens of manufacturing firms, including many producing nonessentials, which were operating far below capacity because of competition from imported goods and high costs of labor and raw materials. In practice, then, the September controls were not so rigorous as they appeared on paper.

At the time of the Emergency Measure promulgated in February 1947 the government returned to its theory that relaxation of credit controls was essential for an increase in production, and that the price and wage ceilings could not be maintained without such an increase in output. In April, therefore, the limit above which individual loans of the government banks were subject to the approval of Joint Administration was raised from CNC $50 million to $200 million. To render assistance to productive enterprises, rates of interest on industrial loans were to be kept at a minimum and manufacturers were again permitted to use buildings and machinery as partial security for loans. At this time also the rediscount and remortgage facilities of the government banks were liberalized. Under the directive of May 1946 rediscount and remortgage were obtainable only in respect to funds provided jointly by groups of private banks for allocation by the Central Bank of China to approved enterprises.

The new governor of the Central Bank of China, who had succeeded to office in March 1947 after the failure of the gold policy and the emergency measure, was anxious to revive normal banking procedures and to allow the commercial and native banks to exercise their own judgment in assessing the credit-worthiness of prospective borrowers. To this purpose a Loan and Rediscount Committee was set up to which the private banks might apply for rediscount and remortgage on their individual loans.

The Loan and Rediscount Committee was composed of representatives of the government and of the commercial and native banks. It had two subordinate credit control committees, one dealing with industrial advances and the other with loans to exporters. Besides reviewing the applications of the private banks for government bank credit, the committee took over from the Joint Board of Administration the work of screening government bank loans to the private banks.

For some time the remote and detailed control of credit exercised by the Joint Administration had caused widespread dissatisfaction among bankers and businessmen. Until April 1947 a government bank loan of over CNC $50 million (about U.S. $18,410 at the average rate of exchange for 1946) had first to be approved by a branch office of Joint Administration and then referred to the head office where it was examined by a committee of experts. Well-established businesses always received priority over newer or smaller concerns. Borrowers who had access to the Board members, and knew how to prepare the necessary forms, had a much greater chance of having their applications approved regardless of the condition of their businesses. In anticipation of a long delay before the Board announced its verdict, borrowers greatly exaggerated their credit requirements to make allowance for further depreciation of the currency in the interim and routine cuts by the Board of the amount originally specified. These obvious weaknesses led to a general demand for the abolition of the Joint Board of Administration and for the transfer of its powers of credit regulation to the government banks and the big private banks, which were in a much better position to assess the merits of each loan application. With the establishment of the Loan and Rediscount Committee, these demands were translated into official action.

Toward the end of 1947 the monetary policy of the government entered on another stage of extreme restrictiveness, provoked by upsurges in Shanghai price levels during the middle months of the year.

In August regulations were promulgated which were designed to keep the expansion of credit to private enterprise within bounds by increasing the degree of selectiveness of government bank advances. Government bank loans were confined to five categories of borrowers: merchants and producers engaged in the production and distribution of daily necessities in short supply, industrial and commercial enterprises producing essential commodities that could compete with imported products, transport concerns and public utilities, and exporters. The good faith of prospective borrowers was to be thoroughly investigated before loans were approved, and the lending bank was made responsible for ensuring that loan funds were properly employed. No private commercial banks were to conduct speculative transactions or to engage in trading in commodities; and they were to adhere to the principle laid down by the Joint Administration of giving first consideration to the needs of essential enterprises in granting credit. A Banking Control Bureau, with branches in all the big banking centers, was established with powers to conduct intermittent examinations of the accounts of the banks and to suspend the operation of any bank discovered violating government regulations.

Despite the efforts of the government, speculation abounded and prices mounted. In January 1948, Shanghai prices rose by no less than 40 per cent. Swayed by irresponsible opinions, the leader of the government imposed a total ban on all bank loans, execpt those to agricultural and export industries, to coincide with the beginning of the Chinese New Year in February. This extremist measure aroused considerable excitement in the money market.

After the suspension of credit in January the government announced that first priority would be given to meeting the requirements of agricultural enterprises and government industries during the coming year. This meant that the private enterprises would obtain credits from commercial banks or outside of banking channels.

The comprehensive ban on credit was lifted in March 1948, but credit was still being limited as to duration: 15 days was the maximum time allowed for rediscount, 30 days for remortgage, and 20 days for rediscount of documentary bills. Only export credit was permitted to be extended for three months.

The government banks had formerly enjoyed the privilege of negotiating directly with the Central Bank for rediscount and remortgage services. Now they were placed on the same footing as the private banks, being required to submit their applications to the Loan and Rediscount Committee. Furthermore, a new method of extending loans to essential businesses by making advance payments for commodities in the process of production or distribution was encouraged. This practice had been used by the government banks after the suspension of credit in January 1948 as a temporary measure to tide merchants over the Chinese New Year settlements. The products purchased through the Central Bank were at first confined to six categories of daily necessities: textiles, leather goods, paper, soap, matches, medicine; and to three kinds of basic industrial goods: iron and steel, cement and machinery, to which coal was added later. The quantity of products purchased in this way was not to exceed one month's production at the average rate of output during the previous six months; and the purchase price paid by the government via the instrumentality of the Central Bank was to be the average of market prices prevailing in the six days immediately prior to the approval of the loan. These advances were restricted to industries in real need of financial assistance and were to be used by them to increase production.

Manufacturers did not respond enthusiastically to the government's scheme, because raw material, wage, and other costs were mounting with such rapidity that the purchase price offered by the Central Bank when the loan was granted often fell short of production costs by the time the commodities concerned were actually delivered. Since the Central Bank would not agree to pricing goods on the basis of the actual costs anticipated plus a margin for profit, its purchase price was invariably lower than the marketable price of goods on completion. Moreover, loans of this description had to pass through devious administrative channels before final approval, by which time many manufacturers had been forced to seek alternative credit accommodation. It was not until the government began to finance manufacturers' purchases of raw materials that a few essential industries, such as textile and flour mills, began to sell their products to the government in advance of production.

By the middle of 1947, since the private commercial banks had come to dominate a large sector of the money market, alterations in the lending policies of the government banks were not sufficient to yield the changes required in the over-all distribution of credit. A trend toward the concentration of funds in the hands of the private banks, stimulated by the discrepancy between the official and black-market rates of interest, had been in evidence for some time. During 1947 the rate of increase in deposits of the private banks had been much faster than that of the government banks, and at the end of the year the private banks handled 92.9 per cent of total bank clearings in Shanghai. Consequently, the restrictions on government bank credit left the speculative side of the money market untouched.

In an attempt to overcome these deficiencies in its banking controls, the government introduced further measures in December 1947. The government banks were prohibited from maintaining deposits with the commercial banks, and the latter were prohibited from quoting interest rates higher than those approved by the Central Bank.

Early in 1946, with the object of stabilizing interest rates, the Central Bank began to announce its rediscount rate, in the hope that the money market would use it as a standard on which to base its interest quotations, and made it compulsory for the modern and native Bankers' Associations to obtain the approval of the Central Bank for the rates they applied to deposits and loans. To prevent the private banks from using their funds in speculative operations, it was also ruled that their rates on deposits must not exceed their rates on loans. While the Central Bank's rediscount rate remained as comparatively low as 1.8 per cent throughout 1946, the market rate of interest gradually rose following the general rise in prices. The Central Bank, forced to recognize the compulsion behind this trend, approved increases in the rates of the private banks. As a result, these monthly rates of interest in Shanghai rose from 7 per cent in January 1946 to 14 per cent in December of the same year. The government banks quoted a third interest rate which was higher than the rediscount rate and lower than the market rate. Since this approved rate continually lagged behind commodity prices, a much higher black-market rate emerged, which added to the pressure on the Central Bank, government banks, and approved market rates. It was only to be expected that the government banks would exploit the cheap money of the Central Bank as one of their sources of profit, that the private banks would endeavor to draw on the cheaper credit facilities of the government banks, and that individual borrowers, who could profitably take advantage of the lag in interest rates behind prices, would swamp the private banks with demands for credit.

Whether or not the cheap money policy should be maintained became a controversial question at the end of 1946. The advocates of higher interest rates criticized cheap credit on the grounds that it benefited speculators without imposing the least check on price levels. They favored a narrowing of the gap between the Central Bank rate and the approved market rate and the abolition of concessional interest rates used to subsidize certain industries. The defenders of cheap money argued in return that price inflation was moving so rapidly that a rise in interest rates not only would be useless as a means of rationing credit but also would add to the financial difficulties of essential enterprises. Most of the members of the Joint Board of

Administration who were departmental heads, e.g., the Ministers of Finance, Economic Affairs, Defense, and Communications, were against increases in interest rates which would have been added to the financial burdens of their organizations. The general conclusion was that raising the Central Bank rate would have salutary effects only in conditions of moderate inflation. The status quo was therefore maintained despite the fact that at the beginning of 1947 the Central Bank rate was only one-sixth of the approved market rate and one-tenth of the black-market rate (Table 73).

TABLE 73. SHANGHAI—MONTHLY INTEREST RATES AND WHOLESALE PRICE INCREASES, 1946–1947[1]

| Month | Central Bank Rediscount Rate Monthly (per cent) | | Approved Market Interest Rate Monthly (per cent) | | Black-Market Interest Rate Monthly (per cent) | | Percentage Increase of Wholesale Prices Monthly | |
|---|---|---|---|---|---|---|---|---|
| | 1946 | 1947 | 1946 | 1947 | 1946 | 1947 | 1946 | 1947 |
| Jan. | 1.8 | 1.8 | 7.0 | 13.5 | 11.0 | 18.0 | 80 | 19 |
| Feb. | 1.8 | 1.8 | 8.0 | 13.5 | 19.0 | 19.0 | 71 | 60 |
| March | 1.8 | 1.8 | 8.0 | 13.5 | 19.0 | 16.0 | 25 | 5 |
| April | 1.8 | 1.8 | 8.0 | 13.0 | 13.0 | 12.0 | −5 | 21 |
| May | 1.8 | 1.8 | 8.0 | 15.0 | 16.0 | 20.0 | 11 | 54 |
| June | 1.8 | 1.8 | 8.0 | 15.0 | 13.5 | 19.0 | 4 | 12 |
| July | 1.8 | 1.8 | 8.0 | 15.0 | 15.0 | 19.0 | 7 | 15 |
| Aug. | 1.8 | 1.8 | 13.5 | 14.2 | 13.0 | 15.0 | 8 | 9 |
| Sept. | 1.8 | 1.8 | 15.0 | 15.0 | 16.0 | 18.0 | 14 | 27 |
| Oct. | 1.8 | 1.8 | 16.5 | 18.0 | 16.0 | 21.0 | 21 | 57 |
| Nov. | 1.8 | 1.8 | 15.0 | 16.5 | 13.5 | 19.0 | 2 | 13 |
| Dec. | 1.8 | 1.8 | 13.5 | 19.5 | 16.0 | 23.0 | 8 | 21 |

[1] Based on data compiled by the Economic Research Department of Central Bank and by Directorate-General, Budgets, Accounts and Statistics.

At the end of 1947 the governor of the Central Bank suggested to the Joint Board of Administration that the Central Bank rate and the interest charged by the government banks should be raised nearer to parity with the approved market rate. This move was strongly opposed by leaders of the government banks, who represented a strong party view, because the profits they derived from the difference between the Central Bank rate and their own lending rates would have been greatly reduced, while an increase in their own rates would adversely affect the borrowing of party enterprises. The Board approved a compromise scheme providing for differential government bank rates. The old low rates on loans to government enterprises were maintained, rates charged to essential industries were increased slightly, and rates applying to the rest of private business were raised nearer the approved market rate, though they still remained well below parity with the latter. At this time commodity prices got into such a steep upswing that everyone demanded credit to buy one day what would be more expensive the next. The interest rate became an insignificant factor in the expansion or contraction of credit.

In August 1947 the Central Bank launched a scheme to immobilize funds in the hands of the private banks by accepting ten-day fixed deposits from the commercial and native banks at an interest rate of 5 per cent per month, raised to 8 per cent in November. The period of deposit was shortened to one week in February 1948, and the rate of interest increased again to 12 per cent per month. In May the Central Bank offered no less than 15 per cent on these short-term deposits. The average of weekly deposits of the private banks in Shanghai with the Central Bank during the first seven months of 1948 was as shown in Table 74.

TABLE 74. PRIVATE BANK DEPOSITS WITH CENTRAL BANK, 1948

| Month | Average of Weekly Deposits (CNC millions) | Per Cent of Total Private Bank Deposits |
|---|---|---|
| Jan. | 300,000 | 10 |
| Feb. | 680,000 | 13 |
| March | 740,000 | 17 |
| April | 1,110,000 | 14 |
| May | 3,100,000 | 27 |
| June | 2,000,000 | 16 |
| July | 800,000 | 3 |

During the first half of 1948 funds held by the private banks in Shanghai were swollen by an inflow of refugee capital from North China after the government's military setbacks in Manchuria. The Central Bank decided to supplement its efforts to decrease the liquidity of the private banks with measures to draw off funds from the general public. In April 1948 the Central Bank began issuing treasury bills carrying a nominal interest rate of 5 per cent per month, redeemable at the end of a month, and selling at a price fixed from time to time by the Bank. The selling price of the first issue was 87.3, producing a redemption yield of 19.5 per cent per month. In May the price was lowered to 84.5, and later to 83.8, giving yields of 23.3 per cent and 24.3 per cent, respectively. About CNC $1,000,000 million worth of Treasury Bills were sold in the first month of sales, rising to $2,000,000 millions in May and June.

At this time funds could be employed on the market in three ways: in commodity trading, in lending at black-market rates, or in speculating in securities. The estimated yields the investor might obtain are shown in Table 75. It can be seen that speculation in commodities

TABLE 75. ESTIMATED PROFITS FROM SPECULATION, 1948

| 1948 | Monthly Profit Percentage from Increase of Commodity Price (according to Shanghai Wholesale Price Index) | Percentage of Profit from the Increase of Security Price (index of one leading security)[1] | Monthly Black-Market Interest Rate[2] (monthly average) |
|---|---|---|---|
| Jan. | 40 | 45 | 24 |
| Feb. | 43 | 14 | 23 |
| March | 62 | 80 | 29 |
| April | 16 | 10[3] | 26 |
| May | 44 | 20 | 28 |
| June | 88 | 77 | 30 |

[1] Taken from Quotations of Chinese Securities published in Shanghai Bankers' Weekly, September 23, 1948.

[2] Taken from Tables of Interest Rates in Shanghai, published in Monthly Bulletin of Central Bank of China, July, 1948.

[3] Suspension of forward sale by government order.

was the most profitable use of money, with trading in securities next in order although subject to wider fluctuation. Lending money out through the small banks or underground banks on the black market, which were solely concerned with illicit transactions, was a less secure and also less profitable operation.

In May, for instance, yields of 23 per cent on the Central Bank's treasury bills did not compare favorably with returns of 28 per cent from market lending, 44 per cent from holding commodities for a month, and 20 per cent for speculating in securities. Bank deposits with the Central Bank and proceeds from sales of treasury bills were estimated to be about one-tenth of liquid funds flowing in the market. As black-market rates of interest rose higher, eventually to exceed 30 per cent per month, the private banks became less and less willing to keep deposits with the Central Bank. In July the Central Bank decided to discontinue the practice. The private banks, following in the footsteps of the Central Bank, began accepting weekly deposits from the public at very attractive rates of interest, and funds which might have been invested in treasury bills were switched to the private banks. Sales of treasury bills were suspended at the end of July 1948, only to be revived after the failure of the August measures for currency reform. This latter attempt to sell bills was again vitiated by the overwhelming competition for funds in the market.

While the Central Bank endeavored by indirect methods to reduce the lending ability of the private banks, it also applied them to the government banks. The first step was to transfer all government accounts to the Central Bank. On paper the Central Bank had been the sole government fiscal agent since October 1946, but this regulation had never been put into effect because of opposition from the other government banks. The Central Bank made constant appeals to the government to enforce this measure because it was discovered that many officials in military organizations and public enterprises were using government funds in accounts with the government banks in speculative activities which were a disturbing influence in the money market. Repeated instructions from the government to public organizations to transfer their accounts to the Central Bank were openly defied. Finally, because of the insistence of the Central Bank, the accounts were transferred from the government banks early in April 1948. It is a revealing commentary on the activities of the politically influential party members controlling the interests of the government banks that such a simple yet fundamental financial measure was not enforced until the climax of inflation was at hand.

### *The Final Breakdown of the Money Market*

In view of the public's rapidly waning confidence in the currency, it was inevitable that the government's uncoordinated attempts to restore order in the money market would fail and that the financial system would ultimately disintegrate. The growing reluctance of the public to hold cash or bank deposits is reflected in the increasing velocity of circulation of note issue and velocity circulation of deposit currency during 1947 and 1948 as shown in Table 76.

After the breakdown of the emergency controls on prices and wages of February 1947, the velocity of circulation rose dangerously to 5.02 in May; but it was slightly lower during the last six months of the year. Despite the suspension of bank credit in January 1948, people still believed that the currency would continue to depreciate under the impetus of the enormous government deficit, and the flight from currency to goods became more pronounced. The trend was strength-

TABLE 76. SHANGHAI MONEY MARKET INDICATORS, 1946–1948

| | Checks Cleared[1] | | | | | Private Bank Deposits[4] | |
|---|---|---|---|---|---|---|---|
| | Number (000) | Amount (000,000,000) | Ratio of Amount to Note Issue | Velocity[2] of Circulation of Notes | Velocity[3] of Circulation of Deposit Currency | Current Value (000,000) | Real Value at Prewar Prices (000,000) |
| 1946 | | | | | | | |
| July | 1,702.2 | 3,751.1 | 1.78 | 2.52 | 38 | 100,421.5 | 27.0 |
| Dec. | 2,231.2 | 8,124.0 | 2.18 | 2.57 | 36 | 237,052.4 | 41.5 |
| 1947 | | | | | | | |
| July | 3,041.0 | 38,067.8 | 2.82 | 4.18 | 42 | 714,461.1 | 23.8 |
| Dec. | 4,921.0 | 120,813.0 | 3.64 | 5.27 | 56 | 2,419,333.2 | 28.8 |
| 1948 | | | | | | | |
| May | 6,712.7 | 732,042.0 | 5.33 | 5.56 | 80 | 11,247,349.8 | 20.7 |
| June | 5,239.3 | 848,306.6 | 4.31 | 7.00 | 82 | 12,801,656.3 | 6.5 |
| July | 6,705.1 | 1,969,536.7 | 5.25 | 10.82 | 90 | 24,373,433.4 | 8.5 |

[1] Taken from the data in Shanghai Bankers' Weekly.

[2] Derived by dividing the wholesale price index of Shanghai by an index of note issue. Check transactions impair but do not wholly invalidate these indications.

[3] Derived by dividing total clearings by total current deposits.

[4] Based on data compiled by the Auditing Department of the Central Bank of China.

ened by the uncertainties engendered by the successive defeats inflicted on the Nationalist forces by the Communists in North China. By July 1948 the velocity of circulation had risen to nearly eleven times the prewar rate.

Because of the method of calculation used, the figures for the velocity of circulation overstate the actual variations in velocity since they do not allow for the influence of two other factors symptomatic of failing confidence in the currency in the closing stages of runaway inflation. One was the fall in the volume of goods offered for sale in the market, because of the dislocating effects of inflation on production and the hoarding of commodities by all classes of society. The other, which concerns us more in the present context, was the increasing volume of supplementary money entering circulation as the demand for notes outran the capacity of the government printing presses.

When the rate of depreciation in the currency began to accelerate in 1947 the public sought additional means of payment, first of all by evolving its own methods of credit creation. The practice of writing post-dated checks on anticipated deposits which might or might not materialize grew to threatening proportions in Shanghai. There was a pyramiding of credit as successive issues of checks were made against the original unpaid checks received. When a bank refused to honor a check, a string of checks written against it would also be rejected. On many occasions the banks refused payment on perfectly sound checks because they were short of funds to meet their liabilities, but bad checks had achieved such a wide circulation that the banks' refusals were never questioned by the public.

The increasing use of checks is clearly reflected in the statistics in Table 76. Between December 1946 and June 1947 the number of checks cleared in Shanghai increased by more than a third, and their total value amounted to almost three times the note issue. Alarmed by this spontaneous creation of credit which continued irrespective of controls on the banking system, the government promulgated regulations in July 1947 stating that people could draw checks only against cash deposits and cleared checks, and ordering the banks to close the accounts of clients found guilty of disobeying this regulation. However, the government was unable to influence either the banks or the public into observing its directives, and business continued as usual, although most of it was illegal.

In June 1948 the government took steps to make the restrictions on the use of bank accounts less severe, but to impose enforcement of those that remained. Checks could be drawn on cash orders and uncollected checks guaranteed by the banks as well as against cash deposits and cleared checks; otherwise the banks could allow customers, in cases of necessity, to draw on uncollected checks subject to the signing of an overdraft agreement. The long delays involved in obtaining guarantees or in negotiating with the banks for overdrafts made checks an unsuitable means of transacting day-to-day business. The use of checks declined, and the public began to cash checks for notes or banks' cash orders. The latter became an important additional means of payment. Every bank was crowded until late at night with thousands of customers all clamoring for cash, and bank deposits fell drastically.

The rapid depreciation of the currency in 1947 and 1948 caused a very serious deterioration in the moral standards of the community. The circulation of bad checks is a typical instance of the deleterious effects of inflation in this respect. Institutions, including the banks and the government administration, succumbed to the corrosive influence of inflation. The black-market dealings of the banks multiplied as the financial situation worsened. They bought and sold gold and foreign exchange, accepted deposits and extended loans above the approved rates of interest, speculated in commodities, and allowed customers advances on uncollected checks.

With the establishment of the Banking Control Bureau in December 1947, the government itself resorted to measures of dubious moral standing. Secret police forces were used to carry out raids on banks suspected of contravening the official regulations. Radio communications were checked, and telephone lines were tapped. During the period of total suspension of credit in January 1948 the private banks found it impossible not to grant a certain amount of accommodation to their customers and could not avoid breaches of law.

The Banking Control Bureau's search for irregularities drove even the reputable banks to keep secret books and to engage in secret transactions. Yet much of their business was attracted away by the underground banks, which always succeeded in eluding the attentions of the Bureau's officers. Black-market dealings were regarded by the banks as a safeguard against competition from other banks which offered their clients illegal credit facilities, and as the sole means of survival during a time of crisis when increases in wages and other costs would have caused heavy trading losses if income from black-market sources had not been forthcoming. Secret police could not control a spontaneous movement to obtain and create money involving millions of people, nor could they prevent the banks from acting in accordance with economic necessity. Consequently, the policy of suppression adopted in the early months of 1948 provided no solution to the problem of inflation.

In the general atmosphere of declining confidence in the currency, discontent with the government, and moral irresponsibility prevailing in the first six months of 1948, it is hardly surprising that the banking measures of December 1947 and January 1948 and the Central Bank's operations in the money market failed to achieve their objectives. The government was finally prompted into making a last desperate attempt to check the depreciation of the currency. The new Gold Yuan was introduced in August, exchanging at the rate of 1 : 3,000,000 of the old currency.

In order to decrease the amount of liquid funds available to the money market, all banks and financial institutions were instructed to increase their paid-up capital. The legal minimum of paid capital for banks and trust companies in Shanghai, Tientsin, and Canton was fixed at GY 500,000 and for the native banks at GY 125,000. The increased capital raised was to be deposited with the Central Bank for a period of three months. In this way the government hoped to immobilize GY 50,000,000, or one quarter of the maximum limit total note issue. However, no check was made to discover the quantity of funds actually raised by individual banks, and cash deposits received by the Central Bank under this scheme were only a fraction of the amounts contemplated. Other measures adopted at this time included the imposition of a maximum limit on interest rates of 6 per cent per annum and a ban on government bank credit. In its anxiety to hold the fixed wage and price ceilings, the government virtually suspended all government bank credit; and it was not until the end of the year, when prices and costs had begun to rise with great rapidity, that the government agreed to the extension of a certain amount of emergency credit to industry.

Conditions in the Shanghai money market were relatively stable in September and October, during which time the banks and the public were attempting to determine whether there were real grounds for confidence in the new stand taken by the government. As shown in Table 77, in October the number of checks cleared in Shanghai had

TABLE 77. INDICATORS OF SHANGHAI MONEY MARKET ACTIVITY: AUGUST 1948–MAY 1949[1]

| | Checks Cleared | | | | | Private Bank Deposits[4] | |
|---|---|---|---|---|---|---|---|
| | Number (000) | Amount (GY 000,000) | Ratio of Amount to Note Issue | Velocity[2] of Circulation of Notes | Velocity[3] of Circulation of Deposit Currency | Current Value (GY 000,000) | Real Value at Prewar Prices (CNC 000,000) |
| 1948 | | | | | | | |
| Aug. | 7,843.3 | 1,441 | 4.75 | 7.23 | 27 | 57.2 | 30.7 |
| Sept. | 3,064.8 | 2,399 | 2.51 | 2.38 | 12 | 240.8 | 122.2 |
| Oct. | 1,955.9 | 2,905 | 1.84 | 1.60 | 22 | 147.7 | 67.0 |
| Nov. | 2,800.2 | 10,720 | 3.35 | 9.18 | 52 | 213.4 | 8.4 |
| Dec. | 4,164.8 | 35,023 | 4.28 | 5.05 | 76 | 509.1 | 14.2 |

[1] Taken from the data in Shanghai Bankers' Weekly.

[2] Derived by dividing the wholesale price index of Shanghai by an index of note issue. Check transactions impair but do not wholly invalidate these indications.

[3] Derived by dividing total clearings by total current deposits.

[4] Based on data compiled by the Auditing Department of the Central Bank of China.

fallen significantly and the velocity of circulation of money and the ratio of checks to the note issue had both declined to their lowest points since early in 1946.

At the end of September deposits held by the private banks in Shanghai were more than four times those of the previous month. This was a most striking increase, for the real value (at prewar price levels) of deposits at the equivalent of CNC $122.2 millions in October, compared with a real value of CNC $8.5 millions in July. The brief suspension of inflationary trends was the chief cause of the increase in deposits, but another important factor at work was a government directive compelling private persons to surrender all holdings of gold, silver, and foreign exchange to the banks for Gold Yuan, on pain of heavy penalties for noncompliance. Teams of inspectors were mobilized in the larger cities with powers to search private homes and to confiscate illegal hoards of specie or foreign currency.

By the end of October the index of the note issue was four and a half times that of August, price and wage ceilings were in the process of disintegration, and it was abundantly clear that inflation could no longer be contained by the expedient of the currency change. On all sides there was a sudden release of inflationary pressures. In November the value of checks cleared in Shanghai rose to more than three times the note issue, and the velocity of circulation of money jumped nearly six times the October figure. The commercial banks found their deposits disappearing overnight because of the public's soaring demand for money and the transfer of capital to South China for expatriation to Hong Kong. The black-market rate of interest leapt to 120 per cent per month, and conditions in the money market tightened to such an extent that the banks' transactions fell heavily.

From the end of 1948 until the Communist armies entered Shanghai in May 1949 the final stages of runaway inflation showed an inevitable sequence in the credit field. Early in 1949 the commercial banks suspended all loan activities except the discounting of commercial bills, and, shortly thereafter, business was brought to a standstill by the continuing fall of deposits. The demand for money was so great that even the Central Bank became short of notes, and by April the black-market rate of interest stood at no less than 300 per cent per month. Immediately prior to the fall of Shanghai to the Communists, silver dollars and other currencies began to appear in circulation alongside Gold Yuan, signifying that inflation was passing into the concluding phase, the rejection of legal notes as a medium of exchange.

Thus the progressive depreciation of the Chinese currency in the postwar period gradually paralyzed the banking system and destroyed the normal routines of the money market. The ability of banks to function smoothly is contingent on the degree of confidence placed in the currency by the public. After the end of 1946 confidence began to wane steadily until, in the first months of 1948, a general flight from the currency gathered momentum, which the August currency change was powerless to check. As a result, there was a concomitant deterioration in the financial and economic role of the banking system and in the standards of banking practice, climaxed by the ultimate breakdown of the money market in 1949. In these conditions, a belated anti-inflationary policy, no matter how well conceived, was destined to failure.

Chapter 12

# Foreign Exchange

### *Introduction*

Fluctuations in the external value of China's currency and in its balance of trade and international payments had psychological and economic effects which aggravated the problem of inflation.

The Chinese currency standard had been changed from one based on full convertibility in silver to a managed foreign exchange standard only two years before the outbreak of the Sino-Japanese war. Deprived of the right to cash their notes, the public had come to look upon fluctuations in the foreign exchange rate for Chinese paper currency as a substitute for the fluctuations in the value of silver which formerly had measured the value of their money. Foreign exchange rates therefore acquired a new significance. Furthermore, China had long been a country which imported more than it exported. The supply of manufactured goods, raw materials, and even foodstuffs was so dependent on imports that the price of imports dominated the general price structure. As a result, changes in the external value of Chinese currency, and the increase or decrease in imports, affected not only the price of imported commodities but also the price of goods produced within China, including even agricultural products.

Meanwhile, China's foreign reserves against her own currency had traditionally been small because her balance of trade had always been adverse and domestic gold production was insignificant. The size of foreign reserves was extremely sensitive to changes in the balance of payments and in turn provided little cushion for maintaining the stability of the external value of the country's currency.

Fearing that the depreciation of the currency's external value might affect its internal value and create a panic among the public, the government, immediately after the outbreak of Sino-Japanese hostilities, adopted a policy of supplying the market with foreign exchange without any restriction. When the reserves appeared in danger of becoming totally exhausted, the financial and banking authorities began to debate whether foreign exchange should continue to be made freely available at a low fixed rate, whether a flexible rate should be tried to reduce the demand for foreign exchange, or whether the foreign exchange market should be cut free to find its own level. The difference between the external and internal values of the currency, which resulted in excessive profits for importers and speculators and thus led to increasing demand on reserves, forced the adoption of a policy of flexible rates which followed the market trends.

This policy was carried out with the support of British banks, but these efforts were unable to overcome fully the inflationary effects of the continued generation of purchasing power by the government's deficit financing. However, by bringing the independent movements of the external and internal values of China's currency more in harmony with each other the situation was greatly helped. A part of imports, after having arrived in the port cities, flowed to Free China. The enemy blockade of Free China's trade routes and the outbreak of World War II in Europe further helped the new policy to succeed. The balance of payments problem virtually vanished when foreign trade came to a near halt. Moreover, many Chinese anticipated a depreciation in European currencies, and this terminated the outward flight of capital, while overseas Chinese residing in the British, French, and Dutch colonies of Southeast Asia remitted capital to Shanghai. These movements temporarily halted the drop in external value of the Chinese currency.

Unfortunately, at this time the changes in the internal value of China's currency acquired such momentum that the strengthening of the external value had comparatively little stabilizing influence. This condition persisted until, with Pearl Harbor, the official market in foreign exchange was completely suspended and the external value of the currency ceased to be a factor in inflation.

After the war government leaders intended to rebuild the reputation of Shanghai as a center for international trade and foreign exchange transactions in the East. With this in mind, they attempted to establish a free and stable exchange market by making available a liberal supply of foreign exchange. But the situation had changed radically from that prevailing during the war, and even from that in force before hostilities began. Inflation was rampant in both Free and Occupied China; large amounts of liquid funds were in circulation; the huge backlog of deferred purchases entailed a high level of effective demand; and business firms endeavored to keep as much of their working capital as possible in foreign currencies because of the sad lessons they had learned from wartime inflation. Added to these factors was the people's growing preference for foreign currency, engendered by the continuing postwar deficit financing. The demands on the government's foreign exchange reserves were thus greatly in excess of supply.

At last the government, forced to abandon its policy of maintaining a stable exchange rate, proceeded to increase the rate periodically. After fixing the rate at a given level for a certain period, it would impose moderate restrictions and allocations—only to witness the rise of many perplexing problems. The free market rate which emerged followed the movement of general prices, but it also influenced the level of imports; this influence in turn affected the general price level. Whenever the official rate was kept unchanged too long, the widening discrepancy between the official and the free market rate greatly benefited importers and profiteers and seriously hurt exporters. On the other hand, more frequent adjustments of the official rate were a public admission of the depreciation of the external value of the currency and frightened ever more people into expatriating their capital; thereupon the price of imports would rise again, general commodity prices quickly followed upward, and inflation received another impetus.

As long as official market rates existed, moreover, they stimulated the flow of newly generated foreign exchange into the free market rather than into official channels. In these circumstances the increasing drain on its foreign exchange reserves forced the government into even more restrictive allocations of foreign currencies, which in turn decreased imports, increased the price of imports, and further increased the general price level.

After the foreign exchange situation had thoroughly deteriorated, the government once more adopted the policy of letting the market find its own level. At this stage, however, the limited foreign currency supply of the black market was unable to satisfy the snowballing combined demand of legitimate imports and capital flight; and the external value of the Chinese currency went into an uncontrolled slide.

The numerous postwar measures devised by the government to manage its foreign exchange reserves thus remained unsuccessful.

Perhaps this was inevitable, for these measures, too, were aimed at combating the symptoms of inflation rather than its causes.

## 1. Prewar Foreign Exchange Policies

### *The Exchange Rate of the Prewar Chinese Dollar*

The depreciation of the external value of Chinese currency and the reduction of the gold and silver reserves in China had begun before the outbreak of the Sino-Japanese war. This had a very important effect on the exchange rate of Chinese currency after the war. Therefore, before dealing with the foreign exchange rate during the war it seems worthwhile to discuss briefly the prewar exchange rates of the Chinese dollar and the balance of international payments during this period.

Before 1930, when the price of silver began to depreciate under the effects of the world depression, the Chinese currency was based on the silver standard. All government or private receipts and payments were made either in silver bullion or in silver dollars. Although paper money was issued, it was redeemable on demand, and for all practical purposes there was a silver currency standard. There being no fixed exchange rate for legal tender, the so-called foreign exchange rate was in fact the ratio between the value of gold and silver.

In most years after China first began trading with other countries there were, in spite of the almost invariably unfavorable trade balance, imports of gold and silver caused by traditional Chinese demand for these precious metals. There were always accounts of foreign in-payments which could not be verified, but the question of disequilibrium in the balance of international payments seldom arose. Gold and silver could be imported just as freely as all other commodities. Exchange control was altogether out of the question.

The relationship of the Chinese dollar to those foreign currencies in which the largest part of Chinese foreign trade was conducted stood as follows when the world depression began in 1929:

1 Chinese dollar = U.S. 36 cents<br>
= Sterling 1s/6d<br>
= Japanese Yen 76 sen

From 1929 on, the world depression deepened and world commodity prices gradually fell. In the three years 1929–1931 the standard U.S.A. Index fell by 26 per cent, while the silver price depreciated much more than commodity prices. In three years it fell by more than

48 per cent* and the value of China's currency unit, the silver dollar, had depreciated as follows by August 1931:

1 Chinese dollar = U.S. 21 cents
= Sterling 10d
= Yen 42 sen

However, while world prices were falling, Chinese internal prices were showing a tendency to rise. The wholesale price index in three important cities in 1929 and 1931 was as shown in Table 78.

The increase in internal prices in China and the fall in world prices combined were less than the depreciation of the Chinese dollar in terms of gold currencies, a condition which placed Chinese export commodities in a favorable position compared with those of other countries. Moreover, since the same effect brought relative rises in the prices of foreign goods, domestic industry was able to compete successfully with those goods, and there was a resulting boom in Chinese domestic enterprises and activity. Therefore, while the volume of Chinese exports fell somewhat because of reduced world demand, it fell less than the volume of world exports as a whole.

Chinese exports in 1929† = $1,582,441 (thousand)‡
1930 = $1,394,166
1931 = $1,416,963
Fall—10.5 per cent
World exports in 1929 = U.S. $33,035 million
1931 = U.S. $18,922 million
Fall—43 per cent

In 1930 and 1931, therefore, China's balance of international payments position was improving. Silver was also imported.

In September 1931 the pound and Japanese yen went off gold. By late 1932 the Chinese dollar had appreciated rapidly in relation to these two currencies but had continued to depreciate slightly in relation to the U.S. dollar.

1 Chinese dollar = U.S. 19 cents
= Sterling 1s/2d (December 1932)
= Yen 93 sen

* Computed from data obtained from Annual Report of the Director of the Mint (1932), p. 127.

† Chinese Customs Report.

‡ In this chapter all references to dollars refer to Chinese Yuan (silver), before November 4, 1935, and Chinese National Currency (CNC) thereafter, unless otherwise specified.

TABLE 78. WHOLESALE PRICE INDEX

| City | 1929 (1926 = 100) | 1931 (1926 = 100) |
|---|---|---|
| Shanghai[1] (Central China) | 104.5 | 129.2 |
| Tientsin[2] (North China) | 111.08 | 122.55 |
| Canton[3] (South China) | 96.7 | 112.6 |

[1] Based on data compiled by National Tariff Commission.

[2] Based on data compiled by Economic Research Department of Nankai University.

[3] Based on data compiled by the Statistics Bureau of the Kwangtung Provincial Government.

After 1932 the price of silver rose and commodity prices in China began to fall. Commercial and industrial stagnation set in, and the volume of exports fell. Precious metals were exported; for the first time in many decades there was a net export of gold and silver.

In 1933 the U.S. dollar also left the gold standard and depreciated greatly in relation to the Chinese dollar. This was followed by a further depreciation in the pound sterling and the Japanese yen in terms of gold. At the end of 1933 the United States government decided to purchase domestically produced silver at the rate of 64½ cents. In June 1934 the United States Congress passed the Silver Act. This caused the world price of silver to rise, and the Chinese dollar rose higher and higher in terms of the three currencies, viz.:

1 Chinese dollar = U.S. 33 cents
= Sterling 1s/4d
= Yen 1.0
} December 1933

In 1934 the average rate was as follows:

1 Chinese dollar = U.S. 33.785 cents
= Sterling 1s/4.1d
= Yen 1.13
} 1934

In October 1935, during the week preceding the currency reform, the Chinese dollar stood higher than the average rate of the previous year:

1 Chinese dollar = U.S. 36.5 cents
= Sterling 1s/5.7d
= Yen 1.27
} October 1935

However, commodity prices in China were gradually depreciating in contrast to the rising prices in other countries as Table 79 shows.

TABLE 79. WHOLESALE PRICE INDEX IN CHINA,[1] UNITED STATES, AND ENGLAND[2]

China

(1926 = 100)

| Year | Shanghai | Tientsin | Canton |
|---|---|---|---|
| 1932 | 112.4 | 112.87 | 113.0 |
| 1933 | 103.0 | 100.59 | 102.6 |
| 1934 | 97.1 | 91.78 | 94.3 |
| 1935 (September) | 91.1 | 90.68 | 81.69 |

United States and England

(1913 = 100)

| Year | United States | England |
|---|---|---|
| 1932 (whole year) | 92.8 | 86.1 |
| 1933 (whole year) | 94.5 | 86.9 |
| 1934 (December) | 110.2 | 90.4 |
| 1935 (July) | 113.8 | 93.7 |

[1] Same sources as Table 78.

[2] Based on statistics of *The Economist, London.*

Consequently, economic activity in China suffered a depression. Production of manufactured goods was reduced and many factories were closed; in the big cities there was much unemployment. International trade was unfavorable, and there was a large drainage of silver dollars from the interior to the cities, whence they were exported, attracted by the high world price of silver. This caused currency deflation and had a serious effect on the whole economy. Eventually the government was compelled to abandon the silver standard and to adopt a managed exchange standard.

### *The New Dollar Rate: November 4, 1935 to 1937*

A currency reform plan was announced on November 4, 1935. The notes of the Central Bank of China, the Bank of China, and the Bank of Communications were designated the nation's only legal tender (CNC). All government expenditure and receipts were to be in terms of the new currency, and all silver and silver dollars were to be nationalized. The new currency would not be redeemable in silver dollars; instead, it could be bought and sold for foreign exchange. The exchange rate of the new currency was announced to be as follows:

| | | |
|---|---|---|
| 1 Chinese dollar | = U.S. 30 cents | November 4, 1935 |
| | = Sterling 1s/2½d | |
| | = Yen 1.03 | |

The above rate was based upon the average rate during the previous five years, 1930 to 1934.

Considering the world silver prices in effect when the new rate was announced (2s/9.4375d for one ounce), and the silver content of the dollar (0.8816 ounce), on the basis of which the Chinese dollar exchange rate should have been above 2s, the Chinese currency unit was devalued by more than 40 per cent. As a matter of fact, because of the imposition of a silver export duty in April 1934 and an equalization duty in October 1934, the Chinese dollar had been devalued earlier. At first the export duty was 2.25 per cent, equal to the seigniorage on one Chinese silver dollar, but after October 15 the duty was raised to 10 per cent. The equalization duty was levied according to the difference between the domestic price of silver and the price in foreign markets for the purpose of preventing profiteering by exporters of silver. Before the currency reform, the exchange rate of the Chinese dollar in Shanghai was about 1s/4d, about 40 per cent lower than world silver prices. It was generally recognized that from the date when an export duty had been levied on silver China was no longer a country with a purely silver standard.

After the new currency was put into effect there was a bumper crop in 1936 which broke all records established over the preceding few decades. China's imports of agricultural goods were therefore much lower, thus considerably reducing her unfavorable trade balance and improving the balance of international payments position. The United States government agreed to purchase silver from China, and her foreign exchange reserves were increased. All the above factors helped to stabilize the exchange rate, and, in spite of minor speculation late in 1935 and in May 1936 and the political disturbances which followed the Sian incident* in December, the new currency was able to maintain stability of exchange throughout this period. Only in September 1937 were some slight modifications made.

In view of the appreciation of the U.S. dollar in relation to the pound sterling, in order to forestall profiteering in exchange, and to avoid seeming in any way to peg the new currency either to the pound sterling or to the U.S. dollar, and being reluctant to depress the selling

* The kidnaping of Chiang Kai-shek by Chang Hsueh-liang.

rate of the exchange in sterling or to enhance its buying rate in U.S. dollars, the Central Bank resorted to the device of keeping the selling and buying rates farther apart. It quoted the exchange rate as follows:

| | | |
|---|---|---|
| In terms of Sterling | Selling 1s/2½d | September, 1937 |
| | Buying 1s/2¾d | |
| In terms of the U.S. Dollar | Selling 29.50 cents | |
| | Buying 30.50 cents | |
| In terms of the Yen | Selling 1.01 | |
| | Buying 1.05. | |

No disturbance at all was caused by this change. Thus, up to the beginning of the Sino-Japanese war in 1937, the new currency may be said to have successfully maintained a stable exchange rate.

Since the currency reform of 1935 was followed by a bumper harvest, the excess of imports over exports was reduced because of the decrease of imports of agricultural goods. The remittances from Chinese citizens abroad and the remittances from overseas to foreign residents or institutions in China increased, and the flight of capital stopped. Consequently, the balance of international payments became more favorable. Table 80 shows the trade balance and the overseas remittances of 1935, 1936, and 1937.

Table 80. Imports, Exports and Overseas Remittances, 1935–1937[1]
(CNC $ thousands)

| Year | Imports | Exports | Imports over Exports | Overseas Chinese Remittances (Estimate) |
|---|---|---|---|---|
| 1935 | 919,211 | 575,809 | 343,402 | 280,000 |
| 1936 | 941,544 | 705,741 | 235,803 | 320,000 |
| 1937 | 953,386 | 838,256 | 115,130 | 450,000 |

[1] Based on Chinese Customs Report.

These two items, the trade balance and remittances from overseas, were the most important in the international in-payments and out-payments. The unfavorable balance of trade was more adequately met by the increased overseas remittances. The other items, which included Chinese government debt service, business investments abroad, miscellaneous Chinese payments abroad, and miscellaneous foreign expenditure in China, were not large enough to have any bearing on the international balance of payments. This is proof that the balance of payments was greatly improved after the currency reform.

The new currency plan also provided for the nationalization of silver. While this process was under way, from 1935 to June 1936, the various exchange agencies in the country received $308,040,000 worth of silver. The amount of silver reserves held by the government banks, the commercial banks, and the Provincial Bank of Kwangtung, which had the largest issue among the provincial banks in June, 1937, on the eve of the Sino-Japanese war, totaled $800,000,000. So the government obtained about 1,100 million silver dollars. The United States government agreed to purchase China's silver holdings to provide foreign reserve for the new currency. The amount of silver shipped out, according to an announcement made by the Ministry of Finance in May 1937, reached $830,000,000; and the amount held in China waiting for shipment was $62,000,000. The proceeds of sales of silver amounted to about U.S. $270 million. As a result of the more favorable trend of the international balance of payments, this amount was not significantly reduced between late 1935 and mid-1937, and, at the beginning of the Sino-Japanese war, was in the neighborhood of U.S. $250 million.

This would have been adequate to stabilize the exchange rate in peacetime; but, when large quantities of foreign reserve must be spent to import military supplies, the amount of $250 million would necessarily be far from adequate, even allowing for the suggestion that the remaining silver and gold holdings of the public could still be nationalized to increase the foreign reserve. According to one estimate, public gold holdings* before the currency reform were only about $350,000,000,* of which $100,000,000 was exported in 1936 and 1937. Silver holdings were estimated to be $1,600,000,000, of which $900,000,000 had already been exported. Of the balance of gold and silver holdings, valued at $950,000,000, probably only about half—approximately U.S. $150,000,000—could have been mustered because the holdings were spread over the country, some being lost and some buried.

* According to the estimate of the American Mining Industry Association made in 1931, China produced 146,000 tael (nearly one ounce) of gold, based on an average price of $62 per tael, with an annual yield of $9 million. It totaled $780 million during 87 years (1850–1937). Export of gold between 1864, the first year of publication of Custom Report, and 1911 was about $48 million and that between 1912 and 1935, about $376 million. Hence the public holdings of gold in 1935 were estimated to be $350 million.

There were three estimates of silver holdings made by experts in the nineteen thirties: (1) 1.5 billion Chinese dollars (2) 1.6 billion Chinese dollars (3) 1.7 billion Chinese dollars. The net export of silver from 1934–1937 totaled 960 million.

This suggests that China began the war with very little in the way of potential foreign exchange reserves.

## 2. Wartime Foreign Exchange Policies: 1937–1938

### *Early Attempts to Maintain a Stable Exchange Rate, 1937–1938*

At the time of the currency reform of 1935 the government was convinced that the people had a predilection for a currency convertible into other media of exchange, particularly specie, or foreign currency. Since the government felt that it could not convert its paper money into specie, it believed that this popular predilection could be satisfied by providing convertibility in foreign exchange. That was why the currency reform plan stipulated that the Central Bank, the Bank of China, and the Bank of Communications should be able to buy and sell, without limit, foreign exchange with the new currency. The public regarded this stipulation as its only safeguard of the value of the new currency. Early in 1937, when the war was approaching, several leading economists took the view that any change in the foreign exchange rate would cause psychological repercussions and economic disturbances.* They advocated that the exchange rate be upheld as long as possible, suggesting that, at the same time, the government prepare for foreign exchange control to avoid flight of capital. They proposed immediate enforcement of the following measures preparatory to control of foreign exchange:

Ending foreign exchange sales in small amounts, to make it impossible for those who had doubts about the new currency to acquire foreign exchange.

Concentration of all foreign exchange in government banks. In case of any transfers being necessary, the government banks should have priority in its purchase.

Gradual restriction of the supply of foreign exchange to importers, evidence of all forward transactions to be produced, and an amount of Chinese currency equal in value to the foreign currency or currencies needed in the transactions, at the current rate of exchange, to be deposited with the government banks.

Requiring exporters to declare all foreign exchange earnings and to deposit all such foreign exchange in government banks.

Announcement of foreign exchange controls to be imposed should war break out.

* Articles published in Bankers' Weekly, Shanghai, 1937.

At that time the financial authority held the view that it would be necessary to maintain the present exchange rate and, as a corollary, to buy and sell foreign exchange in unlimited quantities, these two measures to be pursued pari passu to the end. Internally, this would enhance public confidence and consolidate the Chinese financial and economic position; externally, it would show Chinese determination for a long struggle, thus winning the support and aid of friendly powers.

The imperfect structure of the Chinese administrative organization and the lack of practical experience in exchange control of her public functionaries tended to lend support to this view. The adoption and enforcement of any control measure would, in all likelihood, entail bureaucratic "red-tape" and malpractices which would cause disappointment and criticism in both the Chinese and foreign communities. Moreover, Chinese financial and economic policies were frequently influenced by foreign opinions in Shanghai. Extraterritorial rights for foreign residents of Shanghai and Tientsin rendered the government unable to enforce its decrees completely; and no exchange control measure could be made fully effective except with the cooperation of the foreign community there. However, the foreigners in Shanghai held fast to their traditional point of view that, as China's politics were not modern or Western in nature, the less the government interfered the better it was for private enterprise, Chinese or foreign. Such policies as trade control and exchange control, to which their own governments had long resorted, and to which they had long acquiesced complacently as a matter of course, would have shocked them exceedingly should China have undertaken them.

These attitudes had a great influence on Chinese administrators as well as on the financiers and industrialists of Shanghai. As a result of the influence of the traditional views of the foreign community, China's economic and financial policies were one or two decades behind those of Western nations. Now that China was confronted with a war of the first magnitude, she still could not get away from her faith in free exchange and free trade.

The continuation of the free exchange policy during the war had a very serious effect—it made the flight of capital possible. Acrimonious disputes on the subject of private holdings of foreign exchange in the latter period of inflation mirrored the public discontent and developed into attacks on the government by the people. The disputes even affected the confidence felt by friendly powers.

It is always difficult to enforce government measures which are liberal at the beginning but become strict afterwards. Thus, as the currency depreciated, the power of the government began to wane, and the government became ever more afraid to undertake anything which might cause public discontent.

Had this effect been anticipated by the advocates of a liberal policy? If the figures for foreign reserves had been carefully examined, the rashness of continuing the free exchange policy would have been clearly seen. The figures announced by the Ministry of Finance in May 1937, immediately before the war were as follows:

> The value of silver deposited with the United States was U.S. $120 million.
>
> That deposited with Britain was £stg. 25 million.
>
> Government holdings of silver in China were 62 million Chinese dollars.

China's silver reserve, therefore, totaled only 830 million Chinese dollars. In addition, a small quantity of gold was held abroad, bringing the total reserves to about U.S. $250 million. This reserve was much too small to support a policy of unlimited supply of foreign exchange at fixed rates.

### *Banking Moratorium in Shanghai*

On July 7, 1937, Sino-Japanese hostilities commenced at Marco Polo Bridge and soon spread to Peiping and Tientsin. On August 3 Shanghai took up arms. In less than a month great alarm spread throughout the entire country, and the people began scrambling for the foreign exchange sold by government banks in unlimited quantities at fixed rates. During this period the amount of foreign exchange sold by the government banks was reported to be about U.S. $40 million.

To halt the run on the government banks and the rush for foreign exchange, a two-day moratorium at Shanghai was announced on August 13. Simultaneously, the following regulations were announced:

> Drawing on current deposits in banks (including native banks) was limited to 5 per cent of the weekly deposits. No depositor was to draw more than $150 weekly. Fixed deposits not yet due were not to be drawn upon. When falling due and discontinued, they were to be changed into current deposits. Mortgages on the security of deposit receipts not yet due were limited to $1,000.
>
> Separate arrangements were made for factories, corporations, mercantile stores, and public and government organizations to pay wages and salaries or to meet military needs.

Thus the bulk of the capital in Shanghai was temporarily frozen to prevent pressure on the supply of foreign exchange and the exchange rate.

### *Gentlemen's Agreement with Foreign Banks in Shanghai*

An agreement was reached between the government and the foreign banks in Shanghai for the joint prevention of flight of capital and for the prevention of depressing buying and selling rates of the Chinese dollar. The agreement provided that:

> The government was to supply foreign exchange at the fixed rate of 1s/2¼d stg. and U.S. 29 cents.
>
> Buying and selling of foreign exchange were to be limited to spot transactions only.
>
> Transactions between the government and foreign banks or merchants, if already begun, were to be settled in Chinese currency.
>
> Chinese and foreign banks were each to nominate two representatives for consultation on foreign exchange and relevant financial problems.
>
> Foreign banks were temporarily to refuse deposits by Chinese in Chinese currency.

These provisions aimed at the dual object of freezing deposits to tighten the currency and narrowing the channels for speculators and persons wishing to send money out of the country to obtain foreign exchange. However, there was a loophole; quantities of government bank notes from various localities were transported to Hongkong for conversion into foreign exchange. Also, bank notes were acquired by discounting Wei-wah money (money used for interbank transfers between native banks) in order to buy foreign exchange without having to use cash. In addition, there were payments on foreign loans and the legitimate needs of trade, so that from August 13, 1937, to March 3, 1938, the day on which the exchange policy was modified, the amount of foreign exchange sold by the government was reported to be around U.S. $50 million.

### *Discontinuance of the Unlimited Supply of Foreign Exchange at Fixed Rates*

Most of the government's critics maintained that the loss of nearly U.S. $100 million, about two-fifths of the foreign exchange reserve, through the policy of unlimited supply of foreign exchange to the market was the result of the lack of foreign exchange control and proved their earlier theory valid. The majority opinion in the government was that since Shanghai, the principal loophole for flight of capital, had now almost fallen into enemy hands and the seat of government had been removed westward into the interior, it had become imperative that the government relieve itself of the burden of supplying foreign exchange to the Shanghai market.

On March 10, 1938, the puppet government of North China announced the establishment of a Federal Reserve Bank with power to issue notes. It decreed that notes issued by the North China Branch of the Bank of China and the Bank of Communications could continue to circulate for one year, but that all other note issues of the government banks must be withdrawn not later than three months from that date. Since eventually all such notes would make their way to Shanghai, it was possible that the Japanese might exchange the new puppet notes to secure foreign exchange. The government took this opportunity, on March 14, to proclaim some measures to control foreign exchange:

> All sales of foreign exchange were to be transacted through the Central Bank, and handled by formal applications to its head office at the seat of government.
>
> To facilitate the work, a correspondent was to be appointed at Hong Kong, where applications for foreign exchange would be received from banks and others and forwarded.
>
> The head office of the Central Bank or its correspondent at Hong Kong should receive such applications at 10 a.m. every Thursday, and, after examining each application, should notify each bank of the results at 10 a.m. the next day. On the day after receiving this notice the applying bank might purchase the amount of foreign exchange approved at the official rate.

These measures were designed to limit the supply of foreign exchange by screening the applications and reducing Shanghai's dependence on the Central Bank for foreign exchange. Because of the Central Bank's remoteness and the cumbersome methods for application, Chinese banks ceased to deal in foreign exchange after the above measures were brought into force. Foreign banks limited the amount purchasable by individuals for personal needs to U.S. $250 or £50.

Both Chinese and foreign banks adopted a temporary attitude of watchful waiting. There was general dissatisfaction on March 17 when it became known that the first allocation of foreign exchange amounted to only 37.59 per cent of what the applicants had asked for and that there was no rational basis for the allocation. Foreign banks renounced the gentlemen's agreement of August 1937 and revoked their obligation to observe the official rate of foreign exchange. The next day the banks set their transactions, inter se, at 1s/– and some even at 11.875d, or at U.S. 21 cents. Henceforth the Chinese currency no longer had a fixed rate.

The examination of applications gradually became more rigid, and the amount of foreign exchange approved and allocated was slowly reduced. The exchange rate on the United States and Great Britain began to fall rapidly (Table 81). In the first month three allocations were made, amounting to 37.59 per cent, 34.3 per cent, and 28 per cent of what had been requested—a total allocation of about U.S. $6.8 million. In the fourth month allocations dropped to 5.7 per cent of applications (about U.S. $2.7 million), and in the eighth month to below 1 per cent (about U.S. $160,000). At the end of March 1939 they were only 0.6 per cent (about U.S. $50,000). In the year from March 1938 to the end of March 1939 a total of about U.S. $23 million in foreign exchange was thus frittered away, although the monthly rate of sales was considerably less than when exchange had been supplied in unlimited quantities. The external value of the CNC dollar was gradually falling and hovered around U.S. 15.625 cents.

It is difficult to judge how effective were the government's early attempts to stabilize the exchange rate. On the one hand, the various measures were counterinflationary in nature, and runaway inflation might have started sooner had the various measures not tended to uphold the external value of China's currency. On the other hand, public confidence in China's currency might have been maintained longer had the government's foreign exchange reserves not been subject to such heavy drainage. One clear defect in the government's policy emerges, however, which could have been remedied while it was still time. This is the lack of restrictions on the flight of capital. This flight not only materially contributed to the exhaustion of China's foreign exchange reserves but also, by its adverse psychological impact, hampered any chance of success which the government's anti-inflationary program might have had. Table 81 shows the monthly market rate from March 1938 to March 1939.

The foreign banks ceased to observe the fixed rate of exchange after March 1938. Importers who could not secure the foreign exchange they needed from official sources therefore went to banks other than the Central Bank and paid higher than the fixed rate for such foreign exchange as they could get. Those eager to send out their capital needed foreign exchange and paid the current market rate for it. The depressed market rate and its fluctuations not only hampered legitimate trade but also caused the government to lose its grip on the foreign exchange rates. Moreover, the limited foreign exchange reserves proved inadequate to meet the needs of the market and military requirements simultaneously. The government now turned to the British government for assistance and concerted action in its

TABLE 81. DECLINE OF OFFICIAL FOREIGN EXCHANGE RATES, 1938–1939[1]
(Foreign currency per Chinese dollar)

| Year | Sterling (d) | U.S. Dollars (cents) |
|---|---|---|
| 1938 | | |
| March (average) | 1s/1.954 | 28.613 |
| April | 1s/0.978 | 26.9049 |
| May | 1s/1.298 | 23.3870 |
| June | 8.970 | 18.5150 |
| July | 8.838 | 18.1719 |
| August | 7.933 | 16.1538 |
| September | 8.082 | 16.2332 |
| October | 8.078 | 15.9792 |
| November | 8.000 | 15.7375 |
| December | 8.000 | 15.6250 |
| 1939 | | |
| January | 8.000 | 15.6250 |
| February | 8.000 | 15.6250 |
| March | 8.000 | 15.6250 |

[1] Based on Central Bank of China reports.

attempt to stabilize the exchange rates. In 1939 the Sino-British Exchange Stabilization Fund was created. After almost two years the fund was exhausted and the United States was invited to join, resulting in the establishment of the Sino-American-British Stabilization Board in April 1941. When it began to operate, the Pacific war had broken out and Shanghai and Hong Kong had fallen into enemy hands. Even though the new fund continued to operate in the interior, it was almost suspended because of the very small number of foreign exchange transactions. In March 1944 the Stabilization Board was abolished at the request of the Chinese government. A brief history of these two funds is summarized here.

### 3. THE SINO-BRITISH STABILIZATION FUND: 1939

The agreement to establish a Sino-British Stabilization Fund with resources of £10 million was reached on March 10, 1939. The Fund's requirements were to be advanced by two British banks and two Chinese banks in the following proportions:

The Bank of China and the Bank of Communications–£5 million.
The Hong Kong and Shanghai Banking Corporation–£3 million.
The Chartered Bank of India, Australia, and China–£2 million.

The management of the Fund was vested in a committee which met in Hong Kong. Known as the Hong Kong Committee, it had five members, two jointly appointed by the Chinese banks, one each by the two British banks, and the remaining member—who had to be a British subject—by the Chinese government in agreement with the British Treasury and on the approval of the British banks.

The function of the Fund was to check undue depreciation of Chinese currency by the purchase and sale of Chinese dollars and by other necessary operations on the exchange markets of Shanghai and Hong Kong. The committee's duties were to determine the day-to-day policy best suited to achieving the objectives of the Fund, and to give instructions to the Hong Kong and Shanghai Bank and the Chartered Bank about the extent and nature of operations in the Shanghai and Hong Kong markets. The Chinese government made the following assurances to the British government:

> During the life of the Stabilization Fund the financial, economic, and monetary policies of the Chinese government would be designed to maintain the stability of the Chinese dollar in terms of sterling. These policies would be made known to the management committee of the Fund in confidence.
>
> The Chinese government would restrict outlay in foreign exchange by government organizations as far as possible in conformity with policies of the Fund. Such organizations would not purchase foreign exchange greater than their immediate commitments, either directly or indirectly, and would purchase all foreign exchange through one or more of the banks represented on the management committee.
>
> The Chinese government banks would co-operate in all ways with the Fund and would not operate in the foreign exchange market in any way which would impede the operations of the Fund.

The main purpose of the Fund's policy was to stabilize the rate on the free exchange market in Shanghai so that the free flow of international trade and the prosperity of enterprises in Shanghai would be maintained and international payments would automatically balance as they had before. Therefore, the policy emphasized the reduction of government commitments in foreign exchange rather than reduction of the unfavorable balance of trade or stopping the flight of capital and stopping the seizing of foreign exchange by the enemy. When the Stabilization Fund began, the market exchange rate of Chinese currency was 7 13s/16d or U.S. 13.9792 cents to one Chinese dollar. The committee decided to maintain the market rate at about 8d or U.S. 15.6250 cents. In the first half of 1939 imports exceeded exports by two-thirds of the figure for the same period in 1938. The figures for Shanghai alone accounted for one-half of the total. Imported cotton and grains registered the largest increases. The bulk of the foreign exchange used to import cotton went to Japanese cotton mills in China.

Meanwhile there were continued setbacks in the war, and the enemy and its puppet government resorted to every possible means to impair the credit of the Chinese currency. The resulting demand for foreign exchange gradually drained the resources of the Fund. On June 7 it was decided to suspend the selling of foreign exchange temporarily to enable the market to find a new level for the exchange rate. The new rate was finally fixed at approximately 6½d sterling and U.S. 11.75 cents to reduce the brisk demand for foreign exchange and to preserve the Fund's reserves. However, the new rate had a disquieting effect on the public mind, leading to endless drawings on deposits to purchase foreign exchange. In ten days over £1 million of foreign exchange was sold at the new rate. The government, aware from the trend of affairs that the problems could not be solved by merely depressing the exchange rates, resorted to various supplementary measures in the hope of curtailing the drain on the resources of the Fund:

> After June 22 a second moratorium was declared enjoining all banks, including native banks, to limit drawings on deposits to $500 a week. Drawings for government purposes or for paying wages were to be treated differently. Amounts over $500 were payable in Wei-wah.
>
> Imports of all commodities not for military use or not absolutely needed in the daily life of the people—or, even if so needed, those for which domestic substitutes were available—were prohibited.

Since the moratorium was confined to Shanghai, it was still possible to go to other places to get bank notes to send to Shanghai to buy foreign exchange. The restrictions imposed on imports could hardly be carried out in Shanghai because that city was outside the control of the Chinese government. Commodities imported into Shanghai, whether they were prohibited imports or not, had to be paid for with foreign exchange obtainable in the free market of Shanghai. Therefore, demands on the Fund for foreign exchange increased in spite of the restrictions. By the middle of July the £10 million originally in the Fund were nearly exhausted, for the second time the sale of the Fund's foreign exchange had to be suspended, and the exchange rate of 6½d or U.S. 11.75 cents had to be relinquished.

On and after July 18 there was a precipitous fall in the exchange rate as the market became panic-stricken. At the end of July the exchange rate was readjusted at approximately 4d sterling and U.S. 7.50 cents. On August 11 the rate fell to 3.25d and U.S. 6.3125 cents. However, at the beginning of September Britain declared war on Germany and Europe took up arms. The pound sterling dropped in terms of U.S. dollars, and the exchange rate of Chinese currency rose in relation to sterling. Then Hong Kong and Malaya commenced exchange control, and flight of capital to Shanghai began. The Fund was able to add more than two million pounds to its reserves through purchases in the market. This stroke of luck enabled it to cope with the vicissitudes of the market for another six months.

After the outbreak of war in Europe to May 1, 1940, the exchange rate fluctuated between 4½d and 4d, and between U.S. 6 cents and 7 cents. On May 1, 1940, when only £200,000 remained in the Fund, the Fund notified the Chinese government that it was unable to carry on without additional resources. Sale of foreign exchange was once more suspended, and the market quotation fell to 3.125d, or U.S. 4.5 cents.

However, when the German invasion of Holland and Belgium caused the Chinese people to grow skeptical about foreign currencies, the Dutch and Belgian banks in Shanghai, to withstand an imminent run on them, decided to sell out their holdings of foreign currencies. On May 20 the exchange rate rose to 4.234375d and U.S. 5.874 cents. Capitalizing on this unexpected turn of events, the Fund purchased over £1 million of foreign exchange, and the Chinese government simultaneously appropriated to it an additional amount of U.S. $3 million. The Fund was able, therefore, to function for another year. The market rate fluctuated between 4d and 3.171875d and between U.S. 6 cents and 5.1875 cents until April 1941, when the Fund was reorganized with the participation of the United States.

Fund operations were further handicapped, as the Fund Committee repeatedly complained, by the government's inability to observe the sanctity of business secrets; and those in close touch with government circles were able to speculate and profiteer in the exchange market so freely that they jeopardized the efforts of the Fund. Experience has taught that the essential keys to the success of a stabilization fund are to have at its disposal resources big enough to command the respect of speculators and to have authority to act quickly, wisely, and secretly.

It was generally admitted that the Sino-British Stabilization Fund, by giving the Chinese people the impression of international backing for their country's currency, had a favorable psychological effect. Likewise, it was an effective counterattack against the Japanese attempts to undermine the credit of the Chinese dollar. However, while operation of the Fund lessened the inflationary pressures on the Chinese dollar, the continued mistake of ignoring the importance of trade and exchange controls finally defeated it. Its proponents had simply underestimated the enormous demand for foreign exchange arising from imports, speculation, and flight of capital. The government's continuous policy of deficit financing, which ran counter to its promise to coordinate its financial policy with the operation of the Fund, was another reason why the Fund was too small to cope with the situation. Had it not been for the European war and the events detailed above, the Fund might have been exhausted long before and the exchange rate might have dropped lower sooner.

## 4. The Sino-American-British Stabilization Board: 1941

On April 1, 1941, a Sino-American agreement and a Sino-British agreement were signed, under which the American and British governments agreed to make loans to the Chinese government of U.S. $50 million and £5 million, respectively, for the purpose of stabilizing the Chinese currency. To coordinate with these external loans the Chinese government banks also subscribed U.S. $20 million for the same purpose. These resources, amounting to U.S. $90 million, were to be used for the purchases of Chinese currency in the market, thereby maintaining its value in terms of the U.S. dollar and the pound sterling. The understanding was that the Chinese currency thus purchased would be repurchased by the Chinese government at the original rate of purchase.

Control of these funds was vested in a Stabilization Board of China with three Chinese, one British, and one American member, each appointed on the recommendations of the Treasuries of their countries. The old stabilization funds were transferred to the new board. Headquarters of the Board were established in Hong Kong, convenient center for supervising the Board's operations in Shanghai as well as in Free China. The Board also had a branch office in Kunming, at that time the most important port of entry for imports coming into Free China via Rangoon and the Burma Road. After the conclusion of the agreement some time elapsed before the American member could arrive and definite policies could be framed by the Board. It was, therefore, not until August 13 that the Board began to function.

The Board was able to benefit from the mistakes of the former Stabilization Fund and to make improvements. In supplying foreign exchange to the Shanghai market the Board's policy was to emphasize the import of raw materials needed to keep in operation the textile and other leading industries, which not only provided employment for Shanghai residents but also supplied consumer goods for Free China and for export. A quota system for imports was devised, and recipients of foreign exchange had to undertake not to acquire foreign exchange from other than official channels and to refrain from selling their imports at free market prices.

At this time, too, the United States, Great Britain, and Holland announced the freezing of Chinese and Japanese funds in their respective countries. This action enabled the board to solve certain difficult problems connected with speculation, flight of capital, and illicit trade. Had it not been for the Pacific War, the Board would have shown better results, would have conducted its operations more efficiently, and would have set a good precedent for future exchange control in China.

## *The Freezing of Chinese and Japanese Funds*

On July 25, 26, and 28, respectively, the United States of America, Great Britain, and the Netherlands announced the freezing of Chinese and Japanese funds held within their boundaries. The following provisions were adopted:

> Only 14 foreign banks of British, American, Dutch, and Russian nationality were authorized to handle foreign exchange transactions in China for Chinese trade with the United States, the other American republics, the British Commonwealth, Soviet Russia, and Holland.
>
> All foreign exchange business transacted by Chinese banks prior to July 26 was to be transferred to the Central Bank. In addition to the Central Bank, the Bank of China, the Bank of Communications, and the Farmers' Bank of China might also deal in foreign exchange.
>
> Only Chinese nationals and such nationals of the three countries as had been domiciled in China for business purposes prior to June 14, 1941, might apply for foreign exchange. Japanese banks or firms which had foreign exchange deposits in British, American, or Dutch banks in China were allowed to draw on them only in Chinese national currency or drafts in foreign currencies. Payments on such drafts had to be approved by the proper authorities.

These provisions made it impossible for the enemy to obtain foreign exchange in China, stopped the flight of capital and speculative transactions, and thus helped the Board to overcome some of the difficulties which lay before it.

### *Co-operative Actions Taken by the American and British Governments*

The American government again took the lead and adopted the following actions at the request of the Stabilization Board. The British government followed suit:

> On September 6, 1941, the British and United States Treasuries instructed British and American banks in the Far East to co-operate fully with the Board in order to maintain the exchange rate fixed by the Board. All banks of other nationalities then followed suit.
>
> On September 11, 1941, the United States and British governments announced that all payments in or out due on trade or other dealings between China on the one hand and Britain or the United States on the other were required to go through the Board, its designate, or an approved bank. Trading in foreign exchange by all banks had to be approved by the Board and conducted according to the Board's regulations. The United States and British Customs were instructed to see that all the conditions imposed by the Board on goods going to China had been complied with. Chinese consular officials stationed in the various ports of the world were also instructed to see that the rules the Board had made were complied with before consular certificates were issued for goods exported from China. Remittances to China from Britain or the United States were permitted whether or not they were from the frozen accounts but were required to go through the banks abroad appointed by the Board.
>
> The government of Hong Kong, to show that it intended to co-operate with the Chinese government and the Board, announced a set of regulations banning all unauthorized transactions in Chinese currency. These provided that no one without a proper license from the Hong Kong government might engage in any transaction involving the use of Chinese national currency, or might possess, acquire, pay, import, or export the same currency. Only banks authorized or approved by the Chinese government might apply to the Board for permission to engage in transactions in Chinese national currency, and then only at the official exchange rate.

These actions provided a check on financial arrangements for Chinese exports and imports and hindered the growth of a black market. They strengthened the hand of the government in controlling the import of nonessential goods and concentrated foreign exchange coming in from overseas remittances with the Central Bank. The Hong Kong government's action in controlling transactions in Chinese national currency reduced the black-market supply of foreign exchange and Chinese national currency, preventing illicit traders, smugglers, and importers of goods not complying with the Board's requirements from obtaining foreign exchange from the black market. The freezing order and the co-operation of the Allied Nations, while maintaining the Shanghai market and international interests in Shanghai, helped the Board to prevent foreign exchange from flowing into enemy hands and improper channels, and thus helped it to accomplish what the former Stabilization Fund had not done. The Pacific war did not allow the Board sufficient time to show its ability; but it proved that, so long as China lacked a stable currency, the Central Bank lacked full control of the foreign exchange market, and the free exchange market of Hong Kong still existed, the success of foreign exchange control in China depended upon the full co-operation of foreign powers. Had the Board let its foreign expert members explore policies and methods for postwar trade and exchange control and possible ways of co-operating with foreign governments, the postwar mistakes made in these areas might well have been avoided. It was unfortunate that, because of its fears of possible interference by the creditor nations in the utilization of foreign loans, the Chinese government abolished the Board, thus depriving itself of needed skill and advice for planning a long-range foreign exchange policy for China.

### *Operation of the Stabilization Board*

In the three months after the Board commenced operations, i.e., in September, October, and November 1941, it classified commodities, negotiated with trade representatives on the quota system, and devised methods for the prevention of irregularities. The system built up gradually in these months was the embryo of trade control in China. Although necessarily incomplete, it had many rational and praiseworthy features which could have become cornerstones in the Chinese import quota system instituted in November 1946.

When the Pacific war broke out, the Shanghai market was abandoned. Although the Board was still able to function at Chungking and Kunming, the dislocation of China's trade routes and the shrinkage of the exchange market reduced its position to near impotence. Table 82 is a summary of estimates of the foreign exchange resources used up by the Board during its operation.

The tabulation shows that the Board used about U.S. $8 million more than the U.S. $20 million advanced by the Chinese government banks. This was repaid by the Chinese government.

When the Board was first established the market remained almost unaffected because its policy was not yet known and the public had the impression that it might be as weak as the Fund of 1938 to 1941 had been. However, when the various governments announced their freezing orders and the foreign exchange supply was cut off, importers began to seek their foreign exchange requirements in the free market. Speculators purchased extensively in the free market, ostensibly to cover their imports. Within ten days of the inception of the Board the black-market value of CNC fell from 3.3125d to 2.84375d and

TABLE 82. FOREIGN EXCHANGE SALES BY THE STABILIZATION BOARD OF CHINA, 1941–1944

| | U.S. Dollars | Pounds Sterling |
|---|---|---|
| Allotments from Aug. 19, 1941, to Nov. 22, 1941 | 12,430,548.54 | 1,739,960 |
| Allotments from Jan. 1942 to March 1944 | 7,865,835.45 | 2,110,463 |
| Total Allotments | 20,296,383.99 | 3,850,423 |
| Deduct: | | |
| Amount of Hong Kong dollars and Burmese rupees purchased by the Board | | 1,758,708 |
| Total | | 2,091,715 |

from U.S. 5.40625 cents to U.S. 4.78125 cents. But when the Board began to function on August 18 and undertook to supply foreign exchange at 3.1562d and U.S. 5.3125 cents per CNC $1 to those who were lawfully engaged in the import trade, the market became more stable. By October the operations of the Board had halted the scramble for foreign exchange by importers trying to cover their requirements—which had caused the black-market value of CNC to fall to 2d and U.S. 3 cents, the scope of the black market was gradually narrowing, and it seemed that it might disappear altogether if the Board continued to operate for a while longer. In November the Board rate approximated the black-market rate. A summary view of foreign exchange rates in 1939–1941 is given in Table 83.

After the outbreak of the Pacific war there were few exchange transactions, but a small amount of foreign currency notes was bought and sold in the market, the value of which rose in terms of Chinese currency. After July 1942 the Japanese military authorities terminated the market for foreign notes in Shanghai. In Chungking and Kunming the Board maintained the rate of 3.1562d and U.S. 5.6125 cents until July 8, 1943. On that date, acting upon the request of the financial authority of the government, it announced a new rate of 3.01562d and U.S. 5.625 cents. Actual sales by appointed banks then

TABLE 83. FOREIGN EXCHANGE RATES IN CHINA, 1939–1941[1]
(Market rate)

| Year | Sterling (d) | U.S. Dollars (cents) |
|---|---|---|
| 1939 | | |
| April | 8.000 | 15.625 |
| May | 8.000 | 15.625 |
| June | 6.587 | 12.825 |
| July | 5.365 | 10.4141 |
| Aug. | 3.500 | 6.7236 |
| Sept. | 3.640 | 6.0600 |
| Oct. | 4.080 | 6.8175 |
| Nov. | 4.700 | 7.6550 |
| Dec. | 4.271 | 6.9115 |
| 1940 | | |
| Jan. | 4.479 | 7.3333 |
| Feb. | 4.108 | 6.7699 |
| March | 4.000 | 6.2880 |
| April | 4.000 | 5.7933 |
| May | 3.597 | 4.7431 |
| June | 3.7340 | 5.4948 |
| July | 3.7500 | 5.8525 |
| Aug. | 3.6380 | 5.4329 |
| Sept. | 3.4141 | 5.0833 |
| Oct. | 3.6106 | 5.5240 |
| Nov. | 3.72750 | 5.790 |
| Dec. | 3.59380 | 5.6328 |
| 1941 | | |
| Jan. | 3.3780 | 5.3125 |
| Feb. | 3.3390 | 5.370 |
| March | 3.25720 | 5.3050 |
| April | 3.16570 | 5.1322 |
| May | 3.15200 | 5.1741 |
| June | 3.25000 | 5.260 |
| July | 3.18750 | 5.1915 |
| Aug. | 3.04125 | 5.0975 |
| Sept. | 3.15625 | 5.21896 |
| Oct. | 3.15625 | 5.28125 |
| Nov. | 3.15625 | 5.28125 |
| Dec. | 3.15625 | 5.28125 |

[1] Based on Central Bank of China reports.

were at the rate of 3d and U.S. 5 cents. This readjustment of the Board rate was made to bring it to the conversion rate for selling U.S. Dollar Savings Certificates and U.S. Dollar Bonds issued by the Chinese government. At this time the black-market value of American currency notes had already risen in terms of Chinese currency, and the disparity between the Board rate and the black market was becoming greater. By March 1944, when the Board was abolished, the Board rate had become virtually a nominal rate.

## 5. The Foreign Exchange Market during the Pacific War

Communications between Free China and the rest of the world were completely cut off by the outbreak of the Pacific war in December 1941. With foreign trade at a standstill, and the foreign exchange market suspended, even the transactions in American notes were small.

In the spring of 1943 American military forces came to Southwest China bringing with them American currency. Because of the disparity between the official rate and the free market rate, this U.S. currency soon appeared in the market. So did some foreign currency cheques from overseas remittances to foreign residents in China and a certain amount of foreign exchange obtained from exports outside government control. Demand for U.S. currency and foreign cheques existed for hoarding and for remittances to foreign countries. Usually the market rate for U.S. currency notes was higher than that for cheques and the market rate varied from place to place because such transactions were scattered throughout the country in small amounts. Mostly, however, the Chungking rate formed a basis. From 1943 to February 1946 the market rate for U.S. dollar notes reported by the Chungking office of Joint Board of Administration of government banks was as follows:

| Year | Period | U.S. cents per CNC $ |
|---|---|---|
| 1943 | End of June | 1.693 |
| | End of Dec. | 1.191 |
| 1944 | End of June | 0.521 |
| | End of Dec. | 0.1753 |
| 1945 | End of June | 0.0586 |
| | End of Dec. | 0.08165 |
| 1946 | End of Jan. | 0.0680 |
| | End of Feb. | 0.0491 |

Throughout this period the government maintained the official rate at 5 cents. Although there were no commercial transactions, there were foreign remittances for missionary and relief organizations and to diplomatic and consular services, and remittances from Chinese abroad. Such great losses were sustained on these remittances by the receivers that they could not cover their requirements because of the overvaluation of the depreciated Chinese currency. There was a great demand for a change in the official rate, but the government preferred to maintain an official rate because it was impossible to obtain a stable rate at the market level and because it was inadvisable to chase the black-market rate endlessly. Moreover, increasing American military expenditure in China would have demanded frequent changes in the exchange rate and this would have created difficulties for the Chinese government. Therefore the nominal official rate of 5 cents was maintained for four years with two exceptions. In 1944 a subsidy of an equal amount of Chinese dollars on all incoming remittances was given by the government—i.e., an effective rate of 2.5 cents was established; and after 1945 a subsidy of 480 dollars was given on every 100 dollars of Chinese currency purchased, i.e., the rate was 0.172 cent. However, because of the wide disparity between the official rate and the market rate most of the U.S. currency notes and overseas remittances were sold at the black-market rate. Even so, fearing the psychological effect on the currency value, the government still preferred to lose a small amount of foreign exchange rather than abandon the nominal official rate. Indeed, abandoning the official rate could not have helped the situation very much.

After the U.S. $500 million American Treasury Credit had been appropriated to pay for the U.S. Dollar Savings Certificates and to service the U.S. Dollar Bonds and other purchases in the United States, the government had a balance left of U.S. $180 million in gold and U.S. $80 million in currency.

The American government developed and enlarged at its expense airfields in Southwest China in 1943. When the war ended, this and other American military expenditure left an amount of CNC $150,000 million in Chinese currency to be settled for payment. A long dispute about the conversion rate between U.S. dollars and Chinese currency ensued, the Chinese insisting that the official rate should apply and the Americans demanding that the market rate should be used. The compromise finally reached provided that expenditures before February 1944 were to be converted at the rate of 1.66 cents per CNC and expenditures between February and December 1944 were to be settled at a rate of 2 cents. From this settlement the Chinese government received U.S. $400 million.

At the end of 1945 the Central Bank of China held foreign exchange worth about U.S. $140 million and gold and silver taken over from the enemy and from puppet properties worth U.S. $60 million. These three items, the remaining proceeds of the American loan, repayment of American military expenditures, and the Central Bank's own assets, totaled U.S. $856,049,946.48, as follows:

| | |
|---|---|
| Foreign Exchange in U.S. dollars | U.S. $571,366,327.84 |
| Sterling | U.S. $ 44,292,656.19 |
| Gold | U.S. $198,920,962.45 |
| Silver | U.S. $ 43,470,000.00 |
| Total amount | U.S. $858,049,946.48 |

An American official estimate that the Chinese government possessed foreign exchange, gold, and silver holdings at about U.S. $900 million was only a little higher than the actual figure. The Chinese government had never had so much foreign exchange and would probably never have so much again; but, when victory came, the question of how best to use these assets to stabilize the currency began to occupy the financiers and economists. Failure or success of postwar financial and economic reconstruction in large part rested on successful management of this reserve.

## 6. Postwar Foreign Exchange Policy

After Shanghai was reinstated as a center of international trade and banking the Chinese government decided to re-establish the foreign exchange market there. The Central Bank was authorized to buy and sell foreign exchange at the official rate, without any limitation. The unprecedented foreign exchange reserves, so much in excess of anything experienced prewar, created the illusion that the exchange rate could be maintained on a stable basis. It was also felt that using foreign exchange to import commodities would alleviate the general shortage of supplies, and this might lessen inflationary pressures.

But the authorities failed to realize that, although the nominal size of the foreign exchange reserves was large, the economy of China had been so thoroughly disrupted during war and occupation that large-scale imports of all kinds were needed to effect a postwar readjustment. Moreover, the potential demand for imports had been swollen enormously by the combined factors of aggregate demand which expanded during wartime, lack of goods to absorb that demand, and lack of a government policy to absorb excess aggregate demand by appropriate fiscal or monetary policies. When measured against the potential disequilibrium in the balance of payments, therefore, the foreign reserves accumulated during the war were not nearly sufficient. Accordingly, direct controls were called for to protect the reserves from excessive drainage.

The foreign trade and exchange controls which were imposed were at first quite loose, and they largely restricted the import of luxury goods. Demand for exchange for imports was insatiable; merchants were scrambling for any kind of goods, including non-essentials, for which quick delivery was promised. Good profits could be made with goods reaching China quickly.

The authorities became aware of the desirability of trade controls, and a quota system of import licensing was introduced in August 1946. But the total imports permitted were still extremely liberal, motivated by the fear that a restriction of imports would cause greater rises in the general price level. Shortly before the Emergency Regulation of February 1947, about U.S. $400 million, or nearly half of the foreign exchange reserve which the Central Bank had held at the end of the war, had been used up on imports.

As soon as import restrictions, however moderate, were announced, merchants who were either unable or unwilling to obtain foreign exchange through the Central Bank began to bid for exchange on the free market. The gap between the official and the free market rate therefore began to widen, which in turn tended to channel foreign exchange earnings into the free market rather than to the Central Bank. The Emergency Regulation promulgated in February 1947, which strictly prohibited free market transactions and attempted to restrict the free flow of capital, touched off a wave of capital flight, particularly to Hong Kong. Free market exchange transactions were transferred to Hong Kong to avoid regulation and restriction by the Chinese government; the flow of unofficial dealings in foreign exchange between Shanghai and Hong Kong, and between Canton and Hong Kong, thrived. Even had it been possible to throttle foreign exchange dealings in Shanghai, such restrictions would have been ineffective in Canton, where Hong Kong dollars had comprised part of the circulating currency for years.

The flight of capital not only pushed up the free market rate for foreign exchange, and later affected the official rate in the same direction, but also added fuel to the inflation by preventing the use of foreign exchange for the financing of imports. The more restrictive the government's allocations of foreign exchange became, the more importers tended to keep their goods from the market to profit from the constant rise in prices. Thus even the official allocations for imports did not expand supplies of goods as much as they might have under more normal conditions.

In August 1947 the Central Bank abandoned its policy of pegging rates; a Stabilization Fund was installed which was to quote exchange rates in accordance with prevailing market conditions, and imports were to be paid for at the Fund rate. The Fund's intent was to prevent the official rate from lagging behind the free market rate, and it hoped to encourage the flow of proceeds from exports and remittances into official channels. But the rapid progress of inflation made it necessary for the Fund to increase its rates so frequently that

TABLE 84. THE FOREIGN EXCHANGE RATE IN THE POSTWAR PERIOD[1]

| | Open Market Foreign Exchange Rate CNC per U.S. $1 | Official Foreign Exchange Rate CNC per U.S. $1 | Percentage Increase over Previous Period: Open Market Rate | Percentage Increase over Previous Period: Shanghai Wholesale Prices |
|---|---|---|---|---|
| 1945 | | | | |
| Dec. | 1,222 | 20 | — | — |
| 1946 | | | | |
| June | 2,665 | 2,020 | 220 | 430 |
| Dec. | 6,063 | 3,350 | 230 | 180 |
| 1947 | | | | |
| June | 36,826 | 12,000 | 610 | 430 |
| Dec. | 149,615 | 77,636 | 410 | 350 |
| 1948 | | | | |
| June | 2,311,250 | 1,273,000 | 1,550 | 2,000 |
| Dec. | 405,000,000 | 366,000,000 | 17,510 | 5,730 |
| 1949 | | | | |
| April | 2,441,640,000,000 | 615,000,000,000 | 602,900 | 584,000 |

[1] Based on Central Bank of China reports; foreign exchange rate of April 1949 was recorded on the date of April 27.

it engendered political opposition—which had the effect of retarding its flexibility—on the grounds that the constant raising of official rates affected the general price level. By May 1948 the Fund rate had lagged behind the free market rate by one third; the imbalance of international payments increased because of the need to import certain basic commodities in large quantities and the simultaneous decline of exports and remittances from overseas caused by the deterioration of political and economic conditions in China. The exchange reserves dropped to a low point. Rates for the postwar period are summarized in Table 84.

## *Attempts to Maintain a Fixed Rate: 1945–1947*

On the day before victory the price of American currency notes in Chungking had risen to 3,200 Chinese dollars to U.S. $1. In September 1945 their price fell to CNC 680 per U.S. $1; but shortly afterwards they fluctuated between 1,800 and 2,500.

When the war ended, there was a great shortage of shipping, foreign trade could not be re-established, and demand for foreign exchange was not urgent. Early in 1946, however, the business communities in different ports demanded that the government announce an exchange rate in order to facilitate the reopening of foreign trade. Accordingly, following its decision to re-establish the Shanghai exchange market, the government on February 25 announced the following measures:

> The Central Bank would set an exchange rate between Chinese and foreign currencies from time to time, and would buy or sell foreign exchange according to market conditions to stabilize the exchange rate. The first rate so set was 2020 Chinese dollars per U.S. $1.
>
> Trading in gold would be free. The Central Bank would buy or sell gold according to market conditions.
>
> The Central Bank would appoint other banks to buy and sell foreign exchange on its behalf but for certain purposes only: for approved imports, for personal requirements, and for such other payments as might be authorized by the Central Bank.

Approved imports were divided into three groups:

> Those permitted after payment of a luxury surtax equal to half the existing tariff rate.
>
> Those permitted after being licensed by the Chinese Maritime Customs. This group included tobacco leaf, sugar, kerosene, oil, motor vehicles and chassis (whose net F.O.B. factory cost did not exceed U.S. $1200), and developed cinematographic film.
>
> Those permitted without restriction, e.g., essential goods, and raw materials for industry.
>
> All foreign exchange proceeds from exports must be sold to the Central Bank through the appointed banks at the rate fixed by the Central Bank. When an exporter surrendered the exchange proceeds he would receive a certificate from the appointed bank which purchased it. The Chinese Maritime Customs were ordered not to pass any exports unless accompanied by the certificate.
>
> The government appropriated U.S. $500 million as reserve against the note issue. The Central Bank also allocated a part of its foreign exchange reserves to a fund to stabilize the exchange market.

Restrictions on the granting of foreign exchange and control of foreign trade were quite loose, resembling the policy of the Stabilization Fund in 1938. At that time, and again after the war ended, the government believed that one of the main reasons for inflation was the shortage of commodity supplies. The naive belief persisted that if imports of commodities from abroad could be facilitated by reopening of the seaports, the rise in commodity prices would be automatically checked. The more liberal the trade policy, the easier it would be to fight inflation. The Central Bank, after the war, had a reserve of gold and foreign exchange at its disposal which was far above the amount held by the former Stabilization Fund; and the government was confident that it had sufficient strength to control the market, that the Central Bank reserves would be a major weapon to combat speculation, and that open market operations could cushion the effects of deficit financing through excessive note issues.

Such were the major postulates on which the postwar foreign exchange policy was established. Unfortunately, the government overlooked some aspects of the failure of the Stabilization Fund and did not adopt all the remedial measures devised by the subsequent wartime Sino-American-British Stabilization Board. Many important problems had not been resolutely faced; these included reduction of unnecessary imports, allocations of foreign exchange for most essential imports, prevention of speculation, flight of capital and smuggling, stopping overseas remittances from reaching the black market, stopping the black market of Chinese currency in Hong Kong, and securing the continued co-operation of the Allies.

Financial and economic conditions prevailing in 1946, moreover, were different from those prevailing in the period of the Stabilization Fund. In addition to the new and excessive demand for imports and the higher prices of imported goods, the wide discrepancy between the market rate for foreign exchange and the official rate, and the resulting decline in exports and overseas Chinese remittances, would have been enough to exhaust the reserve of foreign exchange and make the government policy fail.

The volume of foreign business gradually shrank after 1939 because of the spread of warfare and because the supply of foreign exchange required to finance imports slowly contracted. But after the victory, the long commodity starvation demanded a larger supply of imports, requiring an unprecedented amount of foreign exchange.

The rate used by the Stabilization Fund had been very close to the market rate. (By contrast, before the end of the war the disparity between the market rate of U.S. 0.035 cent and the official rate of

U.S. 5 cents per 1 Chinese dollar was as wide as 99 per cent.) But after the war, it was impossible to adjust realistically the new official rate to the market rate. As long as inflation continued to grow, the official rate could never catch up with the market rate. This discrepancy inevitably produced a great temptation to importers to get large grants of foreign exchange. Moreover, the closed market rate in the interior at the end of the war could not represent the real level as the open market would. The potential of upward pressures, obscured during the war years, would now become a driving force if inflation continued to increase.

The index of the note issue from January 1939 to December 1941 increased from 164 to 1,071; but now the index had reached 95,403 and was still climbing rapidly. The monthly rate of increase was a thousand times that at the time of the Stabilization Fund. Moreover, since the Allies would not take many co-operative measures in peacetime which they took in wartime, the government could hardly have succeeded in stopping all the loopholes in trade and foreign exchange controls even if it had adopted the Stabilization Board's measures.

### *Failure of the Readjustment*

The rate announced on February 25, 1946, was Chinese currency 2,020 per U.S. $1 (i.e., U.S. 0.0495 cent per 1 Chinese dollar). While occasional readjustments of the first postwar rate were intended according to market conditions, changes in the exchange rate under vicious inflation always caused anxiety among the people and stimulated further increases in commodity prices. Consequently, the government became hesitant about readjusting the official rate, which, therefore, always lagged behind the market rate. The longer the government rate remained stable, the more difficult it was to readjust it; and, when it was altered, the criticism that the government rate was chasing the market rate could not be avoided. It was not until August 19, 1946, that the rate was changed to Chinese currency 3,350 for U.S. $1 (i.e., U.S. 0.0288 cent per 1 Chinese dollar).

After this adjustment the market rate was still about 10 per cent above the official rate. At the end of 1946, because of limitations on the granting of foreign exchange, importers began to scramble to obtain foreign exchange or U.S. dollar notes. The market rate rose about 50 per cent, and export was practically at a standstill. After hesitating over making any adjustment, in February 1947 the government devised a new system for readjusting the rate, similar to instituting a differential exchange rate: giving a 100 per cent subsidy on exports and charging a 50 per cent surtax on imports; but, because of United States government objections to the export subsidy system, it was soon abandoned.

When the Emergency Regulations were promulgated in the same month the rate was readjusted to Chinese currency 12,000 per U.S. $1 (i.e., U.S. 0.00834 cent per 1 Chinese dollar), about 14 per cent below the market rate. The government thought that this new rate could be stabilized because of the freezing of commodity prices and wages; but in less than a month the emergency measures failed, and the market rate jumped again. In March, after a change of cabinet, the new government and the banking authorities began to consider a new policy while still maintaining the existing regulations. During this period the black-market rate kept rising, and by July it was 72 per cent above the official rate. Table 85 shows the changes in the exchange rate and the black-market rate from March 1946 to the end of July 1947.

### *The Crisis of February 1947*

Because of the heavy demands for foreign exchange and gold being sold by the Central Bank, the government had no choice but to amend the export-import regulations in November 1946. All imports were brought under a license system. No free imports or luxury imports were to be allowed, and a quota system was instituted to limit the quantities of licensed imports. This system was more or less the same as the quota system devised by the Stabilization Board. After this amendment was put into effect, the demand for exchange for imports was reduced, but the market rate for foreign exchange kept rising. From November 18, 1946, to March 17, 1947, only U.S. $30 million foreign exchange was appropriated. The official rate, in terms of CNC per U.S. dollar, in January 1947 was about 50 per cent of the market rate. Following the November regulations speculators and people who had been buying foreign exchange to preserve money value turned to gold, and great quantities were sold from November 1946 to March 17, 1947. The price of gold was rising intermittently in spite of the increasing government supply. Commodity prices took their lead from the values of foreign exchange and of gold and rose at the same pace. This result was inevitable since foreign goods were the main source of supply for the urban sector.

As the whole country approached a state of panic, emergency regulations were promulgated on February 17, 1947. Commodity prices and wages were frozen; public transactions in gold were prohibited. The Central Bank of China discontinued the sale of gold, and the circulation and buying and selling of foreign currency notes were prohibited. Private holdings of foreign exchange were to be declared. The measures were prompted by the need to face the emergency but

Table 85. Comparison of the Official and Market Rates of Exchange between U.S. Dollars and Chinese Dollars[1]

| Year | Official Rate (CNC per U.S. $1) | Market Rate (CNC per U.S. $1) | Official Rate as Percentage of Market Rate |
|---|---|---|---|
| 1946 | | | |
| March | 2,020 | — | — |
| April | 2,020 | — | — |
| May | 2,020 | — | — |
| June | 2,020 | 2,665 | 75.80 |
| July | 2,020 | 2,519 | 80.19 |
| Aug.[2] | 2,611 | 2,909 | 89.76 |
| Sept. | 3,350 | 3,576 | 83.90 |
| Oct. | 3,350 | 4,230 | 79.20 |
| Nov. | 3,350 | 4,532 | 73.92 |
| Dec. | 3,350 | 6,063 | 55.25 |
| 1947 | | | |
| Jan. | 3,350 | 6,765 | 49.52 |
| Feb.[3] | 7,369 | 12,222 | 60.29 |
| March | 12,000 | 14,000 | 85.71 |
| April | 12,000 | 16,250 | 73.85 |
| May | 12,000 | 27,204 | 44.11 |
| June | 12,000 | 36,826 | 32.59 |
| July | 12,000 | 43,640 | 27.50 |

[1] Based on data of the Central Bank of China. Before 1946 the official rate was worked out in U.S. dollars; after 1946 in Chinese dollars.

[2] First official readjustment.

[3] Second official readjustment.

were made without any preparation or deliberation. It was only too obvious that they could not produce a lasting effect. Because of the economic chaos, the cabinet resigned.

## *The Drainage of Foreign Exchange and Gold*

In twelve months between February 1946 and February 1947 the government spent nearly U.S. $500 million in sales of foreign exchange and gold, whereas the Chinese currency withdrawn from the market with these resources amounted to approximately one-third of the fiscal deficit of the period. The government deficit amounted to about two-thirds of the government's total expenditure.

The foreign exchange and specie holdings of the Central Bank at the end of February 1947, compared with those held at the end of February 1946, are shown in Table 86.

TABLE 86. FOREIGN EXCHANGE AND SPECIE HOLDINGS OF CENTRAL BANK, FEBRUARY 1946 AND 1947

| | End of Feb. 1947 | End of Feb. 1946 | Net Loss from Feb. 1946 to Feb. 1947 |
|---|---|---|---|
| Foreign exchange in U.S. dollars | 199,072,689 | 546,543,364 | 347,470,675 |
| Sterling | 31,093,208 | 44,652,795 | 13,559,587 |
| Gold | 83,001,139 | 198,920,962 | 115,919,823 |
| Silver | 33,810,000 | 43,470,000 | 9,660,000 |
| Total U.S. dollar value | 346,977,036 | 833,587,121 | 486,610,085 |

## *Attempts to Employ a Flexible Exchange Rate: 1947–1948*

The chain of cause and effect gave the new authorities an almost impossible task. To face the situation, the new government reduced out-payments of foreign exchange and greatly decreased the quota for the second quarter. At the same time it tried to install a flexible rate which was to be readjusted by a newly established Stabilization Fund Committee.

In August 1947 the Central Bank of China announced the following changes in foreign exchange policy:

> The Foreign Exchange Stabilization Fund Committee was established to decide the Fund rate and to maintain an equilibrium between foreign exchange supply and demand, hoping thus to eliminate undue fluctuations in the exchange market.
>
> The Committee consisted of members appointed by the government who worked closely with the Central Bank and leading foreign exchange banks in Shanghai.
>
> The Stabilization Fund Committee would draw its necessary working fund from the Central Bank in either foreign exchange or local currency.
>
> The appointed banks would buy or sell foreign exchange according to the Fund's rate.
>
> Instead of trying to peg the rate at a given level for any period of time, the Stabilization Fund Committee would announce, after consultation with representatives of foreign exchange banks in Shanghai, a Fund rate of exchange from time to time based on market conditions.
>
> Except for foreign exchange needed to import such essential raw mate-

rials as cotton, rice, wheat, flour, coal, and coke, which were purchased by the government and distributed through official channels on a nonprofit basis, and except for a part of the government requirements which the Central Bank would continue to supply at the old official rate of Chinese currency, CNC $12,000 to U.S. $1, all foreign exchange requirements were to be met at the Fund rate.

The main purpose of the new system was to break the deadlock arising from the fixed-rate policy which had been announced during the February crisis. It was hoped that this would reduce the unreasonable profits of importers and reduce the discrepancy between the official rate and the market rate, thus reviving the export trade and inducing an inflow of remittances from overseas. To put the exchange rate readjustments above public suspicion, the work was to be entrusted to an independent committee of men of impartiality and complete integrity. Because the inflation had reached an acute stage, the Committee was careful to discharge its duty faithfully.

It used average wholesale prices from different important cities and the prices of China's chief exports as reference indexes for the rate adjustment. To average these wholesale and export price indexes, proper weights were applied to a ten-day moving average centered on the day concerned. Daily departures from this average were used as a basis for the percentage of adjustment to be made in the Fund's exchange rate. Undue fluctuations of prices of single commodities were usually ignored if they did not represent the over-all condition of the market. Adjustment was usually made when the Fund's rate lagged so much behind that it hampered exports. The Hong Kong exchange rate was also considered, because it was probably the most reliable indication of the market value of the Chinese dollar. Although export promotion was one objective of the Fund's rate adjustment policy, it did not intend to compete for overseas remittances with the black market, because it feared that the diversion of remittances from the black market might accentuate the rise of the exchange rate in the market.

The Fund's rate was adjusted when the Central Bank's foreign exchange reserves began to drain away through being oversold or when there was a large demand for exchange to meet imports already approved. When the rate was adjusted, the Central Bank and other government agents in charge of distributing essential commodities were requested to apply simultaneously measures designed to tighten the money market in Shanghai and minimize the "bullish" effect on prices. Rate adjustment was avoided when there was a large government outlay pouring into the market.

### *Difficulties of Readjustment*

In spite of its precautionary policy, the Committee could not avoid the criticism that it chased the black-market rate and caused prices to rise. It was quite obvious that underlying conditions were now quite different from those obtaining when earlier wartime stabilization activities were undertaken. The new Committee operated under a number of limitations.

> Inflation had almost reached a stage where economic collapse threatened. The people felt so bitter against the government that any measure taken which might lead to an upward movement of prices would be a target for public attack. Rate adjustments would be most conspicuous. Consequently, the Committee found it impossible to make any adjustments based on reality because it had to take public feeling into consideration.
>
> The market rate was rising so rapidly that, unless the official rate was moved up, the market rate and the official rate would be very far apart. But in the circumstances public opinion could not approve the official rate being moved up. However, if the Committee did not follow the market rate, the increase of smuggling, the dispersion of overseas remittances, and the stoppage of exports would make foreign exchange receipts inadequate to provide for imports and other commercial requirements of the market.
>
> The discrepancy between the official rate and the market rate in Shanghai was so wide that the Hong Kong government felt that it was very difficult to control black-market transactions in Chinese currency in Hong Kong. Yet the effect of the Hong Kong black market on Shanghai was becoming so serious that it was almost impossible to control the Shanghai black market by itself.
>
> The Central Bank's foreign exchange reserve was nearly exhausted, and there was no prospect of foreign aid. The Committee did not have access to significant amounts of gold and foreign exchange to stabilize the market.

The first Fund rate at Chinese currency $38,636 to U.S. $1 was announced on August 19, 1947, at the start of the Stabilization Fund Committee's operations. At this time the market rate was $43,000 and the discrepancy was about 10 per cent. The new rate was 11,450 times the prewar rate, but it was still far below the price index, which was already about 32,000 times prewar. The merchants, who knew that they would not now be able to obtain cheap foreign exchange at the Fund Committee rate and that the Fund Committee rate would not be very much lower than the market rate, raised prices of both imports and exports in terms of foreign exchange. Their action affected general commodity prices, particularly rates charged by public utilities which need a great deal of imported raw materials. This in turn reacted on commodity prices and was followed by a rise in the market rate.

The Committee had no option but to readjust the Fund Committee rate to increases in the market rate, which again affected commodity prices and raised the market rate further still. Therefore the Committee rate, which was far below the price index, was unable to keep up with internal prices and could not approximate the market rate, although it kept chasing it.

The increasing tempo of the inflation turned the situation from bad to worse toward the end of 1947 and greatly hampered the operations of the Fund. During the months between February and May 1948 the fund was practically paralyzed by political criticism about the change in the rate, and much of the flexibility in the rate adjustment, envisaged at the time the flexible rate was introduced, was lost.

However, the drain on the Central Bank's foreign reserve was reduced appreciably after the system was put into effect. Exports were maintained at what was a high level in the circumstances—more than U.S. $10 million per month. Overseas remittances also increased during the first three months of the Fund Committee's operations. These improvements, together with the tightening of control over

TABLE 87. COMPARISON OF FUND COMMITTEE AND MARKET RATES OF EXCHANGE BETWEEN U.S. DOLLARS AND CHINESE DOLLARS[1]
(CNC per U.S. $1)

| Year | Committee Rate | Market Rate | Fund Committee Rate as Percentage of Market Rate |
|---|---|---|---|
| 1947 | | | |
| Aug. | 38,636 | 42,759 | 90.36 |
| Sept. | 41,635 | 50,365 | 82.67 |
| Oct. | 53,658 | 81,058 | 66.20 |
| Nov. | 62,640 | 109,387 | 57.26 |
| Dec. | 77,636 | 149,615 | 51.89 |
| 1948 | | | |
| Jan. | 108,350 | 179,045 | 60.52 |
| Feb. | 138,292 | 218,235 | 63.37 |
| March | 211,583 | 449,620 | 47.06 |
| April | 313,385 | 661,154 | 47.40 |
| May | 399,000 | 1,167,154 | 34.19 |

[1] Based on Central Bank of China reports.

imports, resulted in a great reduction in the balance of payments disequilibrium.

From August 19, 1947, to the end of May 1948 the committee rate rose by almost 18 times, the market rate jumped by 28 times, and the Shanghai price index by 15 times. Table 87 compares the average monthly ratio of the Fund Committee's rate with the market rate.

In May 1948, while waiting for decision by a new cabinet about future exchange rate policy, the Central Bank and the Fund Committee introduced a makeshift arrangement in order to avoid a run

TABLE 88. IN-PAYMENTS AND OUT-PAYMENTS OF FOREIGN EXCHANGE FEBRUARY 1947—MAY 1948

| | Out-Payments of Foreign Exchange |
|---|---|
| Government requirements | U.S. $194,000,000 |
| Imports | U.S. $309,000,000 |
| Requirements other than for imports | U.S. $ 21,000,000 |
| Total | U.S. $524,000,000 |
| | **In-Payments of Foreign Exchange** |
| Exports | U.S. $225,000,000 |
| Overseas remittances | U.S. $ 20,000,000 |
| U.S. dollar notes redeemed, and other receipts | U.S. $ 48,000,000 |
| Proceeds of U.S. dollar bonds | U.S. $ 25,819,000 |
| Total | U.S. $318,819,000 |

on available foreign exchange. The expedient provided that a deposit in local currency equal to 50 per cent of the value of the approved import, computed at the Fund Committee's rate on the day of deposit, be made when the import license was issued; and it further provided that the foreign exchange required for the import would be settled at the Fund Committee's rate prevailing when the cargo arrived in China. This regulation caused complaints among businessmen. The Fund Committee was automatically suspended when the new foreign exchange certificate system was announced by the new banking authority. Events proved that, if a government cannot face the reality of the depreciation of external value and the public cannot realize the inevitability of raising the exchange rate while rapid inflation is under way, a policy of flexible rates is bound to fail.

In-payments and out-payments of foreign exchange from the end of February 1947 to the end of May 1948, and the holdings of the Central

Bank and the other government banks and organizations, are shown in Tables 88 and 89.

TABLE 89. GOVERNMENT HOLDINGS OF FOREIGN EXCHANGE
MAY 31, 1948

| Central Bank | Government Holdings |
|---|---|
| Gold | U.S. $ 96,652,898 |
| Silver | U.S. $ 28,959,000 |
| Foreign exchange | U.S. $ 28,305,101 |
| Total | U.S. $153,916,999 |
| Other Government Banks and Government Organizations | U.S. $ 60,000,000 |
| Grand Total | U.S. $213,916,999 |

## 7. FINAL FOREIGN EXCHANGE POLICIES: 1948–1949

### *The Certificate System*

On May 31, 1948, the new Central Bank authority adopted a foreign exchange certificate system. Its chief characteristics may be summarized as follows:

> To purchase foreign exchange proceeds derived from exports and overseas remittances, the Central Bank would issue, through its appointed banks, foreign exchange surrender certificates.
>
> The owner of a certificate might transfer it to a qualified importer or any other person authorized to purchase exchange from an appointed bank at the prevailing certificate rate. Foreign exchange on the certificate could not be drawn from the Central Bank unless the certificates were accompanied by such authorizations.
>
> The certificate rate of exchange was determined by market conditions of supply and demand.
>
> If the supply of exchange certificates in the market did not approximate demand, the Central Bank could intervene by selling or buying certificates in the market.
>
> It was originally stipulated that the validity of a certificate for purchase of foreign exchange should not be more than seven days from the date on which it was issued, and that the validity date could not be extended. Later, validity was extended to thirty days.

In the view of the government and Central Bank authorities, by this system the government could reduce the supply of foreign exchange to the market and also could avoid criticism for pushing up prices because of frequent readjustment of the exchange rate. However, the authorities overlooked once again some of the basic aspects of the problem: that if the government supplied less foreign exchange to the market, the market rate would be forced up by approved imports, the flight of capital, and smuggling; that eventually the certificate rate would become another form of official rate, and the merging of the market rate and the official rate could never be attained; that these two rates would push each other up, and this fact in turn would force up the prices of imports and exports and would aggravate inflation, causing the exchange rate to depreciate further, and, in turn, cause in-payments in CNC or U.S. dollars from overseas remittances and exports to fall still more. This course of events actually ensued.

The failure of the certificate system proved that the previous Fund Committee's operations, even without strong backing, still had certain psychological restraining influences. They moderated rises in the exchange rate and in commodity prices because the people still believed that the government could supply exchange for approved imports and that the official rate had some influence on the market rate, always considered an "indication" rate. The rise of the certificate rate was much faster than the previous market rate. It rose from CNC 849,000 per U.S. dollar quoted on the first day (June 2, 1948) to CNC 7,850,000 on August 19th, which was an increase of 924 per cent in two and a half months. The Fund Committee rate, in contrast, had risen only 650 per cent from January to May 1948. Yet the certificate rate still lagged behind the market rate and the system almost broke down on the eve of the change of currency.

On August 19, the day before the change of the monetary standard, the certificate rate was CNC 7,850,000 per U.S. $1, but the market rate was $12,000,000, the discrepancy being about 35 per cent.

### *The Fixed Rate Gold Yuan*

When the issue of "Gold Yuan" was announced on August 20, 1948 the rate was fixed at:

1 Gold Yuan = U.S. 25 cents<br>
Sterling 1s/8d

In the next forty days the new rate remained quite steady because the government took strong measures to freeze commodity prices and to prohibit the circulation, sale, and holding of silver, gold, and foreign currency notes. There was no market rate. The Central Bank had over-bought exchange, but the pegged rate policy was short-lived after the ceiling-price policy broke down. A market rate for U.S. dollar notes revived, and late in October the market rate for foreign exchange again prevailed and the government had to abandon the policy.

### *The Clearance Certificates*

The clearance certificate system was then introduced in its place. The modus operandi of the clearance certificate system was practically the same as that of the previous foreign exchange certificate system, with only two differences:

> The clearance certificates would be valid for sixty days from the date of issue. Under the previous certificate system the period of validity was first fixed at seven days and was later extended to thirty days.
>
> Restrictions on the purchase of clearance certificates were much more lenient than under the previous certificate system. Also, the Central Bank established an overseas remittance rate which was usually somewhat higher than the clearance certificate rate.

Because the grant of foreign exchange for imports was reduced and because merchants hesitated to import more goods into China in view of the Communist armies' further victories in Northern and Central China, the commercial demand for certificates decreased. But the flight of capital increased, and the discrepancy between the clearance certificate rate and the market rate appeared again. The Central Bank stopped quoting the overseas remittance rate to avoid criticism from the public. Early in 1949 the Communists approached the Yangtze, and the market rate rose higher and higher. At the beginning of March the difference was only 10 per cent, but in May it was more than 60 per cent. Table 90 shows the fixed rate and the market rate for Gold Yuan in August, September, and October and the difference between the clearance certificate rate and the market rate from November onwards. (The rate given is the rate at the end of each month.)

According to the market rate at the beginning of May, U.S. $1 was worth 9 million Gold Yuan. Converted into old currency, this would equal $27,000 billion. This was two and a quarter million times higher than the rate of the old currency just before Gold Yuan was issued. Late in May, when the Communist army approached Shanghai, the market was in a panic. U.S. $1 was worth 23 million Gold Yuan. Everybody was scrambling for foreign currency rather than holding commodities. Finally, the exchange rate of Gold Yuan disappeared after the fall of Shanghai.

The certificate system was doomed to failure from the very beginning. By this device, which in effect gave official sanction to the black-market rate, the financial and banking authority tended to evade its responsibility for orderly exchange adjustments. When the insufficient inflow of foreign exchange failed to meet the demand, the certificate rate soon took the place of the official rate, while an even higher black-market rate was in effect. The certificate system also failed to ameliorate balance of payments disequilibrium because the

TABLE 90. EXCHANGE RATES OF LATE 1948 AND EARLY 1949
(GY per U.S. $)

| Year | Certificate Rate | Market Rate | Certificate Rate as Percentage of Market Rate |
|---|---|---|---|
| 1948 | | | |
| Aug. (19–31) | 4 | 4 | 100 |
| Sept. | 4 | 4 | 100 |
| Oct. | 4 | 15 | 26.67 |
| Nov. | 28 | 42 | 66.67 |
| Dec. | 122 | 135 | 90.37 |
| 1949 | | | |
| Jan. | 240 | 700 | 34.29 |
| Feb. | 2,660 | 2,980 | 89.26 |
| March | 16,000 | 17,700 | 90.40 |
| April | 205,000 | 813,880 | 25.18 |
| May (up to 21st) | No official rate | 23,280,000 | — |

flight of capital continued and limitations on the official supply of foreign exchange pushed the black-market rate up further, thus widening the gap between the rates.

In spite of the failure of the certificate system, the government reintroduced a substantially similar plan with its clearance certificate system after the creation of the Gold Yuan.

Examination of the government's postwar foreign exchange policy leads to the conclusion that its intent was to neutralize the inflationary forces generated by fiscal policies rather than to obtain rational allocation and utilization of funds as required by the war-damaged economy. The recurring emergency measures taken by the government only intensified the pressures on the external value of the currency. As the foreign exchange situation moved out of control, it inevitably produced increasing deficits in the balance of payments which eventually led to the exhaustion of foreign reserves. When finally the government, under the pretense of currency reform, compelled the surrender of precious metals and foreign exchange at rates resembling outright confiscation, it in effect committed moral suicide because of the manifest injustice done to the patriotic and law-abiding citizens, as contrasted to those who previously had removed their capital to foreign lands.

At this point mention must be made of the Hong Kong free market, which was blamed by the Chinese government for many of its difficulties in the prevention of the flight of capital. The Hong Kong government permitted free dealings in U.S. dollars, gold, and Chinese currency. A substantial supply of U.S. dollars from overseas Chinese remittances flowed into Hong Kong, where they were exchanged into Chinese currency to avoid undue losses to the ultimate recipients in China. Gold was smuggled into Hong Kong from Macao and was sold at free market prices, disregarding the price fixed by the International Monetary Fund. The Hong Kong gold trade spurted after the Chinese government progressively reduced its supply of foreign exchange to the Shanghai market, and especially after it prohibited transactions in gold in China.

Late in 1946 the Chinese government asked the Hong Kong government to restrict dealings in Chinese currency, U.S. dollars, and gold. In 1947 the Hong Kong government did enact import licensing for gold imports, but it failed to move against dealings in Chinese currency on the grounds that the disparity between official and free rates was so great as to render effective controls impossible. Restrictions on dealings in U.S. dollars were resisted because of the probable curtailment of Hong Kong's trade and economy this would entail.

In September 1948, when China adopted the Gold Yuan monetary system, the Hong Kong government restricted dealings in Chinese currency, but it dropped those restrictions shortly after the value of the Gold Yuan began its precipitous slide.

Had the Chinese government adopted more effective measures and provided a more competent administrative machinery for their implementation, dependence on Hong Kong measures for currency stabilization would not have been so heavy and the flight of capital would have been less severe. It has been estimated that between 1947 and 1949 about HK $500 million in Chinese flight capital flowed to Hong Kong (around U.S. $100 million). A capital movement of such magnitude plainly constituted an insurmountable roadblock to any stabilization in the Chinese balance of payments and exchange rate.

Table 91 shows the amount of gold, silver, and foreign exchange collected by the Central Bank after the government ordered compulsory surrender when the monetary standard changed to the Gold Yuan. This showed the strength of the people's patriotism and their loyalty to the government even after a long period of suffering caused by inflation. The irreparable damage the government suffered when the people found that the paper notes which they had received in exchange for their precious metals and foreign currency had become valueless only in a few months' time can be easily imagined.

TABLE 91. GOLD, SILVER AND FOREIGN CURRENCIES SURRENDERED UNDER THE GOLD YUAN DECREE

| | | | |
|---|---|---|---|
| Gold | | 1,677,163 ozs. | = U.S. $ 83,858,150 |
| Silver | | 8,881,373 ozs. | = U.S. $ 6,661,029 |
| Silver dollars | | $23,564,068 | = U.S. $ 11,782,034 |
| U.S. dollar notes | | $49,851,876 | = U.S. $ 49,851,876 |
| Hong Kong dollar notes | HK | $86,097,450 | = U.S. $ 16,378,200 |
| Philippine notes | Pesos | 785,907 | = U.S. $ 383,153 |
| Deposits of foreign currency | | | = U.S. $ 10,697,755 |
| Total | | | U.S. $179,612,197 |

An increase of 80 per cent was made over the holdings at the end of May 1948. But foreign currency and foreign exchange were rapidly exhausted; and, after the restoration of the silver dollar standard in February 1949, silver reserves also were depleted. A minor part of the gold was directly used for military expenditure. The last resources, about three million ounces of gold and a small amount of foreign exchange, were moved to Formosa.

Chapter

# 13

# Foreign Trade

### *Introduction*

China has traditionally had a low level of exports. Between 1912, the first year of the Republic of China, and 1928, the last year before the depression, exports increased 2.7 times; but at the end of this period they approached only about U.S. $500 million and constituted only 83 per cent of imports. The low level of exports was due to the stagnation in the country's agriculture and the competition suffered by some staple commodities such as tea and silk by similar goods of better quality in world markets.

The world depression beginning in 1929, followed by the United States high silver price policy, not only brought about a substantial decrease of China's principal exports but also resulted in greater imports of foreign agricultural products—some brought in by foreign dumping. This increased the unfavorable balance of trade. Historically, such imbalance had been covered by overseas Chinese remittances and other invisible exports. Now the gap became so great that it could be bridged only by drawing down China's silver reserves. During the 1930's these weaknesses were further aggravated by the loss of Manchurian trade and the loss of other traditional markets: and in 1934 exports were only about half the value of imports. In 1937, following the change of China's currency from a silver standard to a managed exchange standard, accompanied by devaluation, exports recovered to 87 per cent of imports; but their average value during 1934 and 1937 was only 70 per cent of that of 1928.

Foreign trade centered on only a few large coastal cities, particularly Shanghai and Tientsin. Because all the facilities related to foreign trade were there, these cities and a relatively narrow hinterland were the only ones benefiting from foreign trade. Barriers to internal trade, the need for standardization of export products, and the lack of domestic processing facilities in areas away from the coast limited the involvement of interior regions in foreign trade. Without progress in internal trade, no improvement in production could be looked for, nor did any improvement in standardization in commodities and processing facilities take place. Thus, with the Treaty Ports not subject to government control and virtually cut off from the interior, China's ability to obtain necessities by exporting was almost nil.

These characteristics of foreign trade before the war kept any foreign trade policies from having beneficial effects on inflation; and they persisted after the war to hamper measures to offset inflation.

## 1. Wartime Import Policies

From the time when war broke out, in the middle of July 1937, foreign trade in the whole of China was at a standstill. In Shanghai especially, trading activity was reduced to a minimum as the city was surrounded by fighting and cut off from the hinterland. In the five months from August to December 1937 the monthly average of Chinese imports was 21 per cent of the corresponding figure during the previous seven months; but, because stocks of goods at the ports were fairly high, the monthly average of exports was only reduced to 46 per cent of the figure for the previous seven months. After February 1938, when fighting ceased in North China and the center of fighting gradually moved away from Shanghai into the interior, the import trade of the whole country revived; but, because communications in the interior were halted by the heavy fighting, export trade was at a standstill.

Through the first three months of 1938 the adverse balance of trade increased over that in the corresponding period in 1937. Moreover, demand for foreign exchange became excessive after the beginning of hostilities. The government took this opportunity to abandon its unlimited supply of foreign exchange to the market, replacing it with a policy of foreign exchange control and foreign trade control.

This was the beginning of import control in China. It was gradually tightened because of the increasing imports into Occupied China and the fear of Japanese goods entering Free China. Imports in terms of U.S. currency into all of China in 1938 were reduced by 32 per cent and in 1939 by 38 per cent; imports in 1940 and 1941 declined at the rate of 20 per cent. Supplies to Free China were nearly cut off after the latter part of 1940, and import control was relaxed again.

Following are details of the different methods, both indirect and direct, used to control trade, starting indirectly with a gradual reduction of foreign exchange allocations, followed by application of direct control by restrictions on the kinds of goods which might be imported (at one time these restrictions were relaxed), and ending with government management of the export trade.

### *Permit System: March 14, 1938*

The Chinese government began to control foreign trade by means of moderate control of foreign exchange. On March 14, 1938, the government stipulated that any bank which, after balancing payments from its own and from commercial resources, needed foreign exchange should apply to the Central Bank, which would approve the application if the exchange was for commercial or any other legitimate purpose.

This regulation was interpreted to mean that any application for commercial purposes would be approved, but because of the decline of foreign exchange reserves only 37.5 per cent of funds applied for were granted at first. Gradually, allocations were reduced to an insignificant amount.

Early in May the government required all banks applying for foreign exchange to supply full details, such as the name of the firm, the import commodity, and its uses, but it did not expressly indicate that any differentiation would be made between essential and nonessential imports. Severe criticism of the government for having no clear criterion for its approvals or refusals of applications for foreign exchange ensued, and another method of giving priority to essential goods had to be found.

### *Priority for Essential Goods: June 15, 1938*

On June 15, 1938, the government announced that 65 specific categories of goods would be considered essential imports for the purchase of which priority grants of foreign exchange would be given. No foreign exchange would be granted for importing luxury goods, or for consumer and other goods which could be replaced by domestic products. This marked the beginning of foreign trade control.

But trade through the important coastal cities was already beyond the control of the Chinese government at this time. Shanghai, flooded with people from the interior, many of whom could afford to pay for luxury or consumer goods, became the main port for the import of nonessential goods apart from increasing imports of other consumer goods.

Imports into Shanghai increased by two-thirds over the amount imported in the same period of the previous year. Therefore, the attempt to differentiate between essential and nonessential goods was of no avail.

### *Foreign Exchange for Imports Granted at the Market Rate: March 10, 1939*

Restricting imports by differentiating between essential and nonessential goods had proved to be ineffectual, and abandoning the exchange market in Shanghai was not desirable in the light of its international importance and its position in facilitating the flow of supplies to Free China. The government therefore decided to supply the exchange needed for imports at the market rate instead of at the official rate. It was hoped that increases in prices of imports, because of the higher rate of foreign exchange, would reduce the demand and indirectly restrict imports of unnecessary goods.

However, as communication lines in the interior had been destroyed and the consequent scarcity of agricultural products in the coastal cities changed the increasing trend of imports from nonessential goods to essential goods, such as cotton, rice, wheat, flour, sugar, and tobacco leaf, and increased the latter's price, the new import policy was thus rendered undesirable and ineffective.

### *Differential Exchange Rate for Imports and Exports: July 2, 1939*

In July 1939 the government announced that, to establish an exchange market in Free China, all applications for exchange to cover imports would have to be addressed to the Foreign Exchange Examination Committee, and that when they had been approved the foreign exchange would have to be bought from the Bank of China or from the Bank of Communications. Exchange resulting from exports was to be surrendered to these two banks in Free China.

Every day the two banks quoted their exchange rate as a so-called "commercial rate." Importers had to buy their exchange according to the official fixed rate and to pay the difference between the official rate and the commercial rate as an equalization charge. Exporters had to sell their exchange at the official rate but would be paid the difference between the official rate and the commercial rate as a subsidy.

These measures were intended to restrict imports into and encourage exports from Free China. By this time, however, foreign trade in Free China became insignificant and the movement of exchange rate had very little effect on foreign trade. Moreover, the demand for imports was very strong, and merchants could ship goods either from Shanghai to Hong Kong by sea or through inland routes to Free China and sell them for Chinese currency. Therefore there was no direct correlation between the exchange rate and the volume of imports.

The differential exchange rate lasted until October 1941, when the Sino-American-British Stabilization Board announced a new Board rate, and rate quoting of the commercial rate ceased.

### *The Import Quota System*

In August 1941 the Stabilization Board classified imports in two categories according to the importance of commodities to the livelihood of the population, and to the maintenance of operation of industries in Shanghai. Grants of foreign exchange would be allowed for goods in these two categories with priority going to goods in the first. Trade associations or guilds were collectively to apply to the Stabilization Board, which, after investigating the quantity of existing cargoes and consumer goods, would issue the monthly quota for each commodity. The association or guild would then divide the quota among its members. This marked the beginning of the quota system in China's policy of foreign trade control.

In its first month of operations the Board allocated U.S. $6 million for imports, with Shanghai receiving about half of it. This system lasted only briefly because of the early outbreak of the Pacific War and because the lack of tonnage caused a decrease in the volume of imports.

### *Direct Control*

When the Sino-Japanese war broke out, the Chinese government banned all imports from Japan and from Japan-controlled areas, from firms operated by Japanese in other areas, and from enterprises using Japanese capital. A great number of categories of Japanese and Manchurian goods were placed on the prohibited list. Although this action could be classed as economic warfare, it was not trade control.

To reduce out-payments of foreign exchange, in November 1939 the government prohibited the import of certain goods considered replaceable by domestic commodities or non-essential. However, this prohibition could not be effectively implemented because most of the customs checking points were beyond the government's control, and also because imports into occupied areas shifted in character from non-essential to essential and thus were no longer on the prohibited list.

Free China's growing population and the growing aggregate demand for consumer goods combined to bring pressure on the government to encourage a greater volume of imports to Free China. In July 1939 the government issued a list of goods freely importable irrespective of origin; moreover, importers of those goods were promised transportation facilities and financial aid. In July 1940 the prohibited list was virtually superseded by a new list which defined a few commodities as luxuries and implicitly removed import restrictions on all other goods.

In May 1942 the government abolished the ban on importing enemy goods and issued new regulations for wartime control of exports and imports. Import bans were also lifted from a great number of commodities which were placed under special license control instead. Even artificial silk and goods made from it, fine wool, tobacco, papers, feathers, timbers, and articles made from them could again be imported. Except for the prohibited luxury and non-essential goods, merchants could ship any commodity irrespective of its place of origin.

The following month the government again announced a campaign for securing materials. Its main points were:

> The government specified the kinds of commodities to be secured and designated the department in charge of each.
>
> Any company, firm, or individual could provide capital to buy goods from Occupied China or from abroad.
>
> Such commodities could be sold on the market, or the importers could apply to the department in charge, asking it to purchase the goods.
>
> The parties who secured materials would receive a bonus subsidy, a reduction in tax, facilities for remitting money for transportation or insurance, and other protection.

However, these efforts were in vain because the Burma Road had been closed by blockade. The limited capacity of the air lift could provide only small quantities of military supplies, and only 1,000 tons of civilian goods could be brought into the country each month.

In summary, early wartime import policy was to reduce imports, but later the government reversed its objective and sought to encourage the inflow of supplies to fight inflation. Unfortunately, in each case other forces were stronger and frustrated the government's foreign trade objectives, not only because of the enemy blockade but also because of the war in Europe which cut off the movement of goods from there. Imports into both Free China and Occupied China were sharply reduced. Even the flow of trade from Japan to Occupied China declined because the Japanese needed the goods for their own war effort.

## 2. Wartime Export Policies

A very important wartime problem facing the Chinese government was how to increase exports to get foreign exchange to import essential military and civilian supplies for the war effort. Realizing this, the enemy intensified the blockade and his bombing aimed to sever lines of transportation which had not yet even been properly developed. Only a small quantity of goods could therefore be shipped out. Such shipments were subject to indefinite delays, difficulties, and risks before reaching their destinations. Increased transportation charges and interest on overdue loans increased the cost of exports tremendously. At the same time the government, needing it, made exporters surrender their foreign exchange at a fixed rate. Therefore, in spite of all the government's encouragements, exporters could not overcome all their difficulties. The risks they faced were too great for them to continue in business, and the government had to take over the export trade.

Early in the war there was very little reduction in export trade because quantities of many export commodities were waiting in various ports for sale or shipment. These were hurriedly shipped out in the latter part of 1937. From August 1937 to the end of July 1938 the export trade for all of China fell 25 per cent compared with the previous twelve months. Free China handled 41 per cent of the total.

In June 1938 the government specified that 90 per cent of the foreign exchange resulting from the export of 24 kinds of commodities* was to be sold to the government at a rate it would fix. The remaining 10 per cent could be retained by the merchants. Exporters could get a Customs clearance for their goods only by showing the certificate of settlement of foreign exchange to the Customs. They also had to apply for a tonnage allocation to the Government Trans-

* Wood oil, bristles, buffalo and cow hides, tea, eggs and egg products, mineral ores, gallnuts, goat skins, medical substances, wool, silk, straw braid and hats, human hair, ramie, animal intestines, cotton, groundnuts, sesame, tobacco, timber, bamboo, apricot seeds, duck feathers, hides and skins.

portation Control Organization. At that time, since the only transportation line to Hong Kong was the Canton-Hankow Railway, export control was easy and effective.

The market rate for foreign exchange rose nearly 25 per cent higher than the official rate soon after the measure demanding the surrender of 90 per cent of foreign exchange derived from exports had been introduced. Not only did exporters lose profits because of this discrepancy but also it became impossible for them to compete with exporters in Occupied China because the latter could sell their exchange at the market rate. The merchants asked the government to compensate them for their losses arising from this difference so that they could compete with the exporters in Occupied China. The government disallowed their appeal on the ground that it did not recognize the market rate, but in July 1938 it made several concessions to compensate for the exchange rate differential.*

After Hankow and Canton fell in October 1938, the Canton-Hankow Railway was cut off and the only export route remaining was through Indo-China, either by the long highway going through Kwangsi Province to the rail point in Indo-China or by highway to Kunming for transshipment by the Indo-China-Yunnan Railway. Such long haulage caused great inconvenience and created difficulties for exporters because they were liable to lose either through fluctuations in commodity prices in the foreign market or through damage, loss, or deterioration in transit. Trying to help the exporters, the government agreed that, under certain circumstances, it would reduce the amount of foreign exchange it was necessary for exporters to surrender if the circumstances prevented the exporters from realizing the foreign exchange for surrender. Such adjustments were allowed:

> When the price of commodities in Hong Kong was lower than that agreed on when the exchange amount was settled with the government banks.
>
> When the quantity of the commodity was reduced by accident, loss or pillage.
>
> When the quality of the commodity deteriorated.

* If verified by the Foreign Trade Commission, export commodities would be insured by the government. Exports verified by the Foreign Trade Commission would be exempt from transit duty. Priority of transportation would be given. When the cost of export commodities was found to be higher than the price in the foreign market, the Foreign Trade Commission, basing its calculations on the cost of production, would fix the price at the place of production and at the place of marketing for government purchase. The commodities purchased by the government would be either resold at a reasonable price to merchants for export or entrusted to merchants to be sold abroad on behalf of the government.

Because of the futility of its method of compensating exporters for the difference between the official and market rates, the government announced on July 13, 1939, that the exchange resulting from trade in all except four of the exports on its list would have to be surrendered, at the official rate, to the Bank of China or to the Bank of Communications. The banks would pay the difference between the official rate and the banks' "commercial rate" to the exporters. This implied that, to reduce exporters' losses, the exchange derived from exports would be surrendered to the government at the commercial rate, which was close to the market rate.

The government announcement also stipulated that the exchange would have to be surrendered to the banks irrespective of whether the exports were handled by government organizations or by private individuals or firms. The four exports the exchange from which was exempted from surrender and which were under complete government control were wood oil, tea, bristles, and mineral ores.

On March 15, 1940, the government excluded human hair, straw braids and hats, groundnuts, tobacco, apricot seeds, and sesame from the list of 24 commodities the exchange from whose export had to be surrendered. Twenty per cent of the exchange realized from exporting the other 18 listed commodities was to be retained by the exporters instead of the previous 10 per cent. However, exporters from Southwest China could retain 30 per cent because of heavy transport charges in the area. The list of commodities was further reduced to 12* by the Stabilization Board when it began operations on September 1, 1941. Because of transport difficulties from 1940 to the beginning of the Pacific war late in 1941, however, there was very little export trade from Free China.

After the blockade of the seaports, the coast, and the rivers, the main transport routes were cut off and there were left only a few trading routes and limited means of transport which had to give priority to military supplies. Merchants, unable to calculate the costs of transport or estimate arrival times of cargoes, were compelled to close their businesses.

Government trading was actually in existence before the war. The National Resources Commission controlled the purchase and sale of wolfram and antimony. The Central Trust, a subsidiary of the Central Bank of China, conducted the purchase of government supplies. Two months after the Sino-Japanese war started, in October

* Egg products; feathers; animal intestines; hides, leather and skins; wool; vegetable dyestuffs; medical substances; oils, tallow and wax; seeds; timber; silk and silk cocoons; and ramie.

1937, a Trade Readjustment Commission was set up under the National Military Council. Its function was to provide financial and transport facilities so that Chinese exporters could continue their business notwithstanding the difficulties incurred through military operations.

As the fighting spread, and more positive and constructive measures were required to improve the export trade, in February 1938 the Foreign Trade Commission was established to replace the Trade Readjustment Commission. This new Commission became responsible for conducting the purchase and sale of certain commodities, besides assisting private exporters. Tea was the first product it handled. Under the regulations of March 1939 the Commission undertook the purchase of tea for export. It gave credits to tea merchants and co-operatives who sold their products for export at a fixed rate to the China National Tea Corporation, which was under the control of the Foreign Trade Commission.

The Foo Shing Trading Corporation was organized in April 1939 as a government corporation to purchase and export tung oil to the United States in payment of the principal and interest on the Tung Oil Loan concluded between China and the United States in 1938. The purchase and shipment of tung oil began in October 1940. Dealers and firms handling the oil had to register with the Corporation and sell their products to it at a fixed price.

Meanwhile, in February 1940, control of the collection and export of bristles was transferred from the Central Trust to the Foo Shing Corporation. Bristle dealers had to register with the Corporation before they could trade. After processing, the bristles were to be sold at a fixed price to the Corporation for export. In 1943 the purchase and sale of silk and wool were also transferred to the Corporation.

In 1938 trade in six minerals—tungsten, antimony, tin, mercury, bismuth, and molybdenum—was placed under the control of the National Resources Commission. The Commission bought the refined and concentrated products at a fixed price. Merchants could not export the minerals without a Commission license. Most of the mineral exports were used to repay the American loans and to fulfill obligations under the barter credit concluded with Great Britain and Russia.

The Foo Shing Corporation had a sister organization, the Universal Trading Corporation, which was established in New York in 1939. It mainly marketed tung oil to get money to repay American loans. It also conducted the purchase of government supplies with the proceeds of the American loans. The National Resources Commission also had an agency in New York.

The main exports—wood oil, bristles, tea, and minerals (chiefly tungsten, antimony, and tin)—maintained a reasonable level during the war years. Among all the measures the government adopted during the war time, the government trading appears to have been the most effective because the government agencies could obtain adequate financial and transportation facilities and no loss or risk would be incurred through the fluctuation of exchange rate or world commodity prices.

The export of mineral ores from Free China in 1940 and 1941 exceeded that of 1936 from the whole country, and the export of tea in 1940 was nearly equal to the 1936 figures. In spite of transport difficulties, tung oil exported amounted to 30 per cent of the prewar volume. These figures indicate that export trade could have been greatly increased had the government paid it the same attention prewar as it did during the war. Had the Burma Road not been cut off, the volume of exports could have been maintained at the level of 1940 and 1941; but, after the enemy invaded Chinese territory from Burma, only a few military supplies and personnel could be carried in by air-lift, which backloaded mineral ores, silk, tea, and bristles; and the export of tung oil was nearly suspended. In 1942 total exports were valued at only U.S. $9 million, and in 1943 the value had fallen to U.S. $3 million. In 1944 the air service across the Hump started, and exports were kept at the same level.

## 3. Postwar Import Policies

After the end of the war the government became so concerned with the increase of supplies from abroad that almost no restrictions were imposed on imports. Industrial materials and daily necessities were allowed to be imported without prior approval. Only a few items, such as sugar, tobacco leaf, kerosene, and developed film, needed import licenses. Luxury articles could be brought in after payment of a surtax of 50 per cent of the existing tariff rate. Prevailing demand for almost any kind of goods and the excellent profits available to the importers, coupled with the lavish allocation of foreign exchange, before long led to a foreign exchange crisis which brought about the re-imposition of import controls.

### *Reimposition of Trade Control*

On November 17, 1946, trade regulations were revised. The import licensing system was extended to cover all imports, and imports were classified in four groups: machinery and other industrial equipment, which had top priority and could be imported without any restriction; raw materials for industry, which could be imported within the limits of the quota set by the government; non-quota goods which were ordinarily required and which were subject to approval of applications; and prohibited imports. The quota would be allocated to the various Trade Associations, which in turn would divide it among the different firms within the trade. The system had first been tried by the Sino-American-British Stabilization Board in 1941.

In February 1947 the government announced its intention to supply U.S. $472 million for imports of raw materials and industrial equipment, and that U.S. $200 million of that amount were to be allocated from February to June. The estimated supply of foreign exchange announced by the government seemed to exceed the amount of foreign exchange which was available at that time, as reserves had dropped to only U.S. $350 million. This announcement was made for the obvious purpose of steadying the market; but, because of this promise, the people looked on subsequent quotas as the barometer showing the rise or fall of the government's foreign exchange reserves, and so pointing to the rise or fall of prices. In spite of its desire to maintain the quota as high as possible, the government had to reduce it because of the gradual decrease of its foreign exchange reserves. Actual allocations by quarter were as follows:

| | |
|---|---|
| 1st Quarter (Feb.–April 1947) | U.S. $99,675 (Unit 1,000) |
| 2nd Quarter (May–July 1947) | 72,610 |
| 3rd Quarter (Aug.–Oct. 1947) | 67,873 |
| 4th Quarter (Nov. 1947–Jan. 1948) | 53,393 |
| 5th and 6th Quarters (Feb.–July 1948) | 73,476 |
| 7th and 8th Quarters (Sept. 1948–March 1949) | 42,141 |

From February 1947 to February 1948 the amounts of foreign exchange actually allocated for the four quarters was only U.S. $290,000,000, which was U.S. $180,000,000 less than the original estimate by the government.

In addition the government itself spent approximately U.S. $100 million in each of the years 1946 and 1947 on imports of fuel, bank notes, and military, communication, and transportation equipment.

### *Dependence on American Aid*

At the end of 1947 the government's foreign exchange and metallic reserve reached the very low level of U.S. $187,000,000. This was not enough to allocate a reasonable quota. Fortunately, three events enabled the government to cut the supply for the two quarters from February to July 1948 to U.S. $73,476,000, and the quota for the quarter from September to November 1948 to U.S. $21,000,000. These events were aid from the United States by which food valued at U.S. $38,000,000 was provided from the United States Foreign Relief Program, a certain amount of cotton released by UNRRA, and the immediate prospect of American aid from which U.S. $158,290,000 could be appropriated in 1948. The last was to be used for the purchase of food, cotton, oil, and fertilizer. After June 1948 the foreign exchange certificate system was applied and the government supplied no further exchange. However, had the United States not given assistance, the trade situation would have become critical earlier than it did.

### *Relaxation of Restrictions*

In 1949, after the collapse of the "Gold Yuan" standard and the consequent rapid rise in the foreign exchange rate, and after the military setbacks, commerce came to a standstill and imports were greatly reduced. Supplies of most essential commodities and of industrial raw materials continued to depend on American aid.

When the National government withdrew to Canton in May, import restrictions were almost lifted and encouragements were given to the merchants who had their own foreign exchange. Any merchant who had a foreign exchange certificate could import unrestricted goods within a certain time limit. Those who had their own foreign exchange could import unrestricted goods without any time limit. However, in the latter part of 1949 the territory under the control of the Nationalist government was very limited. All the more important ports had been lost to the Communists, and foreign trade was reduced to an insignificant amount.

### *Prevention of Inbound Smuggling*

The discrepancy between the official rate and the market rate meant profits to the importers and losses to the exporters. Such large profits tempted adventurers to plunge into smuggling even at the risk of their lives. The long coastline of South China increased the difficulties of preventing smuggling. There are many smuggling routes between

Hong Kong and Macao and Kwangtung province because of the short distances between them by sea and because of the proximity of land along the routes.

Smuggling of imports started from Hong Kong and Macao, with transshipment to Canton and other ports along the South China coastline. Smuggling of exports originated from Canton and later, in a small degree, from other ports along the coast. The goods were transshipped to Hong Kong and Macao, where they could be safely sold and exported. The larger the profit from smuggling, the bigger and stronger the smuggling organizations became and the more difficult it became to stop them. Gradually, Hong Kong became the most important center of smuggling.

According to statistics compiled by the research department of the Central Bank of China, the figure for smuggling of imports and exports between China and Hong Kong and Macao was found from the difference between the trade returns of the Hong Kong government and the returns of the Chinese Customs, plus 80 per cent of the trade between Macao and Hong Kong—because the trade between Macao and Hong Kong was eventually either export from or import into China. Commodities smuggled by railway and steamer passengers and by petty traders on the border were estimated to equal about 20 per cent of the trade between Hong Kong and Canton. The figure for smuggled imports in 1947 was estimated to be U.S. $65,200,000, which was 10 per cent of China's total imports for that year.

In November 1946 the Chinese government began negotiations with the Hong Kong government to try to check import and export smuggling between China and Hong Kong. An agreement was concluded on August 15, 1947. The main points respecting the prevention of import smuggling to China from Hong Kong were as follows:

> The Hong Kong government would restrict loading places for exports to China so as to facilitate inspection by Chinese Customs officials.
>
> The Chinese Customs were at liberty to establish centers within Hong Kong at which Chinese duty could be paid or assessed in advance on commodities about to be exported to China.
>
> The Chinese Customs were at liberty to enter and patrol certain specified areas in Hong Kong waters.
>
> The Hong Kong government would limit the number of points in the border through which exports to China passed. The purpose was to hinder or prevent exports going through other points.
>
> All ships carrying cargo to China had to submit manifests to the Hong Kong Harbor Department to be certified. No cargo could be exported without a stamped manifest.

The first four points were covered by a Customs Agreement which was never enforced because it never obtained the full approval of Hong Kong's Legislative Council. The last point came into force in November 1947.

The Macao government followed the Hong Kong government and also agreed that no commodities could be exported from Macao to China unless they were accompanied by an import license issued by the Chinese government.

## 4. Postwar Export Policies

Because of the devastation caused by the war and because the external value of the Chinese currency was officially overvalued, postwar exports did not return to anywhere near their normal prewar volume. In the first half of 1946 the value of exports was only one-fifth of that of imports. In the second half of the year there was a slight improvement and exports increased to one-third of imports. But they were still far below the prewar figures. The government had hoped that exports of soybean from Manchuria could be resumed to boost China's exports, but the National government's inability to regain the area made the realization of its hope impossible.

Many measures were devised to increase exports, among which were bonuses to exporters, government purchase, adoption of a realistic and flexible exchange rate, low interest loans to exporters, provision for extra quota imports for packing and raw materials needed for exports, and the fixing of ceiling prices for export commodities. After these measures were successively carried out exports were much improved during 1947. A part of the increase was attributed to the rise of export of cotton textiles, made possible by a barter arrangement with Pakistan whereby raw cotton from Pakistan was exchanged for cotton yarn and cloth from China, and by the diversion from home consumption to export of cotton yarn and piece goods manufactured from American aid cotton. However, the increased export from the barter agreement could not be considered as an increase in the real level of export. The amounts of exports in U.S. dollars are above the figure for 1936, although, if calculated according to prewar prices, they would still have been considerably less than the 1936 figure:

| Year | Exports |
|---|---|
| 1936 | U.S. $210 million |
| 1946 | U.S. $149 million |
| 1947 | U.S. $230 million |
| 1948 | U.S. $170 million |

### *Export Subsidy*

On February 6, 1947, the government announced that exports would be subsidized by an amount in Chinese currency equal to the amount of foreign exchange surrendered, the figures to be calculated at the official exchange rate. This was meant to avoid frequent readjustment of the official foreign exchange rate, which would cause rises of import prices and would affect the general price level. However, the announcement caused general commodity prices to rise sharply and the cost of producing exports increased. The discrepancies between costs of production and prices in the foreign market became greater. Of course, the discrepancies varied for each export commodity. For example, the cost of producing bristles was 25 per cent higher than the price in the foreign market, while that for tung oil was 50 per cent higher, silk was 120 per cent higher, and tea 100 per cent higher. The subsidy could be effective only where the difference between the cost of production and the price in the foreign market was below 100 per cent, and would be useless where the difference was more than 100 per cent. When the United States objected to export subsidies, the measure was dropped.

### *Government Purchase*

The government found that the subsidy measure was impracticable and that the effect on the general price level of readjusting the foreign exchange rate would be damaging. When the cost of producing exports was close to the foreign market price after a readjustment of the official foreign exchange rate, exports increased. But, after a short while, the price of exports rose again when it followed rises in the general price level and in wages. The result was that export trade came to a standstill once more while exporters waited for the next readjustment of the exchange rate.

The sellers' market for various commodities in the foreign markets also differed from prewar conditions. Since some commodities met keen competition from other supplies unless markets for them were promoted, export of them could be encouraged only by readjustment of the exchange rate or by government purchases. So the government decided to buy exports through government organizations and bear the loss or profit itself. After purchase, the goods would be either entrusted to exporters or handled by government organizations. Government purchases were confined to tung oil, bristles, tea, silk, soybeans, and egg products. When the government adopted a realistic and flexible exchange rate in August 1947, this practice was suspended, but it was revived again at the time when the Stabilization Fund was prevented from adjusting the rate as frequently as it should. Finally it was discontinued under the certificate system.

### *Adoption of a Realistic Exchange Rate*

When foreign trade was resumed in March 1946, the exchange rate set by the Central Bank of China was 2,020 Chinese dollars per U.S. $1—606 times the prewar rate. Since the commodity price index was 2,900 times the prewar rate, the exchange rate lagged 2,280 points behind the price index. The rate could not be readjusted as frequently as had been intended and so became even more overvalued as commodity prices rose. In September the rate was readjusted to 3,350 Chinese dollars per U.S. $1—1,006 times the prewar rate; but the price index was then 4,700 times the prewar rate, a difference of approximately 3,700 points.

In February 1947, when the government intended to freeze prices and wages, the exchange rate was readjusted to 12,000 Chinese dollars per U.S. $1 in the hope that this rate could be maintained along with ceiling prices and ceiling wages. The rate was approximately the market rate, the discrepancy being only 14 per cent (see Table 85). The intention was to bring about a more realistic relation to the internal price level and market conditions. Although the difference between the official and market rates had been reduced, the commodity price index rose to 11,000 times the prewar index in March. As the official exchange rate was only 3,600 times the prewar rate, the lag was 7,400 points, and the gap between the official and market rates increased to 55 per cent by May.

The most significant phenomenon was that exports always became brisk very soon after the official rate had been readjusted but quickly declined again—because exporters held back export commodities while the official rate lagged behind the market, in anticipation of a change in the rate, and, when a new rate was fixed, exported at the new rate to make a profit. A rise in export prices always followed a readjustment in the rate. In the periods between readjustments the export trade was stagnant.

For instance, exports in July 1946 were valued at U.S. $14,922,206; in August, after the rate had been readjusted on the 19th, exports increased to U.S. $24,674,267; in September they fell to U.S. $19,987,408; and in January 1947 there was a further reduction to U.S. $14,384,572. In February, after a readjustment on the 16th, exports increased to U.S. $16,237,229, but in March they fell to U.S. $11,884,456.

Upon the recommendation of the Central Bank of China, the government adopted a flexible exchange rate on August 17, 1947. The average rate was $41,635 Chinese currency per U.S. $1 in September—12,500 times the prewar rate. The price index was 38,400 times the prewar index, and the ratio between the index and the exchange rate was 4 to 1. This was much better than in March 1946, when the ratio was 5 to 1. The government had hoped that this flexible rate could be kept at a realistic ratio. At one time the ratio improved to 2 to 1. This was in the winter, the export season. Exports in September were valued at U.S. $6,800,000. In November they increased to U.S. $24,000,000 and in December to U.S. $27,000,000. In January 1948 exports were U.S. $14,863,000, in February U.S. $9,316,380, and in March U.S. $10,756,000. From March 1948 onward, because politicians criticized the Stabilization Fund Committee for stimulating price rises through rate readjustments, the Committee was hesitant about carrying out its original policy, and the ratio between prices and exchange rate worsened to 5 to 1, while the difference between the official rate and the market rate increased to 50 per cent. Exports in April were only U.S. $8,670,000; and even in May, when there was quite a large exchange rate readjustment, exports increased only to the small amount of U.S. $11,193,000.

### *Low Interest Loans*

On May 2, 1947, the government banks decided to advance low interest loans to exporters. Any exporter who was a member of a trade guild and who conducted a direct export business could apply for a loan from the government banks. It was to be used for purchasing export commodities, for sorting and processing, and for shipment to ports to await exporting. Loans up to 70 per cent of the cost of purchase, processing, and forwarding were granted, with maturities of ninety days. Exporters would also be given packing credit against letters of credit before the commodities left the country. This credit would range from 50 per cent to 80 per cent of the selling price and was limited to thirty days.

At that time commercial banks did not advance loans for a maturity of more than one month. Their monthly interest was about 18 per cent, while interest on government loans was only 6 or 7 per cent, the difference in the interest rate being, therefore, a large subsidy to the exporters. However, the practice was suspended after four months because of the tightening of banking credit.

### *Extra Quota Imports to Secure Packing and Raw Materials Needed for Exports*

On November 11, 1947, the government allowed extra quota imports to secure packing materials needed by exporters. The amount could not exceed 5 per cent of the export value. On March 6, 1948, the government extended the extra quota imports system to cover raw materials needed for exports by the handicrafts industry and by light industry. The amount was not to exceed 40 per cent of the value of the exportable manufactured goods. Manufacturers were to give an assurance that the manufactured goods would be exported within six months and that at the same time they would settle the necessary exchange transaction with the banks. When an importer received from a buyer or agent abroad raw material for processing on the understanding that the buyer or agent would receive the manufactured goods resulting from the processing, the consignee (i.e., the importer) was required to give the bank a written understanding that the raw materials imported would not be sold in China and that the foreign exchange derived from the export of the processed or manufactured goods would be surrendered to the Central Bank. This practice, applied to cotton imported from Pakistan in exchange for cotton yarn, increased textile exports.

### *Floor Price for Exports*

A "floor price" for tung oil was fixed on February 25, 1948. This meant that no tung oil could be exported at a price lower than the "floor price." On April 19 a "floor price" was fixed for bristle, and later all main exports were similarly treated.

There were several reasons for this move. Exporters usually understated the value of exports so as to be able to cover possible losses caused by the discrepancy between the official and market rates of exchange. They also wanted to secure foreign exchange to use as "flight capital." Such practices caused the dumping of Chinese exports in foreign markets and affected the interests of producers and the businesses of legitimate exporters.

### *Prevention of Out-bound Smuggling*

The discrepancy between the official rate and the market rate affected importers as well as exporters, and large profits could be secured from export smuggling to Hong Kong and Macao. It was estimated that smuggled exports from China to Hong Kong in 1947 were U.S. $21,500,000; i.e., 7.8 per cent of China's total exports.

In the agreement of August 15, 1947, concluded between China and Hong Kong it was provided that seven specified Chinese export commodities could not be re-exported from Hong Kong before the Hong Kong Department of Imports and Exports was satisfied that the foreign exchange proceeds from trade in the goods had been surrendered to the appointed banks in China. The commodities were tung oil, bristles, soy beans, tea, silk, eggs, and wool, but later, in January 1949, wool, silk, and eggs were taken out of the list and cotton yarn, wolfram, antimony, and tin were added.

The Macao government agreed that no commodities could be imported into Macao from China unless it was certified that the foreign exchange proceeds deriving from them had already been deposited with the Chinese banks.

### *Conclusion*

Most of the export-promotion measures the government adopted were aimed at removing the handicaps resulting from the discrepancy between the internal and external value of China's currency, being primarily designed to compensate exporters for possible losses arising from inflation.

In view of the large profits accruing to importers as a direct consequence of the inflation which hampered exporters, it is surprising that no system was devised to allocate between them fairly the windfall returns of foreign trade. This would have stimulated exports and removed some of the excessive incentive from imports.

Hardly anything was done to raise the physical volume of export production. It is also characteristic of the postwar period in China that none of the government's schemes which were put in effect was given a fair chance to prove its merit. In many cases, the measures were abandoned before the administrative machinery to handle them was fully set up, and before a full cycle of production-export-import-consumption could be completed. As a result, the various measures became mere gestures rather than effective tools for the re-establishment of a balanced foreign trade.

Thus the failure of the export drives impaired the rebuilding of the government's foreign exchange reserves, and foreign trade failed as a weapon to help combat inflation and keep the cost of living within reasonable limits. The history of China's postwar foreign trade shows that such trade cannot exist in a vacuum but must be supported by and integrated with a country's general economy and its fiscal policy. Only then can foreign trade in turn contribute fully toward the success of the economy.

Chapter

# 14

# Price and Wage Controls

## 1. Wartime Controls

China's price and wage control policies during and after the war did not constitute a comprehensive program to combat inflation; in fact, some individual measures were at cross-purposes with others. Besides these shortcomings in principle, price control measures were sporadic in nature, and the rules and orders which were promulgated were not implemented by efficient, impartial, and universal enforcement. Moreover, whenever one particular measure failed to produce the desired results, either because it was ill-conceived or because of insufficient or improper enforcement, or because insufficient time was allowed for its effect to be felt, an alternative measure—sometimes contrary in spirit—was hastily substituted.

Consequently, the attempt made in the following pages to set out the various controls in an orderly fashion may unwittingly impute a higher degree of rationality to government planning than actually existed. For the reasons set forth, the measures discussed below were not components of a sophisticated plan such as might be employed in a modern industrial society, but were the crude resort of a government faced with an intricate problem of economic cause and effect which was not fully understood.

From the very beginning, the weight of thinking within government circles seemed to oppose price controls as a desirable policy. It was thought that price fixing and physical controls on distribution of commodities would spread fear of scarcity and lead to hoarding, speculation, and other inflationary practices. Government officials who had no previous experience in applying such controls were particularly concerned about the administrative problems involved and endeavored to evade the responsibility of undertaking price stabilization.

A number of major administrative obstacles made the task of enforcing price controls most difficult. First, neither popular and government thinking nor administrative machinery was ready to undertake economic controls of any sort. When the price problem became acute, government at all levels found it hard to delegate authority and responsibility appropriately for the enforcement of control measures; and local governments had little confidence in their effectiveness. Thus local governments failed to put the control orders of the central government in effect; in some of the semi-feudal border provinces the orders were completely ignored.

The public, moreover, was antagonistic to all forms of government controls on the economy; still prevalent was the laissez faire view that market problems would best solve themselves if only the government would not interfere. The continuous outpouring of paper money further decreased popular confidence in government measures. Despite their intense patriotism, the Chinese had not yet developed an awareness of the interrelationship between individual welfare and that of the community.

The second obstacle to effective enforcement of price control measures was the impotence of the trade guilds. The guild system had developed in old China as a means of promoting the solidarity and welfare of the members of the various trades, part of their purpose being to ensure that prices of goods marketed conformed to their quality. These objectives were achieved through the moral influence wielded by the established leaders in each guild and the discipline observed by its members. But after the Nationalist revolution in 1926 the guilds were placed under Kuomintang party control and their moral fabric was destroyed. Party discipline could not replace it because of the poor quality of party designates placed in charge of guild activities; and the division of authority between party and guild leaders gradually led to the disintegration of the system.

Government price control regulations during the war placed the main responsibility for maintaining fixed prices in the guilds. It was soon found that the guilds were not only incapable of disciplining their members but also unable to persuade a large body of firms and dealers to enter their ranks. The government then issued a directive compelling all businessmen to join the guilds of their respective trades; but many of them refused to comply with this order, and carried on business without being registered. The idea of using the guilds to enforce observance of price ceilings thus proved futile.

Another formidable obstacle to the effective administration of price controls was the immaturity of Chinese industry. Industry was still at the handicraft stage of development, and the wide range of quality variation within classes of products complicated the task of price fixing. The divergent processes of production used within one industry, the backwardness of accounting methods, and the absence of statistical records rendered it almost impossible to determine the production costs of most commodities. Inevitably, the price ultimately fixed was a compromise which seldom succeeded if it worked to the detriment of producers and dealers. It was beyond the competence of local government officials to check the accuracy of the cost schedules submitted to them by the trades concerned. In most instances they approved after examination the prices recommended by the guilds, which were based on alleged production and distribution costs. If it so happened that an arbitrary decision on the part of the local price fixing authority was unacceptable to the trade, distributors merely shifted their production to another center where higher prices prevailed or operated black markets in their own localities.

The final and insuperable obstacle to the successful application of price controls was the wide divergence of prices between regions, caused by the varied topography and inadequacy of communications. Marked differences in price levels existed not only between provinces but also between cities within the same province. Under these conditions, price control necessarily had to be decentralized, and could only be enforced by and with the co-operation of local governments. In view of the administrative difficulties in the vast interior, price control became limited to a few large cities, and, not unnaturally, the supply of goods in effectively controlled cities began to dry up and flowed instead to those with weak or no control.

In January 1938 the Ministry of Economic Affairs was empowered to exercise physical controls over all industrial materials and manufactured goods, to fix equitable prices for the sale of all commodities, to adopt measures to encourage the production of essential goods, and to suppress profiteering and speculation. These regulations were introduced with the vague idea that in a war economy the government was entitled to these powers, and not with any serious intention of utilizing them to achieve a stable price level.

After the fall of Hankow and Canton at the end of 1938, price increases accelerated, and the government decided to make its first attempt at price control. In December 1938 the government decreed that the prices of daily necessities should be fixed at fair levels and that hoarding and profiteering should be shunned by all responsible citizens. A price regulating committee was set up in Chungking comprising representatives of the government, the Chamber of Commerce, and the guilds of the different trades. Other large cities of the interior were urged to follow the example of Chungking. To this end, local governments were required to set up commissions to supervise the fixing of prices in the regions under their jurisdiction. The provisions were actually carried out in only two cities, Chungking and Chengtu, which were under the close supervision of the government, but even these official prices always lagged behind market levels and soon became nominal. At the end of 1938 the government also announced a scheme for supplying some of the main cities with a few daily necessities at low prices, and established a Bureau for the Purchase and Sale of Daily Necessities at Equitable Prices, under the Ministry of Economic Affairs.

The half-hearted control in a few cities had very little retarding effect on the rise of prices. This situation continued until November 1942, when a program for strengthening price controls was adopted. The new program was a comprehensive one that included price ceilings on daily necessities, rationing of consumer goods, government buying and selling of commodities, limitations on inventories, restrictions on the use of scarce goods, and wage ceilings.

### *Price Ceilings*

Aware of its administrative deficiencies, the government adopted a less ambitious program of control, limiting controls to eight basic commodities, rice, salt, edible oil, cotton, cotton yarn, cloth, fuel, and paper, and restricting coverage of the regulations to the major inland cities. Prices of other commodities were to be fixed by the guilds as before, subject to approval of local or central government authorities. As the following specific regulations indicate, the government was now determined to employ strong measures to force compliance with its regulations. At every level of government there was to be an agency for regulating prices in conformity with the over-all policy laid down by the central government. In each metropolitan district the prices of commodities subject to control were to be periodically fixed in accordance with local conditions. Black markets were to be suppressed, and government authorities empowered to purchase or seize, hold or sell, goods selling higher than the fixed ceilings. Companies, firms, shops, or members of trade guilds were required to post the fixed prices of commodities selected for control at trading places, or else label the commodities. Capital punishment or life imprisonment could be imposed for serious breaches of the regulations.

The price ceilings introduced in various cities were usually very low and almost invariably resulted in local shortages. On a number of occasions Chungking, the war capital, faced a rice famine because the price of rice in surrounding regions exceeded the metropolitan price ceiling. Local governments placed increasingly severe restrictions on the movement of goods to prevent the escape of commodities subject to price control. Trade barriers sprang up between provinces and even between different cities in the same province as the local governments endeavored to maintain their own price systems. Eventually, internal trade in Free China was threatened with disruption, and the central government was forced to issue a regulation prohibiting the local governments from installing barriers to interprovincial trade. This action immediately furnished an opportunity for officials to abandon their efforts to control prices without losing prestige in the eyes of their constituents. In only a few areas the prices of rice and salt, two of the eight commodities the government had selected for control, were successfully regulated. These successes were not attributable to the efficacy of price ceilings but to the large amount of rice which was collected by the government in land tax and made available for sale to civilians after provision had been made for the requirements of the army and the public servants, and to the government monopoly of salt and the unsuitability of this commodity for hoarding. Ceiling prices for edible oils were enforced only in Chungking; for coal only in a few of the larger industrial centers; and for paper only in Szechwan province, where official prices applied to newsprint supplied to a few leading periodicals. Controls on the prices of cotton yarn and cloth failed completely owing to the acute shortage of supplies, and market prices for textiles rose uninterruptedly.

A statement made by the Chief of the Bureau of Social Affairs in Chungking, who was in charge of price control, explains in simple terms the reasons for the failure of the government's price policy:

> The city of Chungking, which is not a self-sufficient unit, has to satisfy its requirements of numerous kinds of manufactures from outside supplies. Control over the volume and quality of goods supplied and their costs through the various stages of production, transportation, and final distribution was beyond my authority. Moreover, the majority of other centers either did not operate price controls, or else exercised them in an uncoordinated way. How could the city of Chungking alone successfully enforce its price controls?*

* H. K. Pao's article "The Price Control in Chungking" published in a pamphlet "The Problems of Prices" compiled by the Economic Research Department of the Central Bank of China, 1941, Chungking.

### *Consumer Rationing*

The program for strengthening controls on prices at the end of 1942 also specified that the large cities and populous towns should gradually adopt rationing of foodstuffs and other commodities in order to prevent waste and to achieve an equitable distribution of commodities in short supply. But it was soon realized that a workable scheme of rationing could not be devised in the absence of reliable estimates of population and of the supply of commodities available for consumption. The government would have been compelled to market rationed goods itself since it could not rely on individual dealers to distribute quotas fairly. Apart from rice, flour, and salt, rationing of consumer goods was considered impracticable even on a limited scale. When the government had accumulated large stocks of rice and wheat from the land tax in kind, the army was allocated food instead of procuring it on the open market as formerly, and a quantity of food was set aside for public servants. Officers of the central government received a fixed quota of rice or flour beginning in July 1941, and the same privilege was extended to provincial and county government officials in 1943. Public servants of 31 or over were entitled to receive 120 pounds of rice or wheat per annum; those in the age group 26–30, 95 pounds; and those of 25 or below, 70 pounds. This was as far as the Ministry of Food was prepared to go. It dared not undertake the task of rationing civilian food supplies but tried to cater for the needy by establishing auxiliary food supply centers. General rationing of consumer goods in China was impossible just as over-all price pegging was impossible, the basic reason in both cases being the complete absence of comprehensive and co-ordinated administrative machinery.

### *Government Purchases and Sales*

The program known as "Government Purchases and Sales of Goods at Equitable Prices" was, relatively speaking, the most successful of government measures to control prices. Within the limits of its administrative capacity, its transport facilities, and its financial resources, the government engaged in bulk buying of commodities and in selling them through its agents at fixed prices.

Government purchases and sales involved two main classes of goods, daily necessities and export commodities. Originally daily necessities comprised eight commodities, rice, salt, edible oil, fuel, cotton, cotton yarn and cloth, and paper. Between 1942 and 1944 the government also acquired control of all of the output of sugar, matches, and tobacco. The sale of government rice stocks to civilians was entrusted by the Ministry of Food to its own supply agents and private rice shops, scattered throughout 4,083 localities in 18 provinces. In this way part of the supply of rice available to civilians was sold at comparatively low prices. After February 1943 the government required all cotton yarn produced by the mills of Szechwan Province, which accounted for more than half the output of Free China, to be sold to a special government organization called Cotton, Yarn, and Cloth Administration, either for reselling to firms making military clothing or for bartering with manufacturers in exchange for cloth. The government then attempted to ensure that the cloth was sold to the public at the official prices.

Since many mills were finding difficulty in obtaining supplies of raw cotton owing to the dislocation of communications, the government decided to take over the buying and transportation of fiber for allocation to the mills. These government operations prevented producers from hoarding cotton goods; and, within the trade, prices of raw materials were lower than they would have been if the conduct of the industry's affairs had been left entirely to private enterprise. But the government was unable to check rapid increases in wholesale and retail prices of apparel goods, which offset economies effected by the government on the production side. The shortage of clothing remained acute because the production of raw cotton in Free China was small and the productive capacity of the textile industry was limited; and by the end of the war the index of clothing prices stood fifty per cent higher than that for foodstuffs. While the government could exercise a degree of control over prices up to the marketing stage, it could not restrain merchants dealing in cloth from exploiting the public.

The government also controlled the distribution to wholesalers of coal, charcoal, and edible oil for sale to consumers in Chungking and a few other important cities, and handled the sale of newsprint in Szechwan province. In industrial centers the government allocated coal and coke to manufacturers at low prices. The state monopoly of sugar did not contribute to lower prices because output declined as molasses was diverted to the production of alcohol for industrial uses. Additional commodities purchased from producers by the government were tobacco and matches. Though tobacco and matches were daily necessities, the government was less concerned about keeping selling prices low than it was over raising its own revenues.

The government also became the sole buyer of eleven export commodities, tungsten, antimony, tin, mercury, bismuth, molybdenum, tea, bristles, tung oil, silk, and wool. Proceeds from these exports were already committed in repayment of debts in several loan agreements between the Chinese government and the Allies. The loss of export markets would have led to a relatively great decline in the prices of these goods if the government had not assumed control. Yet producers constantly complained that the prices paid by the government were below costs of production.

### *Limited Inventories*

Controls on the volume of inventories of industrial raw materials held by merchants and firms and restrictions on the use of scarce capital goods became urgently necessary after Pearl Harbor, when Free China was severed completely from foreign supplies. At the end of 1942 merchants and manufacturers were required to provide the Ministry of Economic Affairs with a record of their stocks of any of two hundred items considered essential to industry and to keep the Ministry informed of changes in their holdings. Purchases of scarce goods were to be approved by the government, and no shipments could be made without a license. These controls had some effect in minimizing speculation in raw materials and equipment and in curtailing the activities of less important industries which had previously obtained a large share of productive resources.

### *Wage Ceilings*

In December 1942 an attempt was made to freeze wages at the levels prevailing on November 30, that year, with the hope of stemming the rise of production costs. Ceilings were to apply to wages of workers in industries producing daily necessities, machinery, and building materials and to persons engaged in transport organizations. But the success of wage stabilization was contingent on the success of price stabilization; and, since the price level could not be held, wage ceilings could not remain stable for very long.

The foregoing summarizes the reasons why the policy of price controls, originally devised to reduce the pressure of excess purchasing power upon a dwindling supply of goods and services, could not possibly have been successful. As the realization spread in government circles of the futility of attempting to achieve general price stability, the objective was scaled down and became that of preventing, or at least slowing, the rise in the cost of a few basic commodities. These commodities, not quite incidentally, also were key magnitudes in the official cost of living index. The more limited objective in price controlling was in small part successful in the main cities principally because of the collection of the land tax in kind (grains) and because of the economic isolation of the population centers of China from each other due to poor communications. A rough measure of this achievement is provided in Table 92.

TABLE 92. PERCENTAGE INCREASE IN WHOLESALE PRICES IN CHINA: 1941–1945

| Year | Whole of Free China | Chungking |
|---|---|---|
| 1941 | 152 | 177 |
| 1942 | 200 | 179 |
| 1943 | 221 | 201 |
| 1944 | 244 | 223 |
| 1945 (to Aug.) | 277 | 262 |

## 2. POSTWAR CONTROLS

### *Attempts to Suppress Inflation: February 1947*

The rapid progress of inflation during 1946 eventually forced the government to reimpose controls in February 1947. Price and wage ceilings were reintroduced despite the experience of their wartime inefficacy and the fact that early in 1947 inflation was progressing approximately twice as fast as in 1942, when the previous experiment was made. On February 16th emergency measures were announced by which ceiling prices of daily necessities (rice and flour, cotton yarn and cloth, fuel, salt, sugar, and edible oil) were to be strictly enforced in the big cities beginning with Shanghai and Nanking, the capital. Wages were to be frozen in accordance with the January cost of living index, and no change in the basic wage rate was to be allowed. The government also proposed to undertake the distribution of essential consumer goods to industrial workers. Each factory was to be allocated a supply of food, fuel, and cotton cloth for distribution to its employees at the average retail price for January. Each worker was to receive a basic ration of 8.8 pounds of rice, 165 pounds of briquettes, 1.1 pounds of sugar, 5.5 pounds of salt, and 5.5 pounds of edible oil per month; 10.9 yards of cotton cloth per half year. At the end of February, when the wage ceilings were to be introduced, the city government, not having completed preparations for supplying consumer goods to factories, decided temporarily to pay workers a living allowance to take care of the rise in the cost of the basic ration. Under the vigilant attention of the police, the price of these daily necessities steadied during March; but no sooner had the price and wage fixing committees begun working in Shanghai early in April than there was a renewed upsurge in prices of consumer goods (Table 93). All the weaknesses of a partial system of price control, which

TABLE 93. PERCENTAGE INCREASE OVER JANUARY LEVELS OF PRICES OF DAILY NECESSITIES INCLUDED IN THE SHANGHAI BASIC LIVING RATION FOR INDUSTRIAL WORKERS, 1947

| | February | March | April |
|---|---|---|---|
| Rice | 65 | 60 | 118 |
| Edible oil | 70 | 95 | 172 |
| Salt | 47 | 44 | 50 |
| Briquettes | 86 | 105 | 113 |
| Cloth | 170 | 117[1] | 177 |

[1] The drop of price was due to the restriction of movements outside Shanghai.

had brought failure to the wartime attempt to keep a lid on prices, began to reappear. Rice dealers complained that prices in producing centers were higher than the official selling price in Shanghai, and a shortage of rice developed.

Edible oil was diverted to South China, which depended on supplies from other parts of the country and paid high prices. Many industries were caught in the squeeze of rising raw material costs and fixed prices for their products. Coal producers demanded a subsidy to cover their increasing outlays on raw materials, and textile manufacturers threatened to reduce production unless cloth prices were increased to allow for rises in raw cotton prices. The Shanghai government placed restrictions on the movement of cotton yarn and cloth to prevent these commodities from escaping to higher price areas, but the only noticeable result was a flourishing black market for cotton goods in Shanghai. At the end of April turmoil developed with the suspension of the rice market because dealers could not profitably replenish their stocks while the fixed selling price was maintained. This was followed by raids on rice shops by the poor, many of whom were nearing starvation. A number of cities outside Shanghai were also plunged into confusion. Meanwhile, labor unrest was growing despite the government's wage subsidy. The workers complained that they were unable to buy the basic ration of goods even with the government subsidy because they were receiving no compensation for rises in the prices of other necessary commodities not included in the basic wage regimen. In view of the grave situation, the city government relinquished the fixed prices for rice on May 5, and price ceilings on other necessities were also abandoned. The government could no longer afford wage subsidies, and these were discontinued on May 10. Thus, in less than three months, wage and price pegging had broken down.

The events described above suggest in themselves that the imposition of ceiling prices restricted to a few areas and a few commodities was more than impracticable; by disrupting the supply of commodities to certain key cities it actually accentuated the problem the controls were designed to attack. Similarly, the failure of wage freezing not only was a blow to the government's hopes for stabilizing the economy but also damaged its prestige with the general public.

### *The System of Automatic Adjustment*

Prior to the government's effort to freeze wages in February 1947 there had been no uniform formula for calculating wage increases in accordance with the cost of living. Wage rates were determined by employers with reference to business trends and the cost of living index, and standard rates applied to each industry. But to compensate factory workers and laborers for the withdrawal of the subsidy on wages in May, and to protect them from further losses of real income, the government announced that wages were to be adjusted on the basis of changes in the prices of essential consumer goods. The new system was as follows: Wages of factory workers and laborers were to be revised monthly according to the cost of living index; where a worker or laborer's wage in the base period (April) was the equivalent of thirty prewar CNC dollars or less per month, the wage was to be fully adjusted each month by the cost of living index, but the cost of living adjustment on each additional ten dollars in excess of thirty was to be applied at a ten per cent discount; in cases where employers were unable, owing to unfavorable business conditions, to conform with this formula, wage payments could be reduced subject to negotiations between employers and employees, and, if no agreement could be reached, the dispute could be referred to an Arbitration Committee constituted by the municipal government; changes in the base rate for each industry were not permissible.

The great majority of workers and laborers affected by these provisions were earning well under the equivalent of thirty prewar dollars per month. For purposes of adjusting wages the cost of living index used was that published by the Shanghai municipal government each month, comprising 60 items: food 31, clothing 11, rent 3, fuel 8, miscellaneous 7, weighted according to the importance of each item in the average family budget.

Businessmen generally were strongly opposed to the government's cost of living formula, believing that important lines of manufacturing activity would become unprofitable owing to increasing labor costs. They argued that the new wage regulation would impose special hardships on industries producing goods of which the prices were rising more slowly than the cost of living, or of which labor costs formed a major part of total costs; and on firms already operating on smaller profit margins than others in the same industry. Another argument used was that once workers and laborers, who represented only a small proportion of the total labor force, were granted the privilege of automatic wage increases, other working people would demand the same treatment and the costs of personal and distributive services would rise. Economic trends in the latter half of 1947 appeared to support these popular contentions. A majority of industries, excluding those producing the more essential consumer goods such as textiles and flour, found their profit margins falling and reduced production. But the rise of money wages was not the actual reason for the depressed state of industry, which arose from a different set of circumstances. Costs of raw materials and equipment and the market rate of interest were mounting rapidly under the inflation pressures, and firms were finding increasing difficulty in obtaining sufficient working capital to enable them to maintain inventories.

Beginning late in 1947, inflation brought forth a marked change in income distribution. As the real purchasing power of lower-income groups diminished—in spite of an abundance of paper money—their demand became effective mostly on a few basic commodities. Meanwhile, higher real incomes tended to accrue to those groups who engaged in hoarding and speculation rather than to those who invested in productive enterprise; this led to reduced employment of workers or a lowering of real wages, which in turn further reduced the aggregate purchasing power of the working group. The volume of industrial output soon began to shrink, beginning with silk textiles, rubber goods, cotton weaving, cement, and tobacco, and eventually spreading to underwear, cosmetics, matches, woolen textiles, and finally affecting the cotton textile industry.

Most businessmen, clinging to the view that the automatic adjustments of wages were causing the industrial malaise, strongly voiced their belief that the welfare of the community should not be jeopardized in the interests of a small group of workers. Demand for changes in the method of wage payments was widely publicized. The main suggestion was that labor productivity and the business outlook for each industry, as well as the cost of living, should be taken into account in wage fixing, so that different wage adjustments would be made for different industries. But, as inflation intensified, the hardships of the working people were becoming so severe that the municipal governments did not consider it politically feasible to modify the wage system. All the local government officials could do was to search for some excuse for understating increases in the cost of living. When it was discovered that the government was manipulating the cost of living index, there was a strong protest from the workers, who demanded the publication of the procedure used in calculating the monthly figures. After runaway inflation set in early in 1948 many workers agitated for half-monthly adjustments to wages; in July the Shanghai city government acceded to this demand. It was clear that, while prices continued their meteoric rise, the system of automatic adjustments to wages could not be superseded.

### *Controlled Distribution*

After the breakdown of price and wage ceilings imposed by the Emergency Regulations of February 1947, inflationary forces which had been temporarily suppressed by government controls began to operate with renewed vigor. In May the cost of living in Shanghai jumped to 70 per cent above the April level; it rose by another 8 per cent in June. It was clear that the new system of adjusting wages in accordance with the cost of living would contribute to the process of rising prices and wages unless something could be done to stabilize the prices of foodstuffs and other consumer goods. By now the leader of the government and his political advisers, despairing of solving the economic problem by resorting to further political stratagems, appealed to the Central Bank to devise effective measures for combating inflation. At this time a new governor was appointed whose opinion was that the Central Bank could do little more than temper inflation by allocating daily necessities, and that the fundamental cure must be to reduce the government's drawings on the Central Bank and to stimulate increased supplies of goods.

In July 1947 the Central Bank introduced a system of controlled distribution of daily necessities to assist the Shanghai municipal government in its efforts to slow down the rise of the cost of living. The government-owned Central Trust of China conducted the actual buying operations with Central Bank financing. Allocation committees, composed of representatives of the Central Bank, the Trust, and the municipal government, were set up for each commodity to regulate distribution. Buying of commodities began in Shanghai and Nanking, and distribution was at first confined to organized groups such as civil servants, public school teachers, students, factory workers, and employees of philanthropic and cultural organizations. Three kinds of commodities were covered, rice, briquettes, and edible oil, and the monthly rations for each person were as follows: rice 16.5 pounds, briquettes 110 pounds, edible oil 2.2 pounds. Rice distribution was later extended to include industrial workers on the records of the unions and people reported by the municipal government to be living in extreme want. The distribution prices of these commodities were from 5 per cent to 30 per cent lower than those prevailing in the open market.

Undoubtedly, the introduction of controlled distribution did enable low income earners to maintain a subsistence standard of living. In addition, since the commodities distributed were the main components of the cost of living on which wages and salaries were adjusted, the comparatively low prices of allocated goods helped to slow down the rate of increase in wages and salaries.

In May, June, July, and August, before the Central Bank's rationing scheme began to take effect, the rise of the cost of living in Shanghai seemed close to the general level of prices; but for the following months the wholesale price index remained above the cost of living, suggesting that the Central Bank's endeavors to slow the momentum of price and wage inflation were not entirely in vain. But these measures could not stem the tide of general price inflation in China since they were confined to a few cities only part of whose population had the privilege of receiving the ration. This may be seen from the comparison of trends in the cost of living and in general price levels given in Table 94.

The distribution of certain essential raw materials was also controlled by the government at this time. For instance, imported cotton was allocated to the mills, and yarn produced therefrom was distributed to the weavers. The prices of cotton yarn and cloth were approved by the government and had to be below open market prices. Coal and imported fuels were rationed among private firms and public utilities. Prices of controlled raw materials were ostensibly decided by the allocation committees; but the Central Bank had the deciding voice in fixing official prices since it was responsible for financing manufacturers' purchases of these goods. These physical controls on the movement and use of commodities were effective in eliminating speculation in the goods involved, and were beneficial both to manufacturers and the general public in a time of economic emergency. But it is interesting to note that the Central Bank was severely criticized at the time for exercising what were regarded as authoritarian powers.

In the early months of 1948 the poverty of the workers was becoming a serious problem, and the municipal governments of Peiping and Tientsin in North China and Canton in the South were demanding physical controls on the distribution of consumer goods similar to those operating in Shanghai. The central government, anticipating

TABLE 94. WHOLESALE PRICES AND COST OF LIVING IN SHANGHAI
(May 1947 = 100)

| Year | Wholesale Prices | Cost of Living |
|---|---|---|
| 1947 | | |
| June | 112 | 107 |
| July | 130 | 122 |
| Aug. | 141 | 131 |
| Sept. | 179 | 146 |
| Oct. | 282 | 208 |
| Nov. | 319 | 226 |
| Dec. | 389 | 290 |
| 1948 | | |
| Jan. | 544 | 405 |
| Feb. | 780 | 642 |
| March | 1,260 | 923 |
| April | 1,460 | 1,100 |
| May | 2,100 | 1,432 |
| June | 7,650 | 3,022 |
| July | 11,100 | 5,863 |

early delivery of foodstuffs under American aid, decided to take the risk of rationing food, mainly rice and flour, in five major cities. Rationing was introduced on March 28th in Shanghai, and from April in Nanking, Peiping, Tientsin, and Canton. Ration cards were issued, and each person was entitled to buy 16.5 pounds of rice or flour per month at a price determined by a price-fixing committee. At the same time people were permitted to buy additional food from the rice shops at the market price so that the drain on the government's stocks of rice would not become excessive and the flow of private trade could be maintained. This scheme was really an extension of commodity controls to embrace a larger number of cities, a manifestation of the government's assurance that it would take action to provide a minimum quantity of foodstuffs to the major consuming cities.

Rationing of rice did promote a political atmosphere more favorable to the government among the people of North and South China, but it failed to exercise any significant influence on price trends generally. Not even the price of rice could be pegged. The reason was that many of the large cities had been isolated from the food producing centers supplying their needs by the rapid spread of the civil war; and this loss of supply more than counterbalanced the increase in the amount of rice supplied by the government.

## *The Third Attempt to Impose Price and Wage Ceilings*

On August 19, 1948, the government adopted a desperate measure to combat inflation, the so-called monetary reform. A new "Gold Yuan" note was issued at the rate of one to three million of the old currency. In the week prior to the change of currency, August 9–16, 1948, the Shanghai wholesale price index was 660,000,000 and the cost of living index was 363,000,000 (on the prewar base). The government was under the illusion that by waving this magic wand prices and wages would be restored to their prewar levels and the vicious circle of inflation would be broken. To achieve these objectives, the government simultaneously froze prices and wages at the levels obtaining on August 19, 1948, reckoned in terms of the new Gold Yuan. Price and wage increases without the express approval of the government department in charge were henceforth prohibited, and the system of automatic wage adjustments was suspended. Strikes and picketing were outlawed. In the past the government had repeatedly tried, without much success, to suppress hoarding for profit. On this occasion the prevention of hoarding was made a central objective of the government's schemes for checking further increases in prices.

It is interesting to compare market prices of food in terms of the new Gold Yuan with those prevailing immediately before the change of currency and with prewar prices:

| | Rice (per 171 lbs.) | Flour (per bag of 49 lbs.) | Edible Oil (per 22 gals.) |
|---|---|---|---|
| 1948 | | | |
| Aug. 22 | GY $20 | GY $6.9 | GY $58 |
| Aug. 19 | CNC $63,000,000 | CNC $21,800,000 | CNC $190,000,000 |
| 1937 | | | |
| July | CNC $12 | CNC $42 | CNC $22 |

The new quotations were considered absurdly low by merchants and traders, and wholesale markets for staple commodities almost came to a standstill. Retailers encountered a clever move by the public to buy goods in order to get rid of their new notes in anticipation of an early depreciation in the value of the currency. The business community hoped that the deadlock would be broken by some government action which would cause prices to rise and give them an excuse for open defiance of price ceilings. Their hopes were soon fulfilled. The government had overlooked the inflationary implications of two further measures which had accompanied the monetary change in August. Sales taxes on commodities had been increased from 70 per cent to 100 per cent; and the official exchange rate, which before the issue of the new currency was only 60 per cent of the open market rate, was revised upwards to bring it into line with the free rate. The price of tobacco was the first affected by the higher rate of tax. Tobacconists closed their shops while awaiting the government's reply to their demands for an increase in selling prices to cover the rise in taxation plus an increase in retailing charges to maintain percentage margins. The government finally acquiesced, and the price of tobacco rose, followed immediately by upward revisions of ceiling prices for all essential consumer goods. Very little business was transacted in imported goods or goods of domestic origin manufactured from imported materials, even after a 50 per cent increase in their prices, because people were speculating on further rises in the exchange rate.

The general increase in prices in September, so soon after the currency change, confirmed the public's suspicions that the government would be unable to check inflation. In the first week of October large crowds of people thronged the shops in a wild scramble for goods of all descriptions, from foodstuffs to expensive luxury items. At first the shops opened late and closed early; then they began withholding goods from sale, keeping their stocks hidden. The poor could not buy rice, bakeries could not obtain flour, bean-cake makers could not obtain beans, restaurants closed through lack of foodstuffs, and even medical goods became unobtainable. Finally, all goods vanished from the markets, and shops were either shut all the time or were compelled by the police to open for a few hours a day even though their shelves were empty. The news of the suspension of trade in Shanghai soon spread to other cities. Local municipal authorities, who had doubted the practicability of ceiling prices from the beginning, now saw that the central government was incapable of enforcing its policy even in Shanghai, where its efforts were concentrated, and immediately began to unfreeze prices. By the end of October, little more than two months after the government had adopted what it regarded as a panacea, the ceiling price system was completely wrecked and wage ceilings automatically became inoperative.

No longer believing that inflation was susceptible to control, the government resigned itself to accepting the compulsion of events. The price of rice was allowed to follow the market price, and prices of other commodities were determined according to costs of production by the municipal authorities responsible for price fixing. It was vaguely indicated also that wages should be readjusted from time to time as the cost of living rose. When ceilings were lifted, prices jumped to more than ten times their levels on August 23rd, as is illustrated by the comparison of prices of rice, flour, and edible oil on August 23 and November 6, 1948:

| | Rice (per 171 lbs.) | Flour (per bag of 49 lbs.) | Edible Oil (per 22 gals.) |
|---|---|---|---|
| 1948 | | | |
| Aug. 23 | GY 20 | GY 7 | GY 58 |
| Nov. 6 | GY 240 | GY 73 | GY 550 |

The wholesale price index number in Shanghai was nearly fourteen times the August figure; the cost of living index had risen slightly less because the controlled distribution prices of a few daily necessities were used in its compilation.

Table 95. Shanghai Wholesale Price and Cost of Living Index: 1948–1949

| Year | Shanghai Wholesale Price Index (Aug., 1948 = 100) | Shanghai Cost of Living Index (Aug., 1948 = 100) |
|---|---|---|
| 1948 | | |
| Sept. | 106 | N.A. |
| Oct. | 118 | N.A. |
| Nov. | 1,365 | 1,170 |
| Dec. | 1,921 | 1,670 |
| 1949 | | |
| Jan. | 6,900 | 6,825 |
| Feb. | 40,825 | 52,113 |

After the breakdown of this attempt to freeze wages and prices the Gold Yuan depreciated at catastrophic speed. Successive military setbacks in the war against the Communists left the central government baffled and demoralized. Its leaders resorted to many reckless and damaging expedients to preserve government revenues, such as fixing public utility rates in terms of U.S. dollars and raising the price of distributed rice higher than the market price. These measures contributed to the disintegration of normal market mechanisms and to the alienation of the working classes. The indexes of wholesale prices and the cost of living are available only up to February 1949; but the figures point to the imminence of economic disaster (Table 95).

In summary, all attempts to control prices and wages in China had only superficial and short-lived effects, and they did not differ much from each other except in minor respects. The leader of the government believed that controls could be made to work if only sufficient political power were to back them up. This belief was the main reason why measures were reintroduced after others of substantially the same kind had failed but a short time before. The failure of each attempt was considered by the leader of the government to be due to the lack of courage and administrative efficiency of the enforcing authorities. The futility of attacking symptoms rather than causes was never fully appreciated.

# Part 4

## Some Lessons and Current Issues

Chapter

# 15

# Some Lessons and Current Issues

Many historical forces contributed to the collapse of the Nationalist government after World War II, but the direct and immediate cause which overshadowed all other factors was undoubtedly the inflation. The story of that inflation is of more than historical interest, for, in similar circumstances, the process may be repeated elsewhere. Unfortunately, there is at the present time an abundance of signs in countries on the periphery of the Chinese mainland that similar inflation-propelled revolutions may be actually in the making. As large defense and, to a lesser extent, development expenditures continue to swell the money supply in these underdeveloped countries with their inadequate fiscal and monetary structures and inexperienced or inefficient governments, a host of palliatives dealing with individual symptoms of inflation, so familiar to students of the Chinese scene, are again being tried, and, it may be added, equally unsuccessfully. It remains to be seen whether a post mortem of the Chinese case will not serve some purpose both as a warning and as a guide to those who hold the destiny of their countries, and of themselves, in precarious balance.

## *Lessons from the Chinese Inflation per se*

At the outset of the Sino-Japanese war, the Chinese government apparently failed to appreciate the extent to which aggregate demand would eventually expand under wartime conditions. Its leadership held to the naive belief that the nation's output of real goods, which was many times the money supply, could be expanded readily and in effect constituted the reserve of the currency. Thus it was under the erroneous impression that an underdeveloped, agricultural economy could in all circumstances provide the basic needs of the population in war, as well as in peace, and was therefore more able to respond to the stimulus of monetary expansion in increasing production than an industrial economy, whereas the opposite is more often true. The leadership failed to realize that the Chinese economy was in effect divided into more or less separate urban and rural sectors and that responses to the uneven inflationary pressures generated in them were not such as to mitigate the total effect. It also overlooked the fact that the tradition-bound Chinese population never had much confidence in the modern money, that its liquidity preference was very low, and that it was not accustomed to save significant amounts of current income.

In fact, China was not equipped with adequate banking facilities to encourage savings. Under these conditions the government failed to appreciate the necessity of undertaking effective measures to expand aggregate supply. It overestimated the readiness with which supply could be raised in the short run, and it grossly underestimated the inflationary effect of the expanding money supply.

Having failed to increase supply in response to the expanding aggregate demand generated by government expenditure, the government compounded this failure by its inability to divert a part of the new income it was creating to savings or partly to offset the inflationary stimulus by greater tax collections. There were certain historical reasons for China's lack of a flexible tax structure, for its lack of savings institutions outside the major established urban centers, and for the absence of an established market for government securities. But the government could not escape responsibility for failing to initiate basic tax and other fiscal reforms when the opportunity to do so presented itself several times during the period in question.

It is axiomatic that, once a vicious spiral of inflation has set in, it becomes increasingly difficult to halt the process. Attempts should have been made to curb Chinese inflation at the earliest possible stage. However, since tax increases and other measures calling for greater sacrifice required strong and broad political support, we concede that the Chinese government may have wished to choose the most favorable and strategic moments to launch sweeping reforms. One such opportunity presented itself in late 1938 and early 1939, when the government was forced to fall back upon the undeveloped hinterland and when the population was heart and soul behind the leadership's announced decision to prosecute a long war for national survival. A second opportunity occurred at the end of 1941, when the entry of the United States into the Pacific war seemed to make final victory for the first time a virtual certainty and provided the much needed psychological lift and financial support to make a determined effort to set the country's finances in order once for all. A third strategic occasion was to present itself at the end of World War II when it should have been apparent to the government that reconstruction could not proceed without monetary stabilization through basic reform and when the call for reform would have united all true patriots. Yet time and again the government failed to launch a program of basic fiscal reform until it was no longer feasible to do so.

To a large extent the government's inability to raise revenue by non-inflationary means and to absorb surplus demand through savings and taxation was due to its fear of losing popular support, of offending vested interests, and of facing a difficult task with courage and determination. Not possessing the wisdom and courage to undertake unpopular measures, the government could of course have reduced the scale of its spending. But it persisted in its refusal to take any effective step to trim expenditure and, overemphasizing the importance of prestige and outward military power, it underwrote political and military expenditures regardless of their economic consequences. It was curiously blind to the fact that in the long run economic health is a prerequisite of political power. It sought an easy way out of its financial difficulties, only to court eventual disaster.

Given the inflationary pressures which its policy failures helped to generate, the government then sought to suppress the symptom of inflation by price control and to increase production by further expansion of credit. Thus the momentum of inflation was given further impetus while the increase of prices refused to respond to the application of political pressure. In fact, direct controls could not be effectively enforced because the government lacked the means of enforcement, namely, an efficient and incorruptible administrative apparatus technically equipped to carry out its detailed assignments with skill, fairness, and loyalty. Yet because of its failure to institute basic financial reforms, the government was increasingly compelled to resort to direct and discretionary controls of credit, production, prices and wages, and foreign trade and exchange, success in which was particularly unlikely in view of the absence of the requisites. In short, it came to concentrate its efforts on the *symptoms* of inflation rather than on its *causes*.

The postwar return of the government to the coast saw a reversion of the economy to its prewar status of division into urban and rural sectors, only the more so this time now that the Communist forces had effectively disrupted communication between the North and the South. While inflationary pressures were built up in the urban centers, the government took no steps to enlarge the supply of goods from the rural sector. Instead reliance was almost wholly placed upon foreign supplies.

It is important to re-emphasize also that at the beginning of the postwar period conditions were strategically favorable to undertake basic readjustments in spending in order to curb further genesis of inflationary pressures, to increase supply potentialities by non-inflationary means, and to reduce inflationary pressures by tax changes. The government rejected these alternatives and instead chose a policy of curbing inflation through disinvestment of its limited supply of foreign assets and government-owned enterprises. That such a short-term palliative was most unlikely to succeed was unfortunately and offhandedly ignored.

It is possible that under the most favorable conditions such a policy of disinvestment might have exerted enough deflationary pressure to provide the initial wedge for more basic adjustment. But to undertake such a policy without a radical change in financial policy and management was to assume a very grave risk. Clearly the government underestimated the seriousness of the Communist military threat and the duration of the civil war, was unduly optimistic regarding the continuation of foreign assistance, and, for some inexplicable reason, grossly overestimated its own political power, especially in regard to the possibility of curbing inflation by political means despite all its wartime experience to the contrary.

When the government had to admit failure in all its economic measures, it once again resorted to political means. It came to stake its political future and prestige on an abortive currency "reform," only to find that its political influence was no longer adequate, that popular confidence had been dissipated through the years, and that it was merely hastening the final debacle.

Chinese inflation also taught the lesson that executive domination of both the budget and the banking system may prove to be a most unwholesome combination. Where the government budget is left in the hands of the political leadership instead of being closely scrutinized by a properly constituted authority, and the central bank is treated as the government's disbursing agent, the ability to create money may become a curse instead of a boon to the economy. In China arbitrary control of the budget and the central bank were vested in the political leadership. This leadership, failing to understand the nature of the economic forces with which it dealt, chose to ignore them. The government could find no alternative with which to finance itself. Inflation was to run its course, and the ultimate fate of the government was sealed. Economic instability finally led to a general loss of confidence in the Nationalist government, and total collapse of political and social morals followed. Into this chaos and political and moral vacuum almost any militant group promising a clean sweep could have moved without strong opposition; and the Communists were there to take full advantage of the situation.

### *Basic Issues Confronting Underdeveloped Countries*

The preceding critical remarks deal specifically with the wartime and postwar experience of China and may not be applicable *in toto* in a different historical context. Over and above the technical issues, however, there are certain underlying attitudes and conceptions which more or less conditioned the course of events in China and which, because of their general applicability in other Asian countries, may bear repeating.

First, it should be recalled that throughout Chinese history the political authority of every new dynasty or era was almost invariably imbued with a consuming desire to perpetuate national and personal glory either through military aggrandizement or through the promotion of gigantic public works. These undertakings almost invariably led to inflationary finance. Although such crude considerations of vain glory may no longer be paralleled in present-day circumstances, the lure of economic development and the paramount desire for national security exert in most underdeveloped countries an almost irresistible pressure toward expanding government expenditure. As one country after another proclaims its own five- or four- or three-year plan of development, the urge to emulate is so strong that similar undertakings become almost imperative. This seems to be the case in most Asian countries at the present time. As for defense, while external threat to national security may be real enough, it is seldom realized that defense expenditures are frequently in joint demand and that one outlay will usually lead to another. Faced with the demand for military power on the one hand and the lure of economic development on the other, the governments of underdeveloped countries do not always possess, it would appear, the wisdom to undertake only what they are capable of doing without inflation. Even with foreign assistance their programs tend to swell local incomes and local spending. This suggests that the financial capacity of the recipient of foreign aid should be carefully considered and guided. Recent Chinese experience has thrown further light on this point.

Second, in the promotion of either defense or economic development the long-run interest of an underdeveloped country is best served by increasing real output and by promoting the accumulation of domestic capital. Chinese experience suggests that, if these are to be accomplished, there must be proper respect for the soundness of private enterprise and banking. Excessive issue of government securities, their forced sale to banks, and relentless deficit financing through direct issue of new currency all served in China to destroy popular confidence in banking institutions as safe custodians of the people's deposits. Chinese experience also suggests that it may be unwise to expand state enterprises merely because private enterprises have developed slowly. Overzealousness in forcing the pace of economic development often results in little more than the destruction of private capital formation, thus defeating the very purpose of development. In the Chinese case, private capital formation during the Nationalist and pre-Nationalist period took place largely through the efforts of the Bank of China, the Bank of Communications, and, to a lesser extent, the major commercial banks. Because of its consuming need for money, the government first monopolized the banks' portfolios through direct borrowing and then followed the process through by partial nationalization. These and other measures nipped in the bud the gradual growth of modern banking institutions through which private savings could have been mobilized more effectively when the need arose during and after the war. The failure to foster rural credit institutions and the mushroom growth of diverse state enterprises had the same adverse effect on private capital formation in China. Parallel developments should be avoided in other underdeveloped countries.

Third, since there is an inherent tendency toward inflation in underdeveloped countries, the establishment of an institutional framework for budget control and the independence of the central bank are of paramount importance for the long-term welfare of the population. We have seen how the absence of such watchdogs contributed to chaotic and reckless management of government finance in China. One cannot be too emphatic in stressing the importance of avoiding the same error elsewhere.

Fourth, once inflation is under way, the government is perforce led to the path of increasing intervention and direct control. Since the number of educated persons and intellectuals is small in an underdeveloped country, as was the case in China, and since such persons are usually concentrated in government service, the teaching profession, and other occupations with relatively fixed incomes, one of the effects of inflation is to diminish the real income of these key groups. This tends to produce disaffection in the very groups upon whose cooperation the success of government depends. Discontent among the articulate is bound to result in a vociferous display of anti-government opinion, not infrequently exaggerating the scale of real grievances. Isolated from these elite groups, precisely at the time when there is the greatest need for efficient administration of its economic controls, government administration tends to become corrupt. Little wonder that the corrupting influence of inflation is compounded in underdeveloped countries. The experience of China has taught us this important lesson.

Finally, again on the basis of recent Chinese experience, it can be stated without equivocation that the complexity of modern economic life defies the grasp of any single individual, least of all a political leader preoccupied with many other responsibilities. To permit absolute and arbitrary control by a single person is to court disaster. Ample examples of the weakness of this power structure may be found in the preceding pages dealing with the Chinese case. It is important, therefore, that a general moral be drawn from the unhappy experience of Nationalist China.

During recent years much has been done by the Free World to aid the economic development of the underdeveloped countries and to bolster their defense. While these efforts are admirable from both a political and humanitarian point of view, the dangers that they pose by threatening inflation should by no means be overlooked. Inflation is no less an enemy of the free society than Communism and, as we have seen in China, may be the harbinger of a Communist triumph.

# Appendix A

## Behavior of Prices*

TABLE A–1. PRICE INDEXES FOR CHINA PROPER: PREWAR PERIOD, 1930–1937
(1930 = 100)

| Year | Shanghai[1] | Northern China[2] | Canton[3] |
|---|---|---|---|
| 1930 | 100 | 100 | 100 |
| 1931 | 110.3 | 105.9 | 111.9 |
| 1932 | 98.0 | 97.5 | 112.1 |
| 1933 | 90.5 | 86.9 | 103.1 |
| 1934 | 84.7 | 79.7 | 92.9 |
| 1935 | 84.0 | 82.5 | 83.4 |
| 1936 | 94.6 | 86.8 | 104.0 |
| 1937 | 112.7 | — | 118.8 |

[1] Based on data compiled by the National Tariff Commission.

[2] Based on data compiled by the Economic Research Department of Nankai University.

[3] Based on data compiled by the Statistical Bureau of the Kwangtung Provincial Government.

TABLE A–2. PRICE INDEXES FOR FREE CHINA: WARTIME PERIOD, 1938–1945
(Base: Jan.–June 1937 = 100)[1]

| Year | Free China | Chung-king | Chengtu | Kang-ting | Sian | Lan-chow | Kun-ming | Kwei-yang |
|---|---|---|---|---|---|---|---|---|
| 1938 | 131 | 126 | 128 | 137 | 146 | 146 | — | 105 |
| 1939 | 220 | 220 | 225 | 225 | 245 | 217 | — | 187 |
| 1940 | 513 | 569 | 665 | 587 | 497 | 399 | — | 413 |
| 1941 | 1,296 | 1,576 | 1,769 | 1,352 | 1,270 | 1,061 | — | 969 |
| 1942 | 3,900 | 4,408 | 4,559 | 4,388 | 4,120 | 2,853 | — | 3,395 |
| 1943 | 12,541 | 13,298 | 14,720 | 12,982 | 16,279 | 10,047 | — | 9,428 |
| 1944 | 43,197 | 43,050 | 56,965 | 49,229 | 39,679 | 26,533 | 62,203 | 34,940 |
| 1945 | 163,160 | 156,195 | 170,379 | 171,053 | 155,341 | 88,655 | 305,711 | 167,025 |

[1] Based on data compiled by the Directorate-General of Budgets, Accounts and Statistics, published in *The China Statistical Abstract,* 1948.

* Tables A–1 through A–3 are computed by simple geometric mean, Table A–4 by weighted geometric mean.

TABLE A–3. PRICE INDEXES FOR CHINA PROPER: POSTWAR PERIOD, JAN. 1946–DEC. 1947

(Jan.–June 1937 = 100)

| Year and Month[1] | | All China | Shanghai | Chungking | Tientsin | Canton |
|---|---|---|---|---|---|---|
| 1946 | Jan. | 182,667 | 160,315 | 209,561 | 134,265 | 214,827 |
| | Feb. | 235,973 | 273,550 | 225,806 | 234,404 | 239,067 |
| | March | 291,596 | 344,383 | 235,728 | 277,525 | 269,481 |
| | April | 309,260 | 325,986 | 248,296 | 278,888 | 310,899 |
| | May | 348,193 | 360,485 | 252,406 | 362,095 | 333,048 |
| | June | 375,273 | 378,217 | 256,963 | 419,200 | 331,370 |
| | July | 412,908 | 403,982 | 273,325 | 425,088 | 365,320 |
| | Aug. | 426,861 | 439,300 | 263,250 | 463,699 | 408,987 |
| | Sept. | 473,966 | 503,122 | 315,515 | 559,843 | 465,036 |
| | Oct. | 547,852 | 612,071 | 357,322 | 665,620 | 539,848 |
| | Nov. | 593,705 | 626,614 | 390,652 | 724,100 | 527,244 |
| | Dec. | 627,210 | 681,563 | 451,035 | 740,983 | 561,091 |
| 1947 | Jan. | 755,000 | 817,750 | 525,300 | 834,587 | 645,916 |
| | Feb. | 1,102,885 | 1,309,848 | 722,986 | 1,264,554 | 1,111,674 |
| | March | 1,219,439 | 1,386,593 | 770,105 | 1,419,989 | 1,160,536 |
| | April | 1,390,200 | 1,669,900 | 780,567 | 1,721,433 | 1,311,971 |
| | May | 1,968,567 | 2,584,000 | 987,186 | 2,673,396 | 1,883,607 |
| | June | 2,483,000 | 2,905,700 | 1,334,382 | 3,172,826 | 2,367,401 |
| | July | 3,122,400 | 3,359,400 | 1,986,598 | 3,778,015 | 2,658,501 |
| | Aug. | 3,439,200 | 3,649,300 | 2,219,269 | 3,936,743 | 3,666,973 |
| | Sept. | 3,836,800 | 4,635,700 | 2,590,240 | 4,574,905 | 4,169,327 |
| | Oct. | 5,931,300 | 7,293,400 | 3,872,665 | 6,494,190 | 5,520,741 |
| | Nov. | 7,696,500 | 8,261,300 | 4,958,040 | 8,158,881 | 7,256,009 |
| | Dec. | 10,340,000 | 10,063,000 | 6,407,078 | 12,100,259 | 9,419,215 |

[1] 1946–47: based on data compiled by the Directorate-General of Budgets, Accounts and Statistics.

TABLE A–4. PRICE INDEXES FOR CHINA PROPER: SHANGHAI AND CHUNGKING, 1948–1949

(Jan.–June 1937 = 100)

| Year and Month[1] | | Shanghai | Chungking |
|---|---|---|---|
| 1948 | Jan. | 14,074,200.0 | 6,327,700 |
| | Feb. | 20,155,200.0 | 8,109,400 |
| | March | 32,576,900.0 | 13,851,900 |
| | April | 37,764,200.0 | 16,678,800 |
| | May | 54,281,300.0 | 21,862,500 |
| | June | 197,690,000.0 | 45,508,000 |
| | July | 287,700,000.0 | 132,500,000 |
| | Aug. | 186.3[2] | |
| | Sept. | 197.0 | |
| | Oct. | 220.4 | |
| | Nov. | 2,543.1 | |
| | Dec. | 3,583.7 | |
| 1949 | Jan. | 12,876.2 | |
| | Feb. | 89,788.0 | |
| | March | 405,320.0 | |
| | April | 20,957,009.0 | |

[1] 1948–49: based on data compiled by the Economic Research Department of the Central Bank of China.

[2] The sharp break in prices after August 20th reflects the conversion resulting from the adoption of Gold Yuan currency.

Appendix

# B

# Factors in Generating Increased Aggregate Demand

TABLE B–1. GOVERNMENT FINANCE: 1937–1948
(All figures in CNC $ millions)

| Year | Expend-iture[1] | Revenue[2] | Deficit | Money Value[3] of Land Taxation in Kind | Note Issue[4] |
|---|---|---|---|---|---|
| 1937 | 1,992 | 1,393 | 560 | | 1,640 |
| 1938 | 2,215 | 723 | 1,492 | | 2,310 |
| 1939 | 2,797 | 740 | 2,057 | | 4,290 |
| 1940 | 5,288 | 1,325 | 3,963 | | 7,870 |
| 1941 | 10,003 | 1,310 | 8,693 | | 15,100 |
| 1942 | 24,511 | 5,630 | 18,881 | 2,896 | 34,400 |
| 1943 | 58,816 | 20,403 | 38,413 | 16,885 | 75,400 |
| 1944 | 171,689 | 38,503 | 133,186 | 50,107 | 189,500 |
| 1945 | 2,348,085 | 1,241,389 | 1,106,698 | 158,498 | 1,031,900 |
| 1946 | 7,574,790 | 2,876,988 | 4,697,802 | 362,735 | 3,726,100 |
| 1947 | 43,393,895 | 14,064,383 | 29,329,512 | 1,156,246 | 33,188,500 |
| 1948 (Jan.–June) | 655,471,087 | 220,905,475 | 434,565,612 | 3,281,380 | 374,762,200 |

Sources:

[1] 1937–45: data compiled by the Statistical Department of Ministry of Finance and Directorate-General of Budgets, Accounts and Statistics; 1946–47: W. Y. Chang, *Money and Finance in China,* p. 243; 1948: records of payments and receipts made by the Central Bank of China.

[2] 1937–44: statistics compiled by the Statistical Department of the Ministry of Finance and the Directorate-General of Budgets, Accounts and Statistics, published in Part III of the *Public Finance Yearbook,* pp. 129–150; 1945–47: W. Y. Chang, *Money and Finance in China,* pp. 140–144 and 244; 1948: records of the Central Bank of China.

[3] Based on the data from the *Abstract of Facts on Finance and Money,* compiled by the Ministry of Finance. Monetary value was calculated from the Central Bank of China's index of food prices in Shanghai.

[4] Based on Central Bank of China records for 1948, Jan.–July.

TABLE B–2. PRIVATE CREDIT, VOLUNTARY SAVINGS, AND INTEREST RATES: 1937–1948

(in CNC $ millions)

| Year | Bank Credit[1] | Deposits[1] | Savings[2] | Interest Rates, Per Cent[3] (Chungking Monthly Market Rate) |
|---|---|---|---|---|
| 1937 | 2,255 | 3,118 | 188 | 1.0 |
| 1938 | 2,614 | 3,902 | 251 | 1.20 |
| 1939 | 3,706 | 5,747 | 312 | 1.30 |
| 1940 | 4,114 | 7,303 | 533 | 1.50 |
| 1941 | 5,589 | 12,741 | 1,104 | 1.92 |
| 1942 | 11,402 | 19,985 | 2,976 | 2.80 |
| 1943 | 22,768 | 28,358 | 7,387 | 6.00 |
| 1944 | 40,423 | 89,903 | 15,456 | 8.57 |
| 1945 | 172,469 | 482,219 | 55,693 | 10.2 |

| Year | Bank Credit | Deposits | Savings | Interest Rates, Per Cent (Shanghai Monthly) Market Rate | Interest Rates, Per Cent (Shanghai Monthly) Black-Market Rate |
|---|---|---|---|---|---|
| 1946 | 1,627,281 | 5,545,583 | 372,592 | 10.7 | 15.08 |
| 1947 | 23,434,073 | 28,855,714 | 1,498,396 | 15.14 | 18.25 |
| 1948 (Jan.–June) | 201,245,341 | 208,656,165 | 5,808,000 | 23.17 | 26.55 |

Sources:

[1] Government Banks; 1937–45: based on data from reports compiled by the Joint Board of Administration of Government Banks; 1946–48: based on data from reports of the Central Bank of China; provincial and commercial banks; 1937–46: W. Y. Chang, *Money and Finance in China,* p. 164; 1947–48: estimates based on statistics of Shanghai banks compiled by the Auditing Department of the Central Bank of China.

[2] 1937–45; based on reports compiled by the Joint Board of Administration of Government Banks; 1946–48: based on statistics compiled by the Auditing Department of the Central Bank of China.

[3] 1937–45: data compiled by the Joint Board of Administration of Government Banks; 1946–48: data from monthly reports compiled by the Central Bank of China.

TABLE B–3. TOTAL MONEY SUPPLY
(Unit: 1926–1934, Silver Dollar; 1935–1948, CNC Dollar)

Prewar Period

| End of Year | Currency Issues[1] | Current Deposits[2] | Total |
|---|---|---|---|
| 1926 | 228,962,163 | 657,646,855 | 886,609,018 |
| 1927 | 262,164,410 | 700,172,666 | 962,337,076 |
| 1928 | 308,818,375 | 808,337,121 | 1,117,155,496 |
| 1929 | 350,236,497 | 957,374,032 | 1,307,610,529 |
| 1930 | 412,968,538 | 1,389,109,572 | 1,802,078,110 |
| 1931 | 393,367,870 | 1,213,334,120 | 1,606,701,990 |
| 1932 | 451,590,418 | 1,255,014,045 | 1,706,604,463 |
| 1933 | 535,190,933 | 1,579,824,899 | 2,115,015,832 |
| 1934 | 622,522,223 | 1,820,621,425 | 2,443,143,648 |
| 1935 | 867,984,374 | 2,324,341,889 | 3,192,326,263 |
| 1936 | 1,633,106,095 | 2,708,005,032 | 4,341,111,127 |

Wartime Period

| End of Year | Currency Issues | Current Deposits | Total |
|---|---|---|---|
| 1937 | 1,640,000,000 | 2,019,000,000 | 3,659,000,000 |
| 1938 | 2,310,000,000 | 2,506,000,000 | 4,816,000,000 |
| 1939 | 4,290,000,000 | 3,214,000,000 | 7,504,000,000 |
| 1940 | 7,870,000,000 | 4,315,000,000 | 12,185,000,000 |
| 1941 | 15,100,000,000 | 7,746,000,000 | 22,846,000,000 |
| 1942 | 34,400,000,000 | 16,391,000,000 | 50,791,000,000 |
| 1943 | 75,400,000,000 | 24,796,000,000 | 100,196,000,000 |
| 1944 | 189,500,000,000 | 85,587,000,000 | 275,087,000,000 |
| 1945 | 1,031,900,000,000 | 474,690,000,000 | 1,506,590,000,000 |

Postwar Period

| End of Year | Currency Issues | Current Deposits | Total |
|---|---|---|---|
| 1946 | 3,726,100,000,000 | 5,455,494,000,000 | 9,181,594,000,000 |
| 1947 | 33,188,500,000,000 | 27,777,060,000,000 | 60,965,560,000,000 |
| 1948 (Jan.–June) | 196,520,300,000,000 | 202,571,339,000,000 | 399,091,639,000,000 |

Sources:

[1] 1926–31: Y. F. Yang, *A Treatise on Chinese Currency,* pp. 119–120; during 1932–35: *China Banking Yearbook, 1936,* Vol. II, Chapter 19, "Banking Statistics," p. S35; 1936: *China Banking Yearbook, 1937,* Vol. II, Chapter 19, "Banking Statistics," p. S53; 1937–48: based on records compiled by the Central Bank of China.

[2] 1926–36: same source for the period as above; 1937–45: government banks, reports compiled by the Joint Board of Administration of Government Banks; commercial and provincial banks, W. Y. Chang, *Money and Finance in China,* p. 164; 1946–48: all figures based on statistics compiled by the Auditing Department of the Central Bank of China. Current deposits of commercial and provincial banks are estimated about 60 per cent of total deposits.

Appendix

# C

# Supply

TABLE C-1. AGRICULTURAL PRODUCTION, 1939–1947
(Unit: 1,000,000 Bushels)

Wartime Period

| Year | Rice (husked) | Wheat | Barley | Cotton | Tobacco | Soybeans | Common Sorghum |
|---|---|---|---|---|---|---|---|
| 1937 | 1,323.51 | 381.66 | 209.87 | 988.888 | 524.800 | 111.742 | 101.83 |
| 1938 | 1,435.78 | 590.47 | 263.03 | 1,041.777 | 446.700 | 106.128 | 98.93 |
| 1939 | 1,466.67 | 576.73 | 266.36 | 1,296.444 | 490.500 | 109.550 | 109.81 |
| 1940 | 1,188.59 | 585.23 | 249.77 | 1,129.333 | 513.450 | 112.256 | 90.97 |
| 1941 | 1,235.94 | 480.50 | 214.75 | 1,000.000 | 425.800 | 101.018 | 86.33 |
| 1942 | 1,220.02 | 609.31 | 260.05 | 842.666 | 378.200 | 85.571 | 69.97 |
| 1943 | 1,170.58 | 579.66 | 235.83 | 1,055.111 | 412.950 | 97.002 | 81.64 |
| 1944 | 1,295.86 | 722.45 | 268.85 | 950.222 | 417.250 | 95.884 | 79.93 |
| 1945 | 1,129.71 | 638.69 | 235.30 | 1,571.555 | 402.700 | 99.080 | 85.12 |
| | | | | Postwar Period | | | |
| 1946 | 1,708.89 | 136.12 | 366.51 | 2,134.777 | 618.650 | 263.914 | 319.41 |
| 1947 | 1,793.00 | 123.40 | 365.26 | 2,412.444 | 606.200 | 272.766 | 303.08 |

Wartime Period

| Year | Millet | Proso-Millet | Corn | Peas | Broad Beans | Rapeseed | Oats |
|---|---|---|---|---|---|---|---|
| 1937 | 69.29 | 27.453 | 197.059 | 80.508 | 98.568 | 94.476 | 8.363 |
| 1938 | 69.30 | 27.051 | 205.083 | 127.149 | 138.644 | 104.302 | 9.073 |
| 1939 | 69.81 | 28.070 | 207.466 | 137.270 | 153.526 | 125.456 | 9.724 |
| 1940 | 61.61 | 25.119 | 195.086 | 125.316 | 138.854 | 141.251 | 8.870 |
| 1941 | 60.25 | 29.414 | 193.614 | 109.253 | 121.996 | 132.783 | 8.375 |
| 1942 | 42.93 | 27.901 | 171.223 | 122.854 | 138.568 | 128.447 | 9.004 |
| 1943 | 52.14 | 32.848 | 188.853 | 110.365 | 127.668 | 143.312 | 8.486 |
| 1944 | 50.80 | 27.185 | 195.959 | 126.097 | 142.986 | 144.481 | 8.474 |
| 1945 | 60.73 | 24.182 | 210.672 | 110.643 | 115.806 | 115.428 | 6.763 |

TABLE C–1. AGRICULTURAL PRODUCTION, 1939–1947 (*continued*)
(Unit: 1,000,000 Bushels)

Postwar Period

| Year | Millet | Proso-Millet | Corn | Peas | Broad Beans | Rapeseed | Oats |
|---|---|---|---|---|---|---|---|
| 1946 | 453.73 | 79.670 | 451.099 | 179.257 | 166.964 | 185.245 | 40.472 |
| 1947 | 378.43 | 69.404 | 413.191 | 187.293 | 179.768 | 216.417 | 44.517 |

Wartime Period

| Year | Sweet Potatoes | Peanuts | Sesame |
|---|---|---|---|
| 1937 | 821.347 | 62.291 | 19.450 |
| 1938 | 804.760 | 63.735 | 12.955 |
| 1939 | 723.606 | 65.242 | 23.273 |
| 1940 | 745.136 | 66.348 | 23.826 |
| 1941 | 806.449 | 66.488 | 21.394 |
| 1942 | 706.083 | 58.631 | 14.084 |
| 1943 | 844.726 | 62.227 | 19.648 |
| 1944 | 883.687 | 63.474 | 20.475 |
| 1945 | 902.403 | 65.731 | 23.315 |
| | Postwar Period | | |
| 1946 | 1,478.792 | 129.867 | 41.636 |
| 1947 | 1,406.368 | 129.251 | 37.457 |

The figures for 1937–45 represent 13 provinces in Free China: Chekiang, Kiangsi, Hupeh, Hunan, Szechwan, Honan, Shensi, Kansu, Ninghsia, Chinghai, Fukien, Kwangtung, Kwangsi. The figures for 1946–47 represent 20 provinces (China Proper); the 13 listed above and 7 additional, Kiangsu, Anhwei, Hopeh, Shantung, Shansi, Chahar, and Suiyuan. The figures for 1937–46 are based on data reported by the National Agricultural Research Bureau; those for 1947 are based on data from the *China Statistical Abstract*.

No adjustments are made in the figures of the production of rice and cotton for 1937–45, as mentioned in footnote 1, Table 59.

TABLE C–2. MANUFACTURING AND MINING PRODUCTION, 1938–1947*

| Year | Cotton Yarn (bales) | Flour (1,000 pounds) | Cement (barrels) | Matches (1,000 boxes) | Paper (metric tons) | Alcohol (1,000 gallons) | Soda Ash (metric tons) | Sulphuric Acid (metric tons) |
|---|---|---|---|---|---|---|---|---|
| Wartime Period | | | | | | | | |
| 1938 | 24,515 | 74,137 | 150,486 | 12 | 492 | 304 | 520 | 170 |
| 1939 | 27,451 | 94,374 | 341,558 | 12 | 526 | 812 | 940 | 124 |
| 1940 | 48,916 | 158,711 | 353,353 | 14 | 660 | 4,590 | 1,486 | 428 |
| 1941 | 88,994 | 220,990 | 178,003 | 19 | 4,200 | 5,408 | 2,079 | 543 |
| 1942 | 102,536 | 239,120 | 278,901 | 26 | 4,250 | 7,885 | 2,263 | 689 |
| 1943 | 127,913 | 202,370 | 245,616 | 24 | 3,580 | 7,714 | 3,251 | 624 |
| 1944 | 121,021 | 141,169 | 284,508 | 33 | 3,669 | 7,346 | 6,101 | 768 |
| 1945 | 69,200 | 100,744 | 295,610 | N.A. | 3,900 | 16,222 | 3,342 | 257 |
| Postwar Period | | | | | | | | |
| 1946 | 2,582,000 | 3,782,359 | 2,047,269 | 289 | 62,361 | 12,379 | 61,177 | 7,205 |
| 1947 | 1,400,000[1] | N.A. | 3,268,398[2] | N.A. | 28,062[3] | N.A. | 36,606[3] | 3,963[3] |

* All figures are based on data compiled by the Department of Statistics, Ministry of Economic Affairs, published in the *China Handbook, 1946* and the *China Statistical Abstract, 1948*. The figures for 1946 and 1947 represent all China; those for 1938 to 1945 represent Free China only.

[1] Production during the period Jan.—Sept.

[2] Production during the period Jan.—Aug.

[3] Production during the period Jan.—June.

TABLE C–2. MANUFACTURING AND MINING PRODUCTION, 1938–1947 (*continued*)

| Year | Nitric Acid (metric tons) | Hydrochloric Acid (metric tons) | Bleaching Powder (metric tons) | Soap (1,000 boxes) | Lubricating Oil (gallons) | Power Engines (horsepower) | Tool Machines (sets) |
|---|---|---|---|---|---|---|---|
| Wartime Period | | | | | | | |
| 1938 | 3 | 99 | N.A. | 82 | — | 610 | 332 |
| 1939 | 2 | 72 | N.A. | 99 | 8,528 | 870 | 639 |
| 1940 | 16 | 151 | 147 | 280 | 39,924 | 2,507 | 1,024 |
| 1941 | 12 | 130 | 521 | 401 | 51,085 | 3,758 | 1,221 |
| 1942 | 17 | 300 | 660 | 320 | 35,358 | 4,476 | 1,147 |
| 1943 | 15 | 368 | 609 | 363 | 5,847 | 7,302 | 1,752 |
| 1944 | 9 | 416 | 797 | 225 | 9,754 | 8,210 | 1,350 |
| 1945 | 5 | 337 | N.A. | N.A. | N.A. | 2,866 | 775 |
| Postwar Period | | | | | | | |
| 1946 | 2,274 | 3,002 | 19,279 | 1,596 | N.A. | 4,765 | 1,052 |
| 1947 | 1,262[3] | 1,651[3] | N.A. | N.A. | N.A. | 3,702[3] | 1,748[3] |

| Year | Industrial Machines (sets) | Generators (kva) | Motors (horsepower) | Transformers (kva) | Copper and Iron Wire (metric tons) | Electric Power (1,000 kw hours) | Coal (1,000 metric tons) |
|---|---|---|---|---|---|---|---|
| Wartime Period | | | | | | | |
| 1938 | 842 | 299 | 600 | 4,390 | — | 73,622 | 4,700 |
| 1939 | 1,512 | 439 | 9,594 | 6,509 | 40 | 91,494 | 5,500 |
| 1940 | 3,775 | 6,308 | 3,102 | 6,124 | 191 | 111,931 | 5,700 |
| 1941 | 2,575 | 5,503 | 11,600 | 10,772 | 571 | 127,302 | 6,000 |
| 1942 | 2,632 | 5,780 | 10,511 | 15,383 | 455 | 136,850 | 6,314 |
| 1943 | 2,110 | 4,790 | 11,451 | 12,484 | 365 | 146,437 | 6,617 |
| 1944 | 3,327 | 4,926 | 6,277 | 11,185 | 266 | 154,220 | 5,502 |
| 1945 | 1,421 | 2,028 | 6,683 | 10,496 | N.A. | 196,695 | 4,989 |
| Postwar Period | | | | | | | |
| 1946 | 2,286 | 4,200 | 4,178 | 12,092 | N.A. | 3,624,654 | 18,408 |
| 1947 | 6,580[3] | 1,680[3] | 2,216[3] | 8,464[3] | N.A. | N.A. | 19,487 |

TABLE C–2. (*continued*)

| Year | Steel (metric tons) | Iron (metric tons) | Antimony (metric tons) | Tungsten Dust (metric tons) | Tin (metric tons) | Gasoline (1,000 gallons) | Kerosine (1,000 gallons) | Diesel Oil (1,000 gallons) |
|---|---|---|---|---|---|---|---|---|
| Wartime Period | | | | | | | | |
| 1938 | 900 | 52,900 | 9,464 | 12,556 | N.A. | — | — | — |
| 1939 | 1,200 | 62,730 | 11,988 | 11,509 | 2,501 | 4 | — | — |
| 1940 | 1,650 | 49,500 | 8,471 | 9,542 | 17,416 | 73 | — | — |
| 1941 | 2,212 | 70,000 | 7,991 | 12,392 | 16,589 | 209 | 113 | — |
| 1942 | 3,300 | 105,600 | 3,510 | 11,897 | 14,003 | 1,896 | 500 | 46 |
| 1943 | 7,480 | 77,000 | 429 | 8,973 | 10,800 | 3,219 | 559 | 51 |
| 1944 | 15,697 | 44,150 | 204 | 3,225 | 5,102 | 4,048 | 2,161 | 155 |
| 1945 | 18,234 | 48,495 | N.A. | N.A. | 2,704 | 4,305 | 1,655 | 216 |
| Postwar Period | | | | | | | | |
| 1946 | 15,700 | 81,000 | 426 | 2,260 | 1,963 | 5,058 | 2,325 | 326 |
| 1947 | 63,000 | 85,000 | 1,580 | 6,402 | 3,790 | 7,880 | 4,002 | 967 |

Appendix

# D

# Foreign Exchange and Foreign Trade

TABLE D–1. FOREIGN EXCHANGE RATE: 1937–AUG. 1948*

| Year | | A. CNC per U.S. $1.00 | | B. U.S. cents per CNC $1.00 | |
|---|---|---|---|---|---|
| | | Official | Market | Official | Market |
| 1937 | June | 3.41 | — | 29.3150 | — |
| | Dec. | 3.42 | — | 29.2500 | — |
| 1938 | June | — | 5.40 | — | 18.5150 |
| | Dec. | — | 6.40 | — | 15.6250 |
| 1939 | June | — | 7.80 | — | 12.825 |
| | Dec. | — | 14.48 | — | 6.9115 |
| 1940 | June | — | 18.21 | — | 5.49480 |
| | Dec. | — | 17.76 | — | 5.63280 |
| 1941 | June | — | 19.00 | — | 5.26000 |
| | Dec. | 18.80 | 18.93 | 5.3125 | 5.28125 |
| 1942 | June | 18.80 | — | 5.3125 | — |
| | Dec. | 18.80 | — | 5.3125 | — |
| 1943 | June | 18.80 | 59.00 (Amer. note) | 5.3125 | 1.693 |
| | Dec. | 20.0 | 84.00 (Amer. note) | 5.0 | 1.191 |
| 1944 | June | 20.0 | 192.00 (Amer. note) | 5.0 | 0.521 |
| | Dec. | 20.0 | 570.00 (Amer. note) | 5.0 | 0.1753 |

* After the outbreak of hostilities in 1937 the official exchange rate was suspended and replaced by a bank rate. In August 1941 a board rate was established and remained until victory in 1945. After Pearl Harbor the market rate for American currency became insignificant and did not reappear until 1943, when American airmen and soldiers arrived in China.

The rates given for the period 1937–42 are based on quotations for the U.S. dollar exchange rate compiled by the Central Bank of China. The rates for 1943–45 are based on quotations for U.S. dollar notes compiled by the Joint Board of Administration of Government Banks; those after 1946 are based on monthly reports compiled by the Central Bank of China.

After the Gold Yuan currency system was adopted, month-end quotations were used in place of monthly averages.

TABLE D–1. (*continued*)

Foreign Exchange Rate after Currency Conversion: Aug. 1948–May 1949

| Year | | A. CNC per U.S. $1.00 | | B. U.S. cents per CNC $1.00 | |
|---|---|---|---|---|---|
| | | Official | Market | Official | Market |
| 1945 | June | 20.0 | 1,705.00 (Amer. note) | 5.0 | 0.0586 |
| | Dec. | 20.0 | 1,222.00 (Amer. note) | 5.0 | 0.08165 |
| 1946 | June | 2,020 | 2,665 | 0.0495 | 0.0375 |
| | Dec. | 3,350 | 6,063 | 0.02884 | 0.0165 |
| 1947 | March | 12,000 | 14,000 | 0.00834 | 0.00714 |
| | June | 12,000 | 36,826 | 0.00834 | 0.002715 |
| | Sept. | 41,635 | 50,365 | 0.00240 | 0.00199 |
| | Dec. | 77,636 | 149,615 | 0.001288 | 0.00668 |
| 1948 | March | 211,583 | 449,620 | 0.000474 | 0.000222 |
| | June | 1,273,000 | 2,311,250 | 0.0000785 | 0.0000433 |
| | Aug. 1–18 | 7,094,625 | 8,683,000 | 0.0000141 | 0.0000115 |

| Year | | A. Gold Yuan dollars per U.S. $1.00 | | B. U.S. cents per Gold Yuan $1.00 | |
|---|---|---|---|---|---|
| | | Official | Market | Official | Market |
| 1948 | Aug. 19–31 | 4 | 4 | 25.0 | 25.0 |
| | Sept. | 4 | 4 | 25.0 | 25.0 |
| | Oct. | 4 | 15 | 25.0 | 6.67 |
| | Nov. | 28 | 42 | 3.57 | 2.38 |
| | Dec. | 122 | 135 | 0.8195 | 0.740 |
| 1949 | Jan. | 240 | 700 | 0.417 | 0.1428 |
| | Feb. | 2,660 | 2,980 | 0.0377 | 0.03355 |
| | March | 16,000 | 17,700 | 0.00625 | 0.005640 |
| | April | 205,000 | 813,880 | 0.000487 | 0.0001229 |
| | May 1–21 | — | 23,280,000 | — | 0.00000431 |

TABLE D–2. CHINA'S BALANCE OF

(In millions of

| | Prewar Period 1935–1936 | | | |
|---|---|---|---|---|
| | 1935 | 1936 | 1937 | 1938 |
| **In-payments:** | | | | |
| 1. Merchandise exports, recorded | 208.8 | 207.7 | 245.7 | 161.3 |
| a. Plus: Adjustment for undervaluation, smuggling, and export duty | 18.0 | 14.7 | 19.6 | 12.6 |
| 2. Gold and silver exports recorded | 35.4 | 85.4 | 133.2 | 16.9 |
| a. Plus: smuggled exports of gold and silver (estimated) | 61.6 | 11.7 | 6.4 | 7.4 |
| 3. Overseas Chinese remittances | 101.5 | 82.2 | 131.9 | 126.9 |
| 4. Foreign expenditure in China: | | | | |
| a. Diplomatic and military | 34.4 | 20.6 | 35.1 | 43.3 |
| b. Philanthropic | 14.5 | 14.7 | 2.0 | 12.6 |
| c. Shipping and tourist | 11.6 | 9.1 | 7.0 | 4.6 |
| 5. Foreign credit and investment, repatriation of capital, and income from Chinese investment abroad | 3.1 | 5.9 | 7.3 | 3.1 |
| 6. Use of foreign reserve | — | — | — | — |
| 7. Unaccounted for | 22.3 | — | — | — |
| Total | 511.2 | 452.0 | 588.2 | 388.7 |
| **Out-payments:** | | | | |
| 1. Merchandise imports, recorded | 333.3 | 277.4 | 279.4 | 187.4 |
| a. Plus: Estimated smuggled imports | 101.5 | 73.8 | 146.5 | 84.8 |
| b. Government imports unrecorded | 18.0 | 25.0 | 42.5 | 24.7 |
| 2. Gold and silver imports | 4.0 | 5.7 | 0.8 | 2.9 |
| 3. Foreign debt service | 36.3 | 31.6 | 33.5 | 24.6 |
| 4. Chinese expenditure abroad | 1.8 | 4.4 | 2.9 | 3.1 |
| 5. Investment abroad and income from investment and business in China remitted abroad | 16.3 | 34.1 | 29.3 | 19.0 |
| 6. Increase of official holdings abroad | — | — | 53.3 | 42.2 |
| 7. Unaccounted for | — | — | — | — |
| Total | 511.2 | 452.0 | 588.2 | 388.7 |

* Data for the years 1935–38 are based on the estimates of Mr. E. Kann, published in Shanghai's *Finance and Commerce Weekly,* and S. W. Chu, published in Shanghai's *Bankers' Weekly,* with some modifications.

For the years 1939–41, import and export figures are from the *Chinese Maritime Customs Report.* Chinese government imports and expenditures abroad are based on the *Ministry of Finance Record.* Foreign Credit for 1939 includes the Sino-British Stabilization Loan, but excludes other credits for military purchases. The remaining figures for 1938–1941 are the author's estimates.

International Payments, 1935–1948*
U.S. dollars)

| War Period 1937–1945 | | | | | | | Postwar Period 1946–1948 | | |
|---|---|---|---|---|---|---|---|---|---|
| 1939 | 1940 | 1941 | 1942 | 1943 | 1944 | 1945 | 1946 | 1947 | 1948 |
| 116.0 | 120.5 | 136.4 | 8.5 | 6.8 | 38.0 | 169.0 | 149.0 | 230.0 | 170.0 |
| 69.6 | 72.0 | 99.5 | — | — | — | — | 30.0 | 46.0 | 67.0 |
| }4.0 | }8.1 | }2.7 | — | — | — | — | — | — | — |
| 112.4 | 91.0 | 122.0 | 27.4 | 60.3 | 37.1 | 37.7 | 76.0 | 74.0 | 90.0 |
| 62.2 | 33.6 | 47.6 | | | | | 60.0 | 30.0 | 22.0 |
| 16.9 | 9.2 | 10.6 | }10.0 | }20.0 | }30.0 | }30.0 | 35.0 | 17.0 | 16.0 |
| 3.6 | 3.0 | 2.9 | | | | | 10.0 | 10.0 | 12.0 |
| 41.1 | 4.0 | — | 200.0 | — | 410.0 | 230.0 | 80.0 | 90.0 | 77.0 |
| — | — | — | 21.9 | 43.0 | 71.7 | 27.5 | 355.0 | 190.0 | — |
| — | — | — | — | — | — | — | 100.0 | 112.0 | — |
| 425.8 | 341.4 | 421.7 | 267.8 | 130.1 | 586.8 | 494.2 | 895.0 | 799.0 | 454.0 |
| 150.6 | 124.0 | 114.5 | 33.0 | 81.0 | 68.0 | 179.0 | 565.0 | 480.0 | 211.0 |
| 138.0 | 168.0 | 253.0 | — | — | — | — | 110.0 | 96.0 | 31.0 |
| 21.0 | 24.2 | 26.7 | 24.4 | 10.2 | 30.2 | 27.6 | 100.0 | 77.0 | 40.0 |
| 7.7 | 1.0 | 1.0 | — | — | — | — | — | — | — |
| — | — | — | — | 19.0 | 66.3 | 41.4 | 25.0 | 36.0 | 46.0 |
| 3.5 | 3.2 | 5.5 | 10.4 | 19.9 | 12.3 | 16.2 | 70.0 | 60.0 | 46.0 |
| 29.0 | 21.0 | 21.0 | — | — | — | — | 25.0 | 50.0 | 80.0 |
| 2.0 | — | — | 200.0 | — | 410.0 | 230.0 | — | — | — |
| 74.0 | — | — | — | — | — | — | — | — | — |
| 425.8 | 341.4 | 421.7 | 267.8 | 130.1 | 586.8 | 494.2 | 895.0 | 799.0 | 454.0 |

For the years 1942–45, the *Chinese Custom Report* distinguished between Occupied China and Free China. The Nationalist government no longer supported the exchange market in Shanghai. The estimates here are confined to Free China for the sake of clarity. Because of the difference between the official rate of U.S. $1 per CNC 20, and the black-market annual average rate of U.S. $1 per CNC 35 (1942), 64 (1943), 255 (1944), and 1,348 (1945), one-fourth of imports and three-fourths of exports have been converted at the official rate, and three-fourths of imports and one-fourth of exports at the black-market rate. The estimates for these years include the following adjustments:

The overseas remittance was limited to the amount brought in through official channels.

Government imports and Chinese expenditure abroad are based on the record of the Ministry of Finance.

Foreign credit (200 million in 1942) was allocated from the American Treasury Credit as a sinking fund for the issuance of U.S. Dollar Savings Certificates and U.S. Dollar Bonds.

Foreign debt service in 1943–45 was largely repayment on the above issues.

Receipts under item 5 for the years 1944–45 (410 million and 230 million, respectively) were in repayment of expenditures made by the Chinese government in Chinese dollars in behalf of United States military forces in China.

All foreign credits obtained for the purchase of military and civilian goods are excluded here because no cash payments were involved.

The remaining estimates for these years are the result of the author's calculations. Detailed figures of foreign expenditure in China and remittance from China abroad are not available, because of the inflexible official rate prevailing during 1942–45 and the resulting flow of foreign currencies and foreign exchange to the black market.

For the years 1946–48 government imports, expenditures abroad, and foreign-credit service are based on the statistics of the Central Bank of China. The following remarks also pertain to this period:

A. Foreign credit in 1946 and 1947 includes only short-term cotton loans from United States banks (1946, $33 million and 1947, $30 million). Repatriation of funds in the same period include the proceeds of the 1947 U.S. Dollar Bonds amounting to U.S. $25.8 million and foreign currencies and foreign exchange surrendered under the Gold Yuan decree valued at U.S. $71 million.

B. Part of the amount "accounted for" in 1946 and 1947 might be imports financed by Chinese merchants' own foreign funds.

C. The remaining figures for the postwar years are based on the *Economic Survey of Asia and the Far East, 1947,* a United Nations document published in Shanghai in 1948, and the *Balance of Payments Yearbook,* published by the United Nations in 1949.

The general trend of average conversion rates between Chinese currency and the U.S. dollar employed for the period 1935–41 is as follows:

One Chinese Dollar per U.S. Cents

| | | |
|---|---|---|
| 1935 | U.S. | 36.2625 |
| 1936 | U.S. | 29.4375 |
| 1937 | U.S. | 29.3125 |
| 1938 | U.S. | 21.1527 |
| 1939 | U.S. | 11.2933 |
| 1940 | U.S. | 6.1175 |
| 1941 | U.S. | 5.2931 |

# Index